Surprise!
You may be reading
the wrong way!

It's true: In keeping with the original Japanese comic format, this book reads from right to left—so action, sound effects, and word balloons are completely reversed. This preserves the orientation of the original artwork—plus, it's fun! Check out the diagram shown here to get the hang of things, and then turn to the other side of the book to get started!

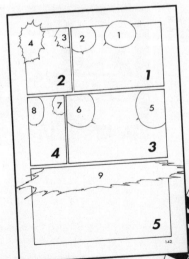

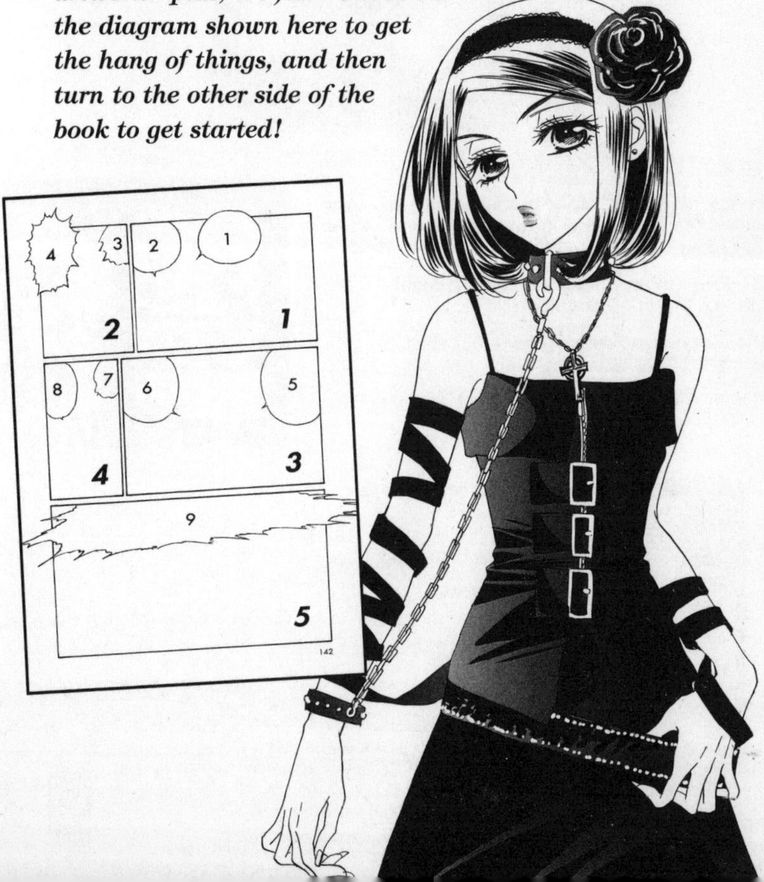

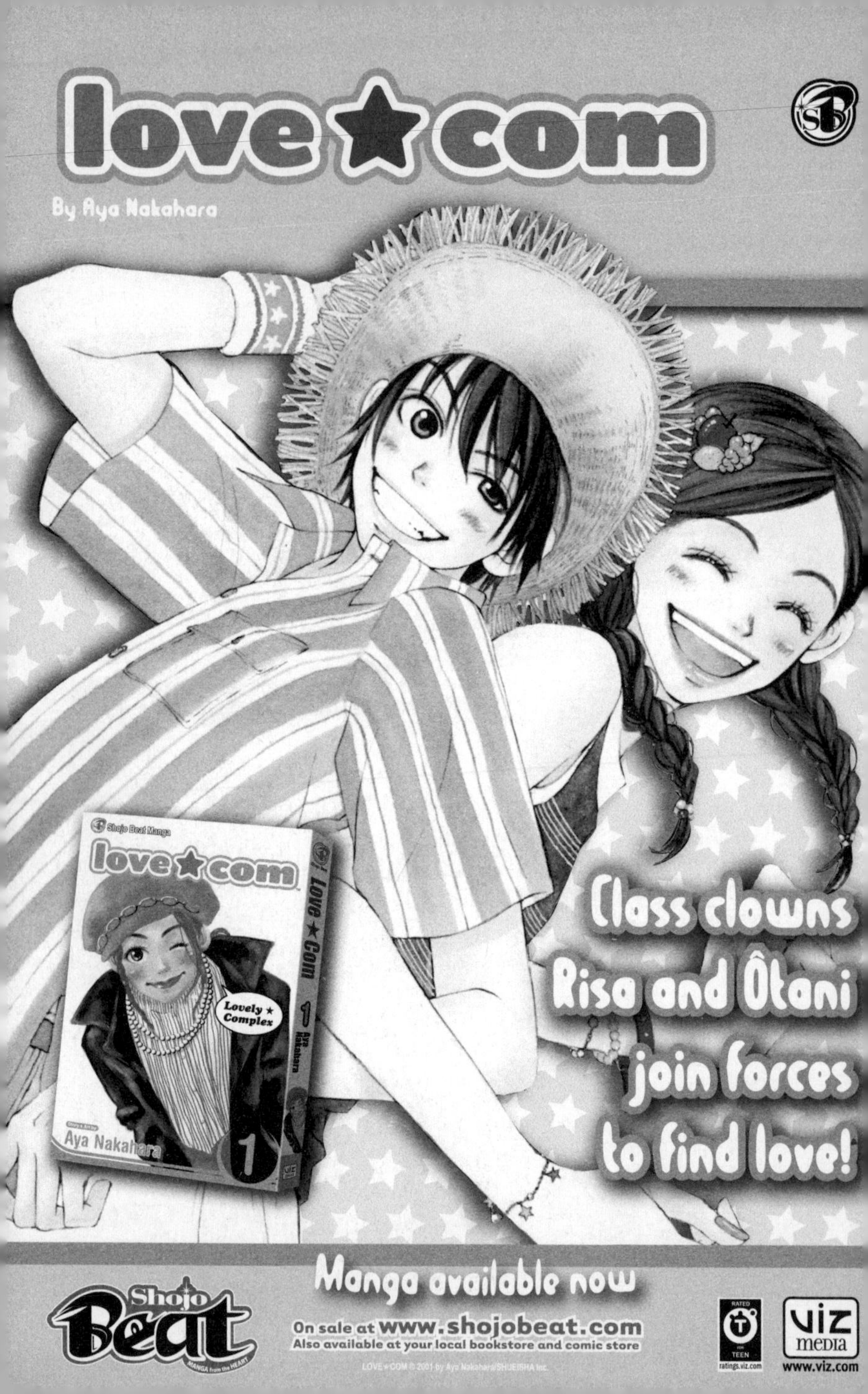
love★com
By Aya Nakahara
Shojo Beat Manga
love★com
Lovely ★ Complex
Love ★ Com 1 Aya Nakahara
Story & Art by
Aya Nakahara
1
Class clowns Risa and Ôtani join forces to find love!
Manga available now
Shojo Beat
MANGA from the HEART
On sale at www.shojobeat.com
Also available at your local bookstore and comic store
LOVE★COM © 2001 by Aya Nakahara/SHUEISHA Inc.
RATED T TEEN
ratings.viz.com
VIZ media
www.viz.com

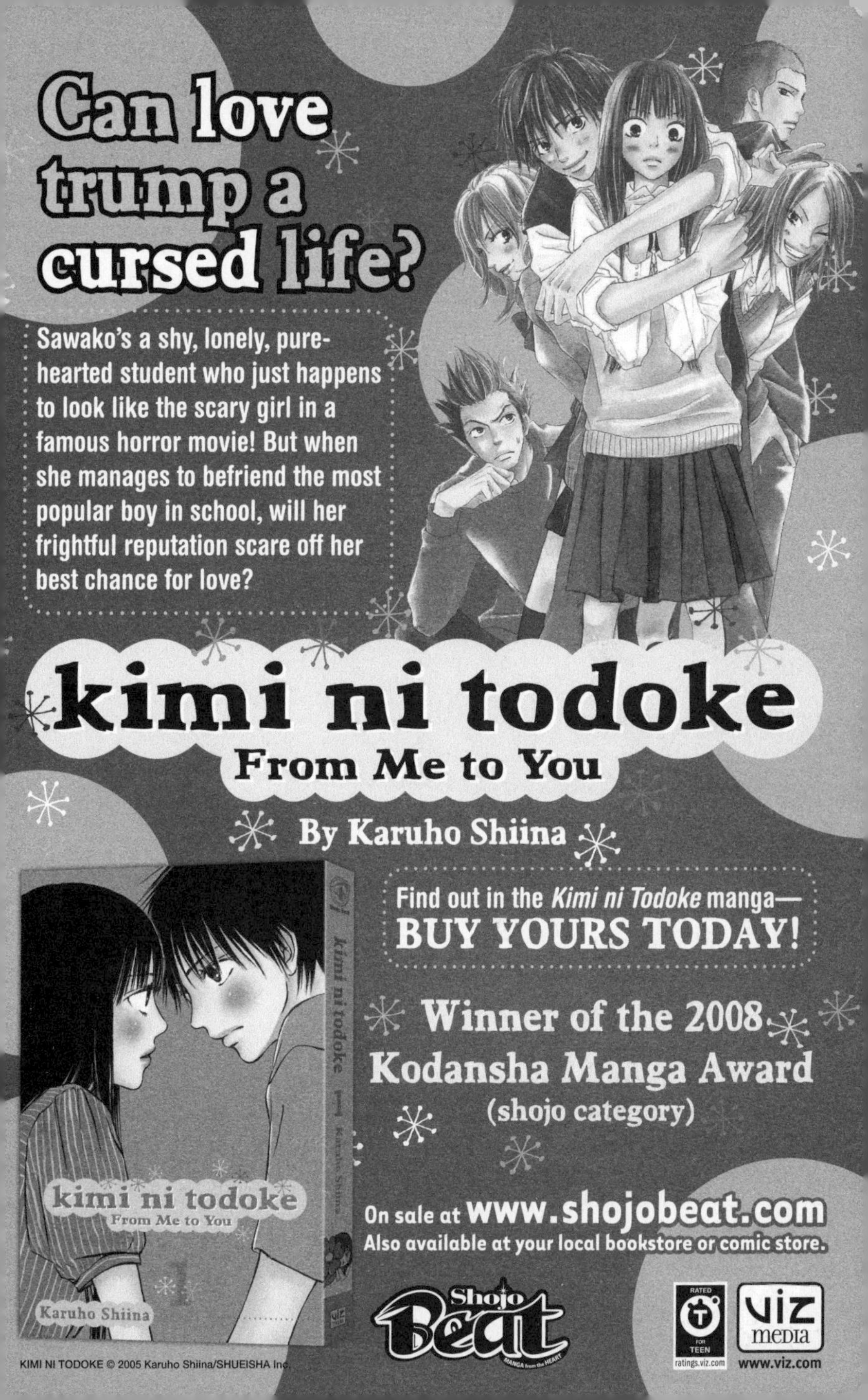
Can love trump a cursed life?
Sawako's a shy, lonely, pure-hearted student who just happens to look like the scary girl in a famous horror movie! But when she manages to befriend the most popular boy in school, will her frightful reputation scare off her best chance for love?
kimi ni todoke
From Me to You
By Karuho Shiina
kimi ni todoke
From Me to You
Karuho Shiina
Find out in the *Kimi ni Todoke* manga—
BUY YOURS TODAY!
Winner of the 2008
Kodansha Manga Award
(shojo category)
On sale at www.shojobeat.com
Also available at your local bookstore or comic store.
Shojo Beat
MANGA from the HEART
RATED T FOR TEEN
ratings.viz.com
viz media
www.viz.com
KIMI NI TODOKE © 2005 Karuho Shiina/SHUEISHA Inc.

A Devil and Her Love Song

Story & Art by
Miyoshi Tomori

Volume 13

The devil makes me LOVELY!!!

STORY THUS FAR

Shin's injured hand shows no sign of improvement, so he chooses to go to the U.S. to get surgery there. Not wanting to hold him back, Maria deliberately tries to put some distance between them. The two of them may be in love, but they each realize they need to go their separate ways.

A month after Shin's departure, Maria responds to how her friends are fussing over her by suggesting that they should all work together to make a music video. Inspired by the result, Yusuke says they should make more, and that he wants to film Maria singing…

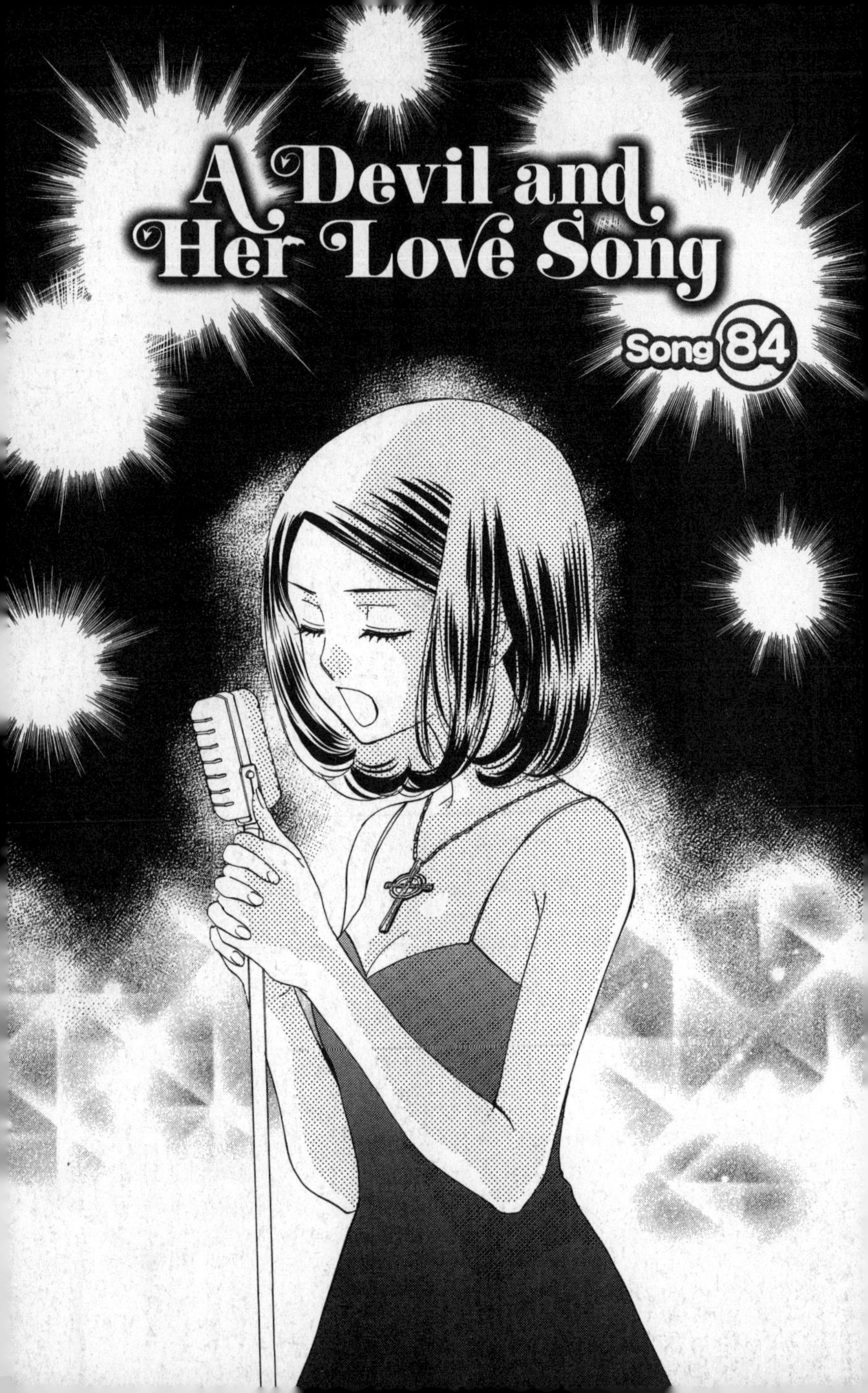
A Devil and Her Love Song
Song 84

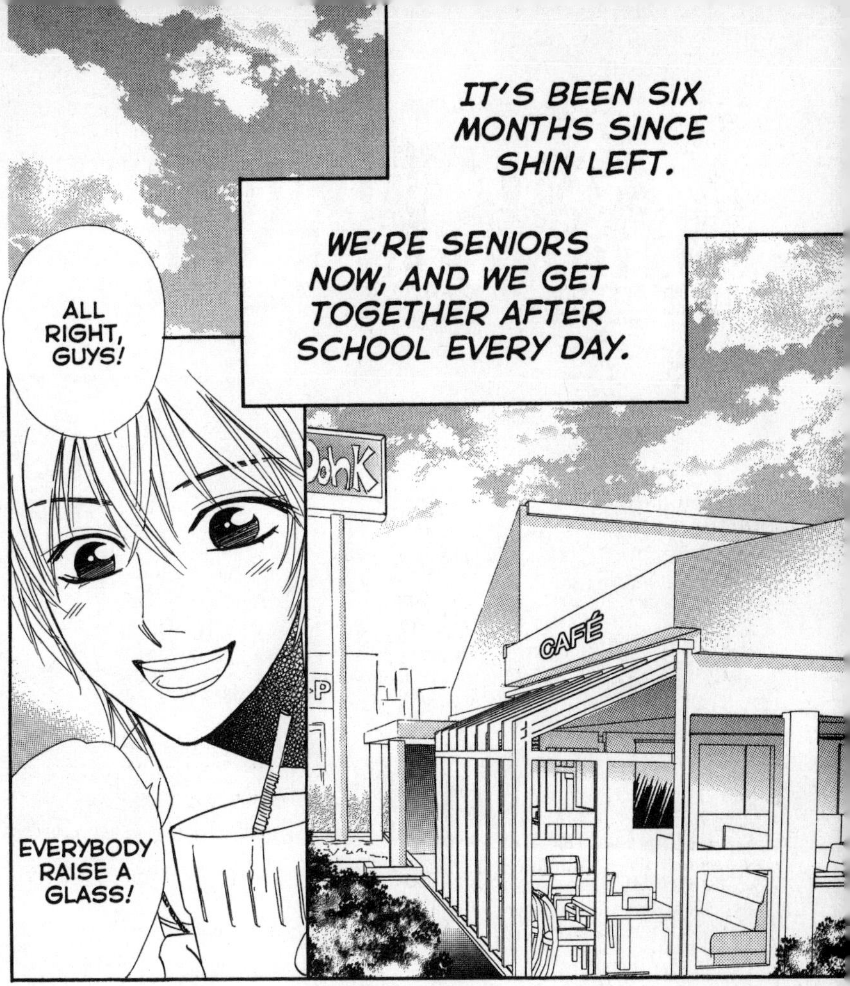
IT'S BEEN SIX MONTHS SINCE SHIN LEFT.
WE'RE SENIORS NOW, AND WE GET TOGETHER AFTER SCHOOL EVERY DAY.
CAFÉ
ALL RIGHT, GUYS!
EVERYBODY RAISE A GLASS!

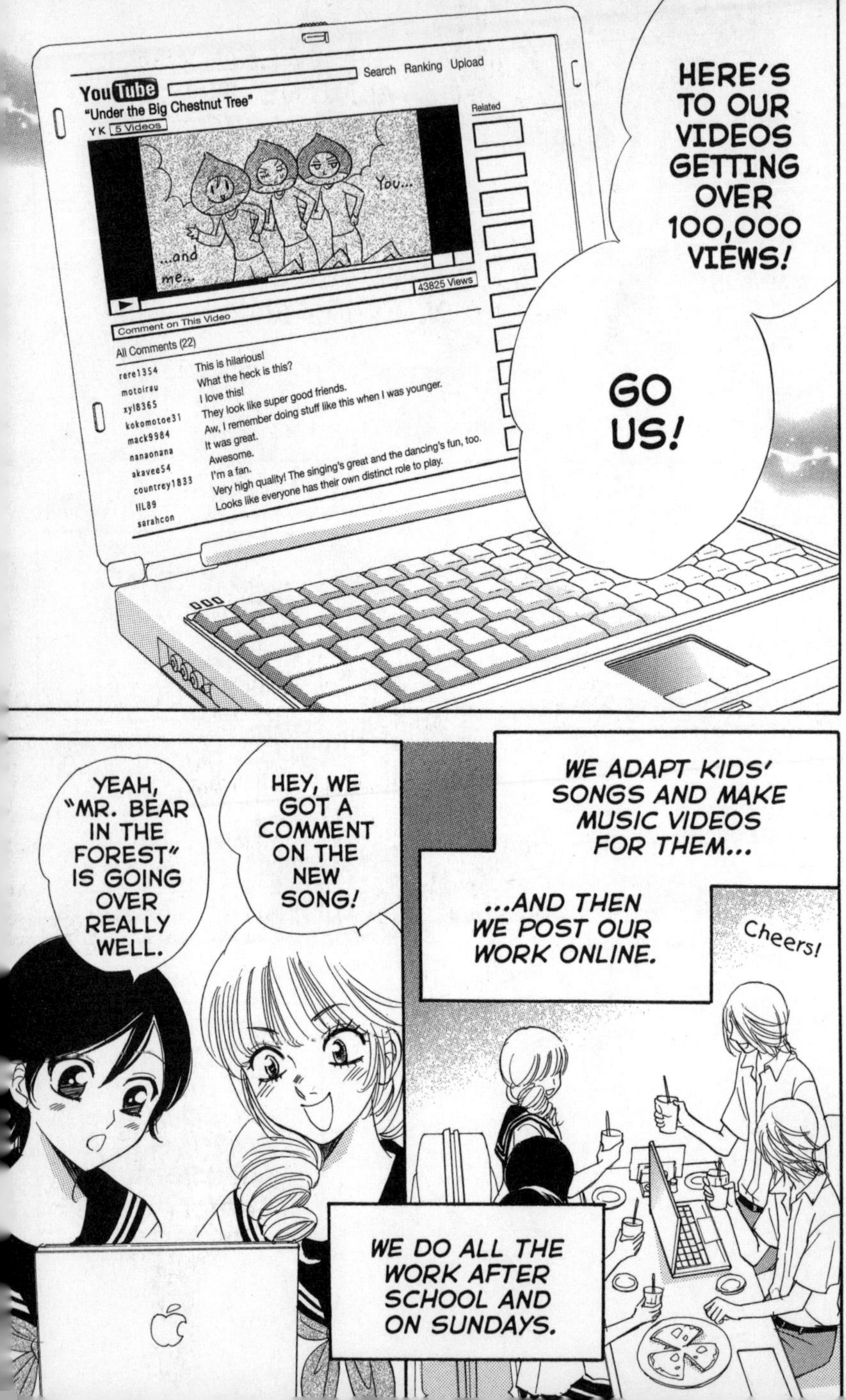
HERE'S TO OUR VIDEOS GETTING OVER 100,000 VIEWS!
GO US!
Search Ranking Upload
YouTube
"Under the Big Chestnut Tree"
YK 5 Videos
Related
You...
...and me...
43825 Views
Comment on This Video
All Comments (22)
rere1354 This is hilarious!
motoirau What the heck is this?
xyl8365 I love this!
kokomotoe31 They look like super good friends.
mack9984 Aw, I remember doing stuff like this when I was younger.
nanaonana It was great.
akavee54 Awesome.
countrey1833 I'm a fan.
IIL89 Very high quality! The singing's great and the dancing's fun, too.
sarahcon Looks like everyone has their own distinct role to play.
WE ADAPT KIDS' SONGS AND MAKE MUSIC VIDEOS FOR THEM...
...AND THEN WE POST OUR WORK ONLINE.
Cheers!
WE DO ALL THE WORK AFTER SCHOOL AND ON SUNDAYS.
HEY, WE GOT A COMMENT ON THE NEW SONG!
YEAH, "MR. BEAR IN THE FOREST" IS GOING OVER REALLY WELL.

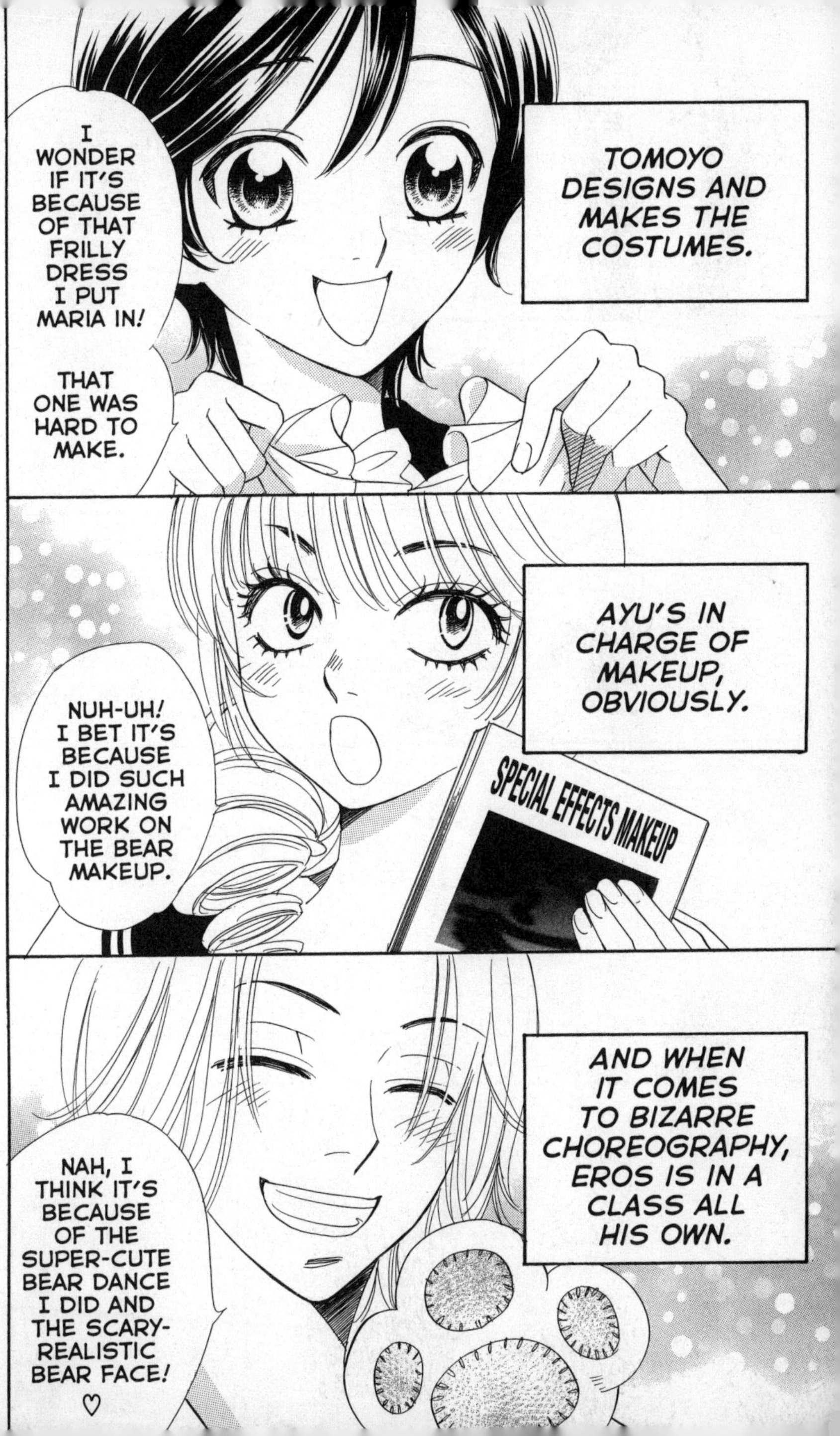
TOMOYO DESIGNS AND MAKES THE COSTUMES.
I WONDER IF IT'S BECAUSE OF THAT FRILLY DRESS I PUT MARIA IN!
THAT ONE WAS HARD TO MAKE.
AYU'S IN CHARGE OF MAKEUP, OBVIOUSLY.
NUH-UH! I BET IT'S BECAUSE I DID SUCH AMAZING WORK ON THE BEAR MAKEUP.
SPECIAL EFFECTS MAKEUP
AND WHEN IT COMES TO BIZARRE CHOREOGRAPHY, EROS IS IN A CLASS ALL HIS OWN.
NAH, I THINK IT'S BECAUSE OF THE SUPER-CUTE BEAR DANCE I DID AND THE SCARY-REALISTIC BEAR FACE! ♡

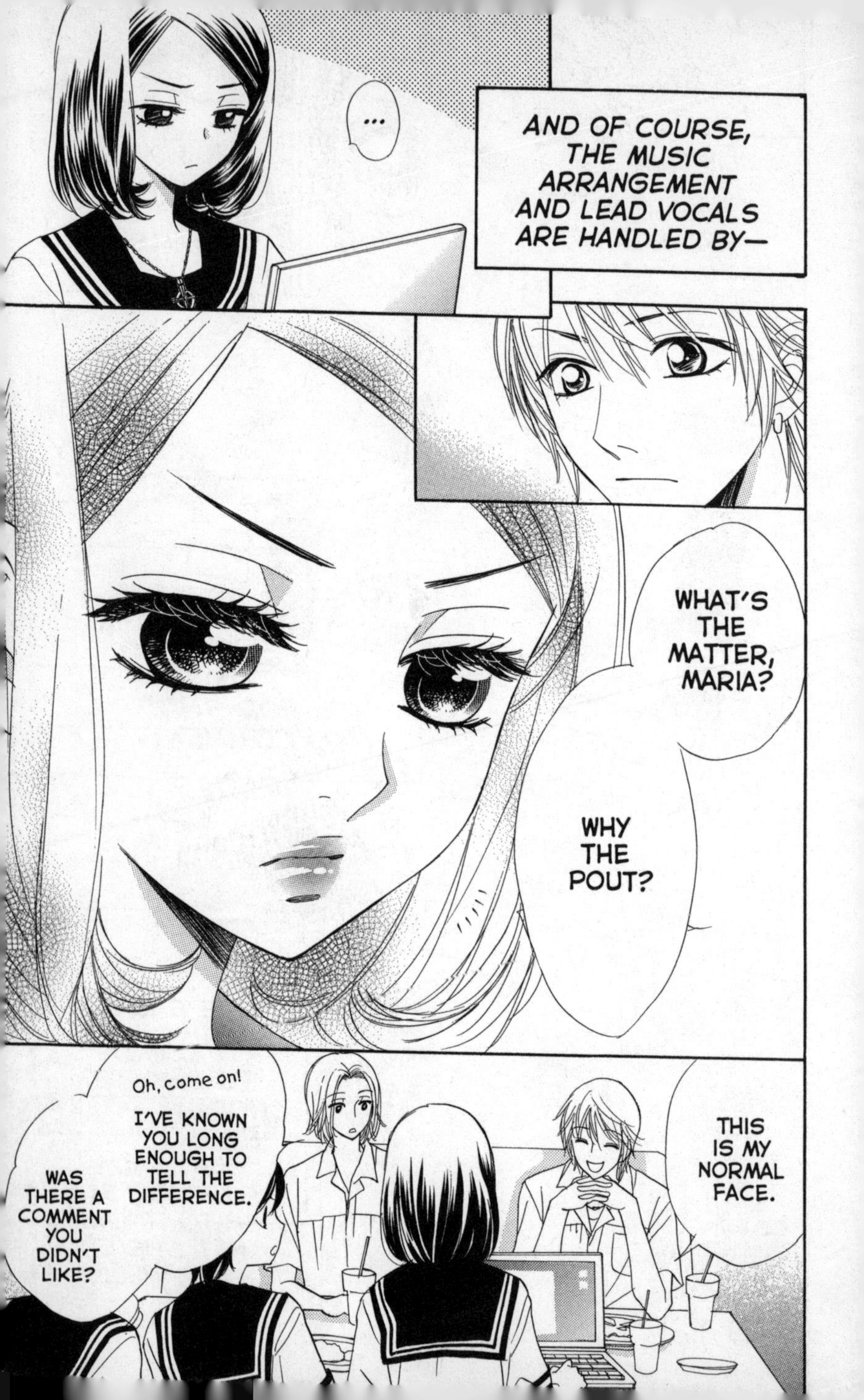
AND OF COURSE, THE MUSIC ARRANGEMENT AND LEAD VOCALS ARE HANDLED BY—
...
WHAT'S THE MATTER, MARIA?
WHY THE POUT?
THIS IS MY NORMAL FACE.
Oh, come on!
I'VE KNOWN YOU LONG ENOUGH TO TELL THE DIFFERENCE.
WAS THERE A COMMENT YOU DIDN'T LIKE?

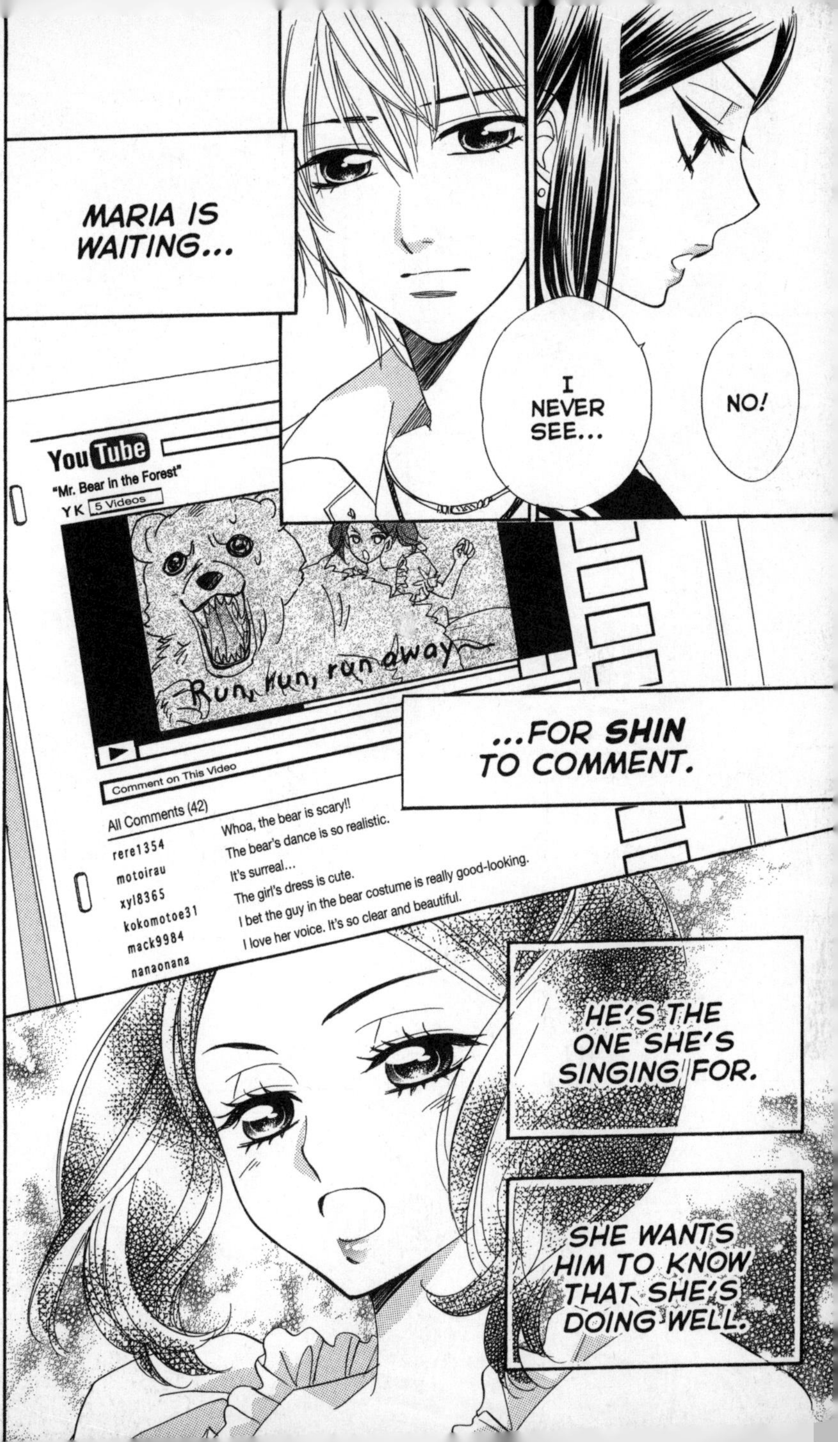
NO!
I NEVER SEE...
MARIA IS WAITING...
YouTube
"Mr. Bear in the Forest"
YK 5 Videos
Run, run, run away~
Comment on This Video
All Comments (42)
rere1354 Whoa, the bear is scary!!
motoirau The bear's dance is so realistic.
xyl8365 It's surreal...
kokomotoe31 The girl's dress is cute.
mack9984 I bet the guy in the bear costume is really good-looking.
nanaonana I love her voice. It's so clear and beautiful.
...FOR SHIN TO COMMENT.
HE'S THE ONE SHE'S SINGING FOR.
SHE WANTS HIM TO KNOW THAT SHE'S DOING WELL.

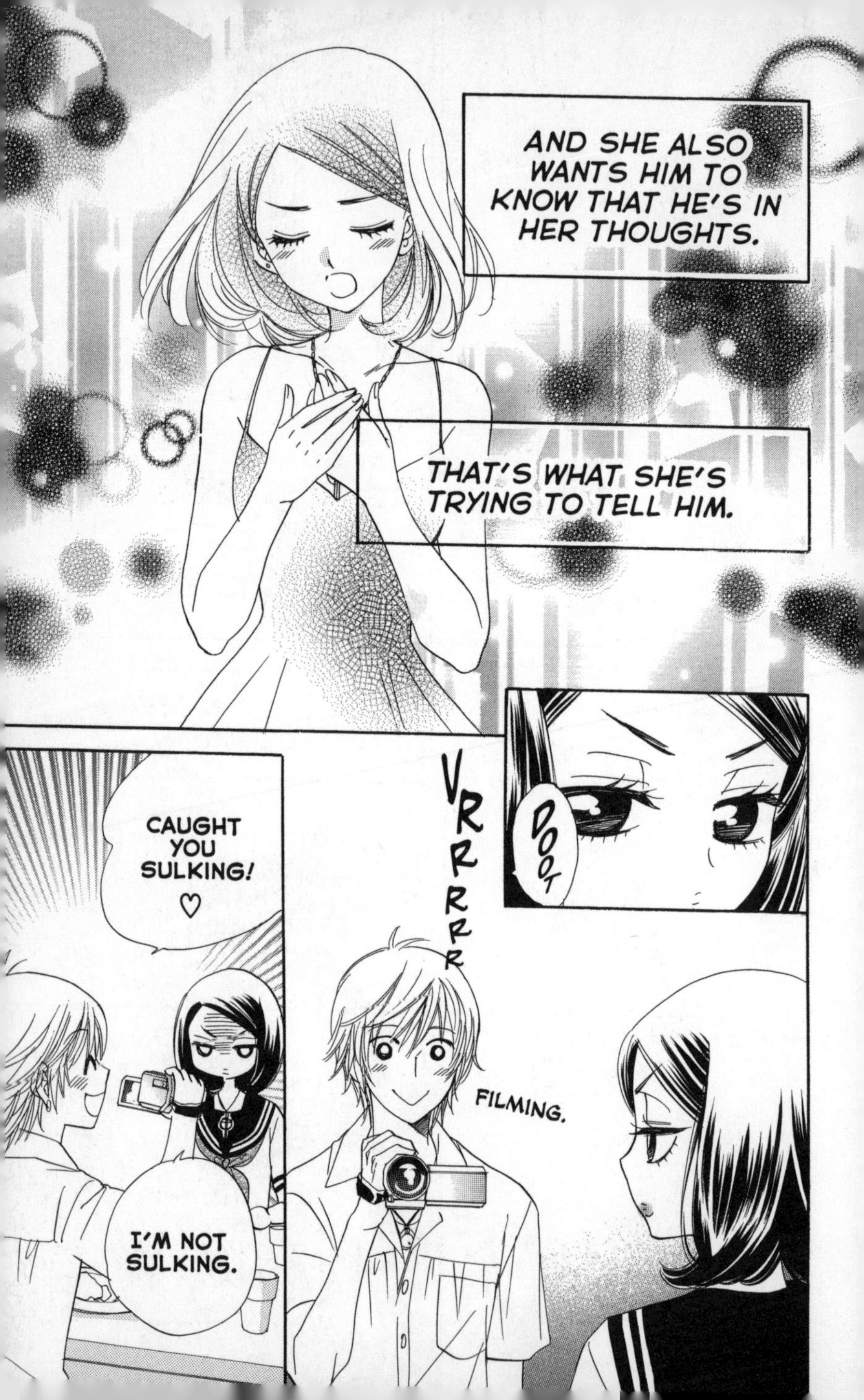
AND SHE ALSO WANTS HIM TO KNOW THAT HE'S IN HER THOUGHTS.
THAT'S WHAT SHE'S TRYING TO TELL HIM.
DOOT
VRRRRRR
FILMING.
CAUGHT YOU SULKING! ♡
I'M NOT SULKING.

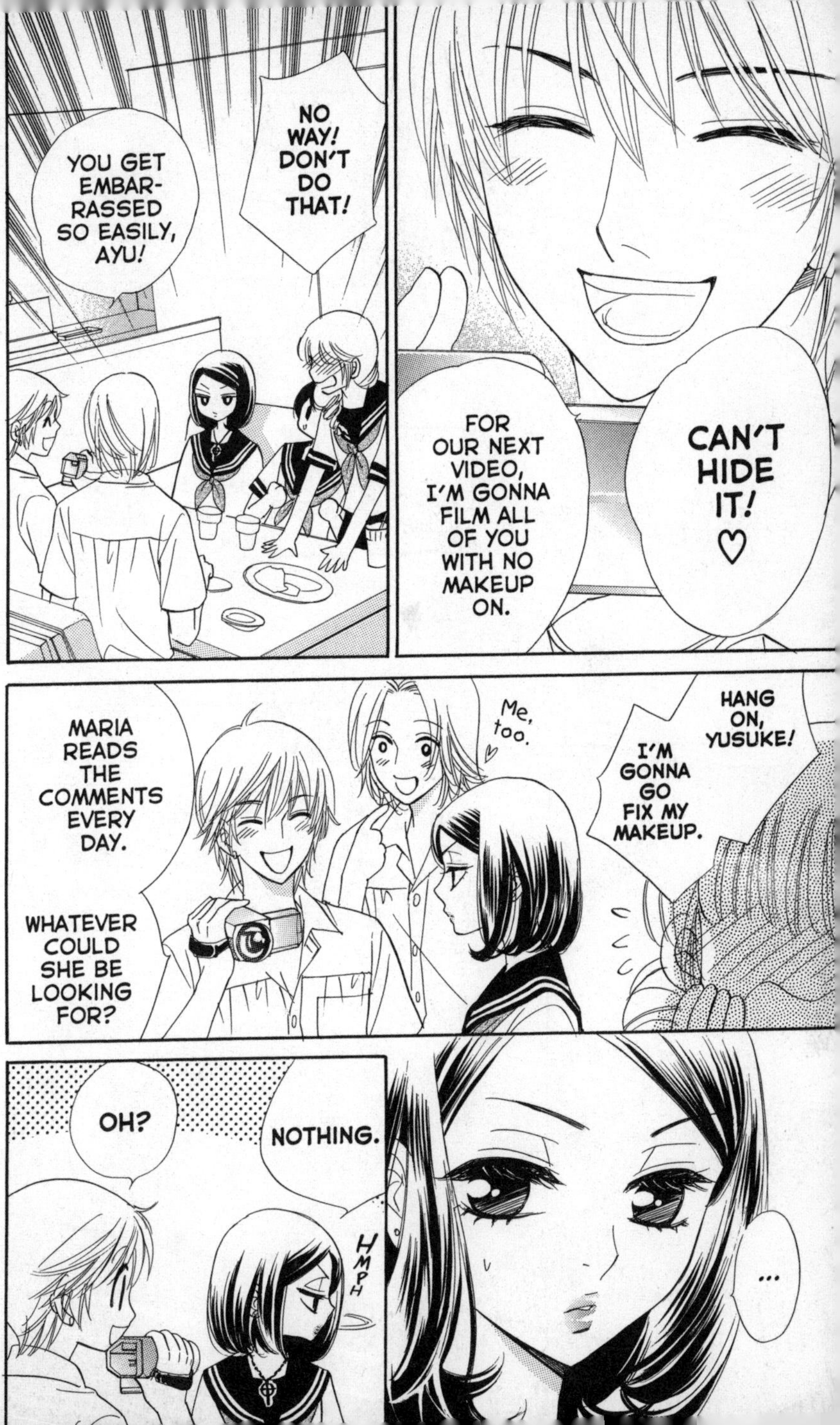
FOR OUR NEXT VIDEO, I'M GONNA FILM ALL OF YOU WITH NO MAKEUP ON.
CAN'T HIDE IT! ♡
NO WAY! DON'T DO THAT!
YOU GET EMBARRASSED SO EASILY, AYU!
HANG ON, YUSUKE!
I'M GONNA GO FIX MY MAKEUP.
Me, too.
MARIA READS THE COMMENTS EVERY DAY.
WHATEVER COULD SHE BE LOOKING FOR?
...
NOTHING.
OH?
HMPH

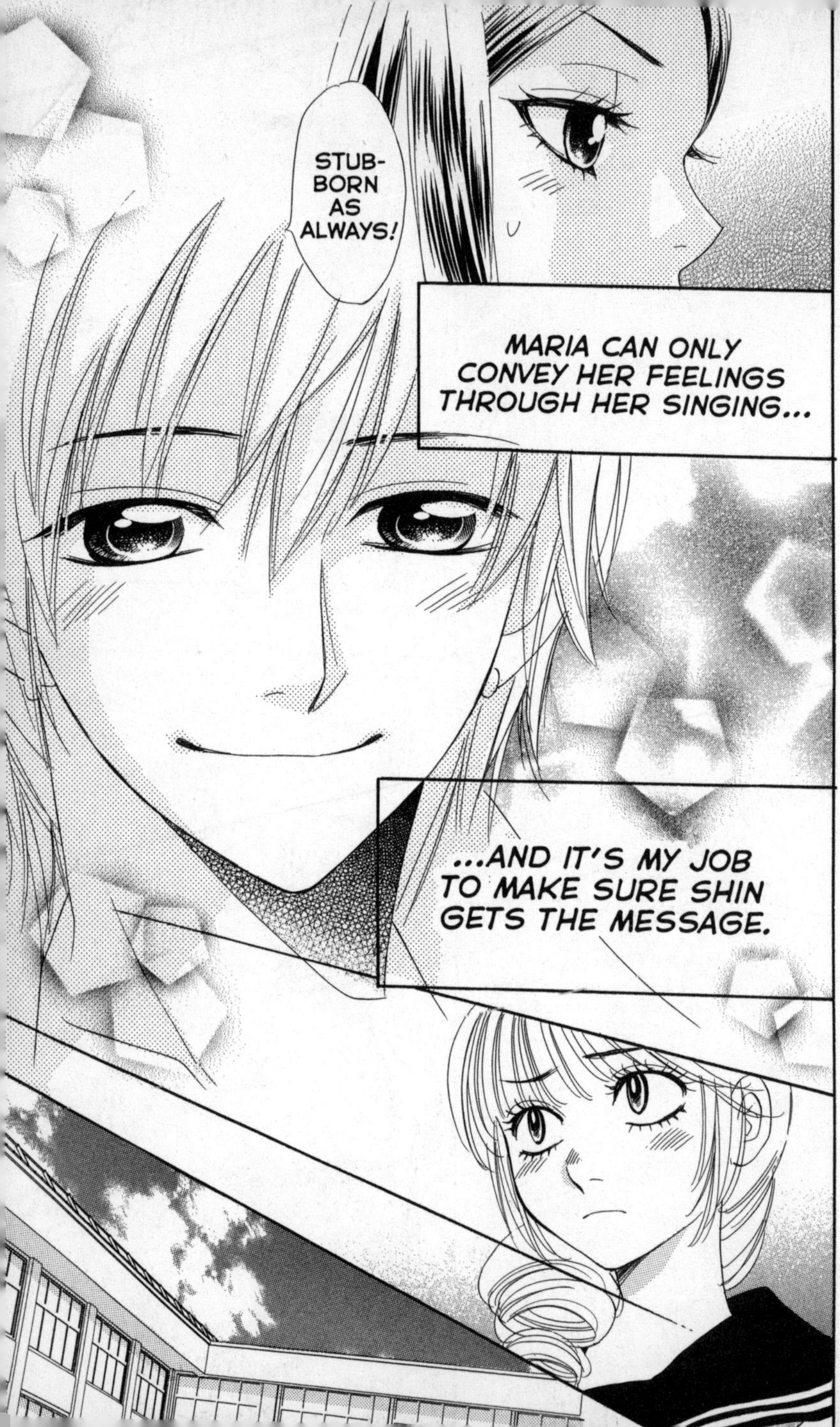
STUB-BORN AS ALWAYS!
MARIA CAN ONLY CONVEY HER FEELINGS THROUGH HER SINGING...
...AND IT'S MY JOB TO MAKE SURE SHIN GETS THE MESSAGE.

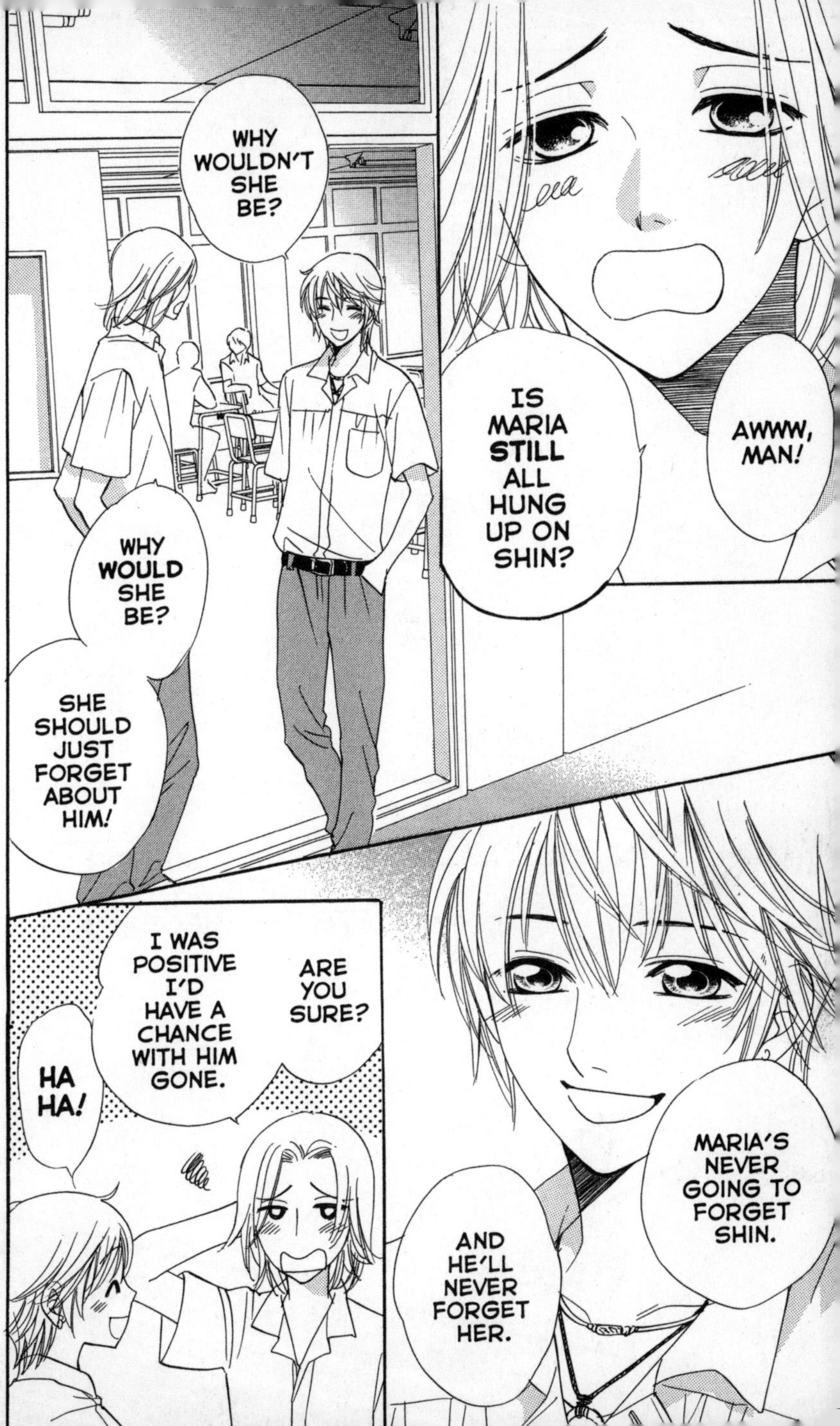
AWWW, MAN!
IS MARIA STILL ALL HUNG UP ON SHIN?
WHY WOULDN'T SHE BE?
WHY WOULD SHE BE?
SHE SHOULD JUST FORGET ABOUT HIM!
MARIA'S NEVER GOING TO FORGET SHIN.
AND HE'LL NEVER FORGET HER.
ARE YOU SURE?
I WAS POSITIVE I'D HAVE A CHANCE WITH HIM GONE.
HA HA!

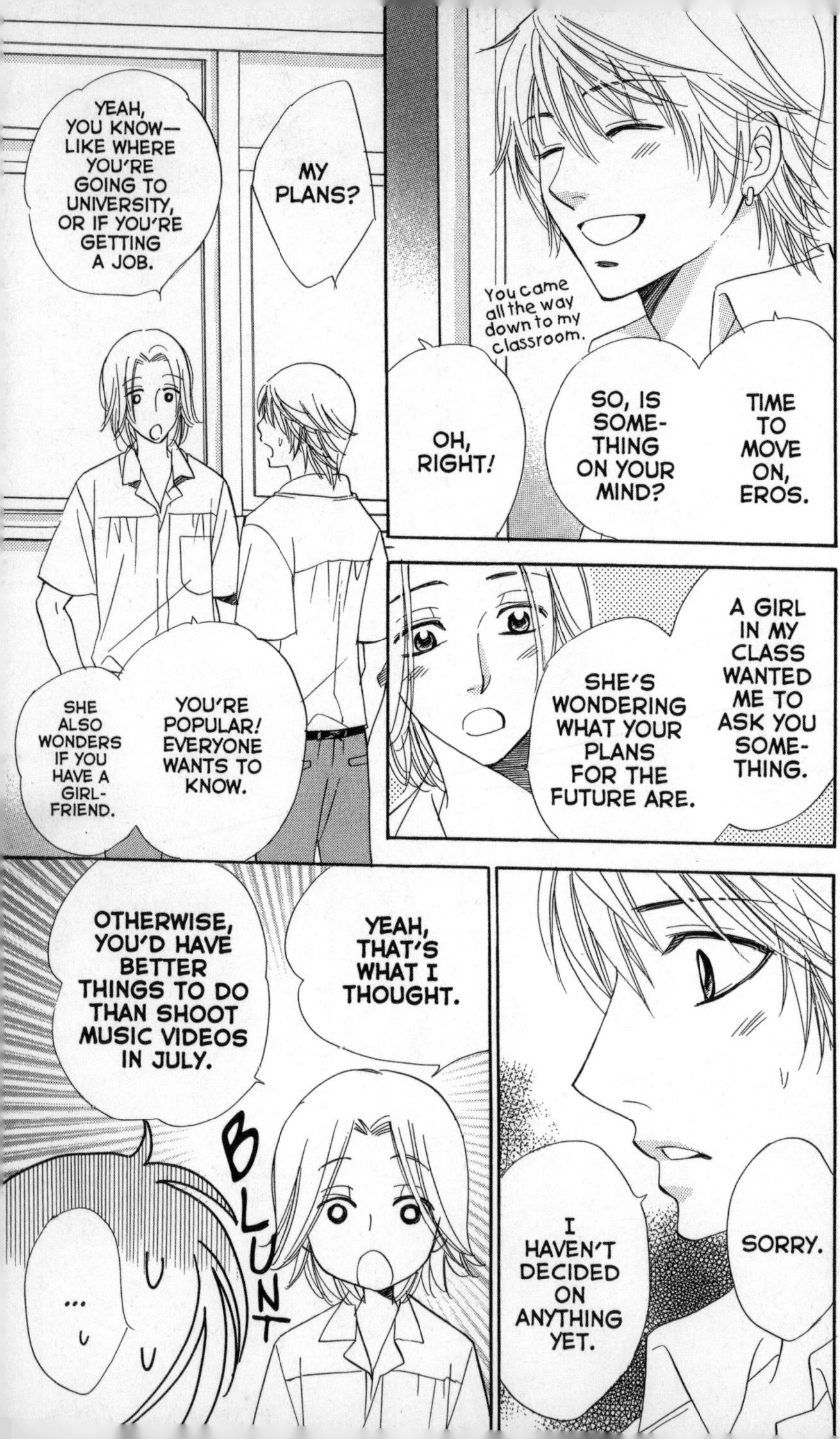
TIME TO MOVE ON, EROS.
SO, IS SOMETHING ON YOUR MIND?
You came all the way down to my classroom.
OH, RIGHT!
A GIRL IN MY CLASS WANTED ME TO ASK YOU SOMETHING.
SHE'S WONDERING WHAT YOUR PLANS FOR THE FUTURE ARE.
MY PLANS?
YEAH, YOU KNOW— LIKE WHERE YOU'RE GOING TO UNIVERSITY, OR IF YOU'RE GETTING A JOB.
YOU'RE POPULAR! EVERYONE WANTS TO KNOW.
SHE ALSO WONDERS IF YOU HAVE A GIRL-FRIEND.
SORRY.
I HAVEN'T DECIDED ON ANYTHING YET.
YEAH, THAT'S WHAT I THOUGHT.
OTHERWISE, YOU'D HAVE BETTER THINGS TO DO THAN SHOOT MUSIC VIDEOS IN JULY.
BLUNT
...

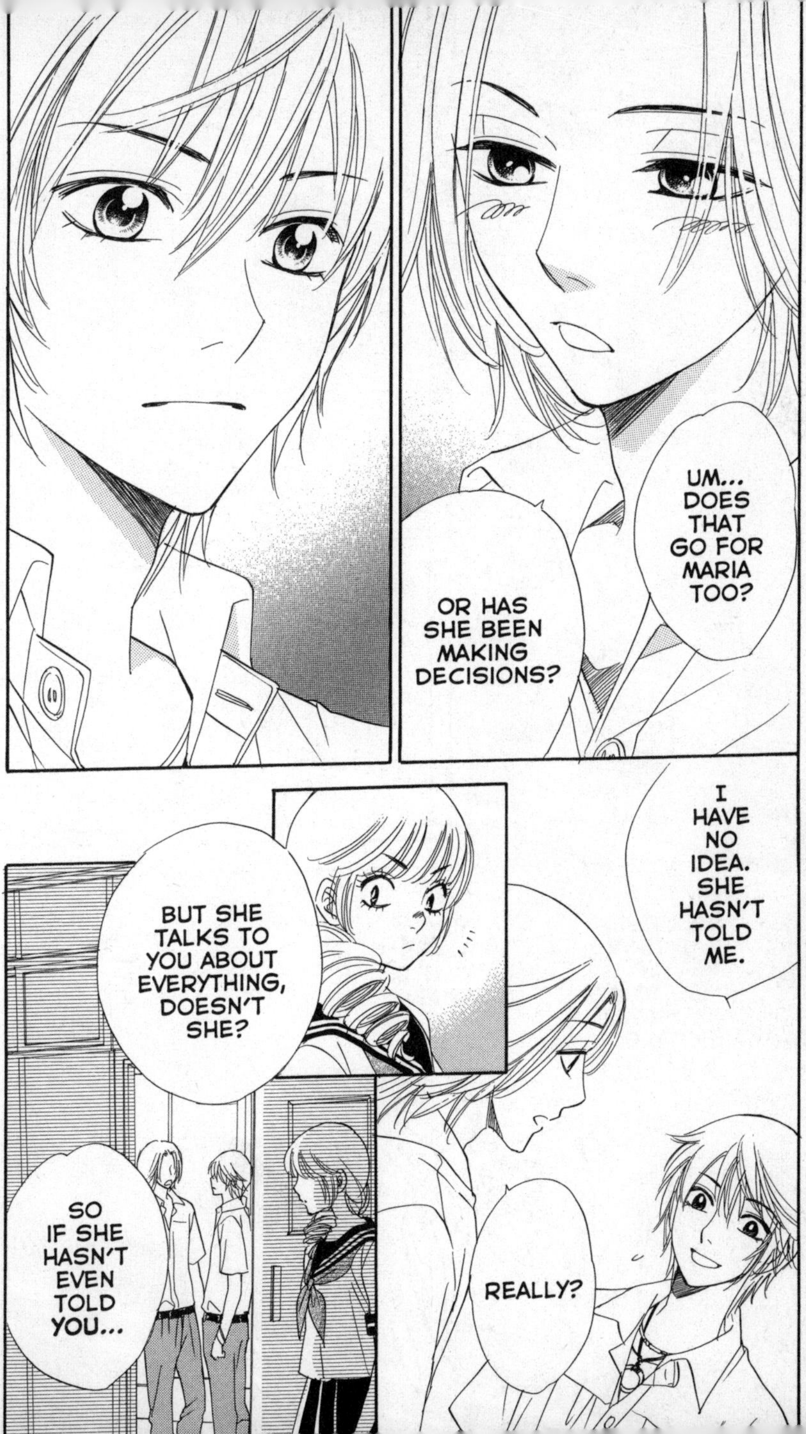
UM... DOES THAT GO FOR MARIA TOO?
OR HAS SHE BEEN MAKING DECISIONS?
I HAVE NO IDEA. SHE HASN'T TOLD ME.
BUT SHE TALKS TO YOU ABOUT EVERYTHING, DOESN'T SHE?
REALLY?
SO IF SHE HASN'T EVEN TOLD YOU...

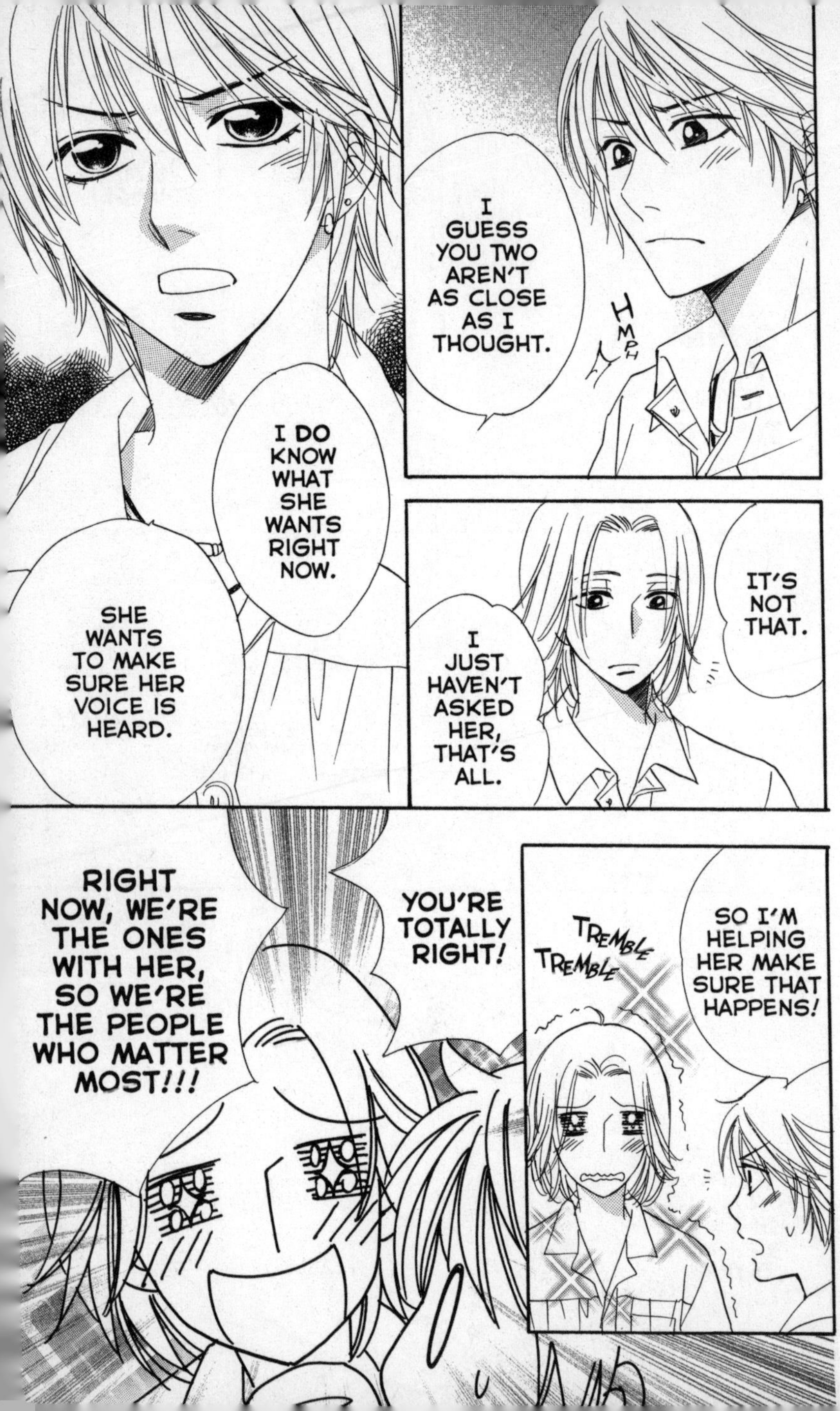
I GUESS YOU TWO AREN'T AS CLOSE AS I THOUGHT.
HMPH
IT'S NOT THAT.
I JUST HAVEN'T ASKED HER, THAT'S ALL.
I DO KNOW WHAT SHE WANTS RIGHT NOW.
SHE WANTS TO MAKE SURE HER VOICE IS HEARD.
SO I'M HELPING HER MAKE SURE THAT HAPPENS!
TREMBLE
TREMBLE
YOU'RE TOTALLY RIGHT!
RIGHT NOW, WE'RE THE ONES WITH HER, SO WE'RE THE PEOPLE WHO MATTER MOST!!!

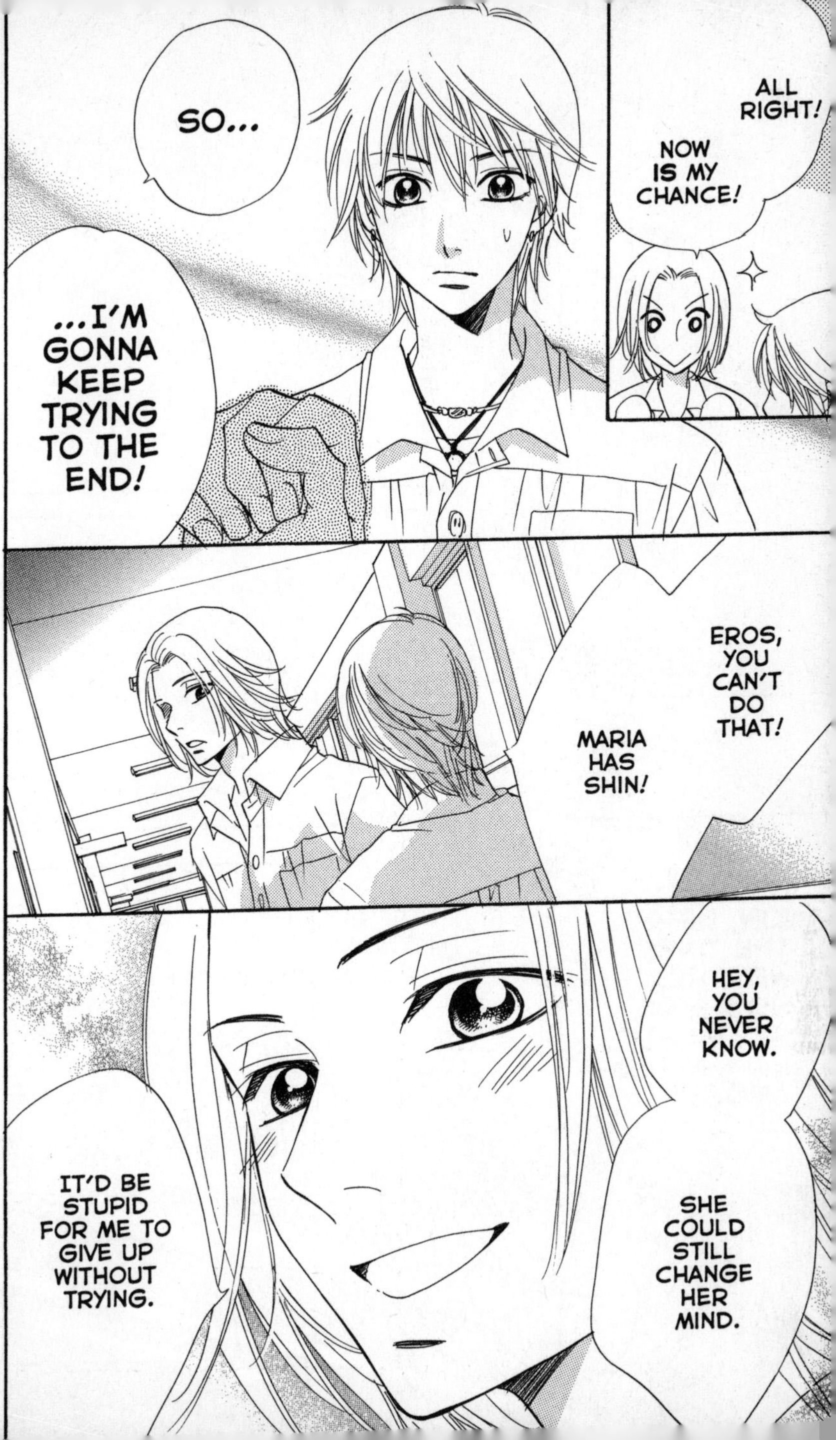
ALL RIGHT!
NOW IS MY CHANCE!
SO...
...I'M GONNA KEEP TRYING TO THE END!
EROS, YOU CAN'T DO THAT!
MARIA HAS SHIN!
HEY, YOU NEVER KNOW.
SHE COULD STILL CHANGE HER MIND.
IT'D BE STUPID FOR ME TO GIVE UP WITHOUT TRYING.

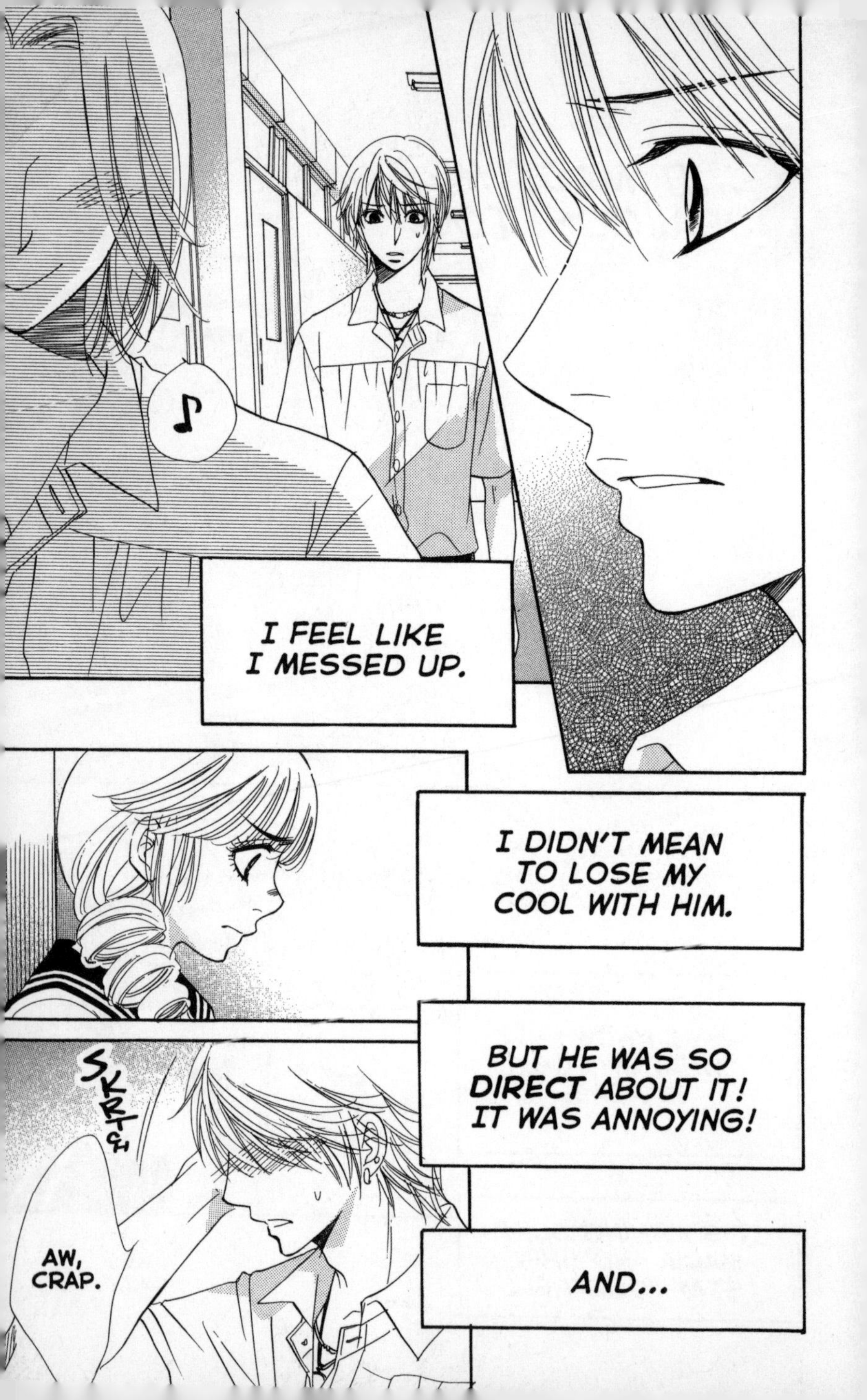
♪
I FEEL LIKE I MESSED UP.
I DIDN'T MEAN TO LOSE MY COOL WITH HIM.
BUT HE WAS SO DIRECT ABOUT IT! IT WAS ANNOYING!
AND...
SKRTCH
AW, CRAP.

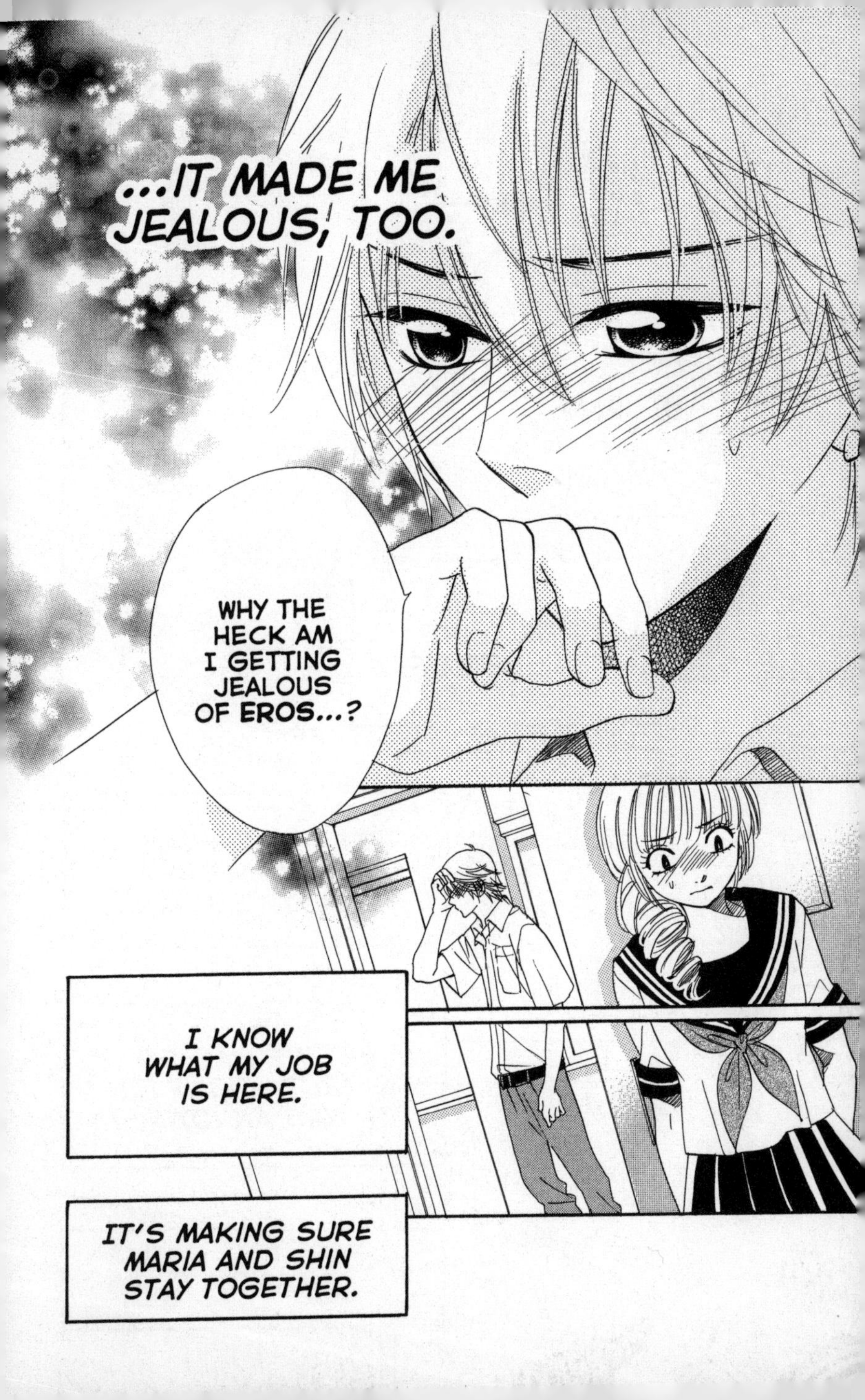
...IT MADE ME JEALOUS, TOO.
WHY THE HECK AM I GETTING JEALOUS OF EROS...?
I KNOW WHAT MY JOB IS HERE.
IT'S MAKING SURE MARIA AND SHIN STAY TOGETHER.

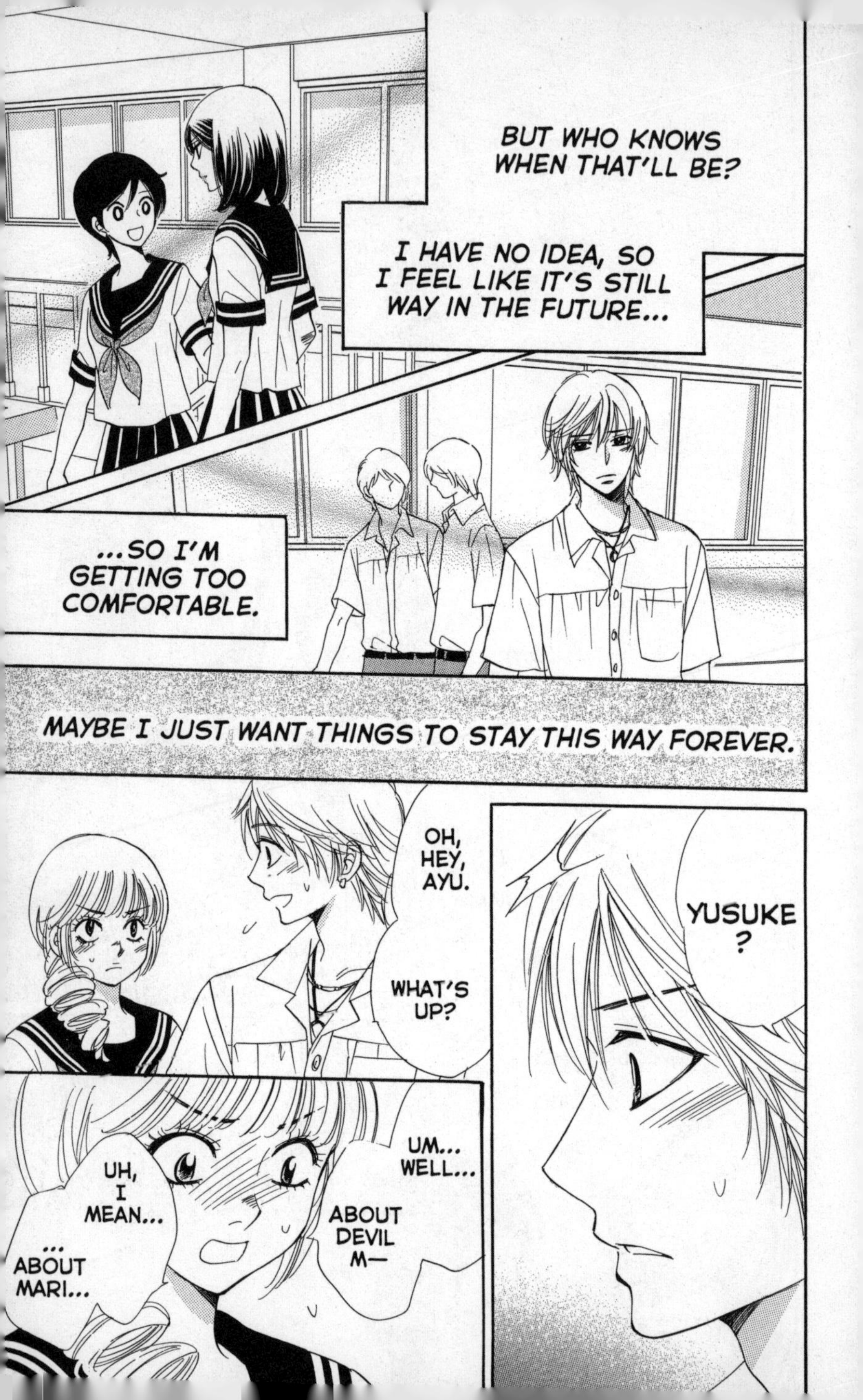
BUT WHO KNOWS WHEN THAT'LL BE?
I HAVE NO IDEA, SO I FEEL LIKE IT'S STILL WAY IN THE FUTURE...
...SO I'M GETTING TOO COMFORTABLE.
MAYBE I JUST WANT THINGS TO STAY THIS WAY FOREVER.
YUSUKE?
OH, HEY, AYU.
WHAT'S UP?
UM... WELL...
ABOUT DEVIL M—
UH, I MEAN...
...ABOUT MARI...

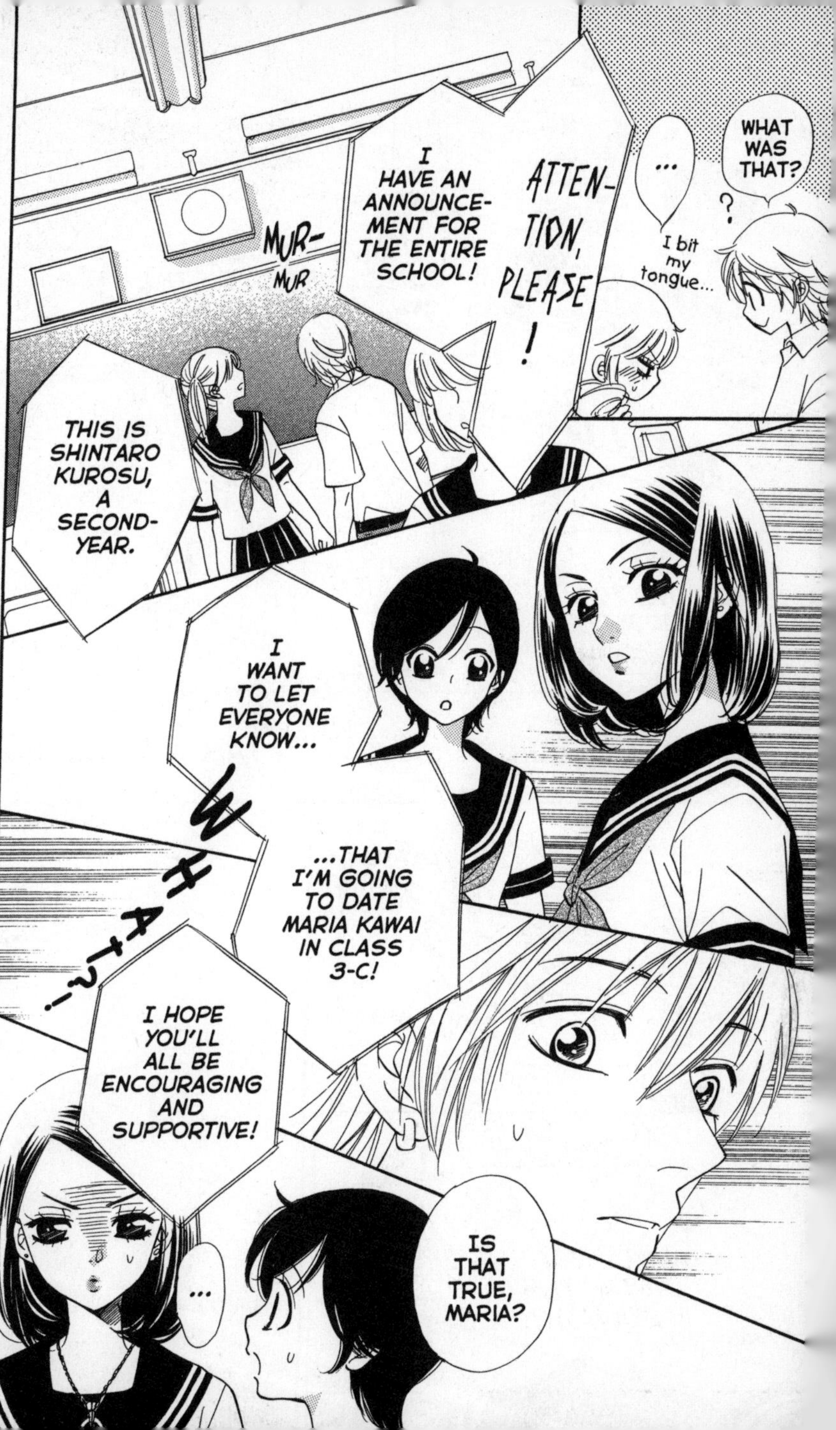
WHAT WAS THAT?
?
...
I bit my tongue...
ATTEN-TION, PLEASE!
I HAVE AN ANNOUNCE-MENT FOR THE ENTIRE SCHOOL!
MUR-MUR
THIS IS SHINTARO KUROSU, A SECOND-YEAR.
I WANT TO LET EVERYONE KNOW...
...THAT I'M GOING TO DATE MARIA KAWAI IN CLASS 3-C!
WHAT?!
I HOPE YOU'LL ALL BE ENCOURAGING AND SUPPORTIVE!
IS THAT TRUE, MARIA?
...

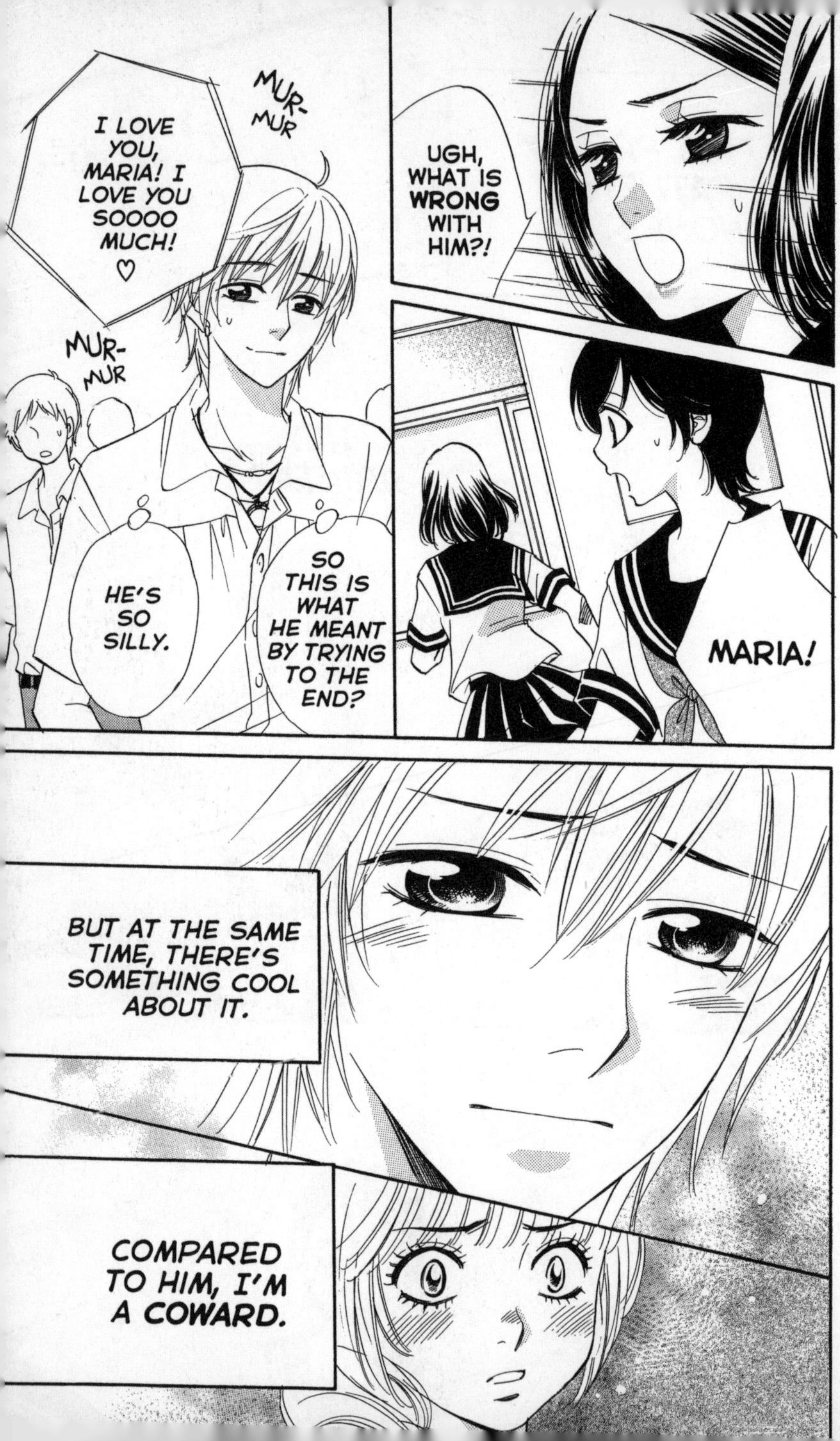
UGH, WHAT IS WRONG WITH HIM?!
MARIA!
MUR-MUR
I LOVE YOU, MARIA! I LOVE YOU SOOOO MUCH! ♡
MUR-MUR
SO THIS IS WHAT HE MEANT BY TRYING TO THE END?
HE'S SO SILLY.
BUT AT THE SAME TIME, THERE'S SOMETHING COOL ABOUT IT.
COMPARED TO HIM, I'M A COWARD.

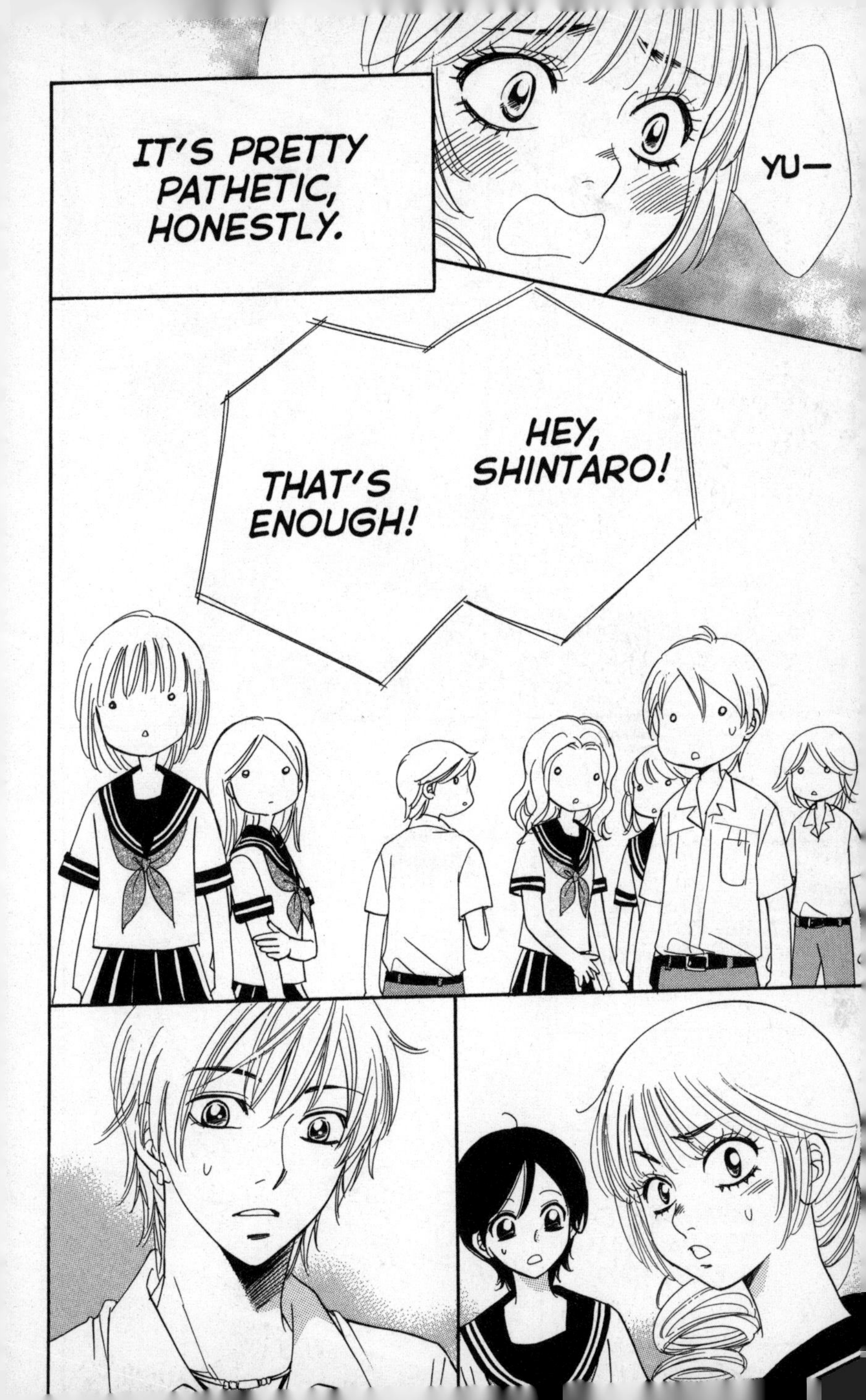
YU—
IT'S PRETTY PATHETIC, HONESTLY.
HEY, SHINTARO!
THAT'S ENOUGH!

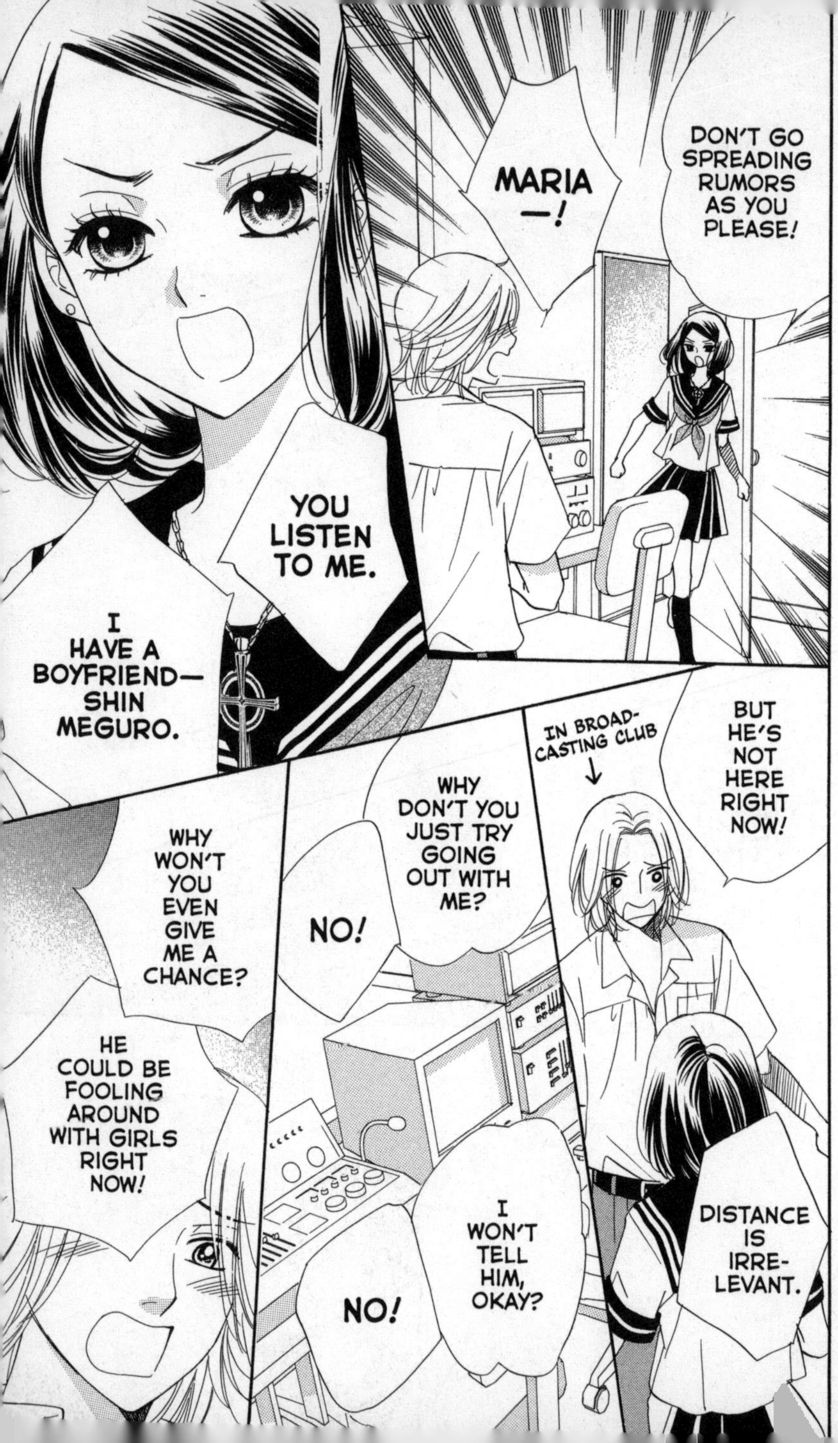
DON'T GO SPREADING RUMORS AS YOU PLEASE!
MARIA—!
YOU LISTEN TO ME.
I HAVE A BOYFRIEND—SHIN MEGURO.
BUT HE'S NOT HERE RIGHT NOW!
IN BROADCASTING CLUB
DISTANCE IS IRRELEVANT.
WHY DON'T YOU JUST TRY GOING OUT WITH ME?
NO!
I WON'T TELL HIM, OKAY?
NO!
WHY WON'T YOU EVEN GIVE ME A CHANCE?
HE COULD BE FOOLING AROUND WITH GIRLS RIGHT NOW!

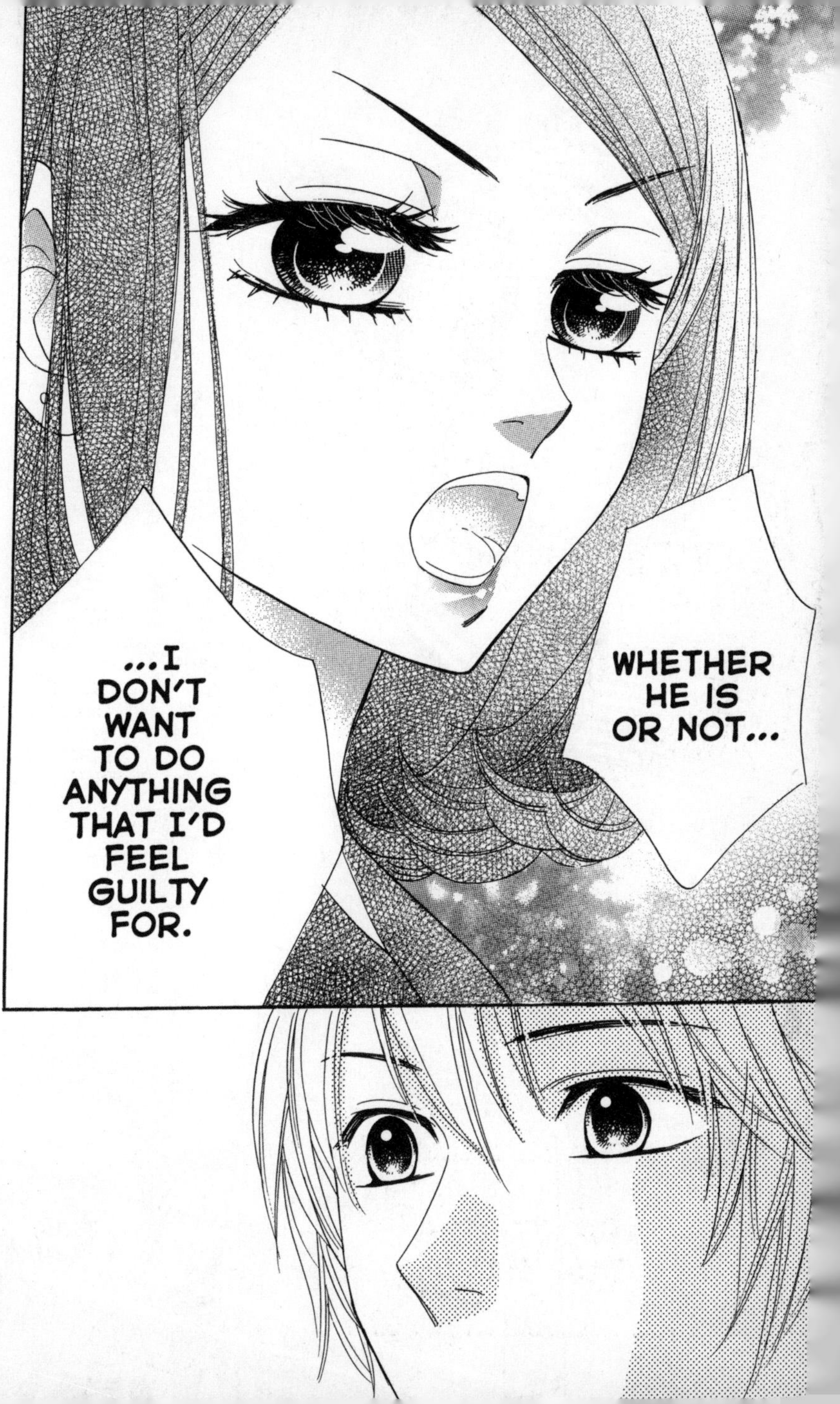
WHETHER HE IS OR NOT...
...I DON'T WANT TO DO ANYTHING THAT I'D FEEL GUILTY FOR.

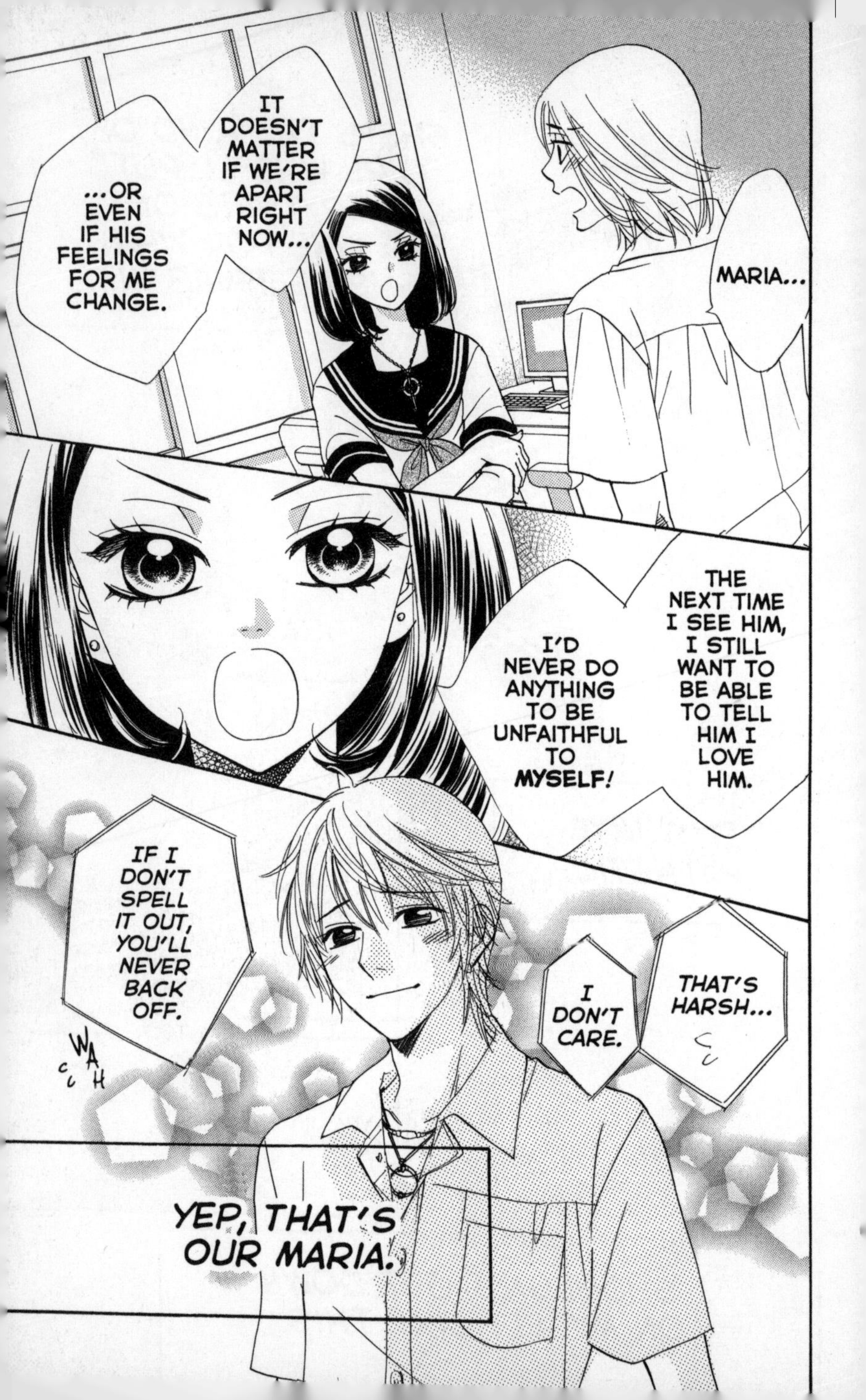
MARIA...
IT DOESN'T MATTER IF WE'RE APART RIGHT NOW...
...OR EVEN IF HIS FEELINGS FOR ME CHANGE.
THE NEXT TIME I SEE HIM, I STILL WANT TO BE ABLE TO TELL HIM I LOVE HIM.
I'D NEVER DO ANYTHING TO BE UNFAITHFUL TO MYSELF!
THAT'S HARSH...
I DON'T CARE.
IF I DON'T SPELL IT OUT, YOU'LL NEVER BACK OFF.
WAH
YEP, THAT'S OUR MARIA.

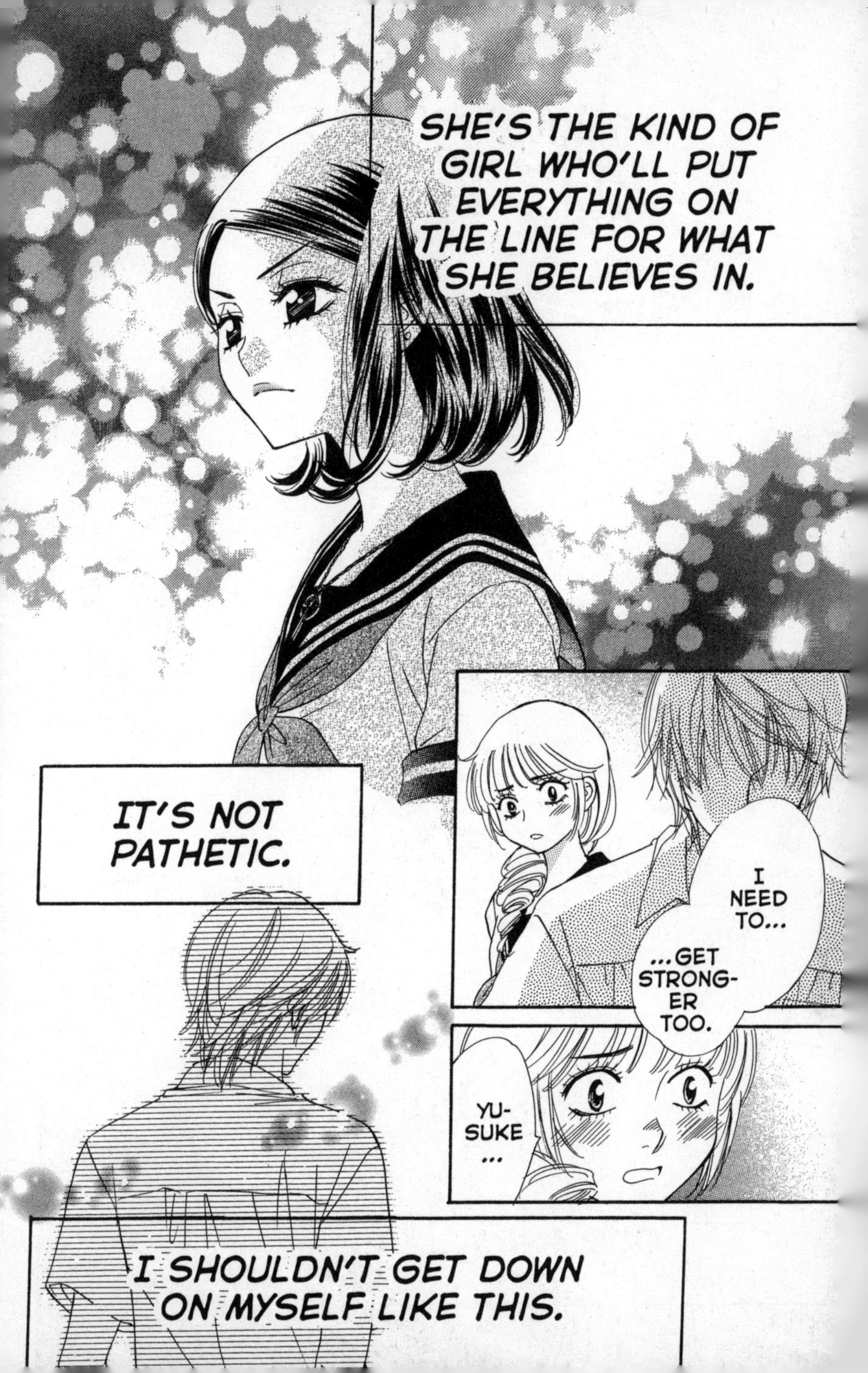

SHE'S THE KIND OF GIRL WHO'LL PUT EVERYTHING ON THE LINE FOR WHAT SHE BELIEVES IN.
I NEED TO...
...GET STRONGER-ER TOO.
YU-SUKE...
IT'S NOT PATHETIC.
I SHOULDN'T GET DOWN ON MYSELF LIKE THIS.

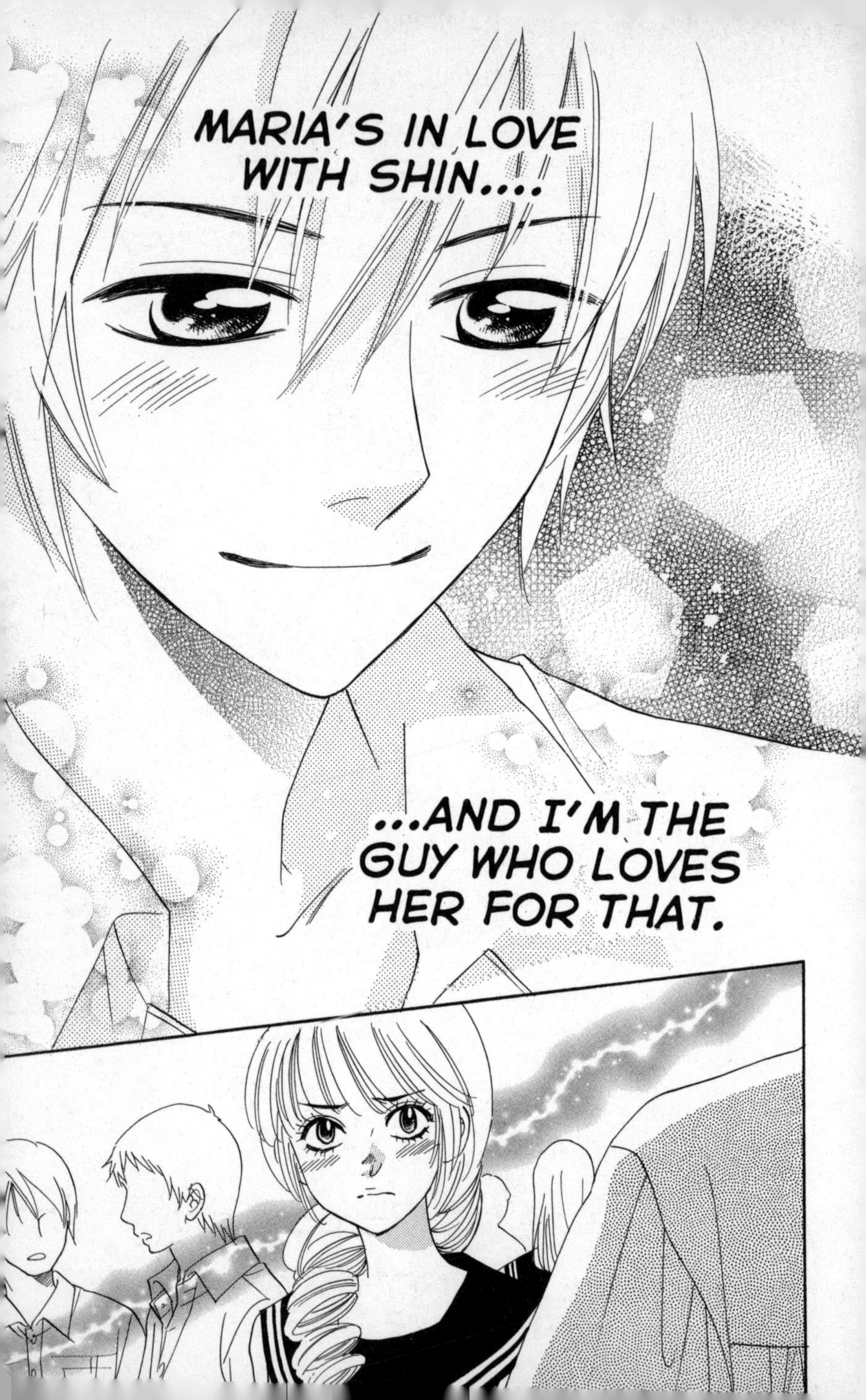
MARIA'S IN LOVE WITH SHIN....
...AND I'M THE GUY WHO LOVES HER FOR THAT.

A Devil and Her Love Song

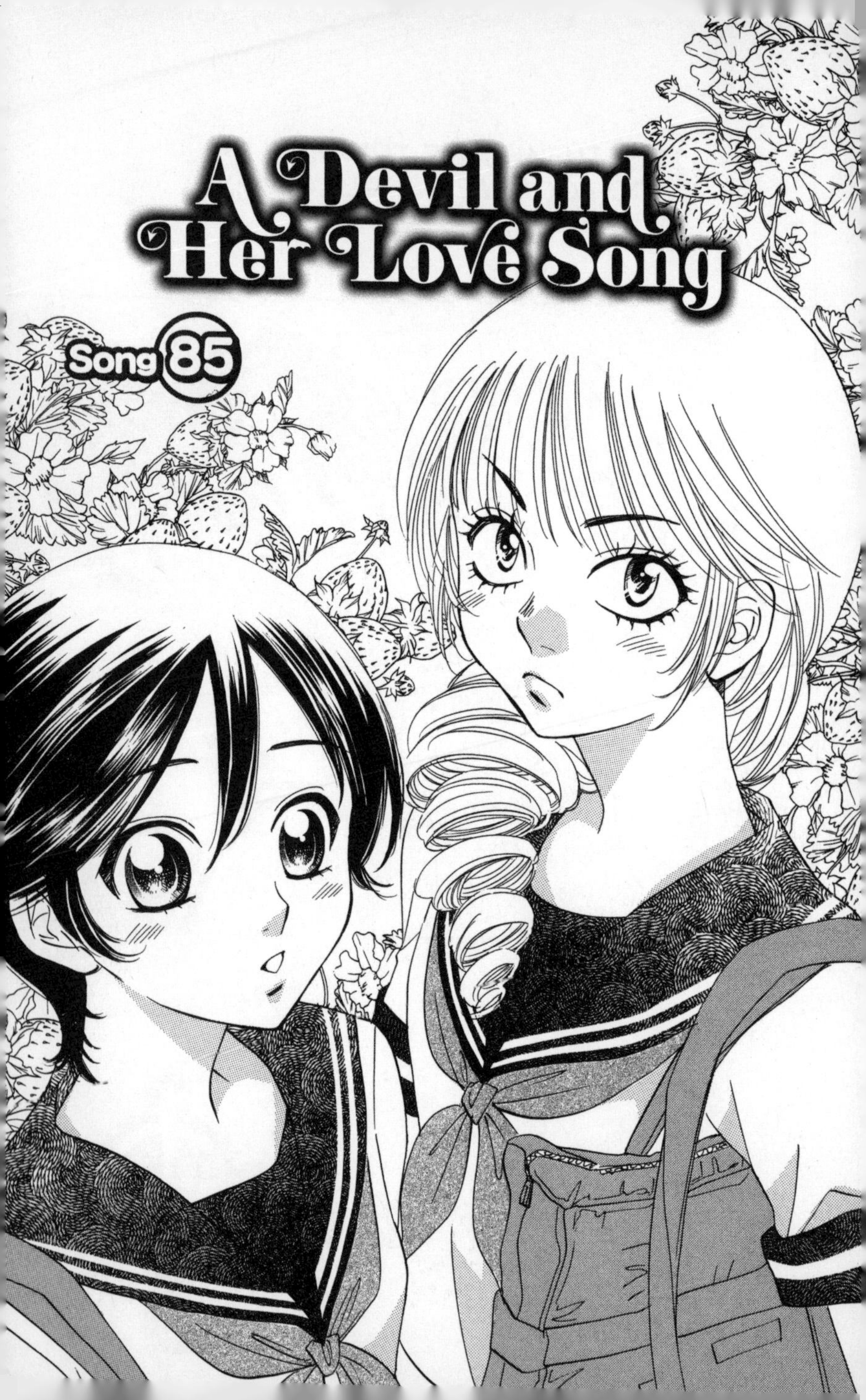
A Devil and Her Love Song
Song 85

IT'S THE WAY OF THE WORLD—GOOD-LOOKING PEOPLE ALWAYS GET WHAT THEY WANT.

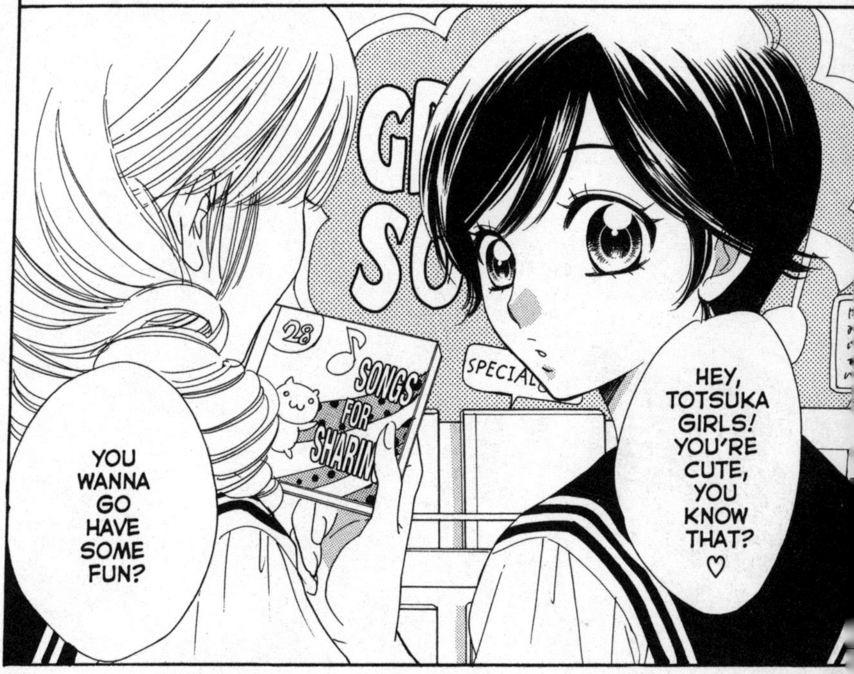
HEY, TOTSUKA GIRLS! YOU'RE CUTE, YOU KNOW THAT? ♡
SPECIAL
28
SONGS FOR SHARIN
YOU WANNA GO HAVE SOME FUN?

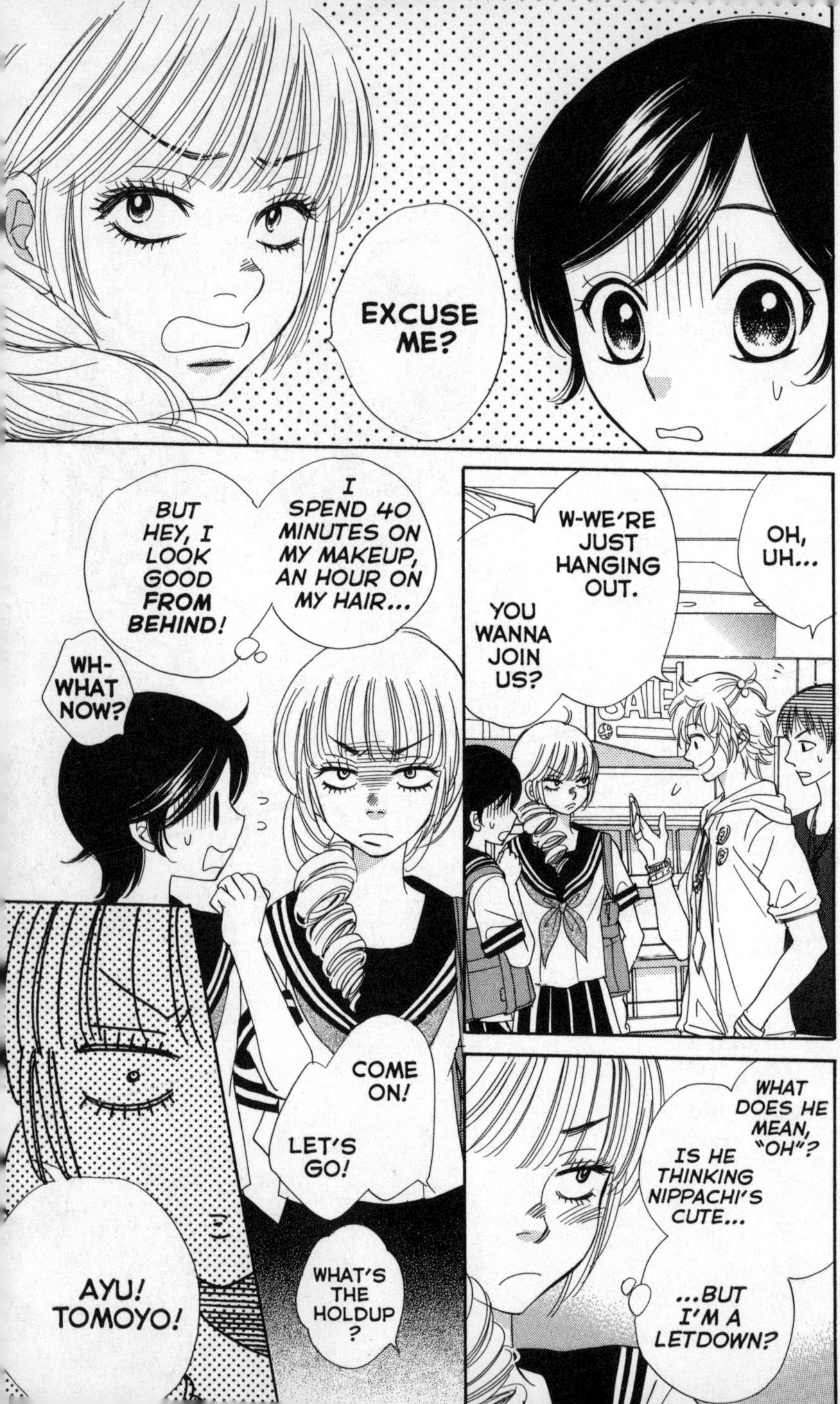
EXCUSE ME?
OH, UH...
W-WE'RE JUST HANGING OUT.
YOU WANNA JOIN US?
WHAT DOES HE MEAN, "OH"?
IS HE THINKING NIPPACHI'S CUTE...
...BUT I'M A LETDOWN?
I SPEND 40 MINUTES ON MY MAKEUP, AN HOUR ON MY HAIR...
BUT HEY, I LOOK GOOD FROM BEHIND!
WH-WHAT NOW?
COME ON!
LET'S GO!
WHAT'S THE HOLDUP?
AYU! TOMOYO!

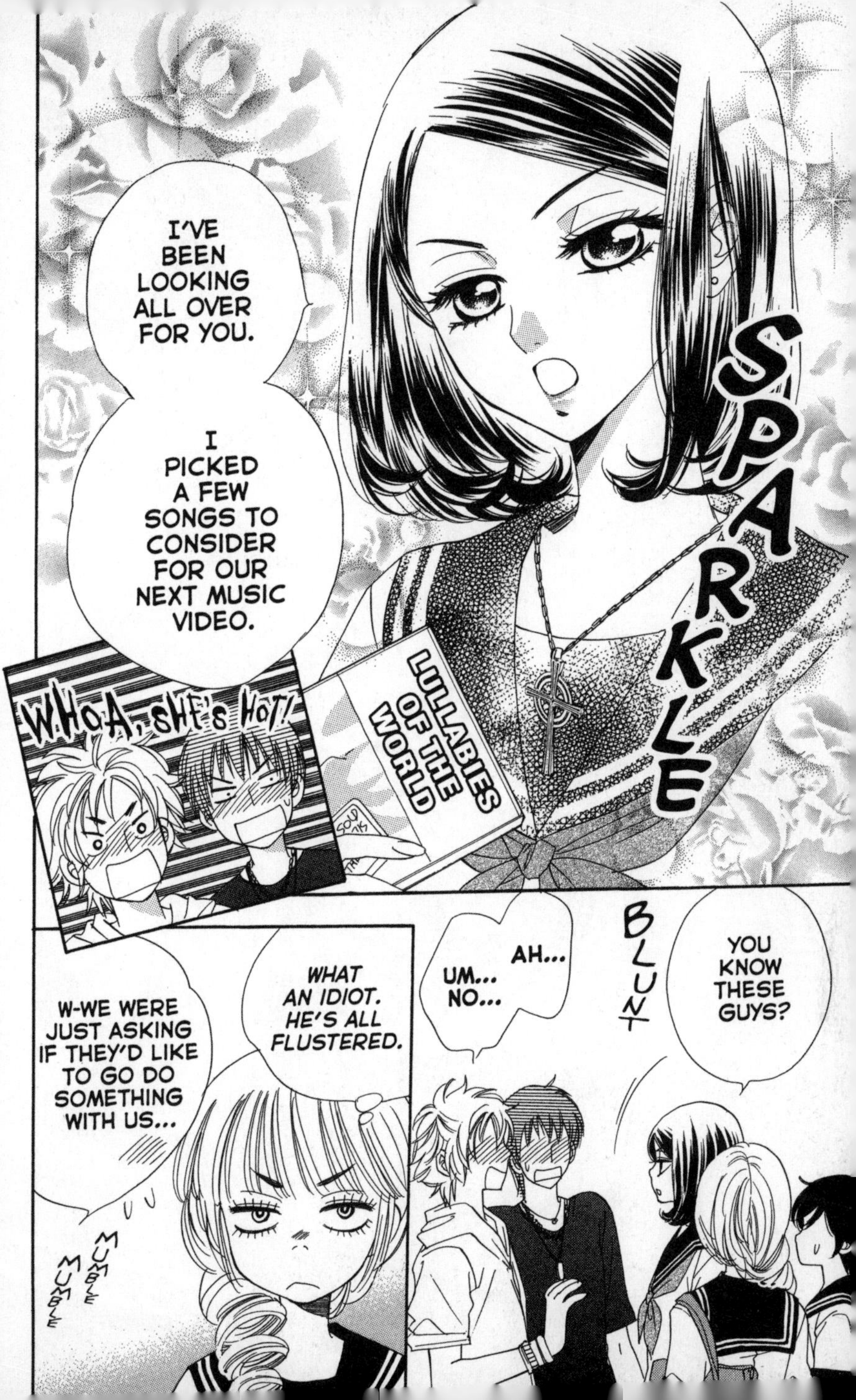
I'VE BEEN LOOKING ALL OVER FOR YOU.
I PICKED A FEW SONGS TO CONSIDER FOR OUR NEXT MUSIC VIDEO.
SPARKLE
LULLABIES OF THE WORLD
WHOA, SHE'S HOT!
YOU KNOW THESE GUYS?
BLUNT
AH...
UM... NO...
WHAT AN IDIOT. HE'S ALL FLUSTERED.
W-WE WERE JUST ASKING IF THEY'D LIKE TO GO DO SOMETHING WITH US...
MUMBLE MUMBLE

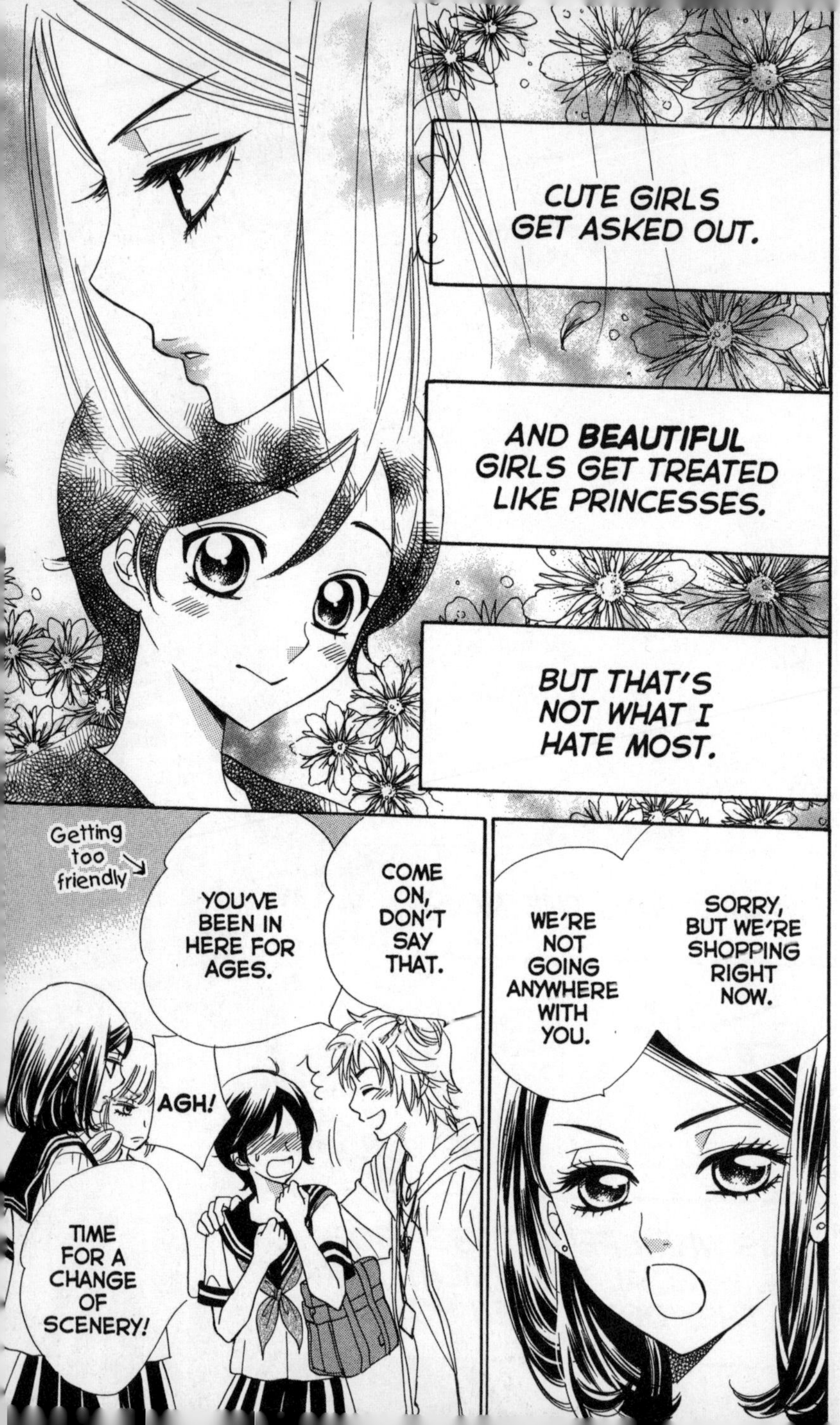
CUTE GIRLS GET ASKED OUT.
AND **BEAUTIFUL** GIRLS GET TREATED LIKE PRINCESSES.
BUT THAT'S NOT WHAT I HATE MOST.
SORRY, BUT WE'RE SHOPPING RIGHT NOW.
WE'RE NOT GOING ANYWHERE WITH YOU.
COME ON, DON'T SAY THAT.
YOU'VE BEEN IN HERE FOR AGES.
Getting too friendly
AGH!
TIME FOR A CHANGE OF SCENERY!

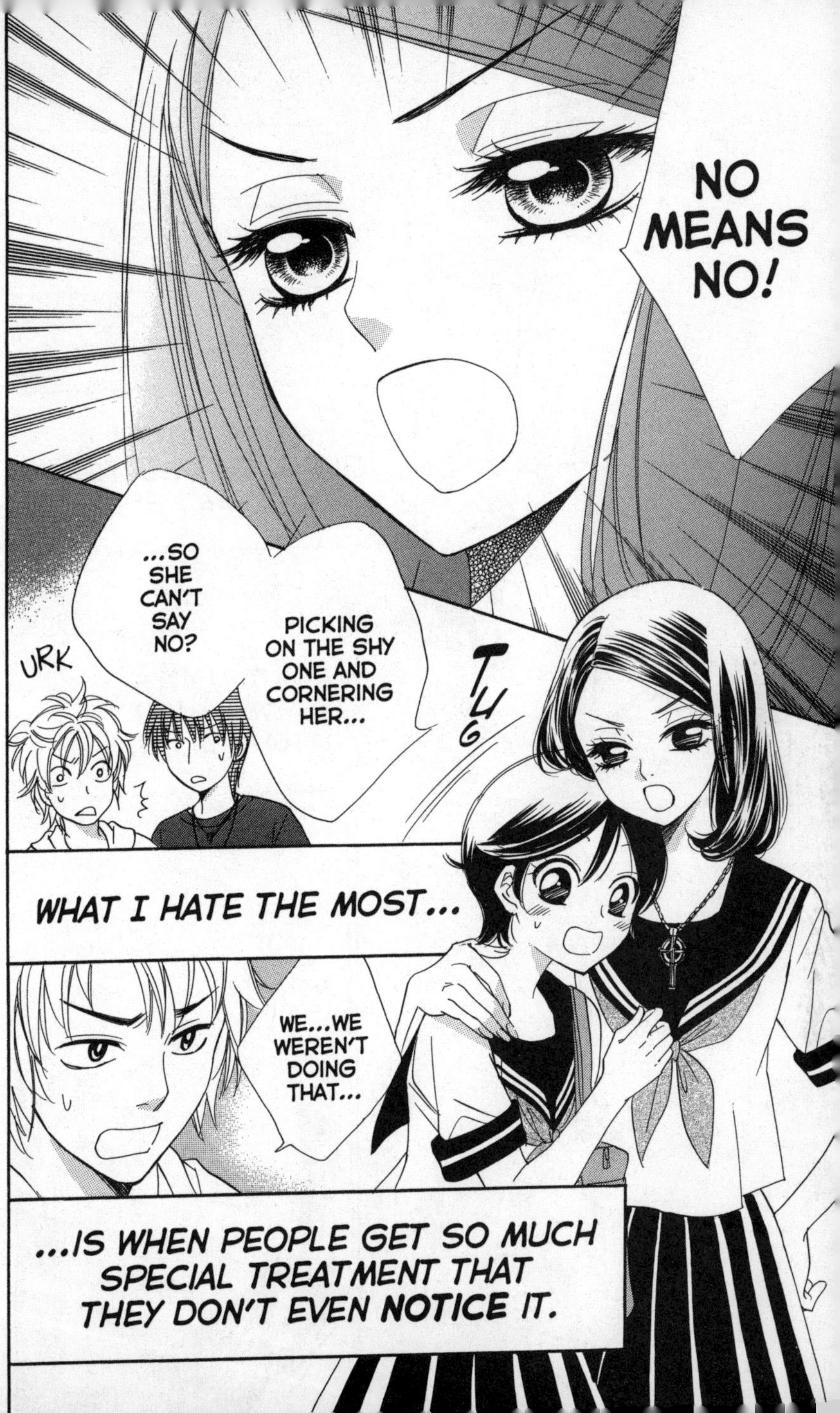
NO MEANS NO!
PICKING ON THE SHY ONE AND CORNERING HER...
...SO SHE CAN'T SAY NO?
TUG
URK
WHAT I HATE THE MOST...
WE...WE WEREN'T DOING THAT...
...IS WHEN PEOPLE GET SO MUCH SPECIAL TREATMENT THAT THEY DON'T EVEN NOTICE IT.

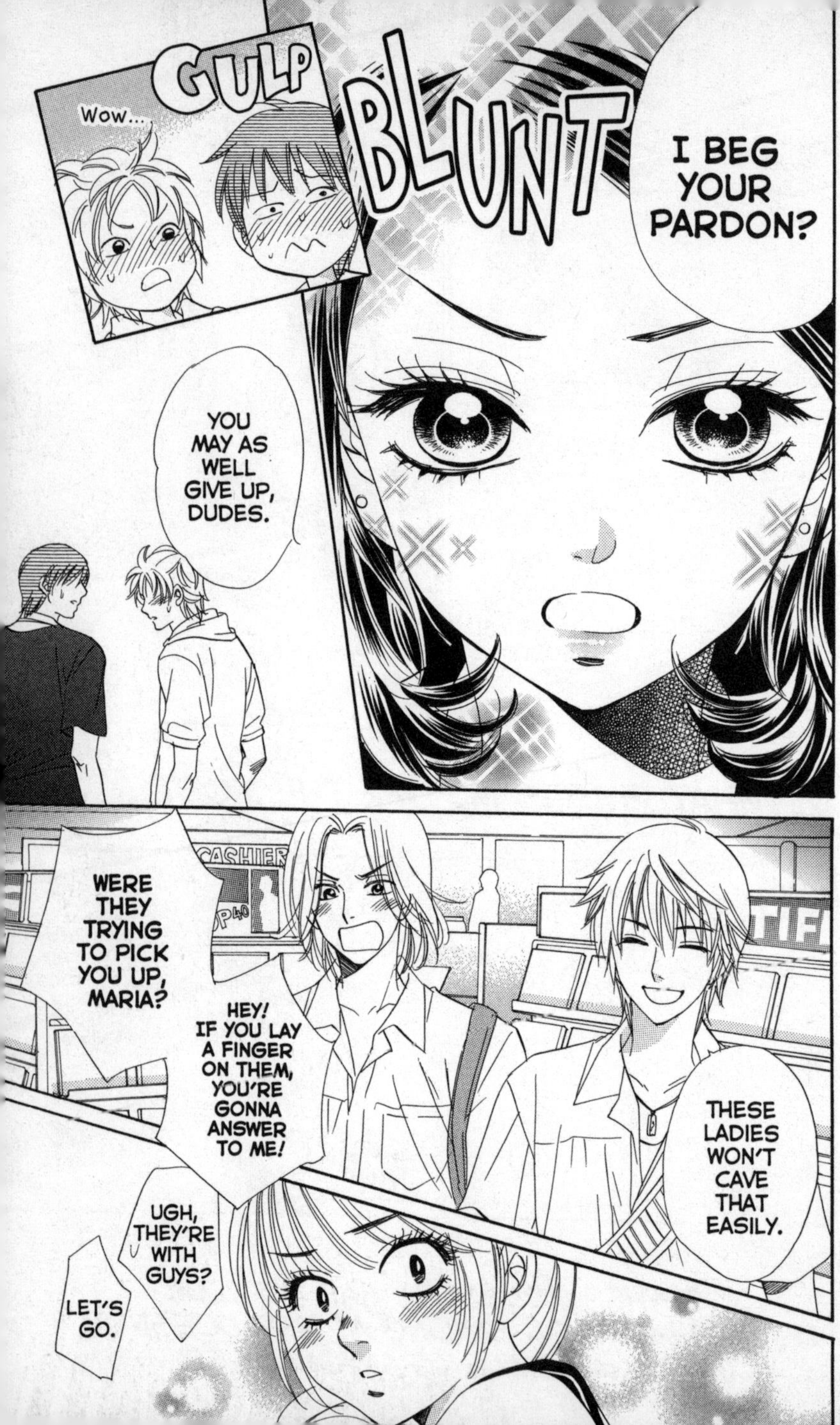
BLUNT
I BEG YOUR PARDON?
GULP
Wow...
YOU MAY AS WELL GIVE UP, DUDES.
WERE THEY TRYING TO PICK YOU UP, MARIA?
THESE LADIES WON'T CAVE THAT EASILY.
HEY! IF YOU LAY A FINGER ON THEM, YOU'RE GONNA ANSWER TO ME!
CASHIER
UGH, THEY'RE WITH GUYS?
LET'S GO.

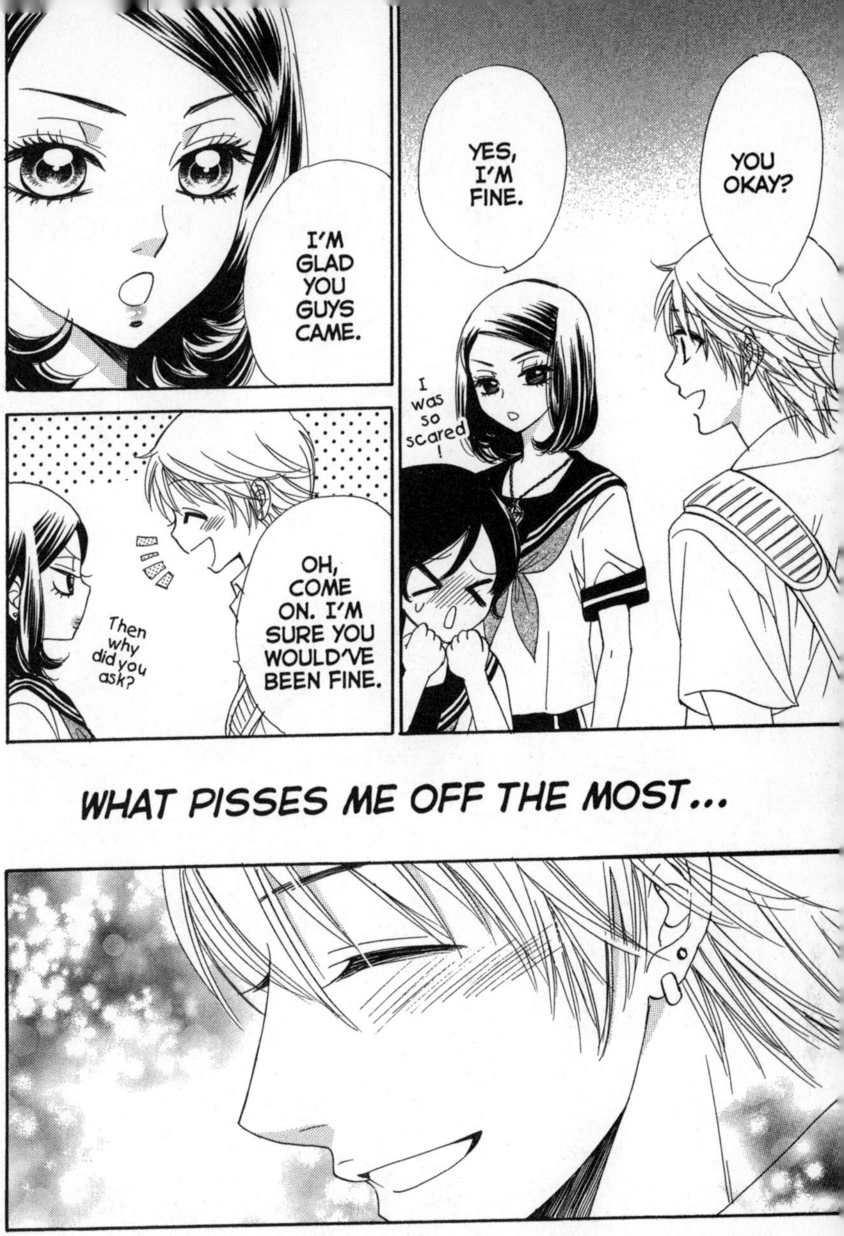
YOU OKAY?
YES, I'M FINE.
I was so scared!
I'M GLAD YOU GUYS CAME.
OH, COME ON. I'M SURE YOU WOULD'VE BEEN FINE.
Then why did you ask?
WHAT PISSES ME OFF THE MOST...

...IS WHEN SOMEBODY HAS NO CLUE THAT THE PERSON SMILING AT HER DOESN'T GIVE THAT SMILE TO ANYONE ELSE.

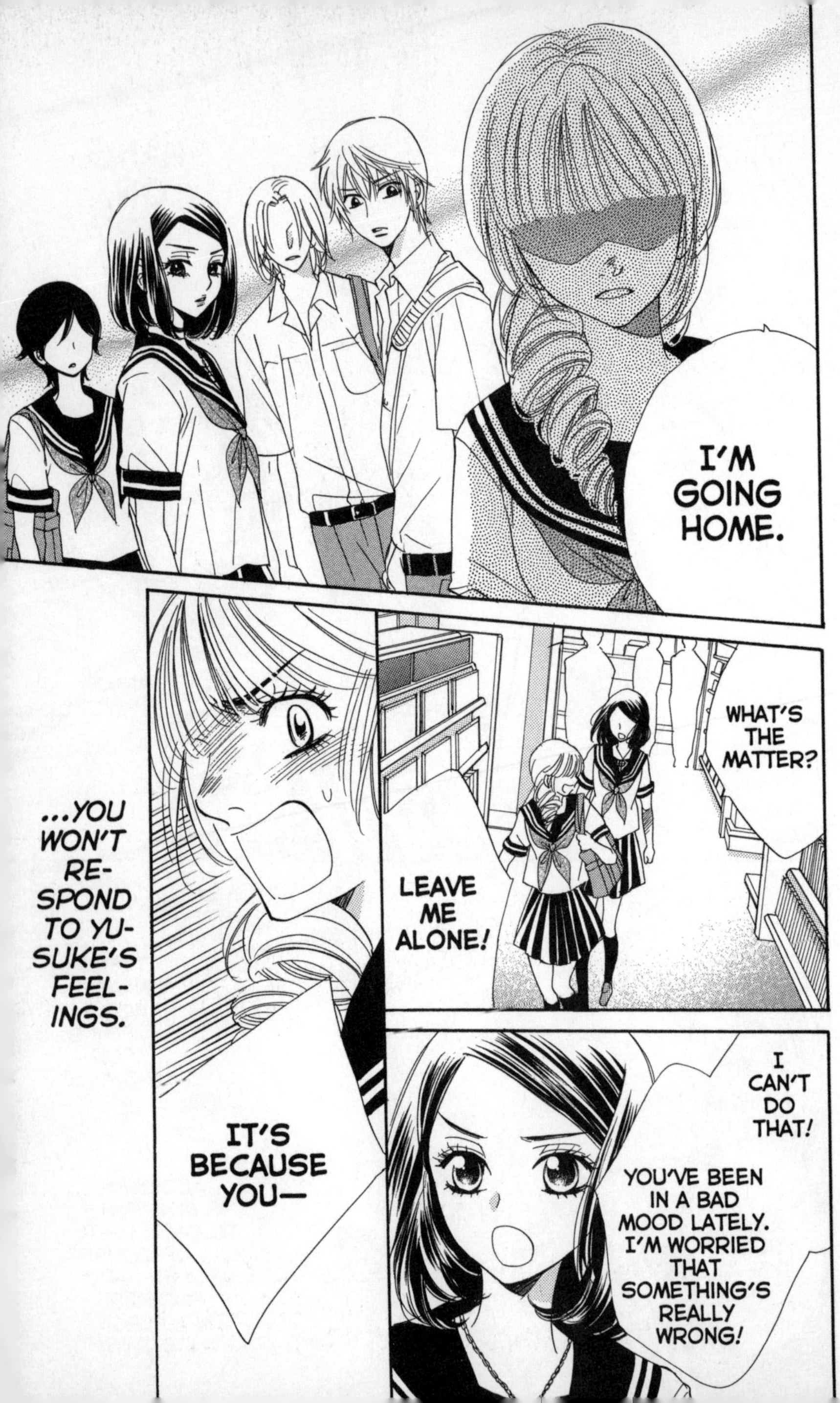
I'M GOING HOME.
WHAT'S THE MATTER?
LEAVE ME ALONE!
I CAN'T DO THAT!
YOU'VE BEEN IN A BAD MOOD LATELY. I'M WORRIED THAT SOMETHING'S REALLY WRONG!
IT'S BECAUSE YOU—
...YOU WON'T RE-SPOND TO YU-SUKE'S FEEL-INGS.

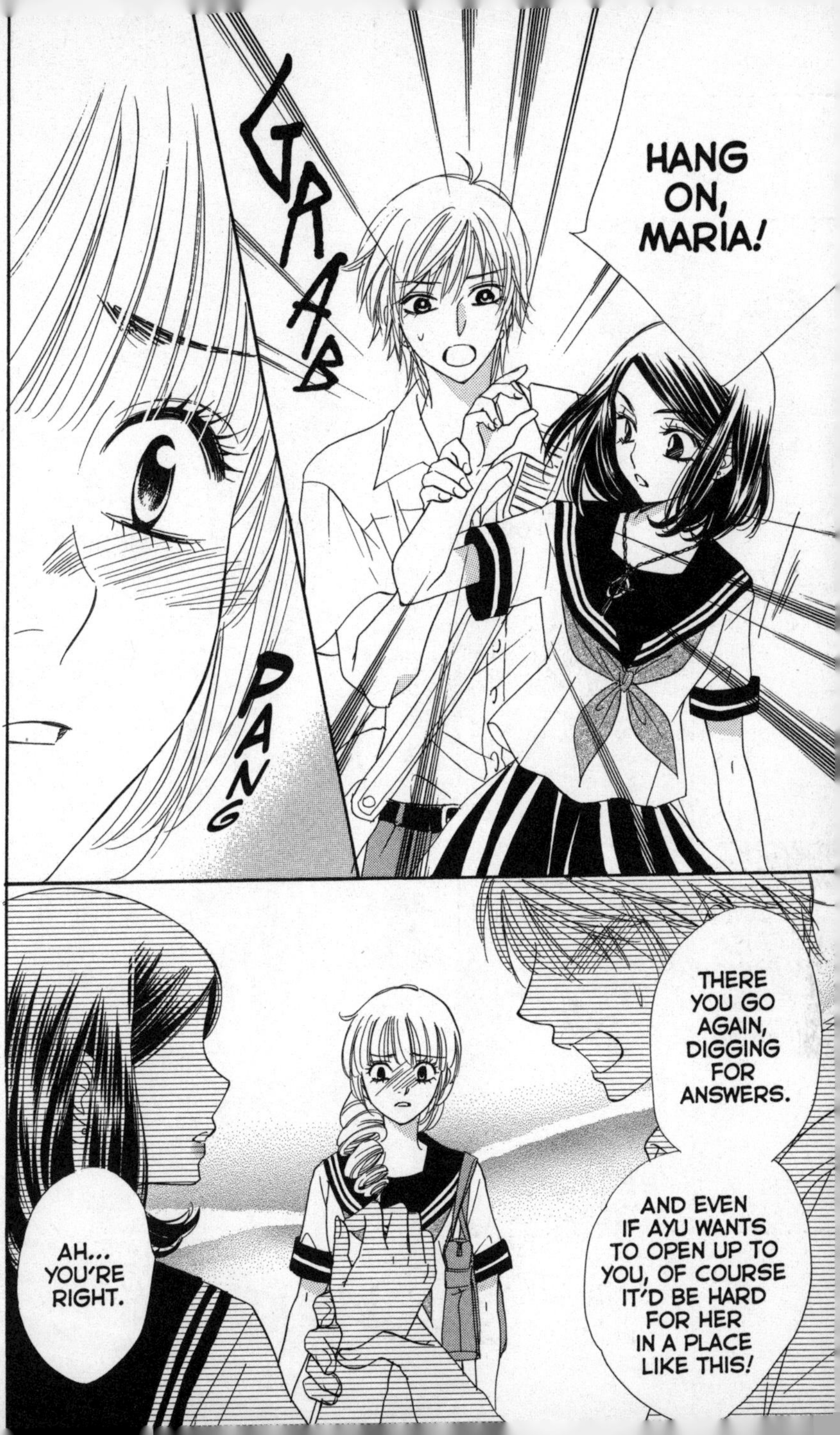
HANG ON, MARIA!
GRAB
PANG
THERE YOU GO AGAIN, DIGGING FOR ANSWERS.
AND EVEN IF AYU WANTS TO OPEN UP TO YOU, OF COURSE IT'D BE HARD FOR HER IN A PLACE LIKE THIS!
AH... YOU'RE RIGHT.

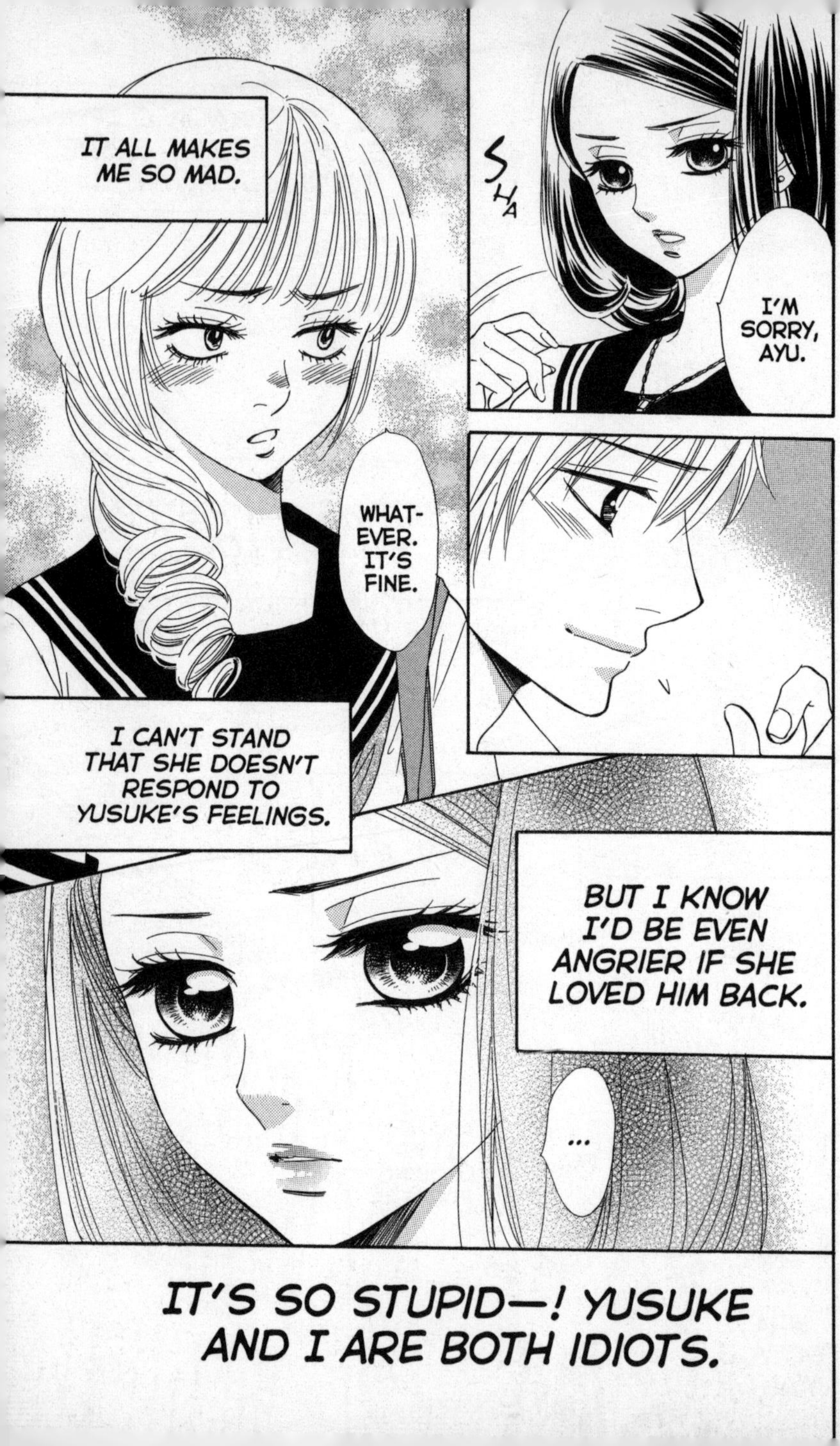
SHA
I'M SORRY, AYU.
IT ALL MAKES ME SO MAD.
WHAT-EVER. IT'S FINE.
I CAN'T STAND THAT SHE DOESN'T RESPOND TO YUSUKE'S FEELINGS.
BUT I KNOW I'D BE EVEN ANGRIER IF SHE LOVED HIM BACK.
...
IT'S SO STUPID—! YUSUKE AND I ARE BOTH IDIOTS.

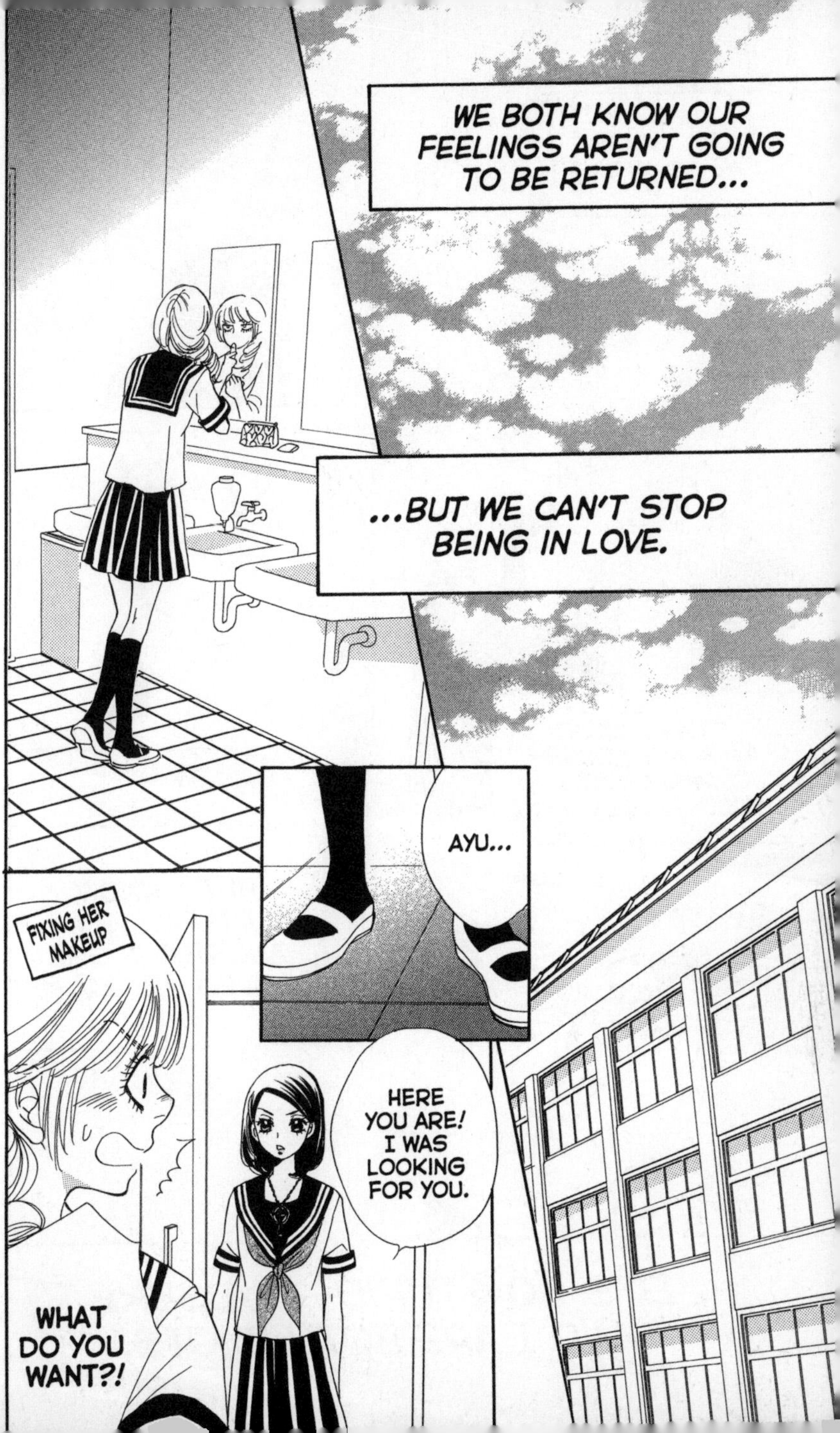
WE BOTH KNOW OUR FEELINGS AREN'T GOING TO BE RETURNED...
...BUT WE CAN'T STOP BEING IN LOVE.
AYU...
HERE YOU ARE! I WAS LOOKING FOR YOU.
FIXING HER MAKEUP
WHAT DO YOU WANT?!

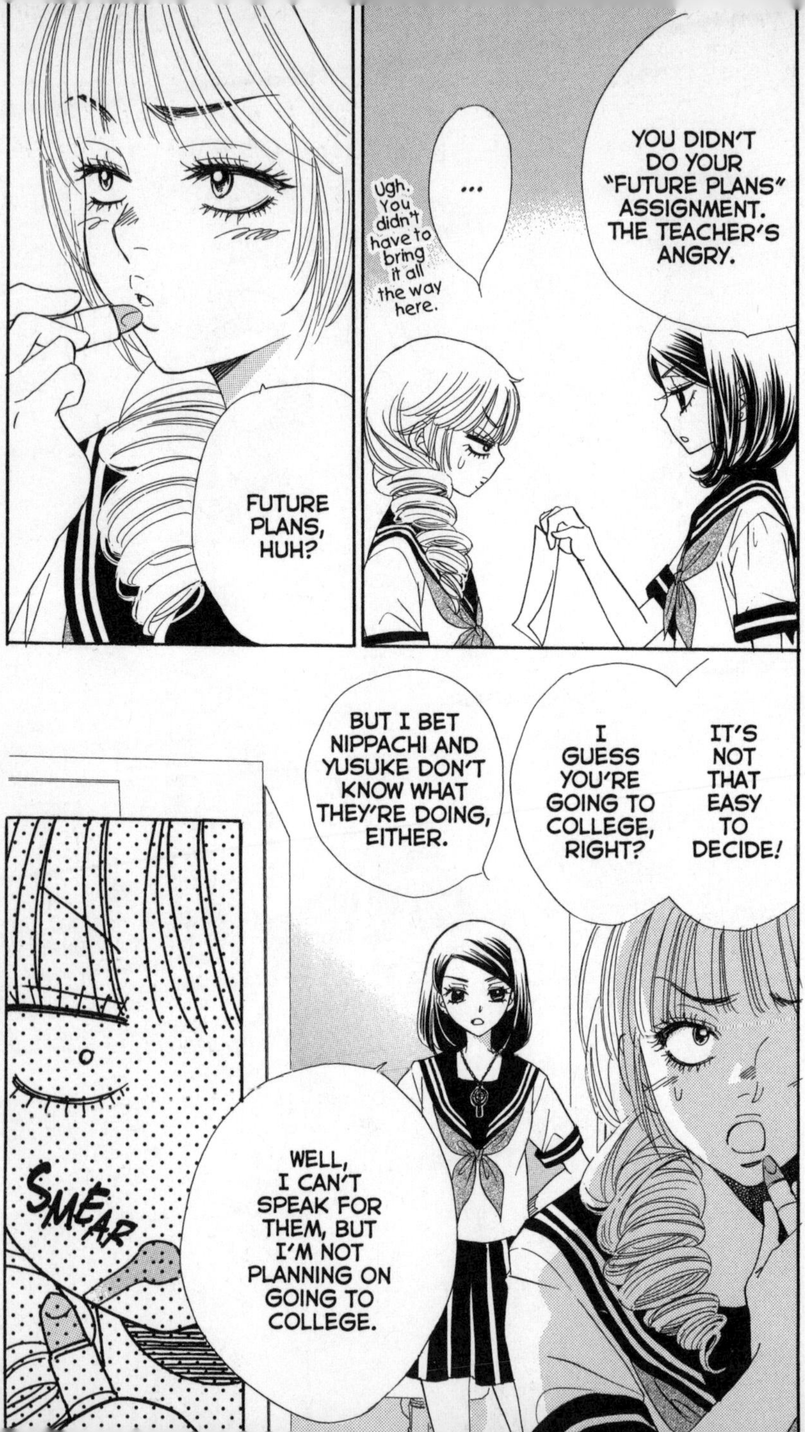
YOU DIDN'T DO YOUR "FUTURE PLANS" ASSIGNMENT. THE TEACHER'S ANGRY.
...
Ugh. You didn't have to bring it all the way here.
FUTURE PLANS, HUH?
IT'S NOT THAT EASY TO DECIDE!
I GUESS YOU'RE GOING TO COLLEGE, RIGHT?
BUT I BET NIPPACHI AND YUSUKE DON'T KNOW WHAT THEY'RE DOING, EITHER.
WELL, I CAN'T SPEAK FOR THEM, BUT I'M NOT PLANNING ON GOING TO COLLEGE.
SMEAR

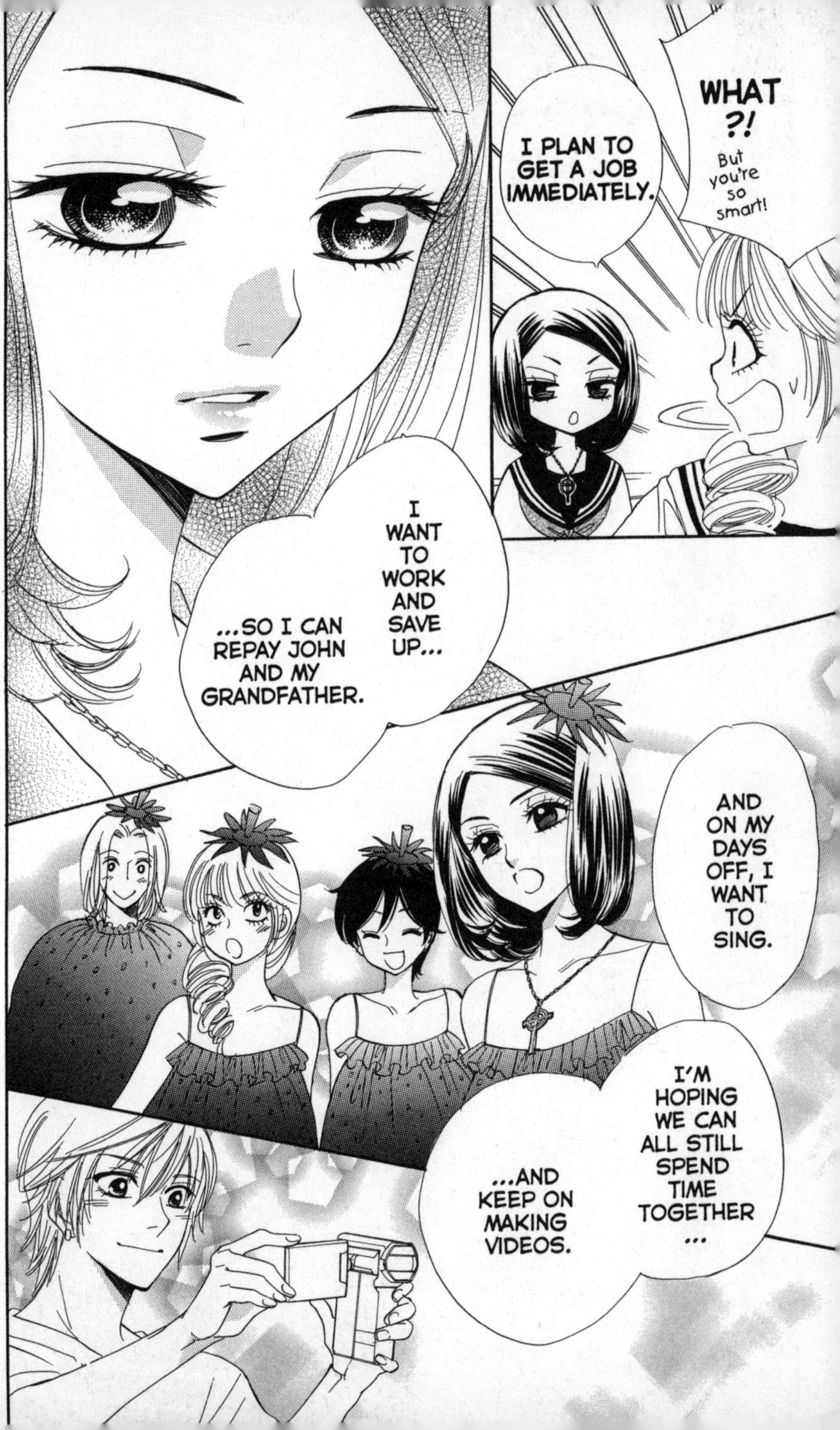
I PLAN TO GET A JOB IMMEDIATELY.
WHAT ?!
But you're so smart!
I WANT TO WORK AND SAVE UP...
...SO I CAN REPAY JOHN AND MY GRANDFATHER.
AND ON MY DAYS OFF, I WANT TO SING.
I'M HOPING WE CAN ALL STILL SPEND TIME TOGETHER...
...AND KEEP ON MAKING VIDEOS.

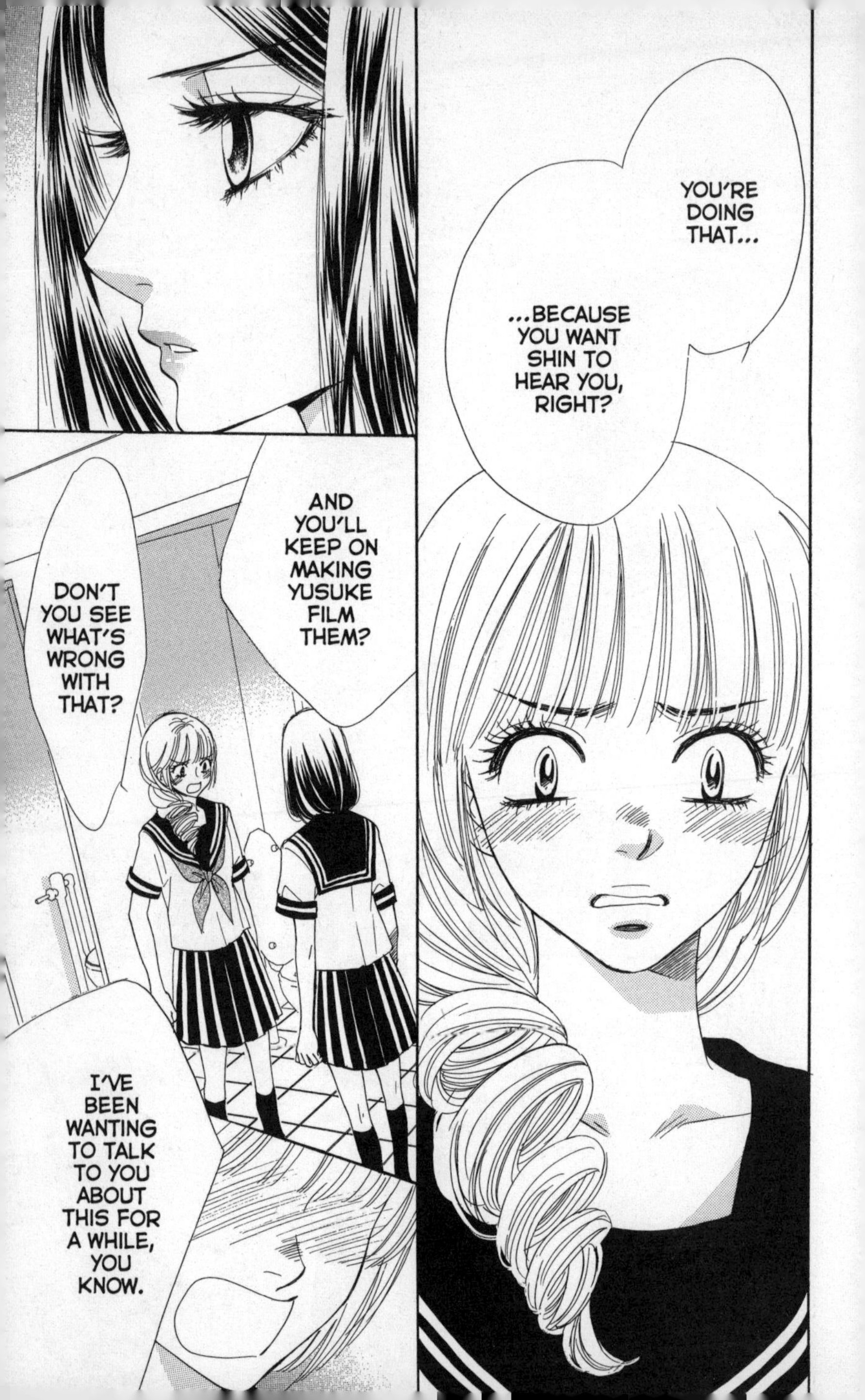
YOU'RE DOING THAT...
...BECAUSE YOU WANT SHIN TO HEAR YOU, RIGHT?
AND YOU'LL KEEP ON MAKING YUSUKE FILM THEM?
DON'T YOU SEE WHAT'S WRONG WITH THAT?
I'VE BEEN WANTING TO TALK TO YOU ABOUT THIS FOR A WHILE, YOU KNOW.

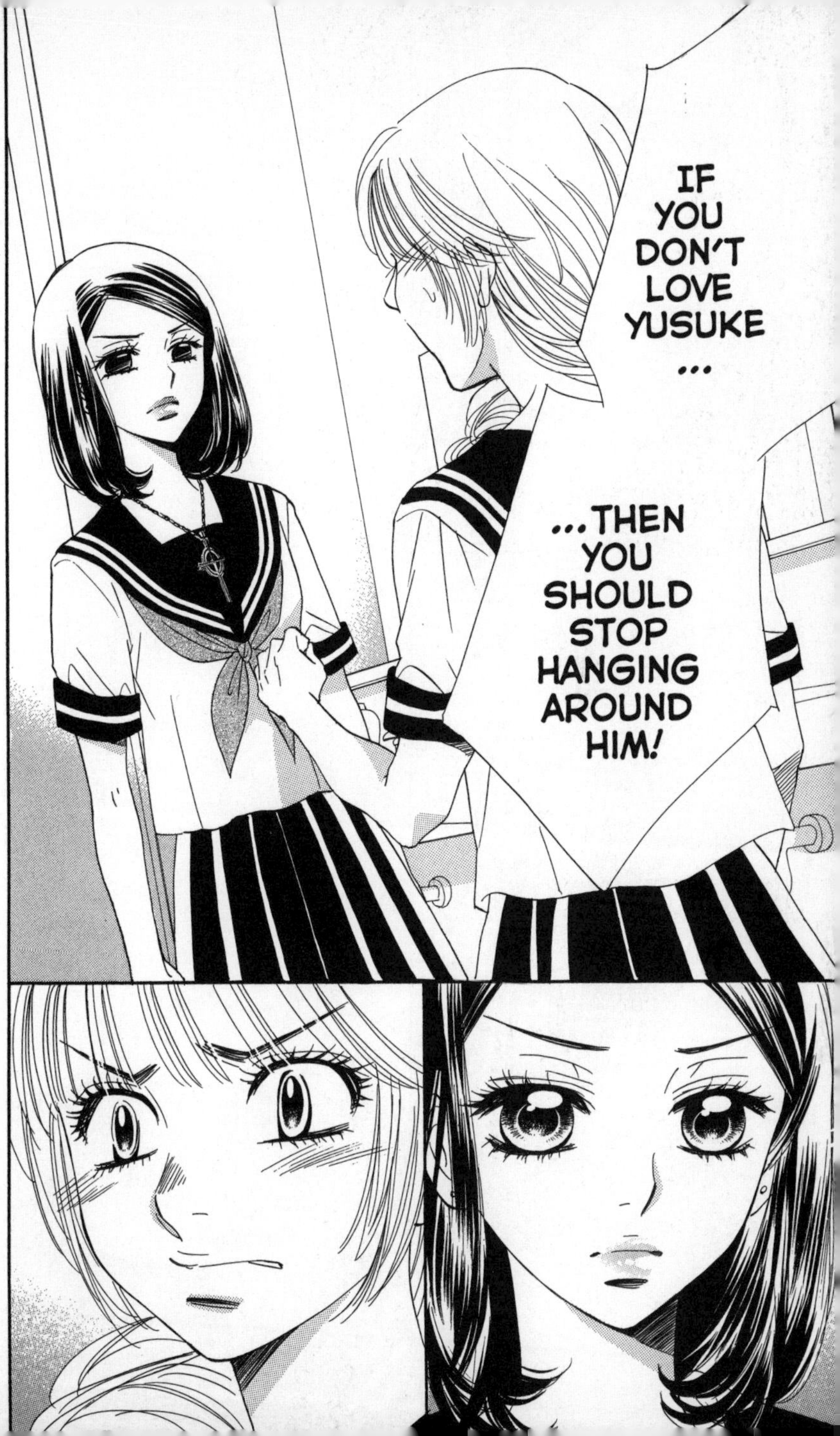
IF YOU DON'T LOVE YUSUKE ...
...THEN YOU SHOULD STOP HANGING AROUND HIM!

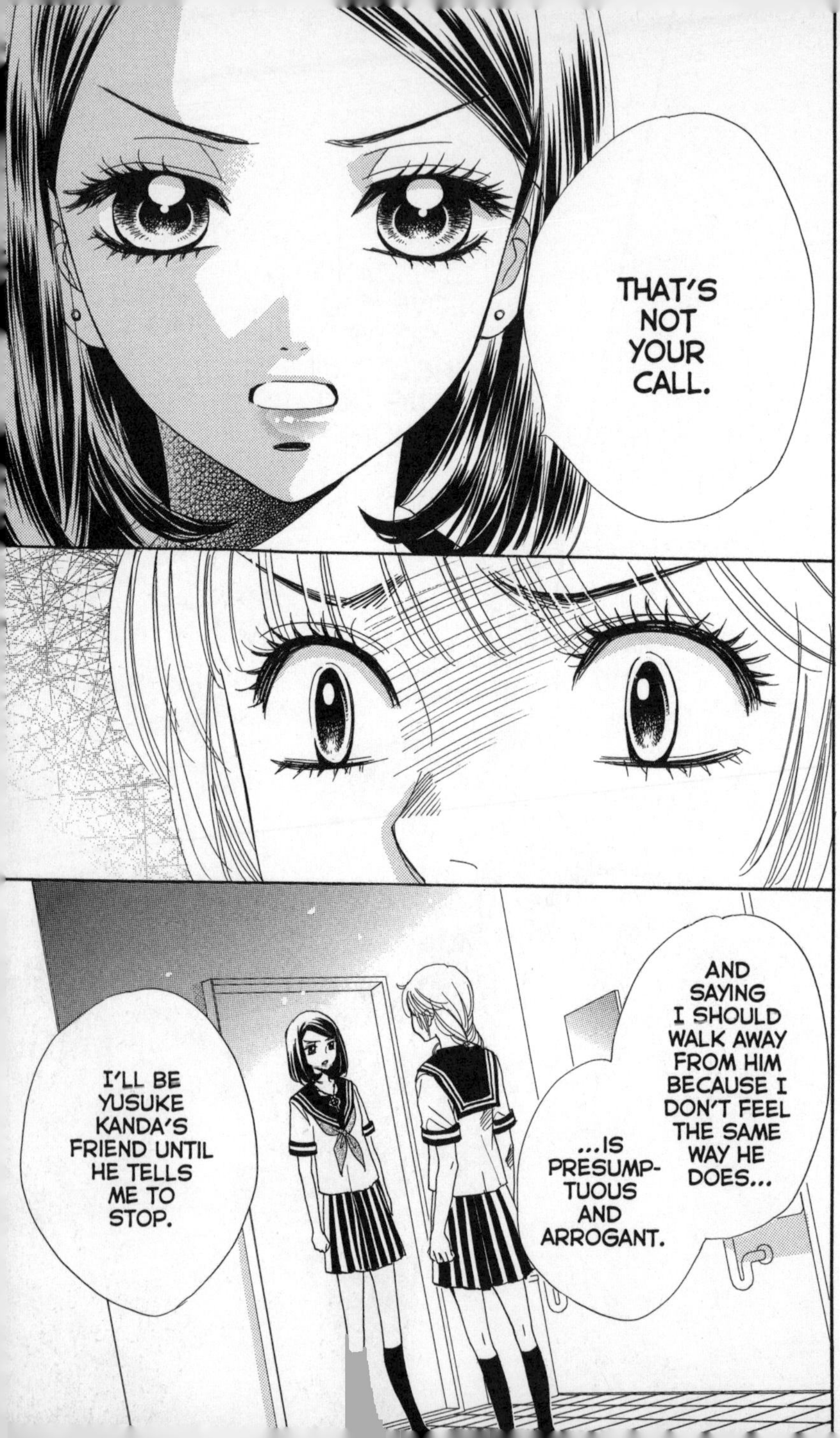
THAT'S NOT YOUR CALL.
AND SAYING I SHOULD WALK AWAY FROM HIM BECAUSE I DON'T FEEL THE SAME WAY HE DOES...
...IS PRESUMP-TUOUS AND ARROGANT.
I'LL BE YUSUKE KANDA'S FRIEND UNTIL HE TELLS ME TO STOP.

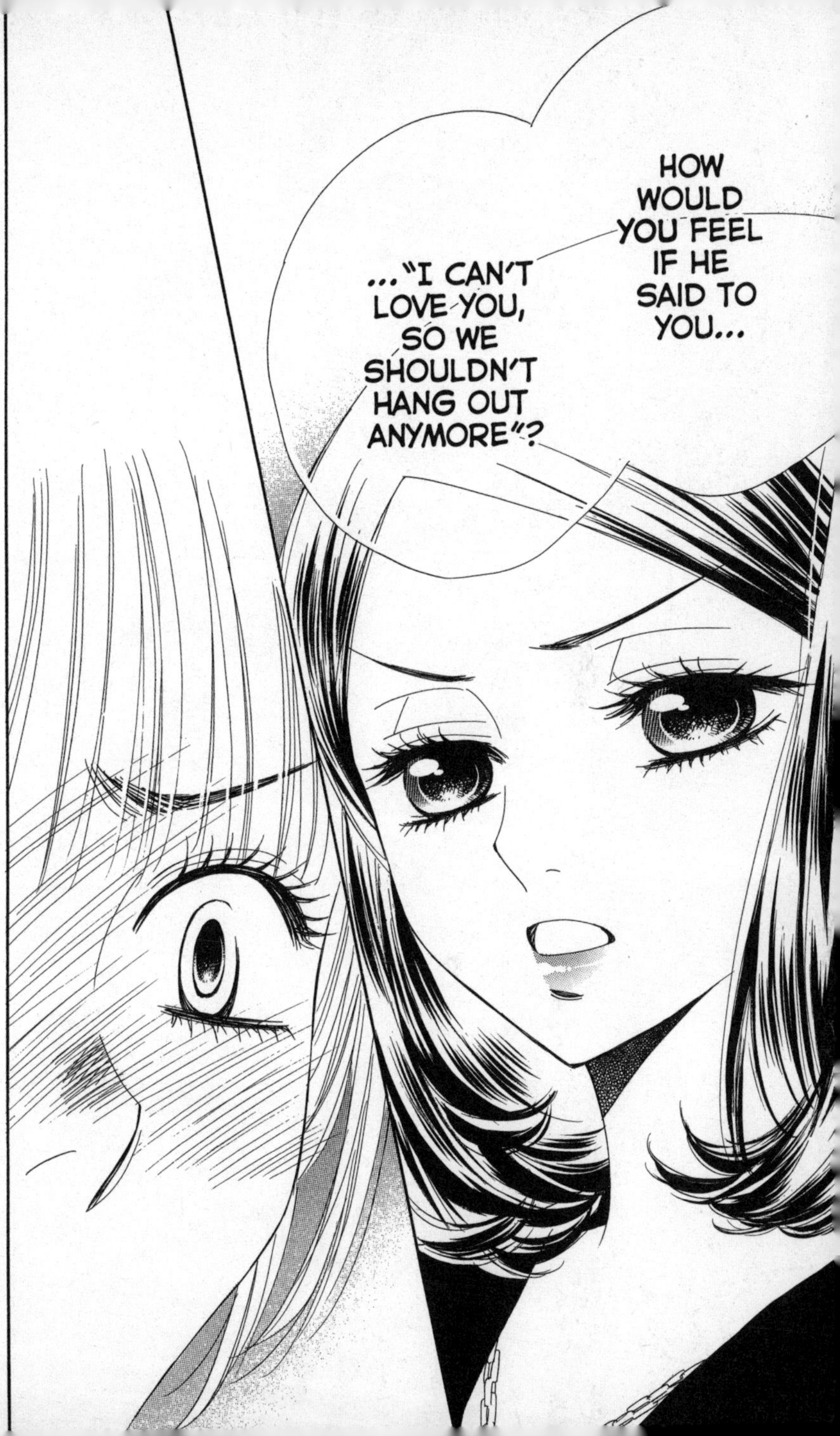
HOW WOULD YOU FEEL IF HE SAID TO YOU...
..."I CAN'T LOVE YOU, SO WE SHOULDN'T HANG OUT ANYMORE"?

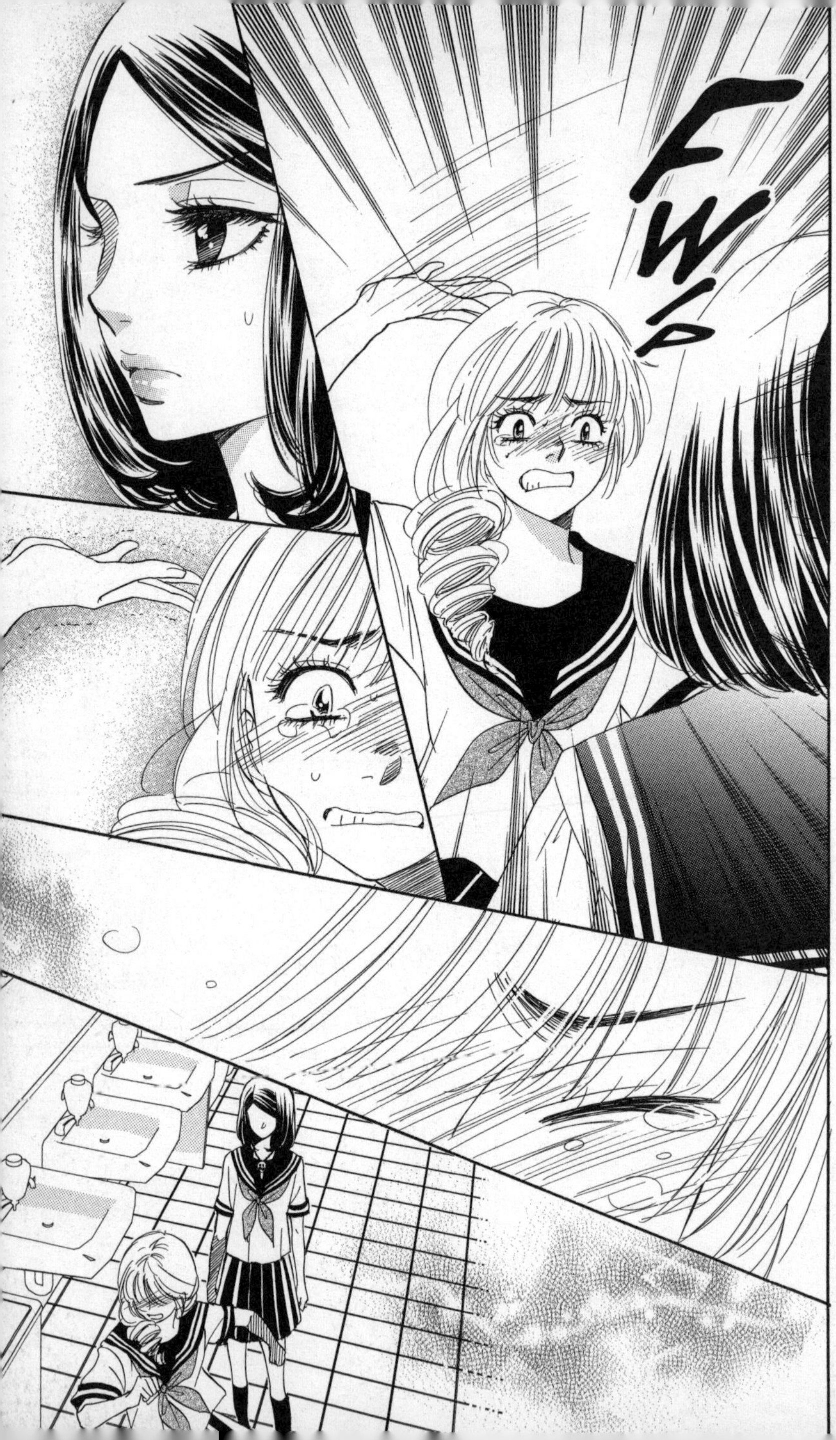
FWIP

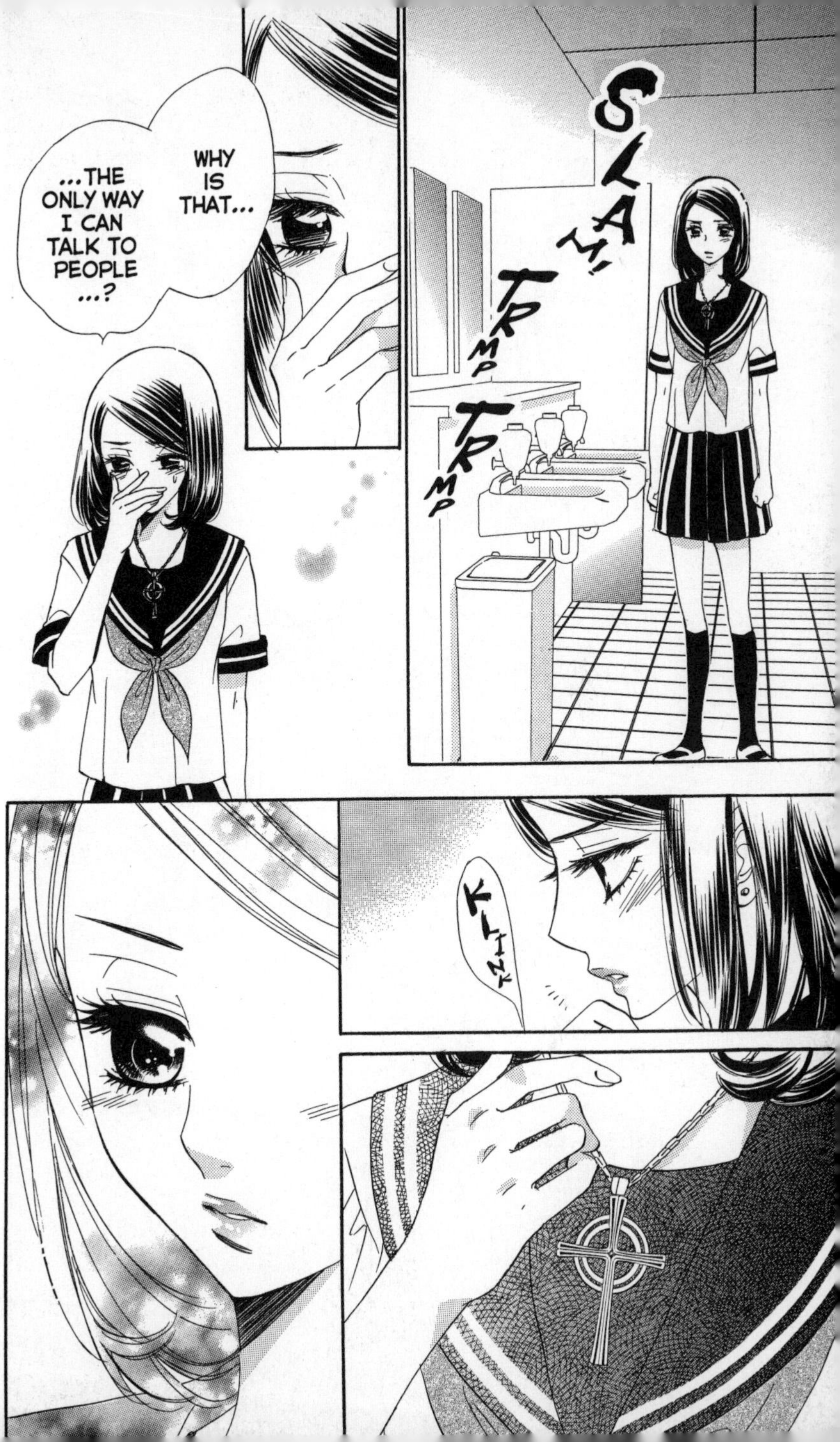
SLAM!
TRMP TRMP
WHY IS THAT...
...THE ONLY WAY I CAN TALK TO PEOPLE ...?
KLLINK

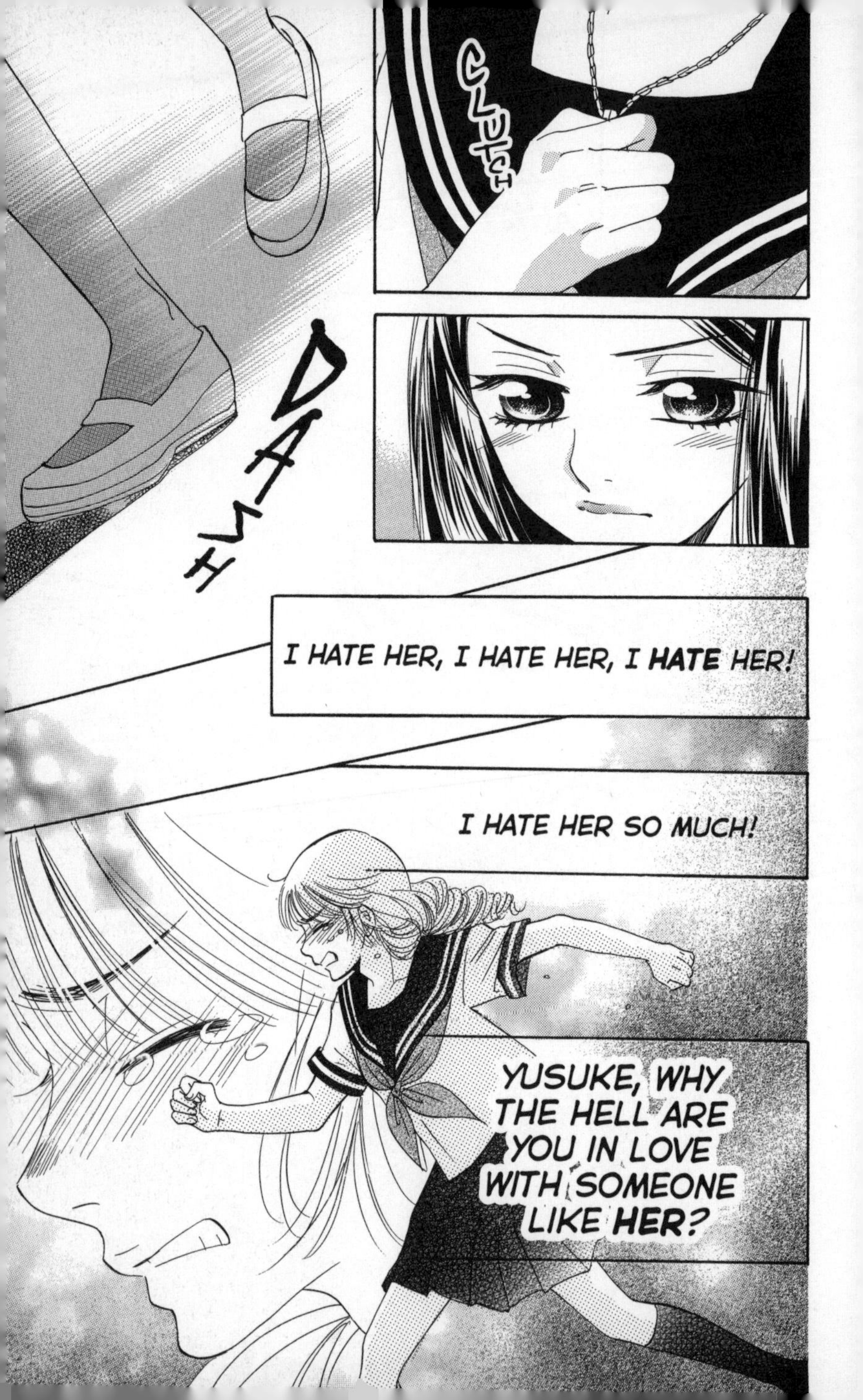
CLUTCH
DASH
I HATE HER, I HATE HER, I HATE HER!
I HATE HER SO MUCH!
YUSUKE, WHY THE HELL ARE YOU IN LOVE WITH SOMEONE LIKE HER?

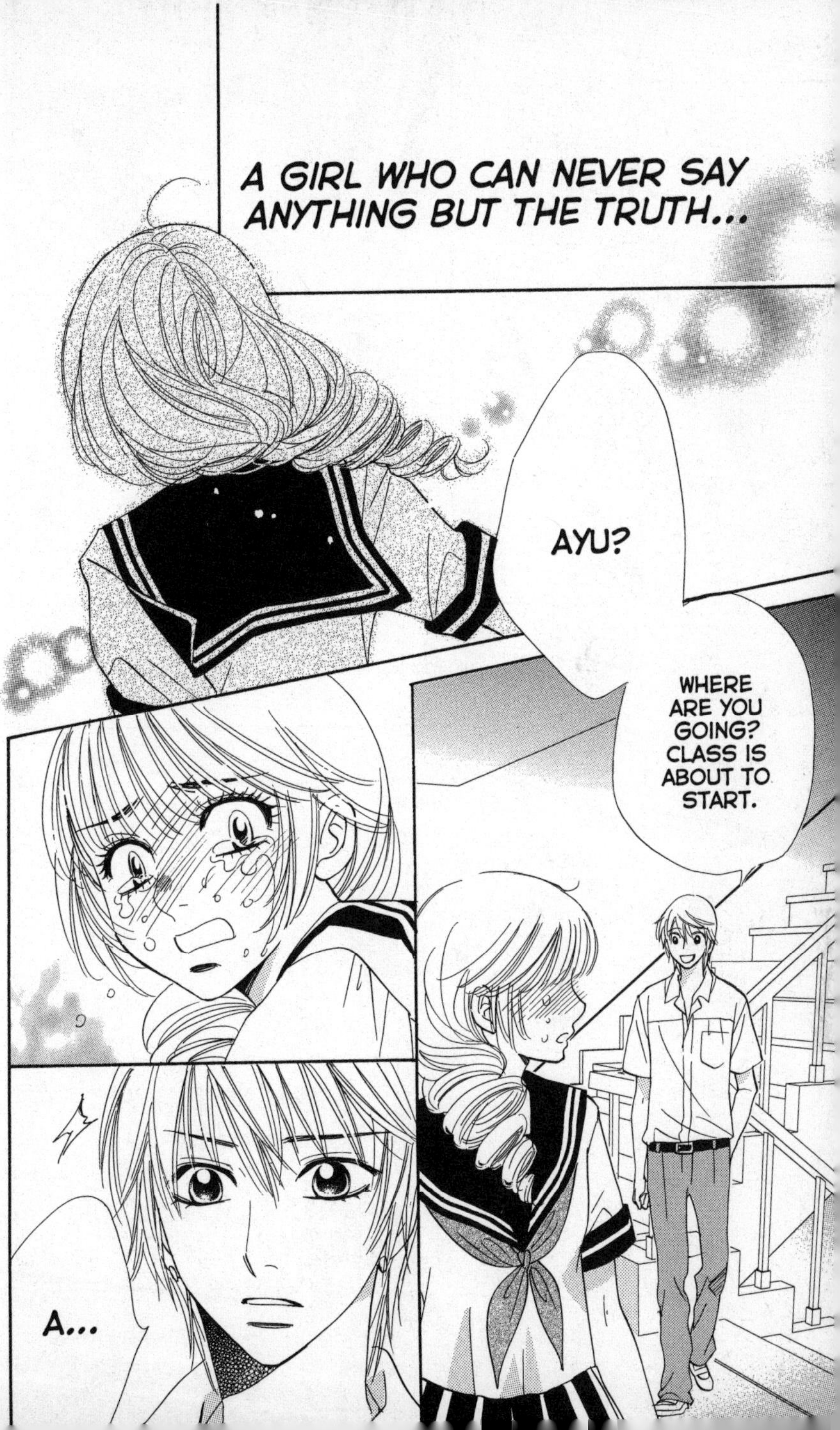
A GIRL WHO CAN NEVER SAY ANYTHING BUT THE TRUTH...
AYU?
WHERE ARE YOU GOING? CLASS IS ABOUT TO START.
A...

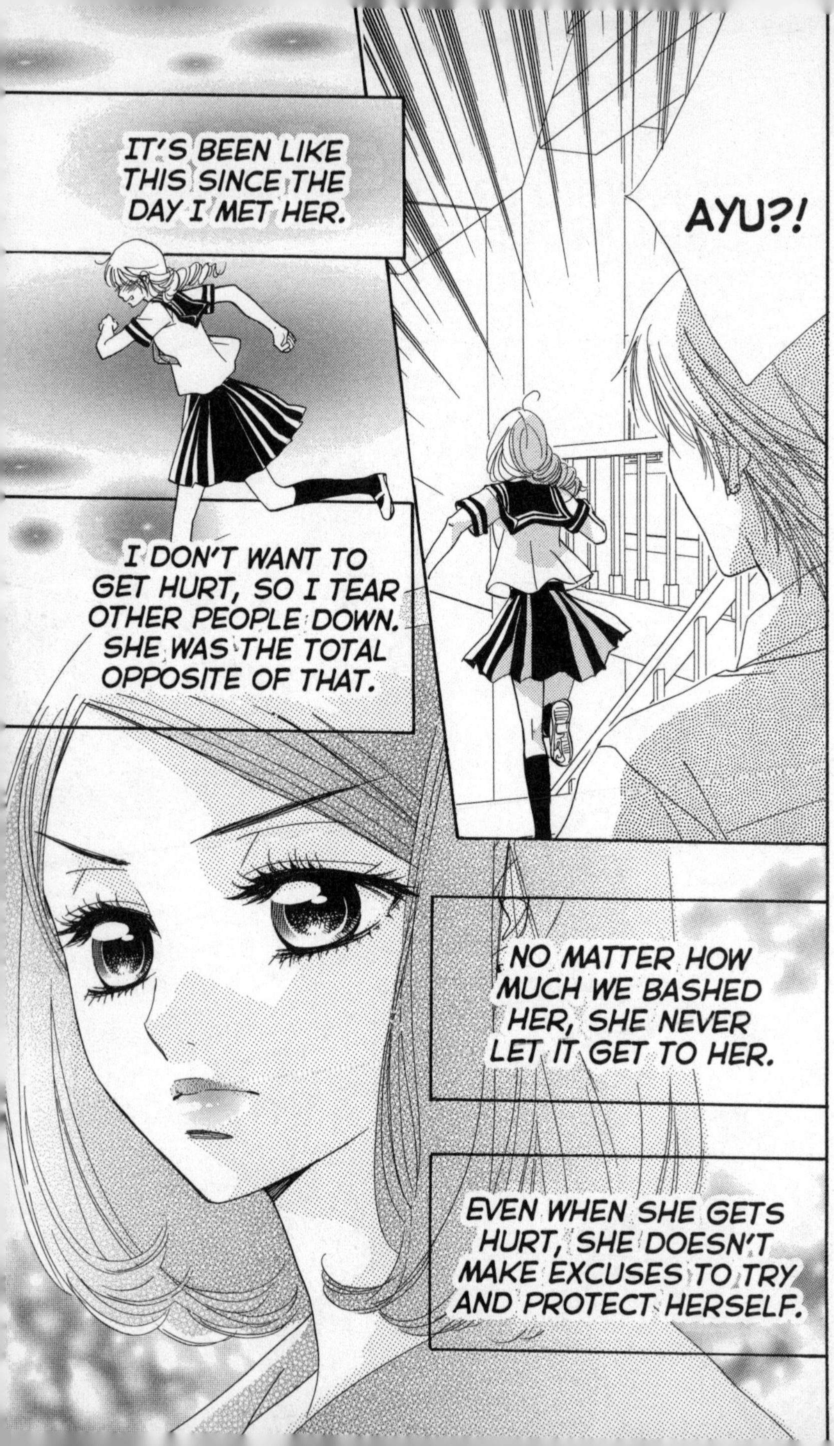
AYU?!
IT'S BEEN LIKE THIS SINCE THE DAY I MET HER.
I DON'T WANT TO GET HURT, SO I TEAR OTHER PEOPLE DOWN. SHE WAS THE TOTAL OPPOSITE OF THAT.
NO MATTER HOW MUCH WE BASHED HER, SHE NEVER LET IT GET TO HER.
EVEN WHEN SHE GETS HURT, SHE DOESN'T MAKE EXCUSES TO TRY AND PROTECT HERSELF.

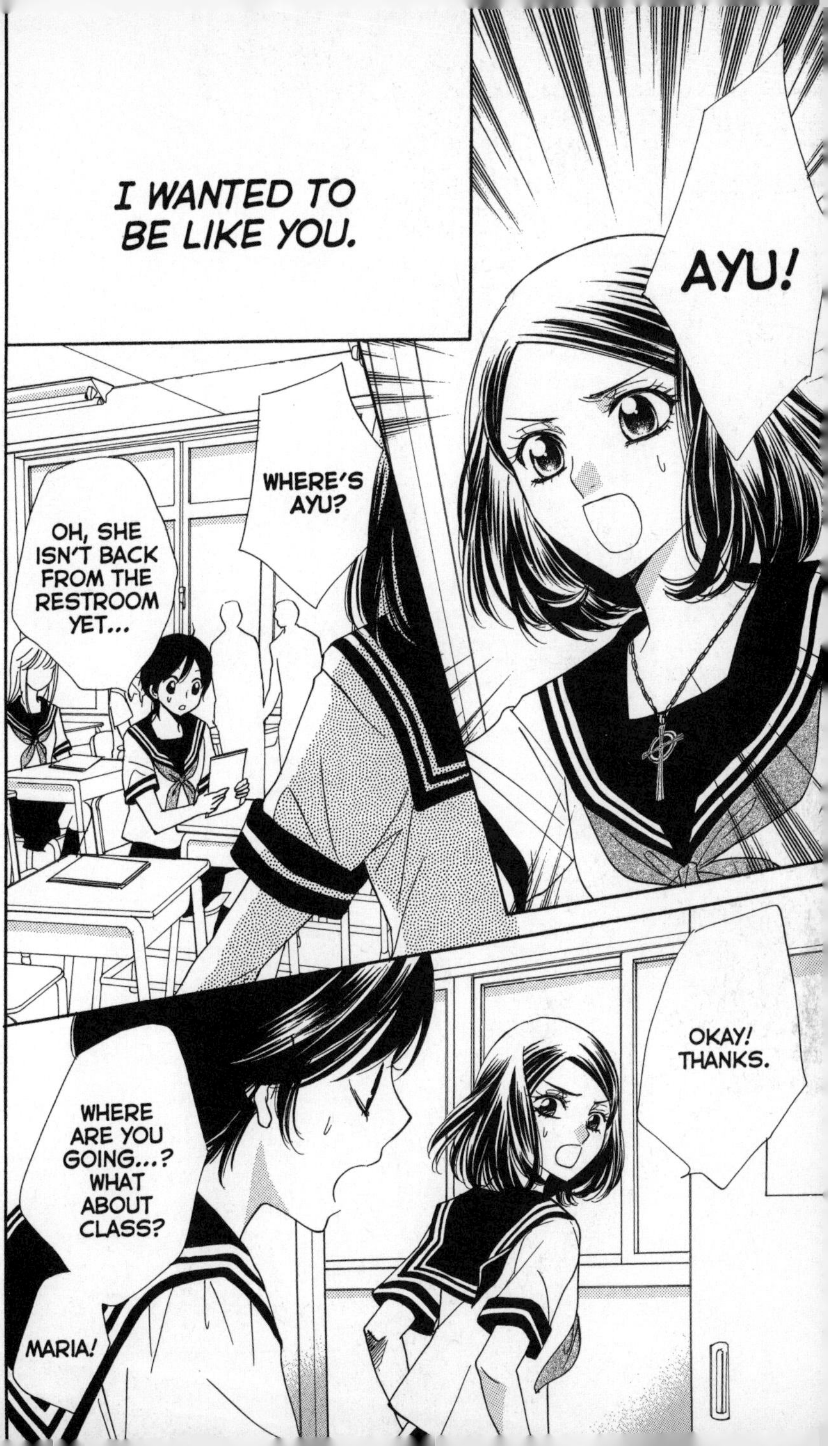
AYU!
I WANTED TO BE LIKE YOU.
WHERE'S AYU?
OH, SHE ISN'T BACK FROM THE RESTROOM YET...
OKAY! THANKS.
WHERE ARE YOU GOING...? WHAT ABOUT CLASS?
MARIA!

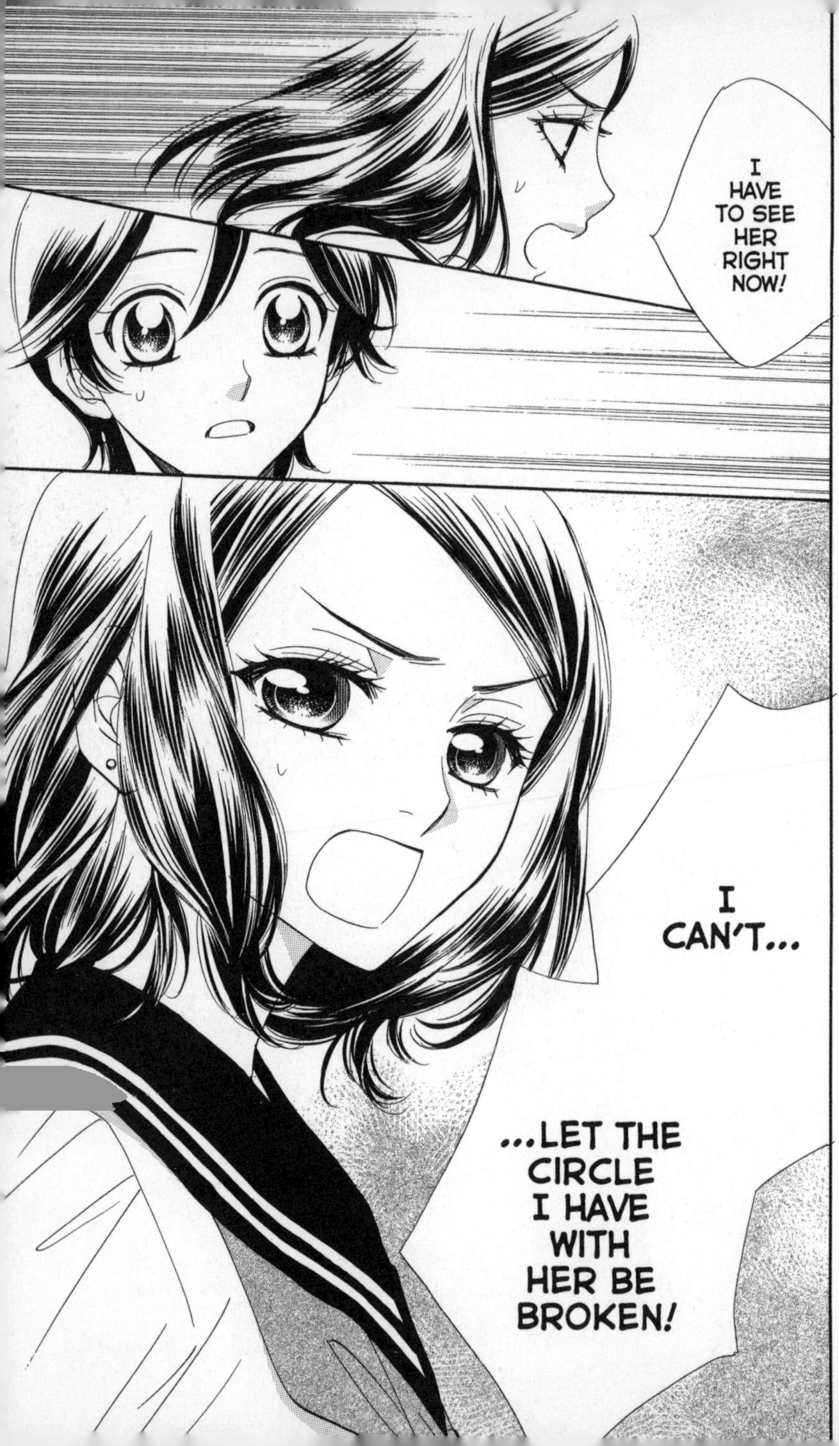
I HAVE TO SEE HER RIGHT NOW!
I CAN'T...
...LET THE CIRCLE I HAVE WITH HER BE BROKEN!

A Devil and Her Love Song

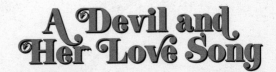

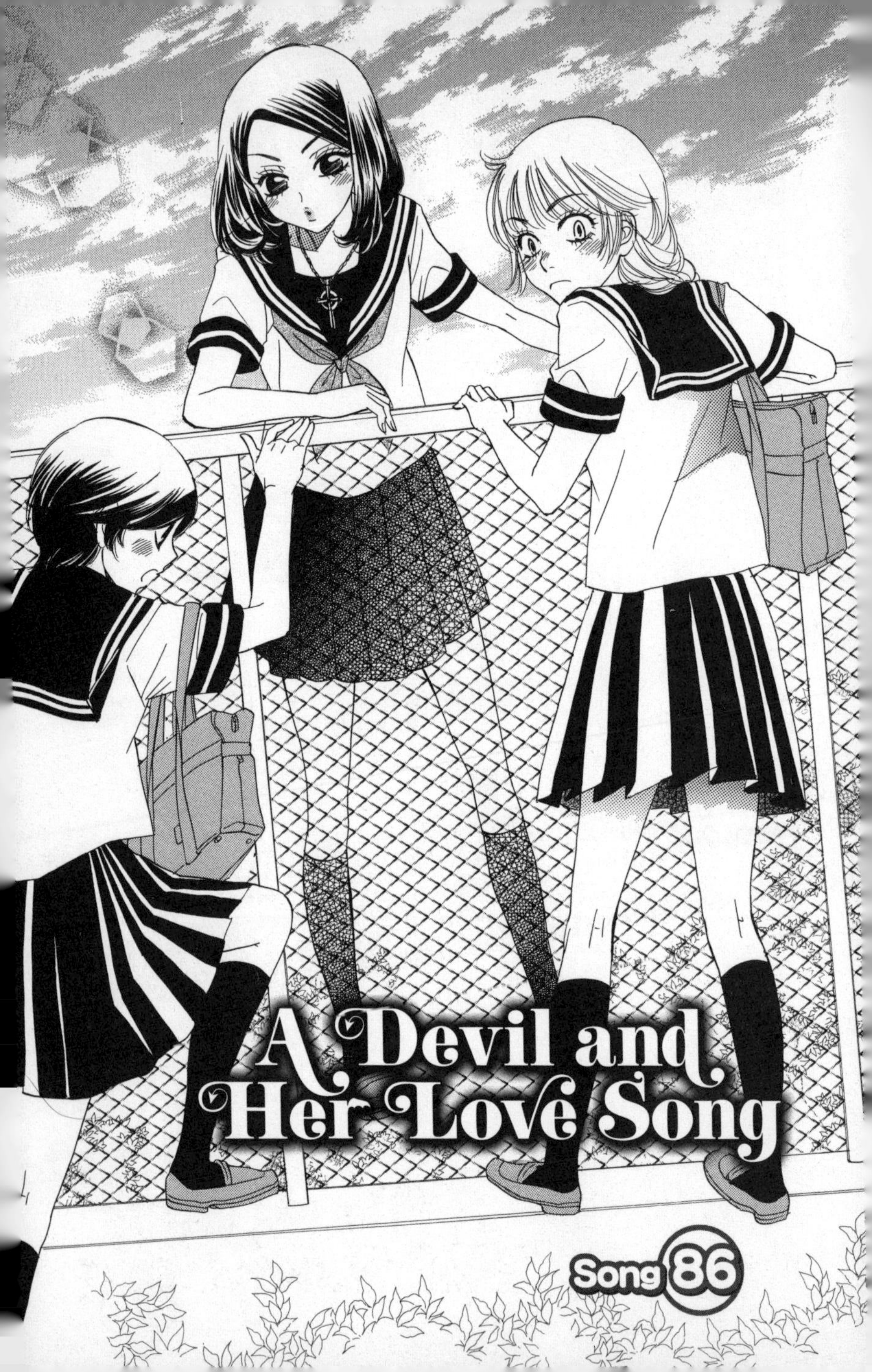
A Devil and Her Love Song
Song 86

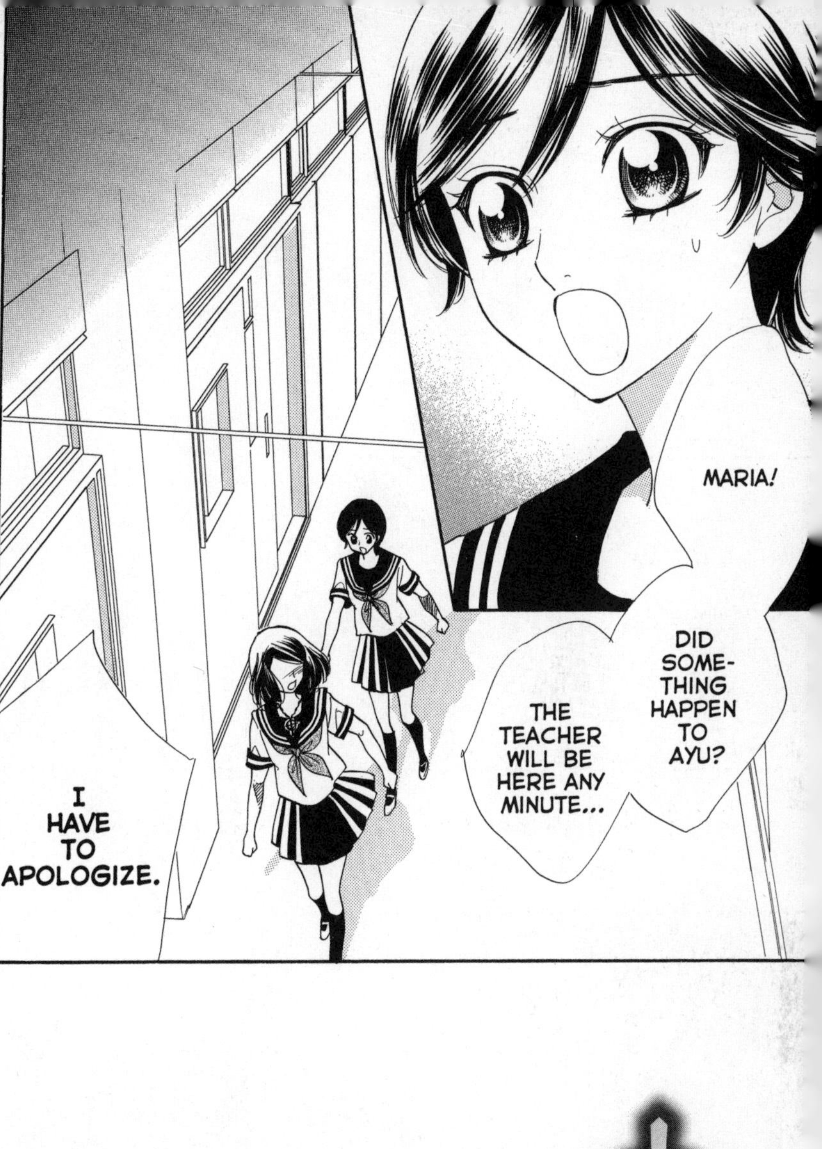
MARIA!
DID SOMETHING HAPPEN TO AYU?
THE TEACHER WILL BE HERE ANY MINUTE...
I HAVE TO APOLOGIZE.

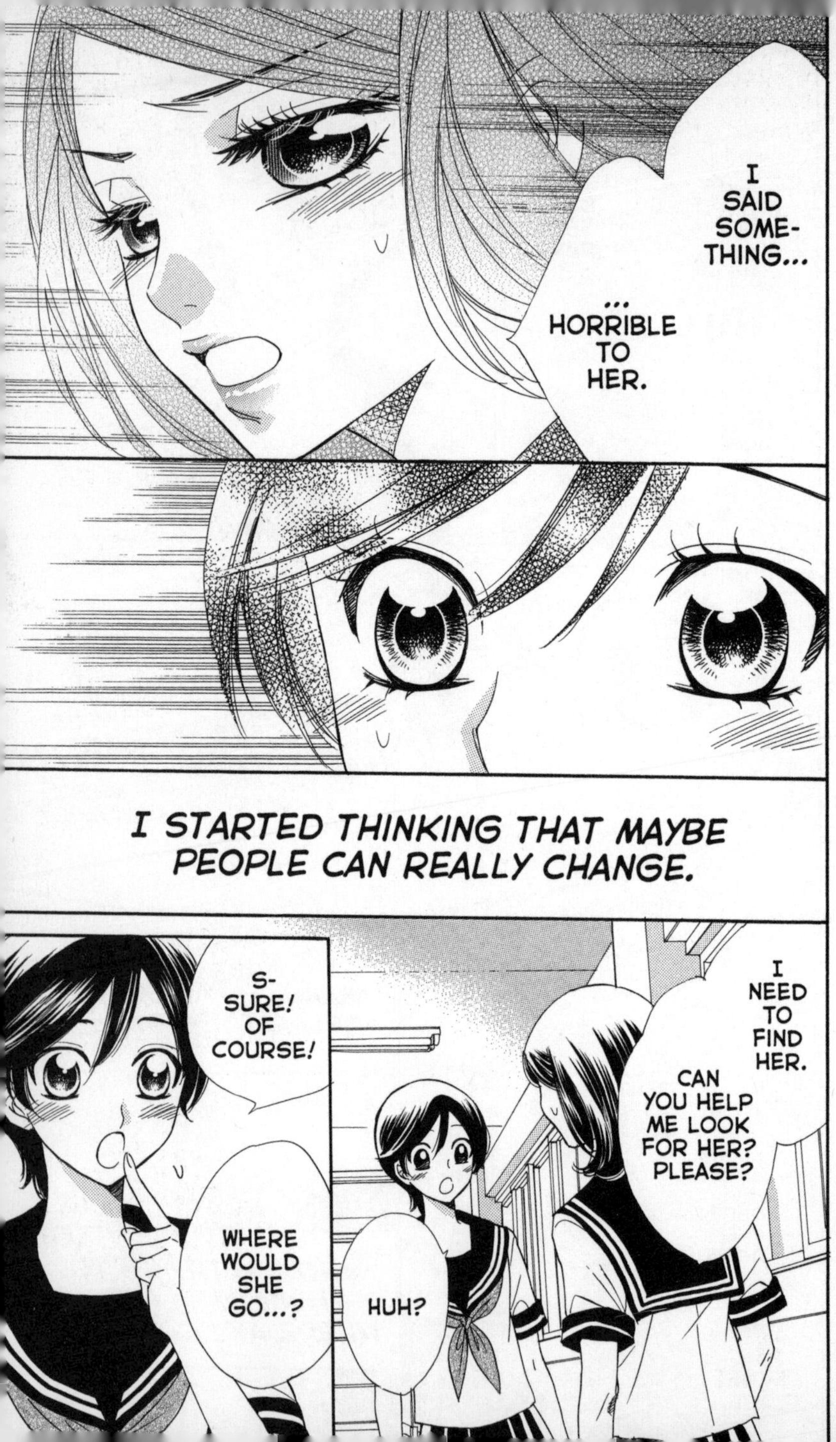
I SAID SOME-THING...
...HORRIBLE TO HER.
I STARTED THINKING THAT MAYBE PEOPLE CAN REALLY CHANGE.
I NEED TO FIND HER.
CAN YOU HELP ME LOOK FOR HER? PLEASE?
HUH?
S-SURE! OF COURSE!
WHERE WOULD SHE GO...?

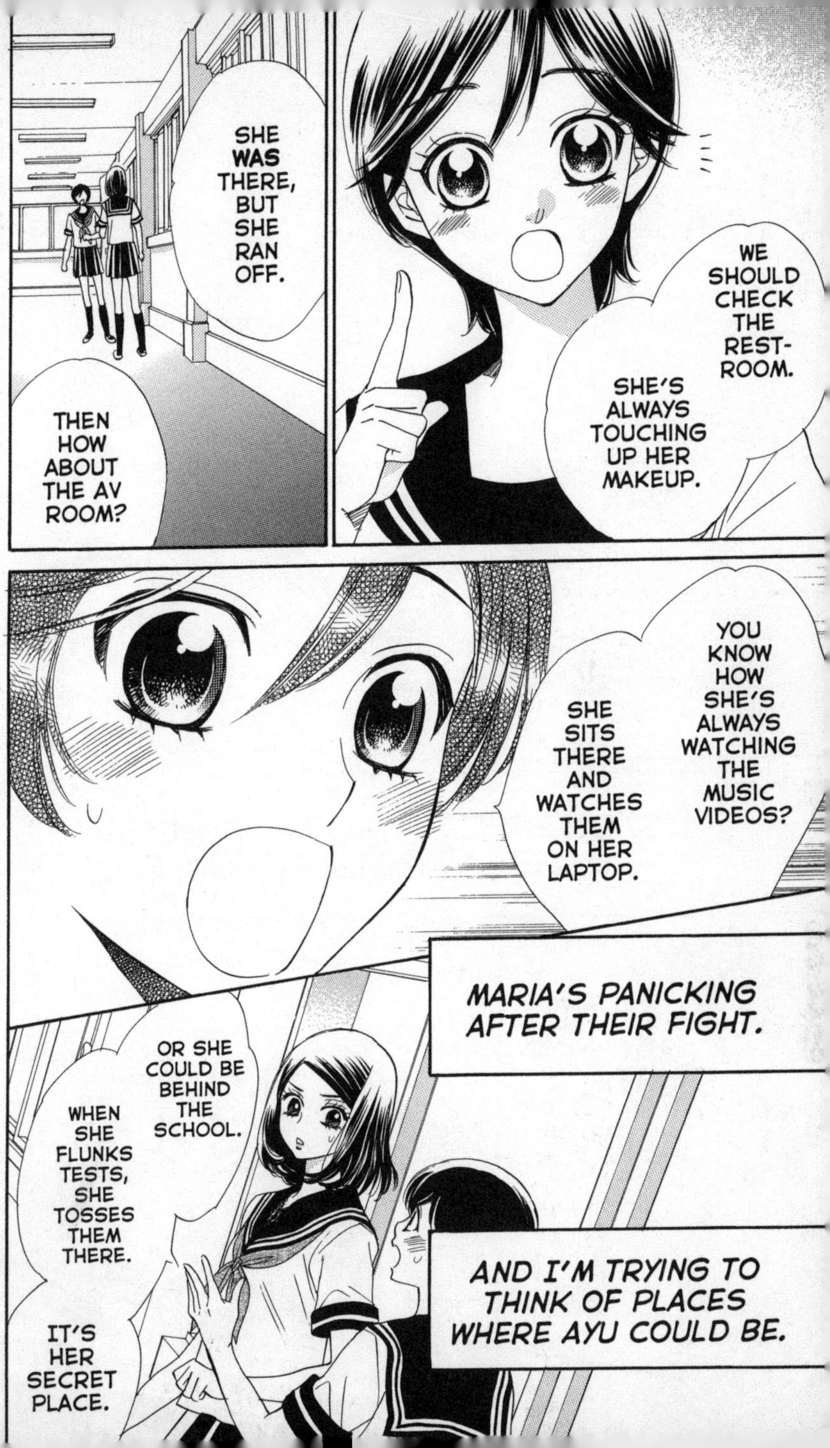
WE SHOULD CHECK THE REST-ROOM.
SHE'S ALWAYS TOUCHING UP HER MAKEUP.
SHE WAS THERE, BUT SHE RAN OFF.
THEN HOW ABOUT THE AV ROOM?
YOU KNOW HOW SHE'S ALWAYS WATCHING THE MUSIC VIDEOS?
SHE SITS THERE AND WATCHES THEM ON HER LAPTOP.
MARIA'S PANICKING AFTER THEIR FIGHT.
OR SHE COULD BE BEHIND THE SCHOOL.
WHEN SHE FLUNKS TESTS, SHE TOSSES THEM THERE.
AND I'M TRYING TO THINK OF PLACES WHERE AYU COULD BE.
IT'S HER SECRET PLACE.

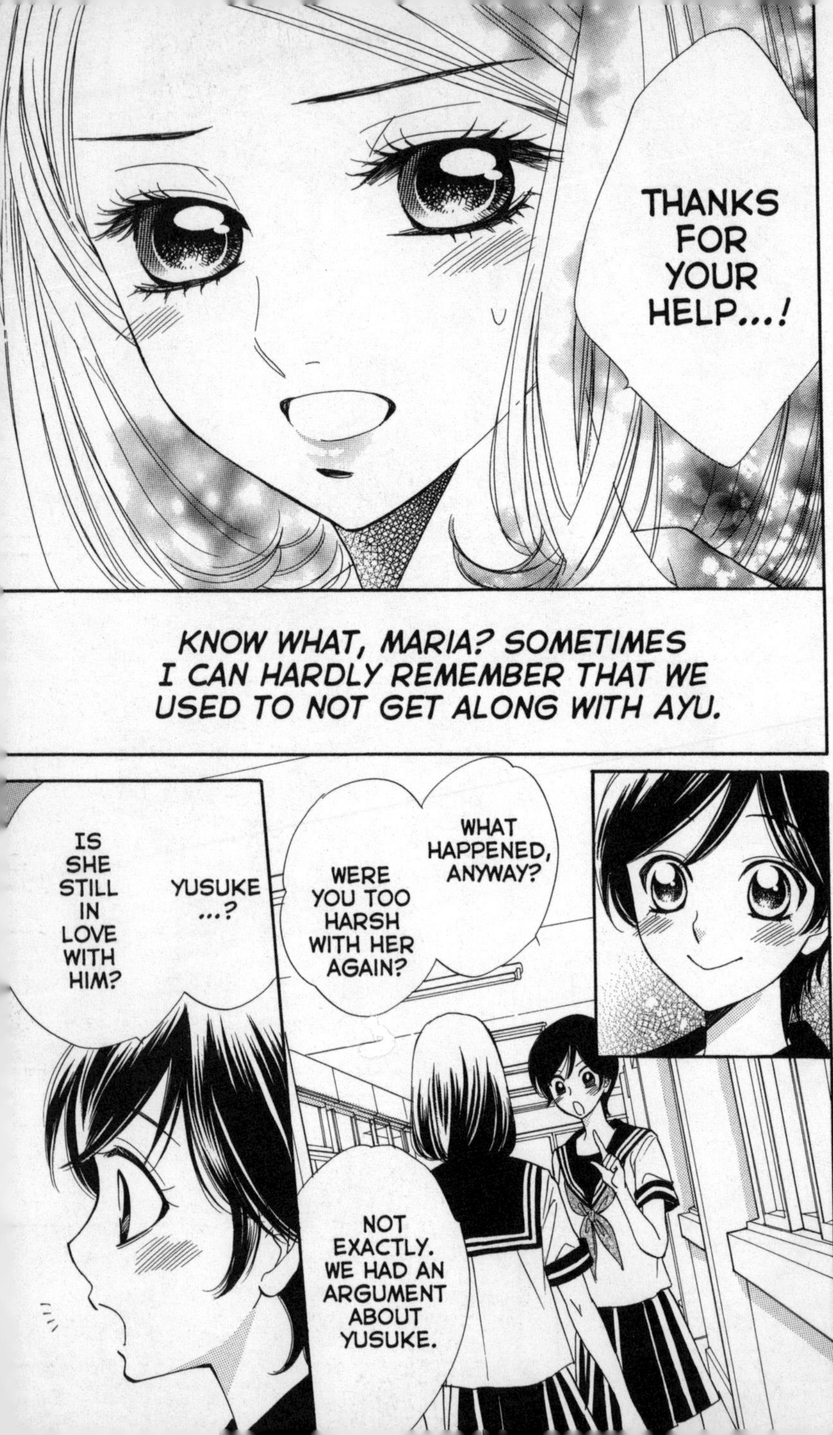
THANKS FOR YOUR HELP...!
KNOW WHAT, MARIA? SOMETIMES I CAN HARDLY REMEMBER THAT WE USED TO NOT GET ALONG WITH AYU.
WHAT HAPPENED, ANYWAY?
WERE YOU TOO HARSH WITH HER AGAIN?
NOT EXACTLY. WE HAD AN ARGUMENT ABOUT YUSUKE.
YUSUKE ...?
IS SHE STILL IN LOVE WITH HIM?

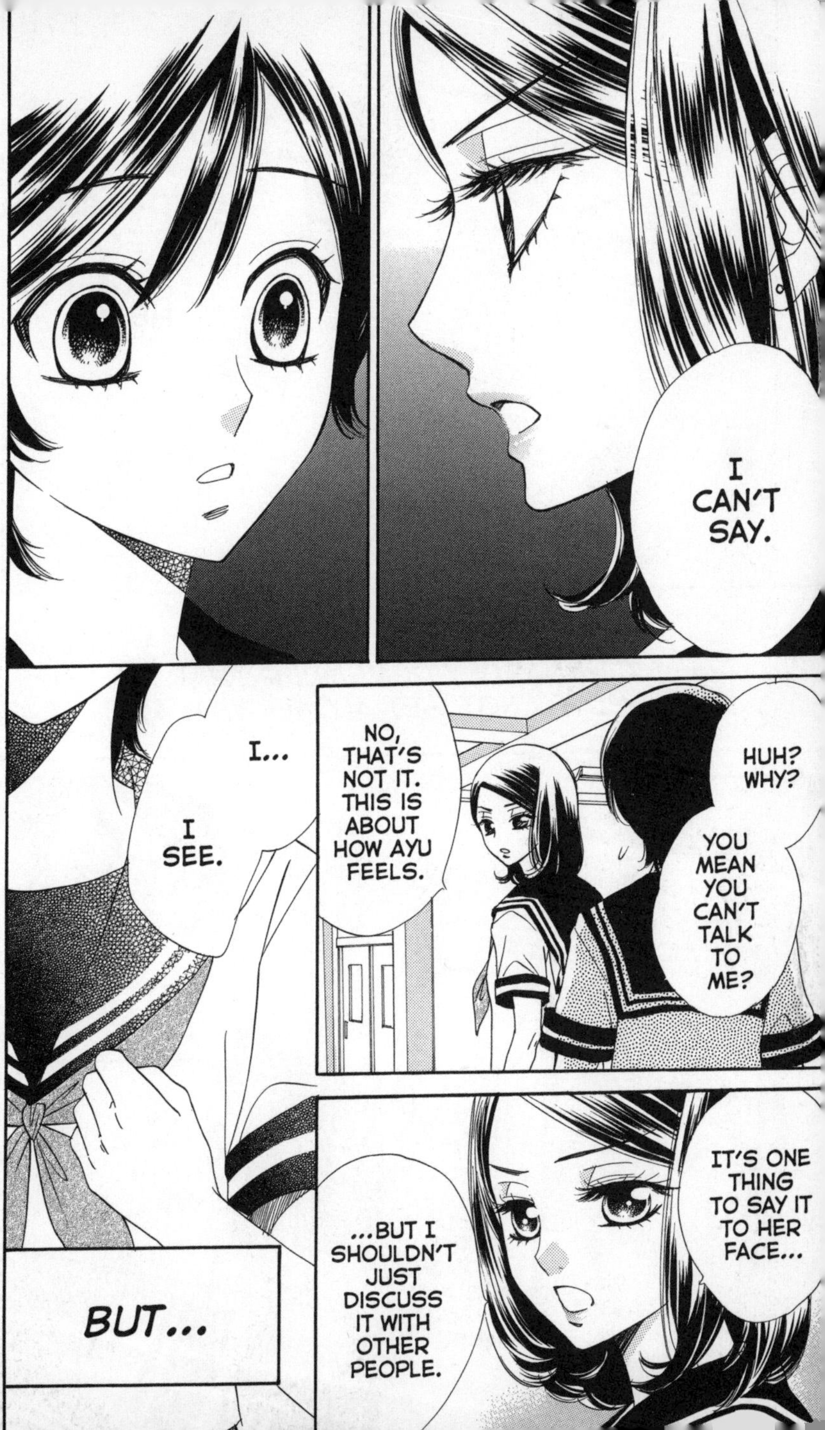
I CAN'T SAY.
HUH? WHY?
YOU MEAN YOU CAN'T TALK TO ME?
NO, THAT'S NOT IT. THIS IS ABOUT HOW AYU FEELS.
IT'S ONE THING TO SAY IT TO HER FACE...
...BUT I SHOULDN'T JUST DISCUSS IT WITH OTHER PEOPLE.
I...
I SEE.
BUT...

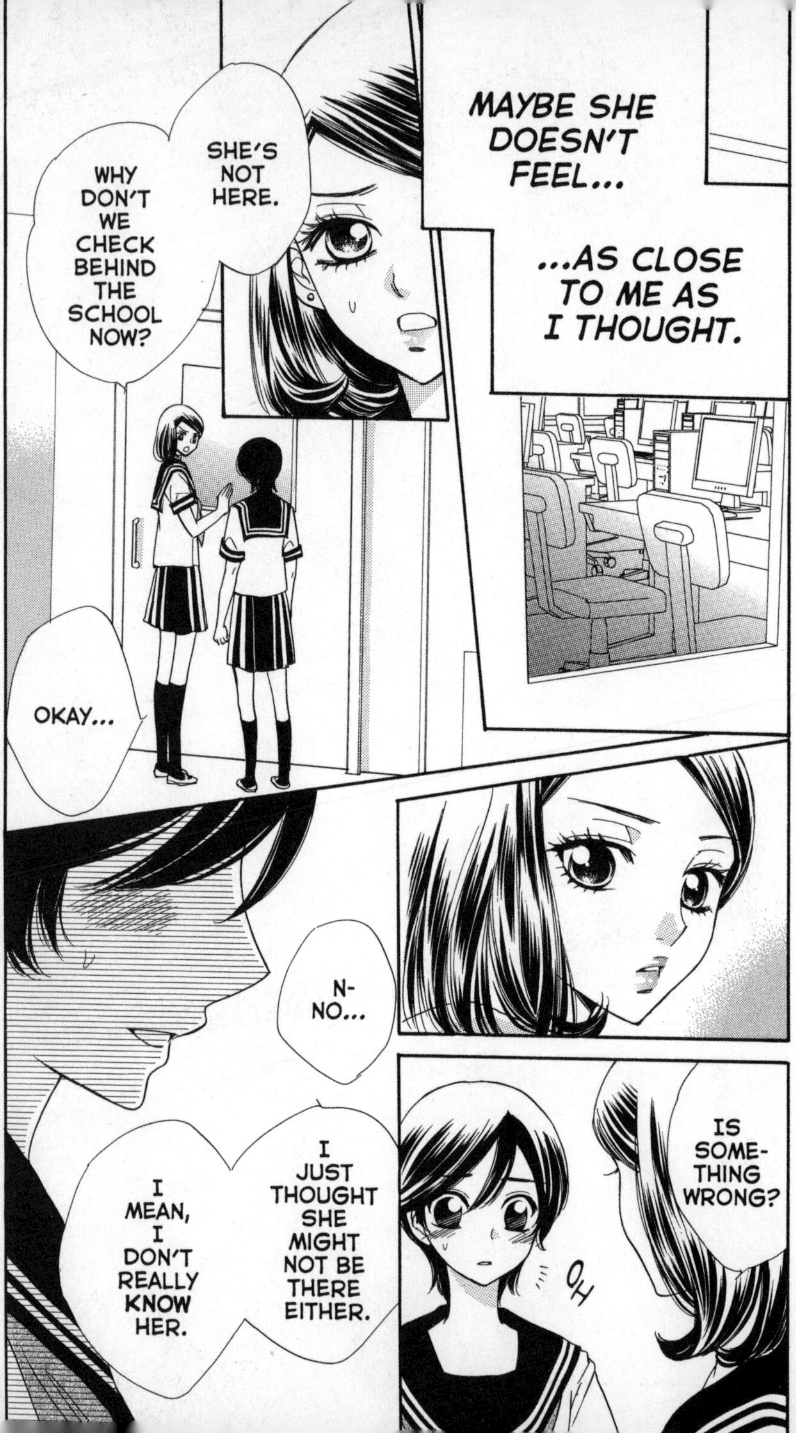
MAYBE SHE DOESN'T FEEL...
...AS CLOSE TO ME AS I THOUGHT.
SHE'S NOT HERE.
WHY DON'T WE CHECK BEHIND THE SCHOOL NOW?
OKAY...
IS SOME-THING WRONG?
OH
N-NO...
I JUST THOUGHT SHE MIGHT NOT BE THERE EITHER.
I MEAN, I DON'T REALLY KNOW HER.

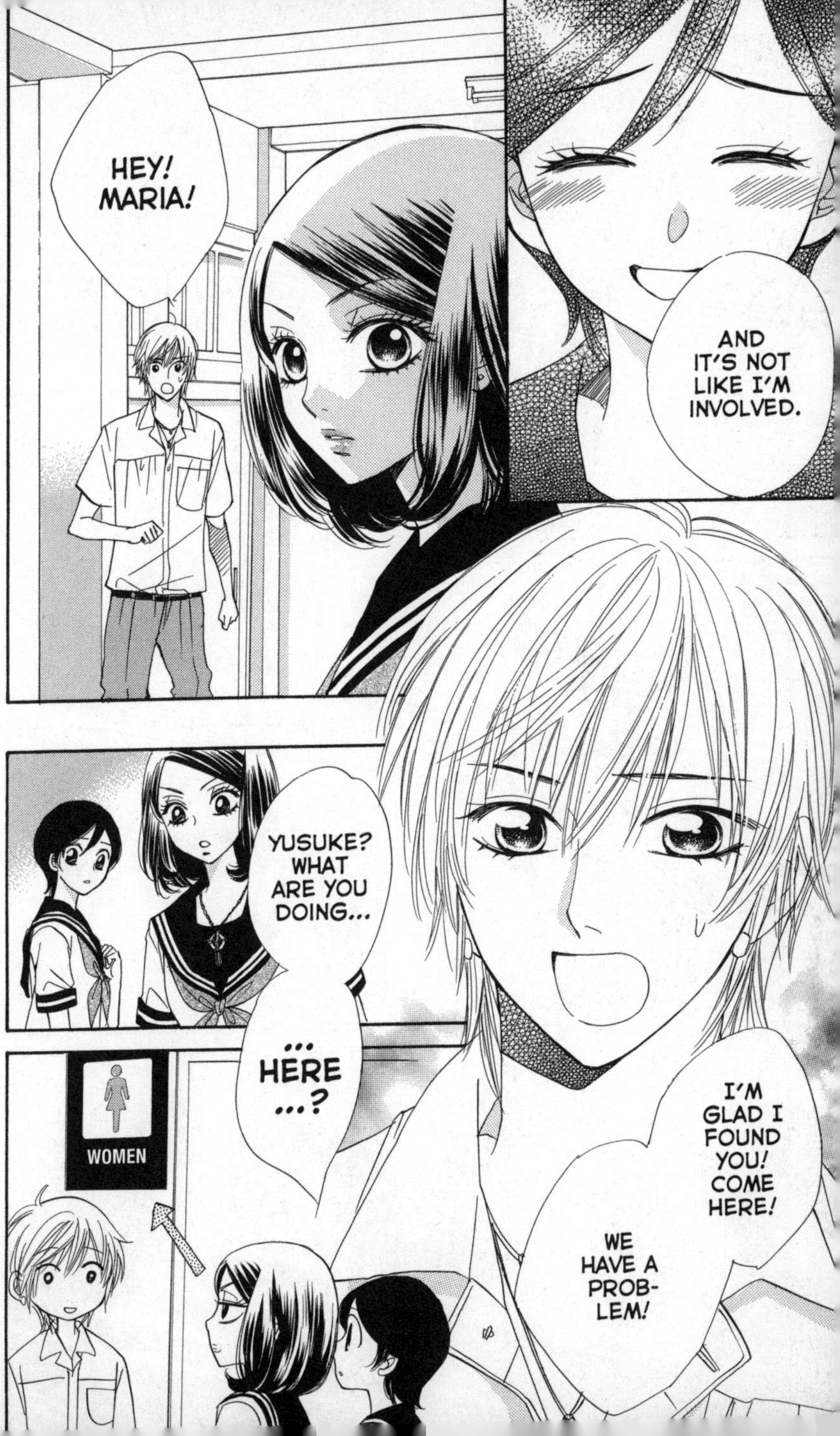
AND IT'S NOT LIKE I'M INVOLVED.
HEY! MARIA!
I'M GLAD I FOUND YOU! COME HERE!
WE HAVE A PROB-LEM!
YUSUKE? WHAT ARE YOU DOING...
... HERE ...?
WOMEN

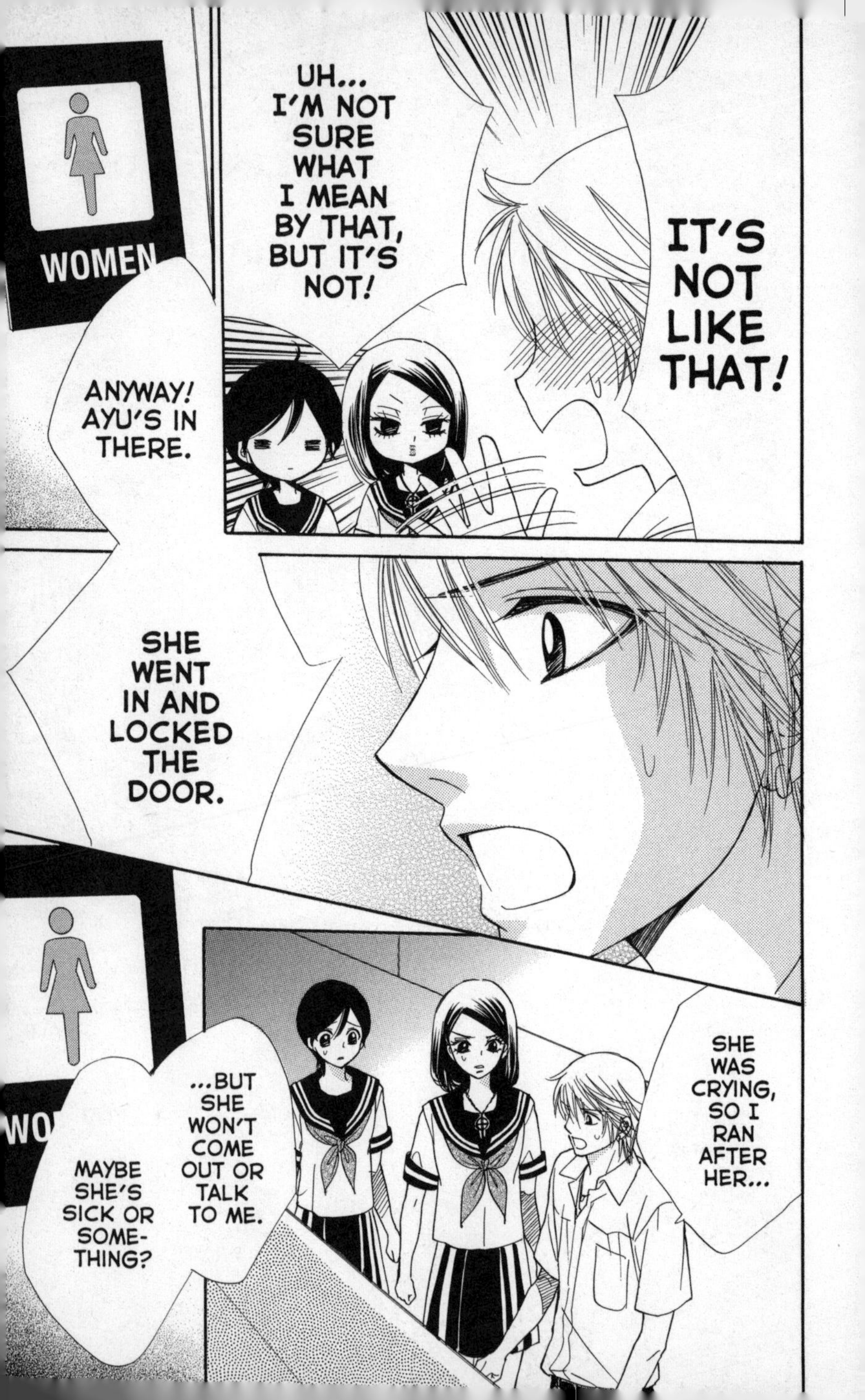
IT'S NOT LIKE THAT!
UH... I'M NOT SURE WHAT I MEAN BY THAT, BUT IT'S NOT!
WOMEN
ANYWAY! AYU'S IN THERE.
SHE WENT IN AND LOCKED THE DOOR.
SHE WAS CRYING, SO I RAN AFTER HER...
...BUT SHE WON'T COME OUT OR TALK TO ME.
MAYBE SHE'S SICK OR SOME-THING?

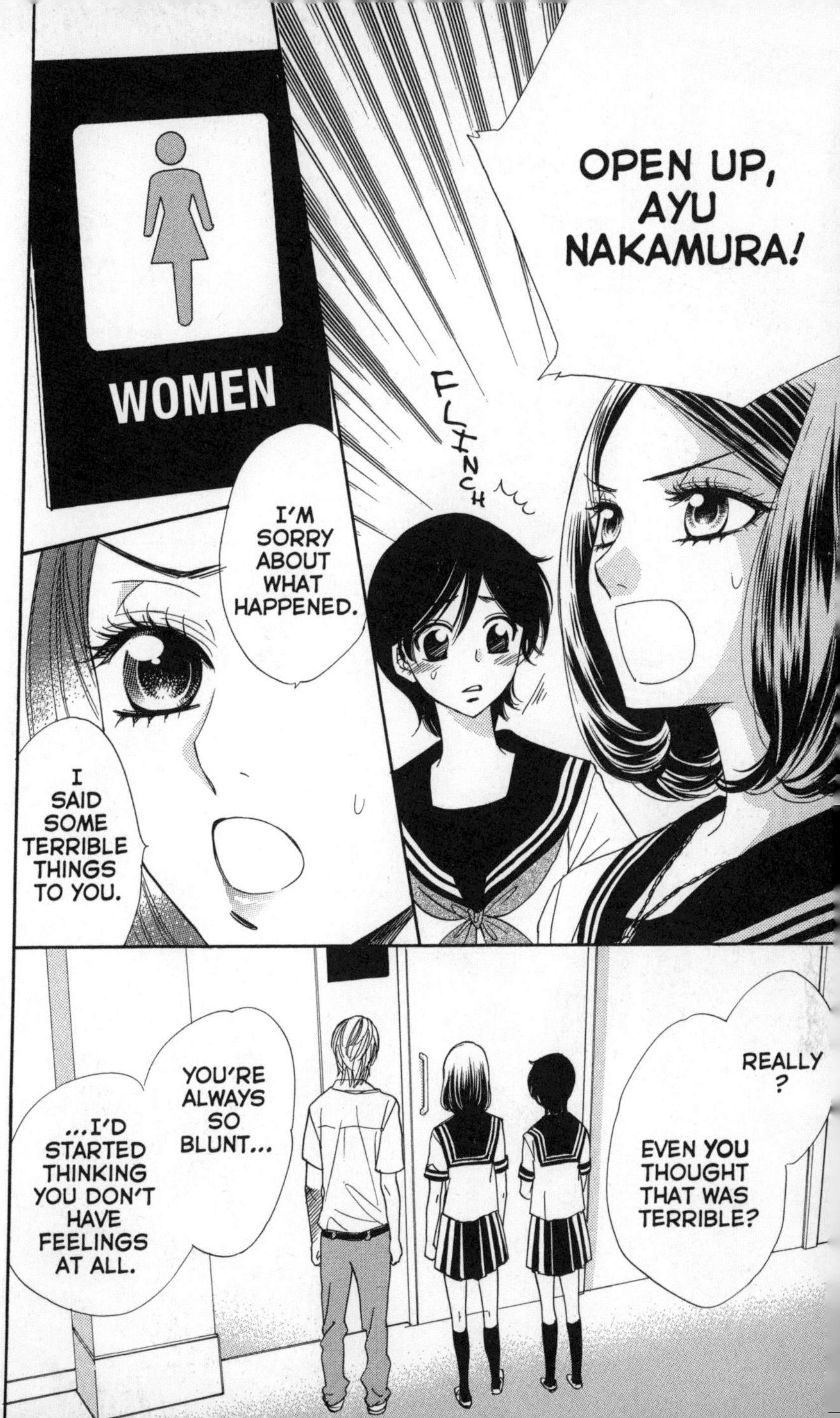
OPEN UP, AYU NAKAMURA!
FLINCH
WOMEN
I'M SORRY ABOUT WHAT HAPPENED.
I SAID SOME TERRIBLE THINGS TO YOU.
REALLY?
EVEN YOU THOUGHT THAT WAS TERRIBLE?
YOU'RE ALWAYS SO BLUNT...
...I'D STARTED THINKING YOU DON'T HAVE FEELINGS AT ALL.

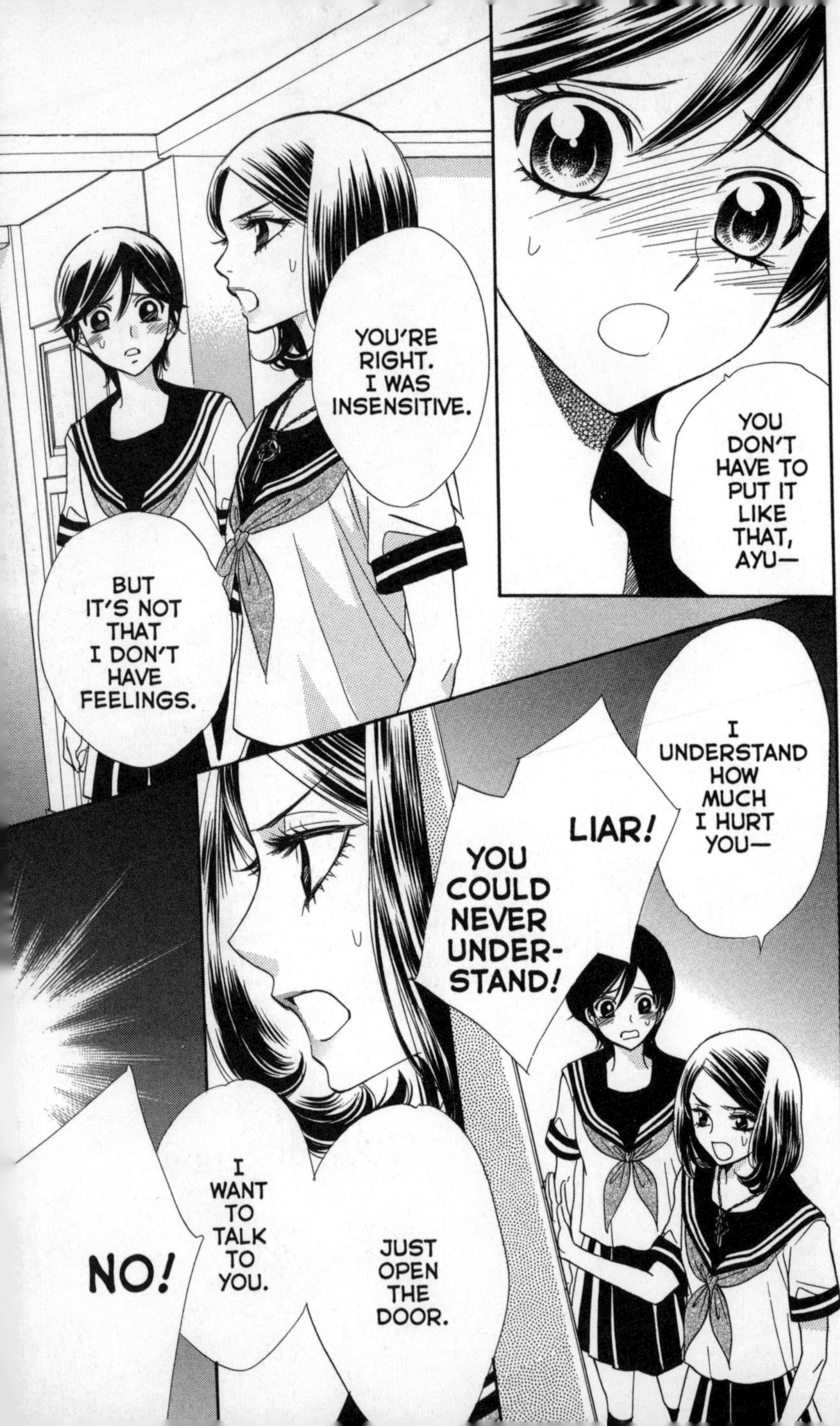
YOU DON'T HAVE TO PUT IT LIKE THAT, AYU—
YOU'RE RIGHT. I WAS INSENSITIVE.
BUT IT'S NOT THAT I DON'T HAVE FEELINGS.
I UNDERSTAND HOW MUCH I HURT YOU—
LIAR!
YOU COULD NEVER UNDER-STAND!
JUST OPEN THE DOOR.
I WANT TO TALK TO YOU.
NO!

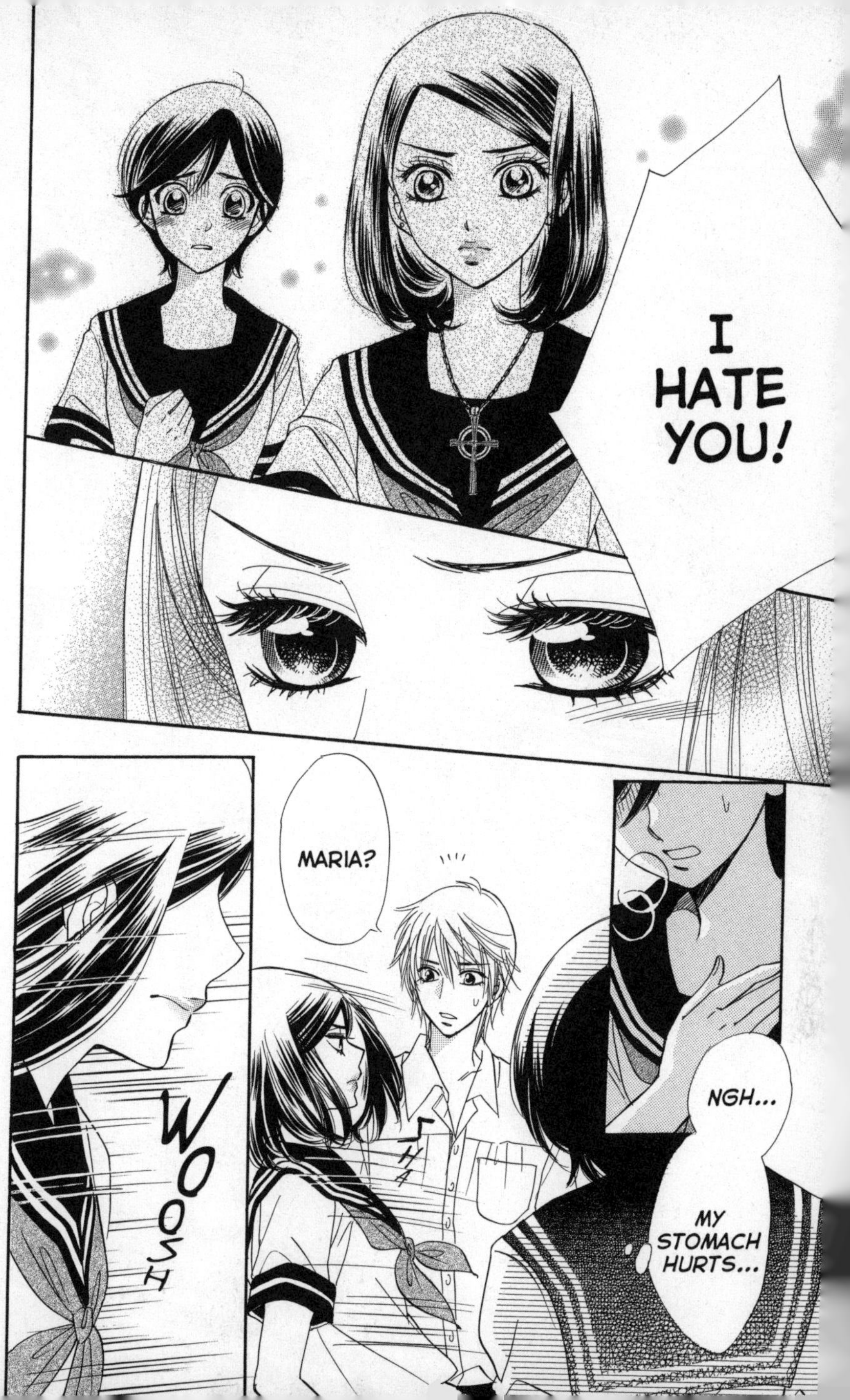
I HATE YOU!
NGH...
MY STOMACH HURTS...
MARIA?
HA
WOOSH

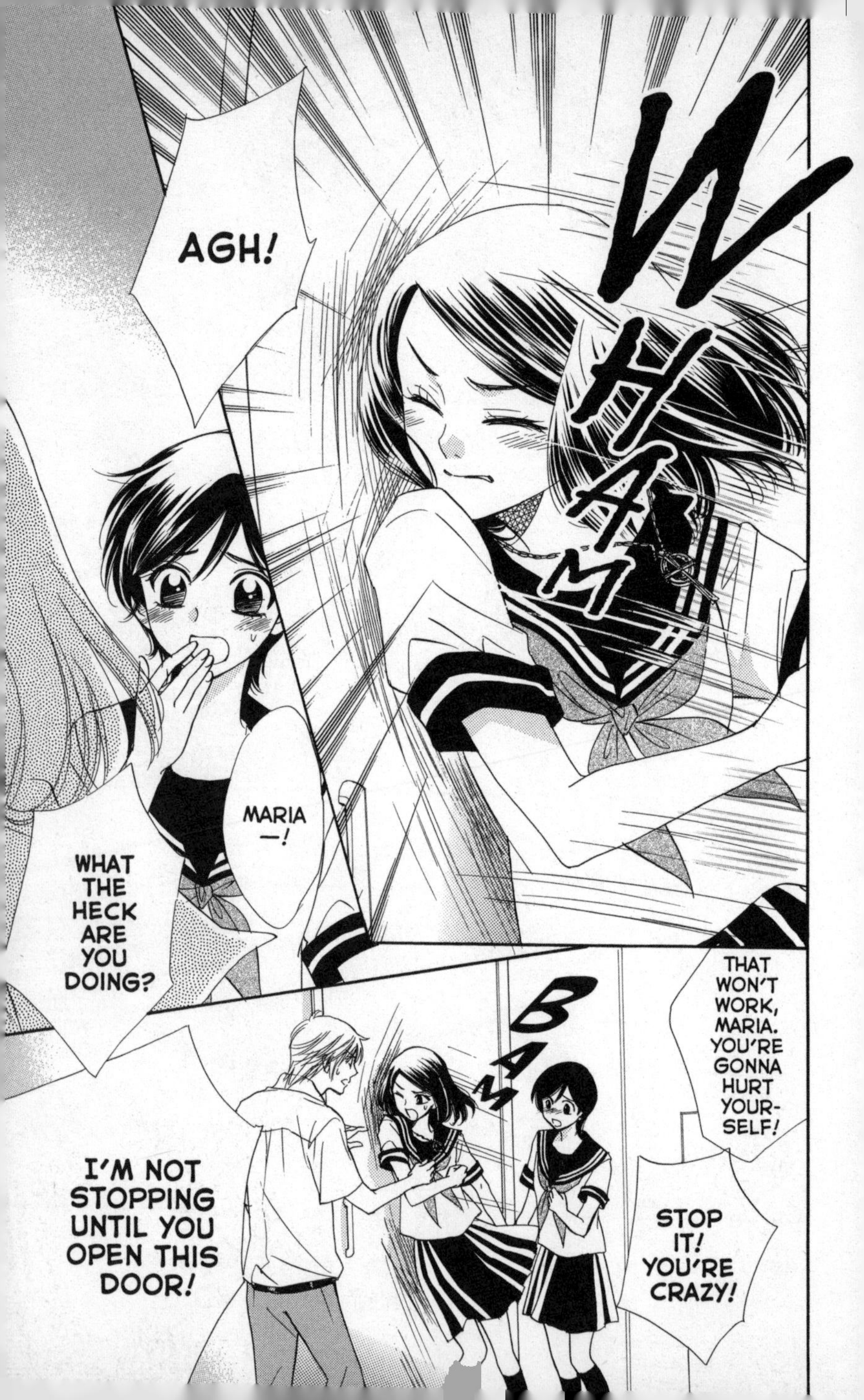
WHAM
AGH!
MARIA —!
WHAT THE HECK ARE YOU DOING?
THAT WON'T WORK, MARIA. YOU'RE GONNA HURT YOURSELF!
BAM
STOP IT! YOU'RE CRAZY!
I'M NOT STOPPING UNTIL YOU OPEN THIS DOOR!

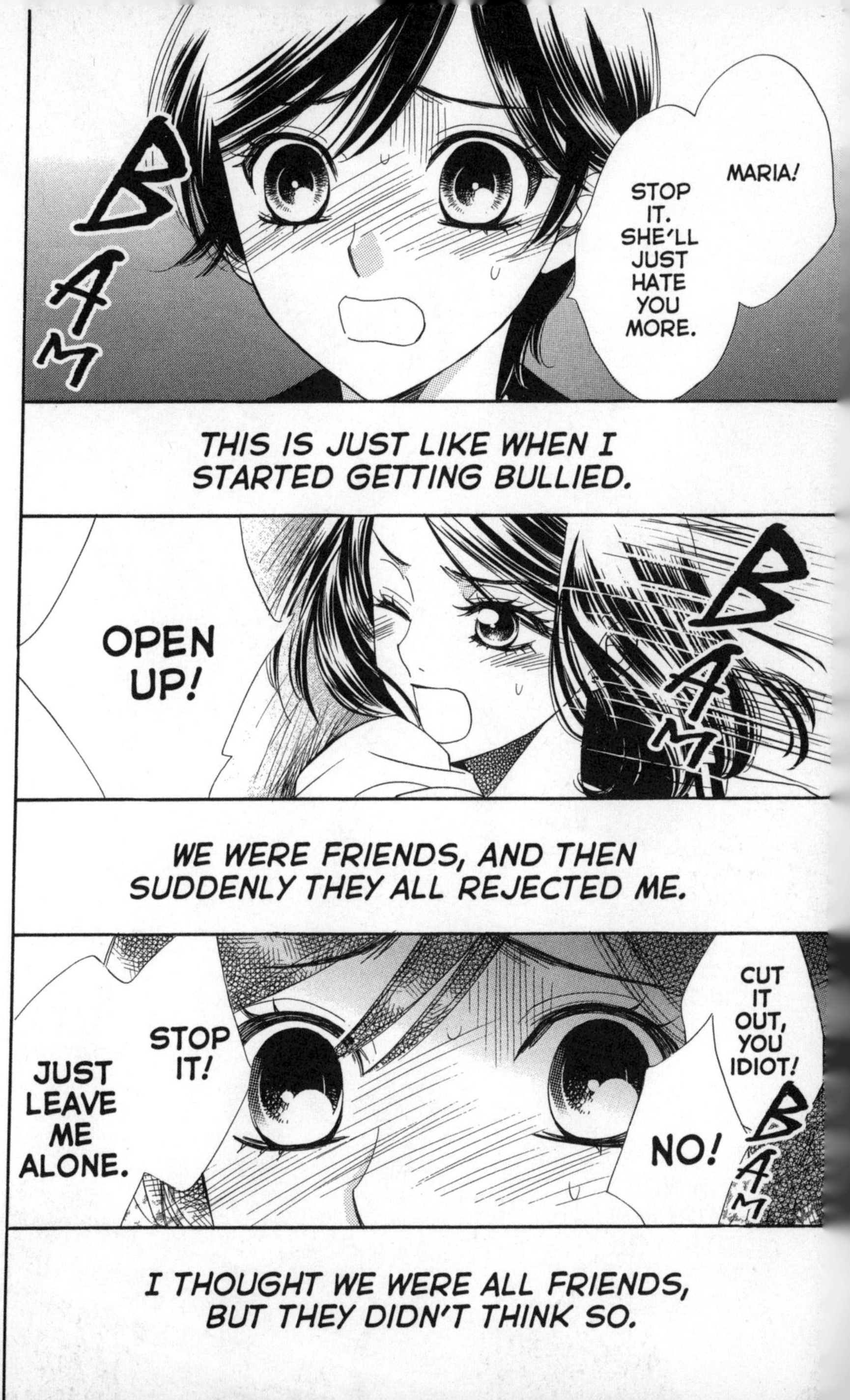
MARIA!
STOP IT. SHE'LL JUST HATE YOU MORE.
BAM
THIS IS JUST LIKE WHEN I STARTED GETTING BULLIED.
BAM
OPEN UP!
WE WERE FRIENDS, AND THEN SUDDENLY THEY ALL REJECTED ME.
CUT IT OUT, YOU IDIOT!
BAM
NO!
STOP IT!
JUST LEAVE ME ALONE.
I THOUGHT WE WERE ALL FRIENDS, BUT THEY DIDN'T THINK SO.

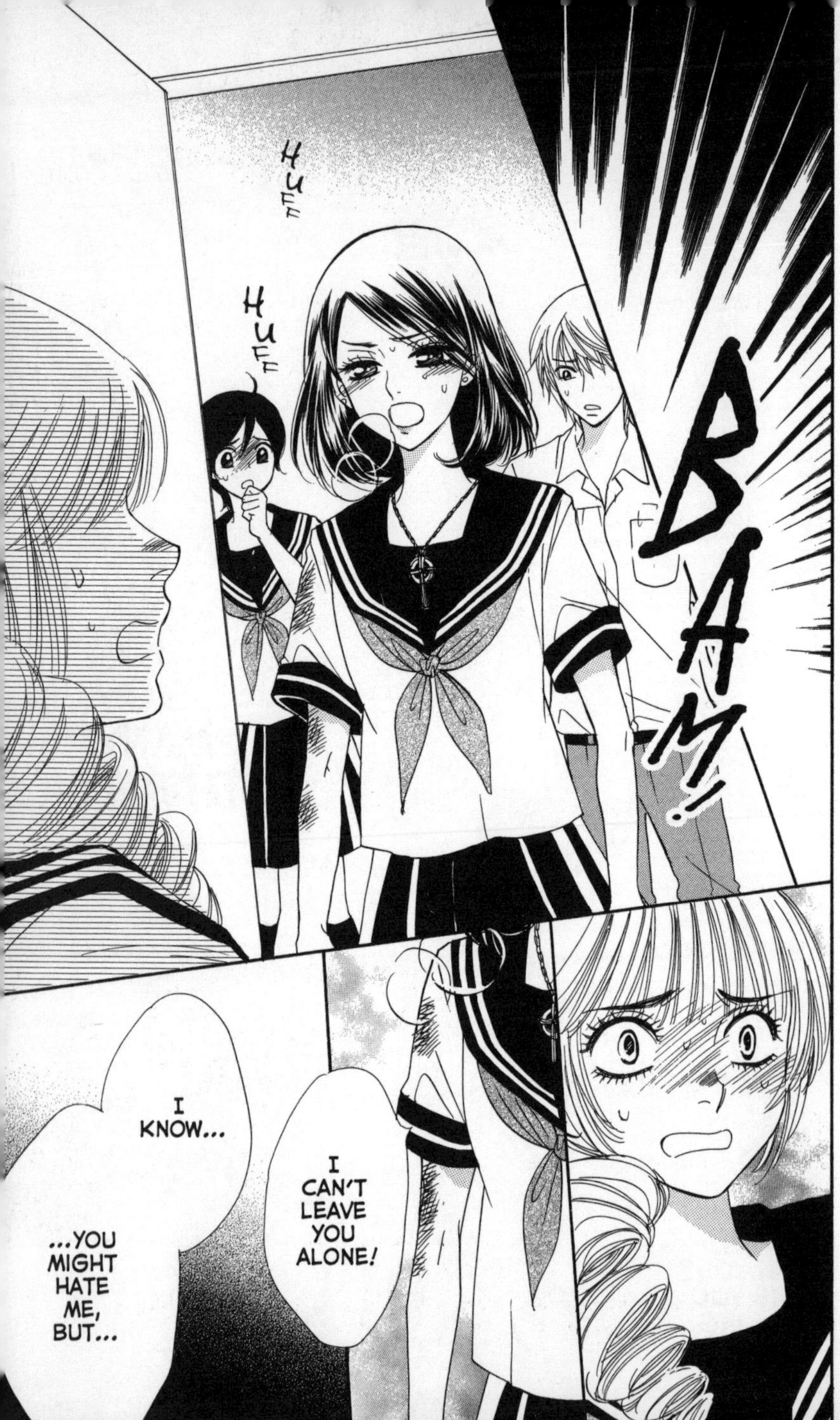
BAM!!
HUFF
HUFF
I CAN'T LEAVE YOU ALONE!
I KNOW...
...YOU MIGHT HATE ME, BUT...

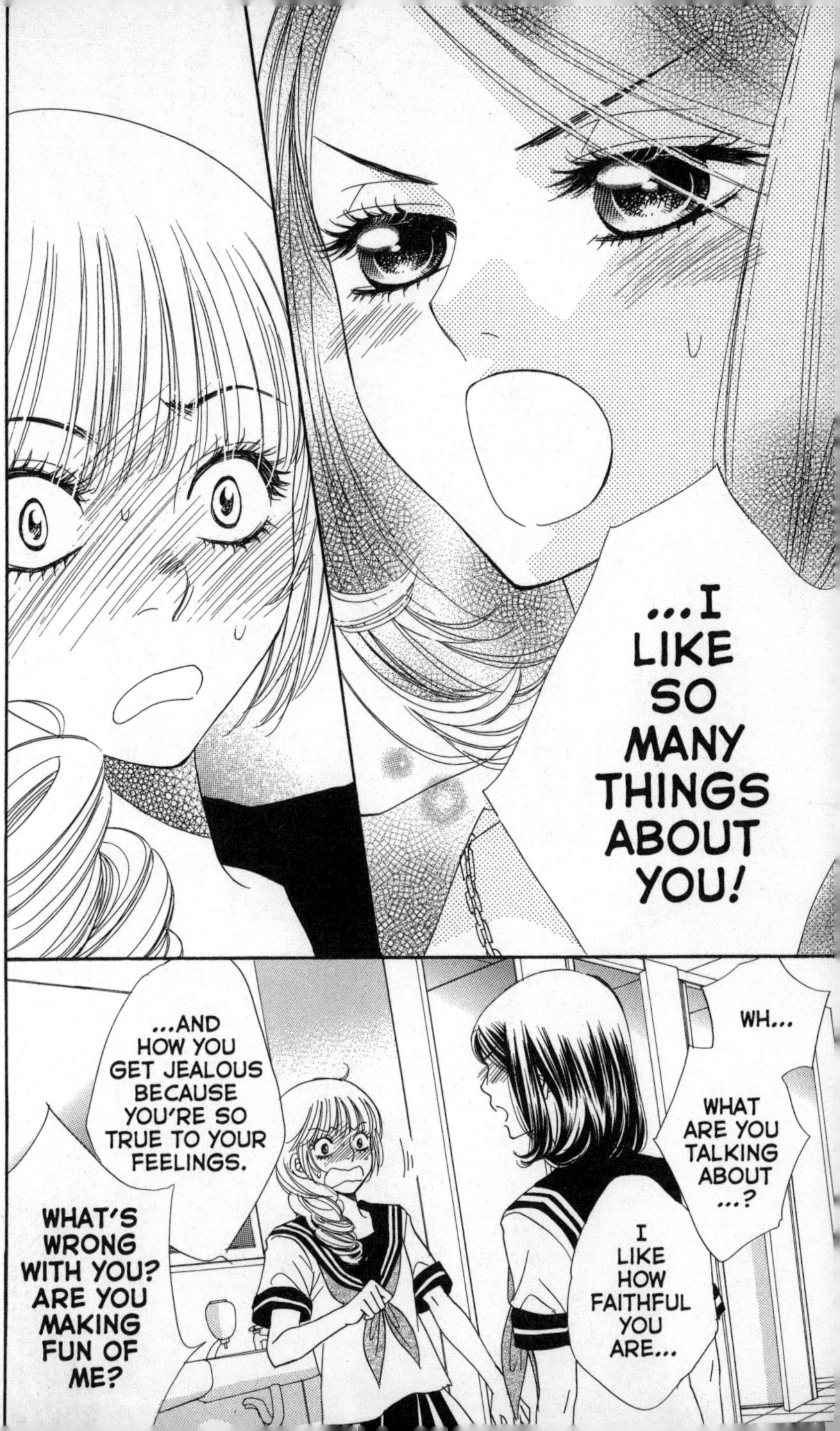
...I LIKE SO MANY THINGS ABOUT YOU!
WH...
WHAT ARE YOU TALKING ABOUT ...?
I LIKE HOW FAITHFUL YOU ARE...
...AND HOW YOU GET JEALOUS BECAUSE YOU'RE SO TRUE TO YOUR FEELINGS.
WHAT'S WRONG WITH YOU? ARE YOU MAKING FUN OF ME?

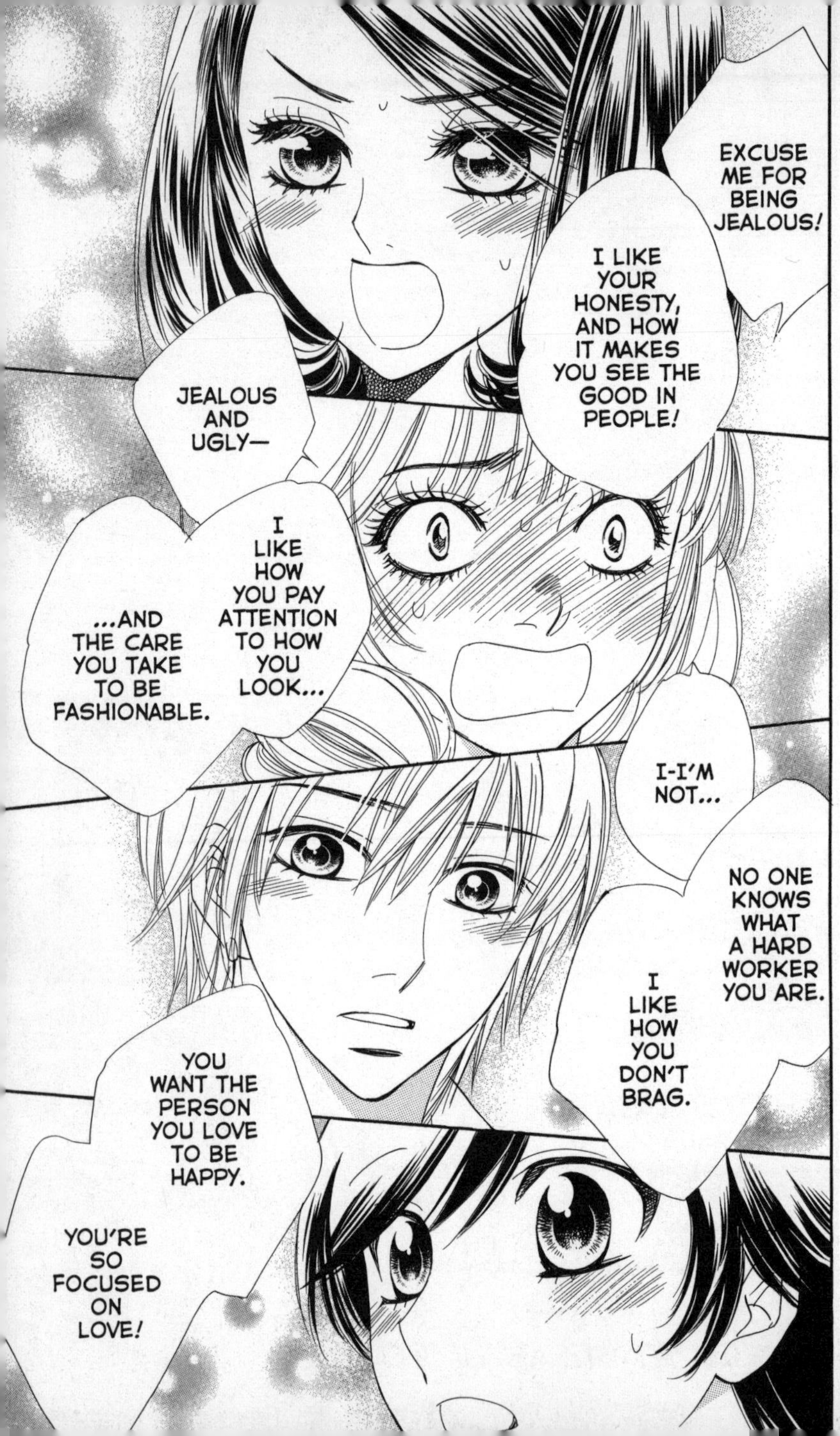
EXCUSE ME FOR BEING JEALOUS!
I LIKE YOUR HONESTY, AND HOW IT MAKES YOU SEE THE GOOD IN PEOPLE!
JEALOUS AND UGLY—
I LIKE HOW YOU PAY ATTENTION TO HOW YOU LOOK...
...AND THE CARE YOU TAKE TO BE FASHIONABLE.
I-I'M NOT...
NO ONE KNOWS WHAT A HARD WORKER YOU ARE.
I LIKE HOW YOU DON'T BRAG.
YOU WANT THE PERSON YOU LOVE TO BE HAPPY.
YOU'RE SO FOCUSED ON LOVE!

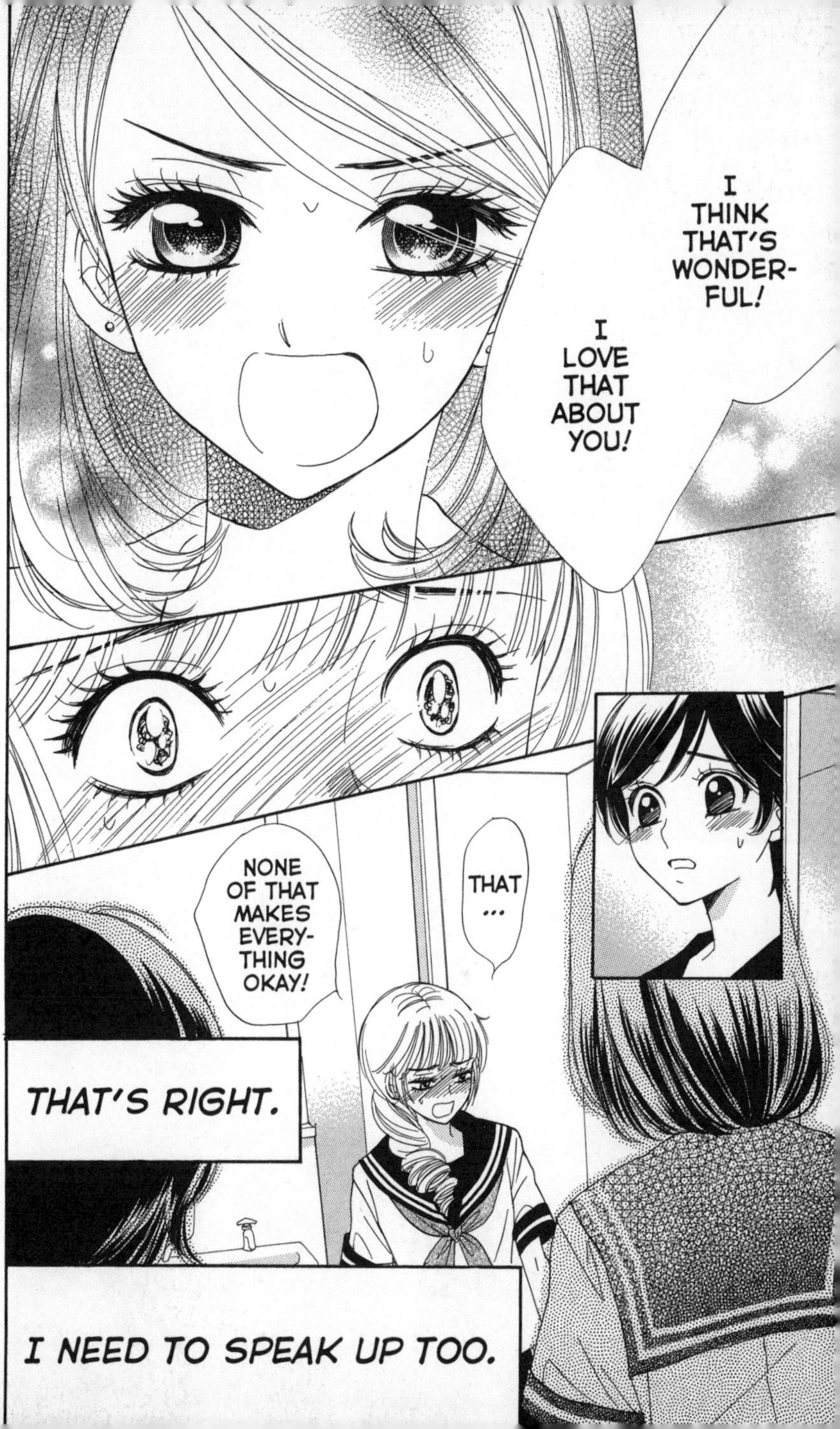
I THINK THAT'S WONDERFUL!
I LOVE THAT ABOUT YOU!
THAT...
NONE OF THAT MAKES EVERYTHING OKAY!
THAT'S RIGHT.
I NEED TO SPEAK UP TOO.

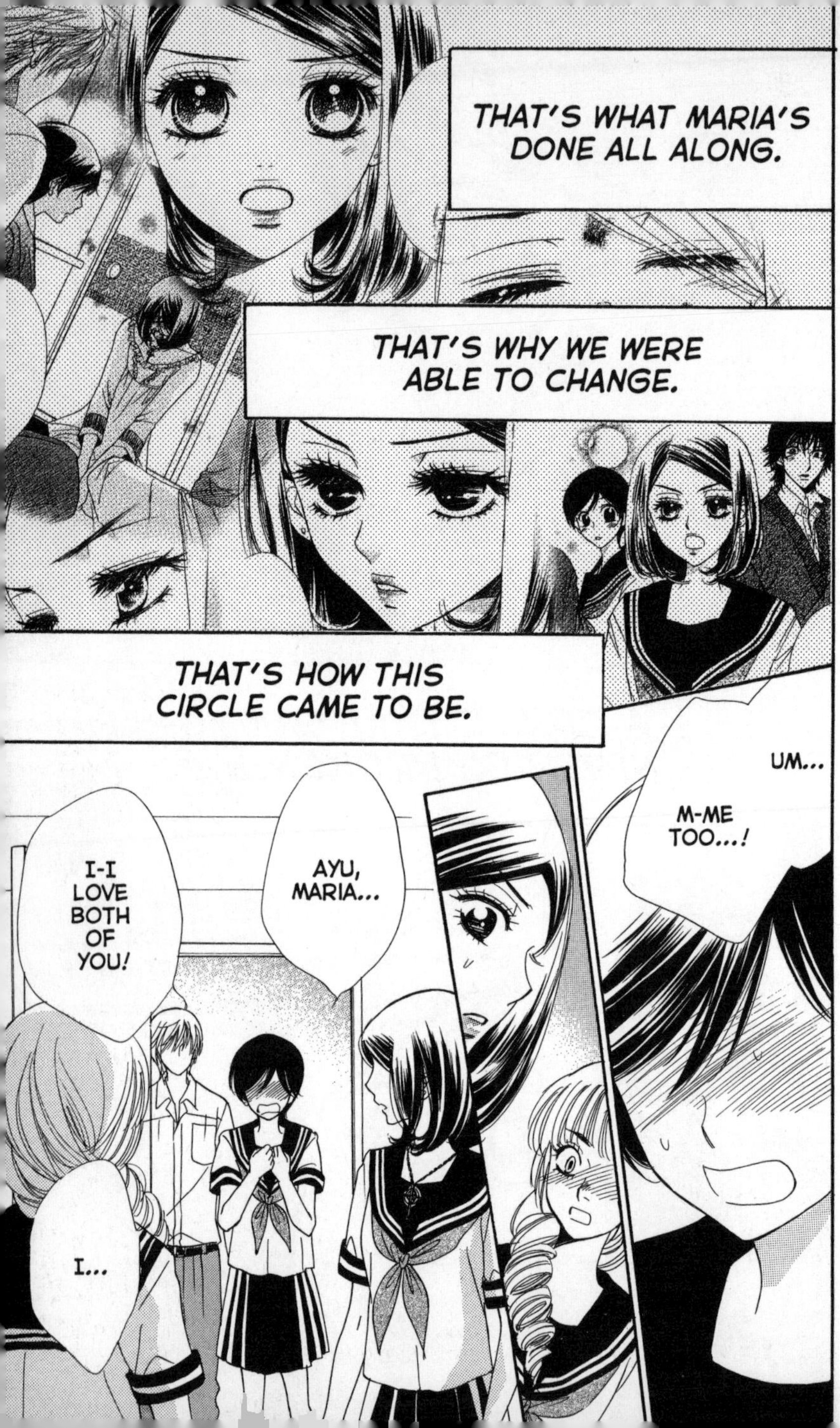
THAT'S WHAT MARIA'S DONE ALL ALONG.
THAT'S WHY WE WERE ABLE TO CHANGE.
THAT'S HOW THIS CIRCLE CAME TO BE.
UM...
M-ME TOO...!
AYU, MARIA...
I-I LOVE BOTH OF YOU!
I...

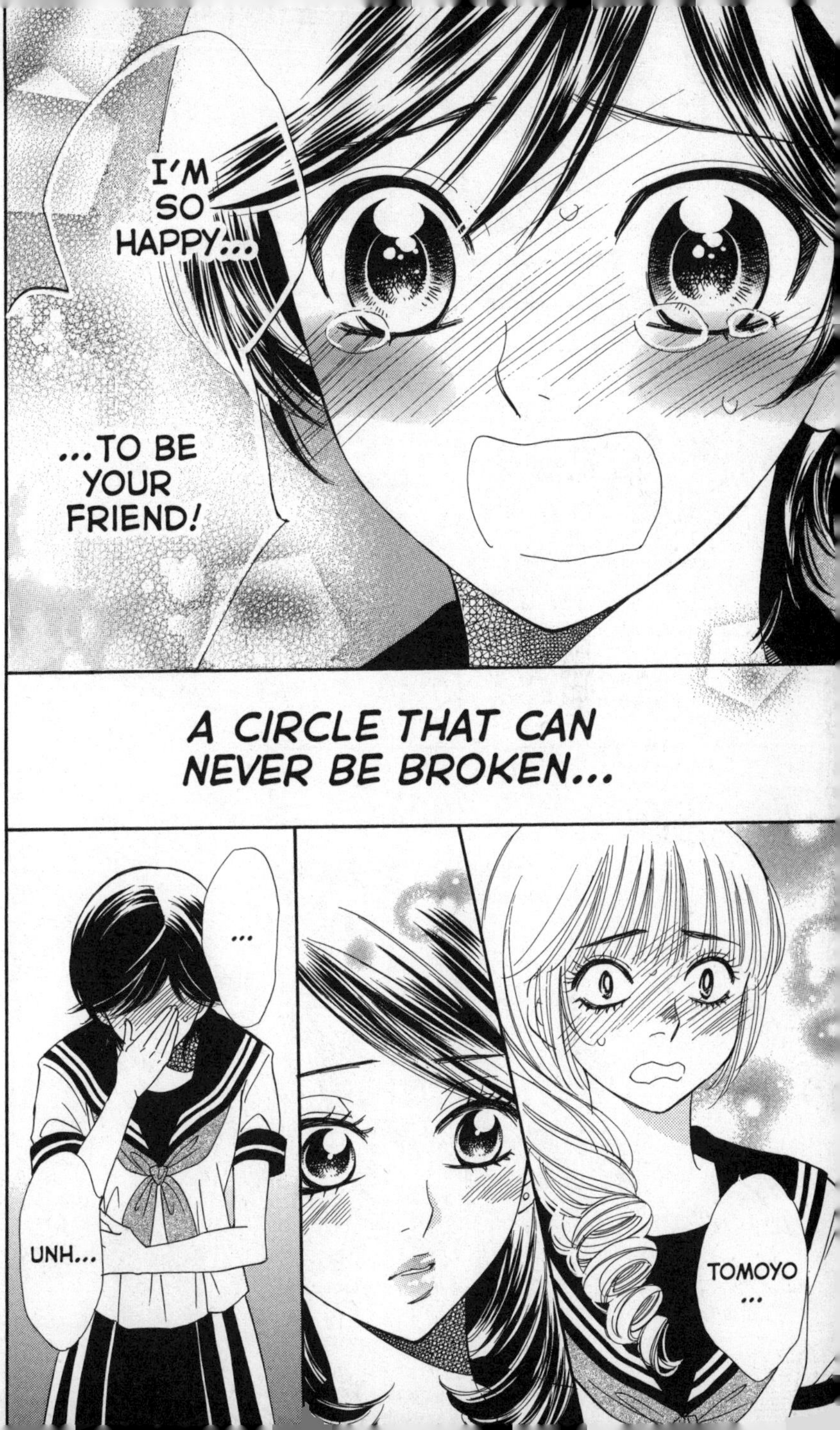

I'M SO HAPPY...
...TO BE YOUR FRIEND!
A CIRCLE THAT CAN NEVER BE BROKEN...
TOMOYO ...
...
UNH...

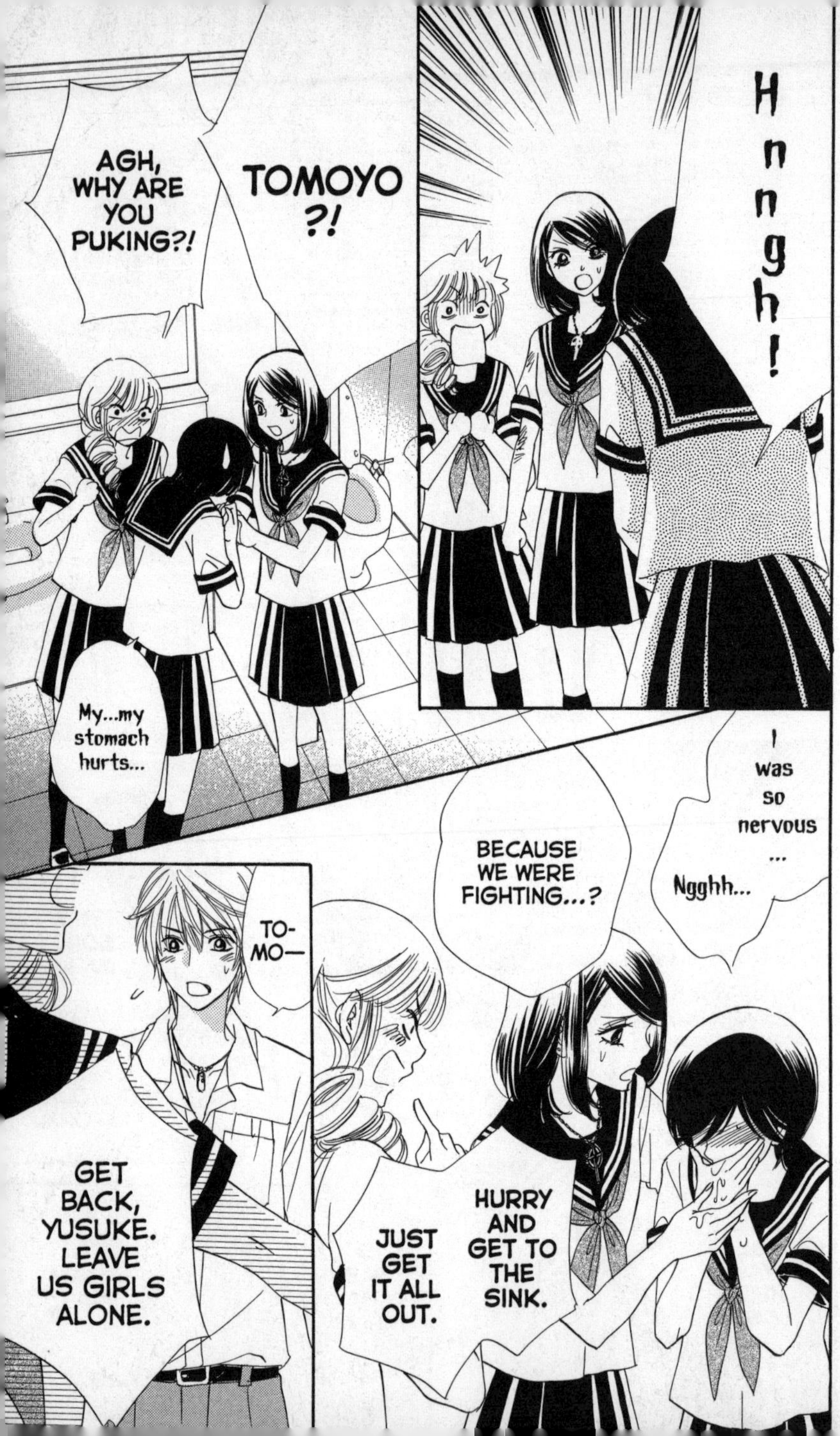
Hnngh!
TOMOYO?!
AGH, WHY ARE YOU PUKING?!
My...my stomach hurts...
I was so nervous...
Ngghh...
BECAUSE WE WERE FIGHTING...?
HURRY AND GET TO THE SINK.
JUST GET IT ALL OUT.
TO-MO—
GET BACK, YUSUKE. LEAVE US GIRLS ALONE.

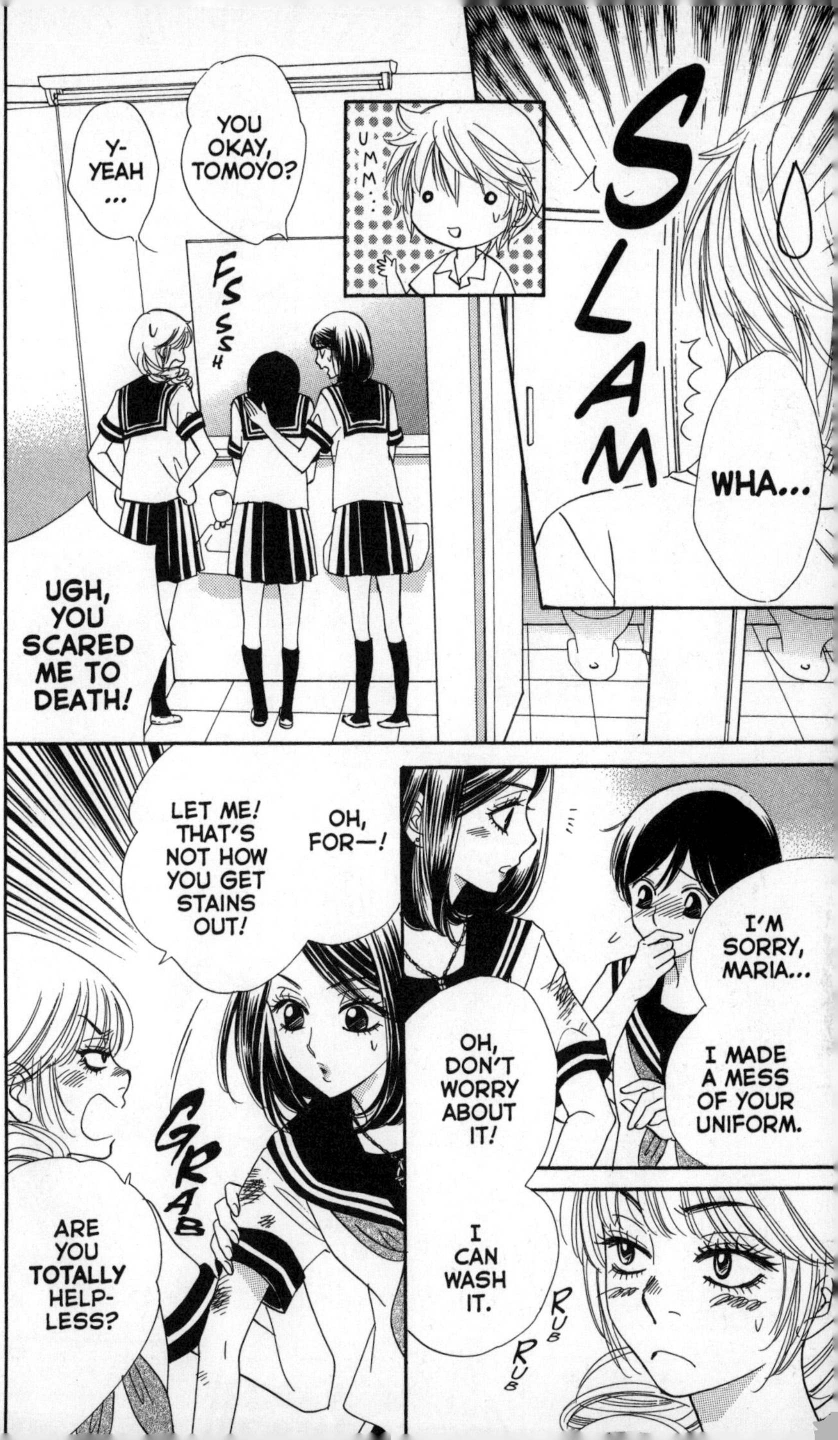
SLAM
WHA...
UMM...
YOU OKAY, TOMOYO?
Y-YEAH...
FSSSH
UGH, YOU SCARED ME TO DEATH!
I'M SORRY, MARIA...
I MADE A MESS OF YOUR UNIFORM.
OH, DON'T WORRY ABOUT IT!
I CAN WASH IT.
RUB RUB
OH, FOR—!
LET ME! THAT'S NOT HOW YOU GET STAINS OUT!
GRAB
ARE YOU TOTALLY HELP-LESS?

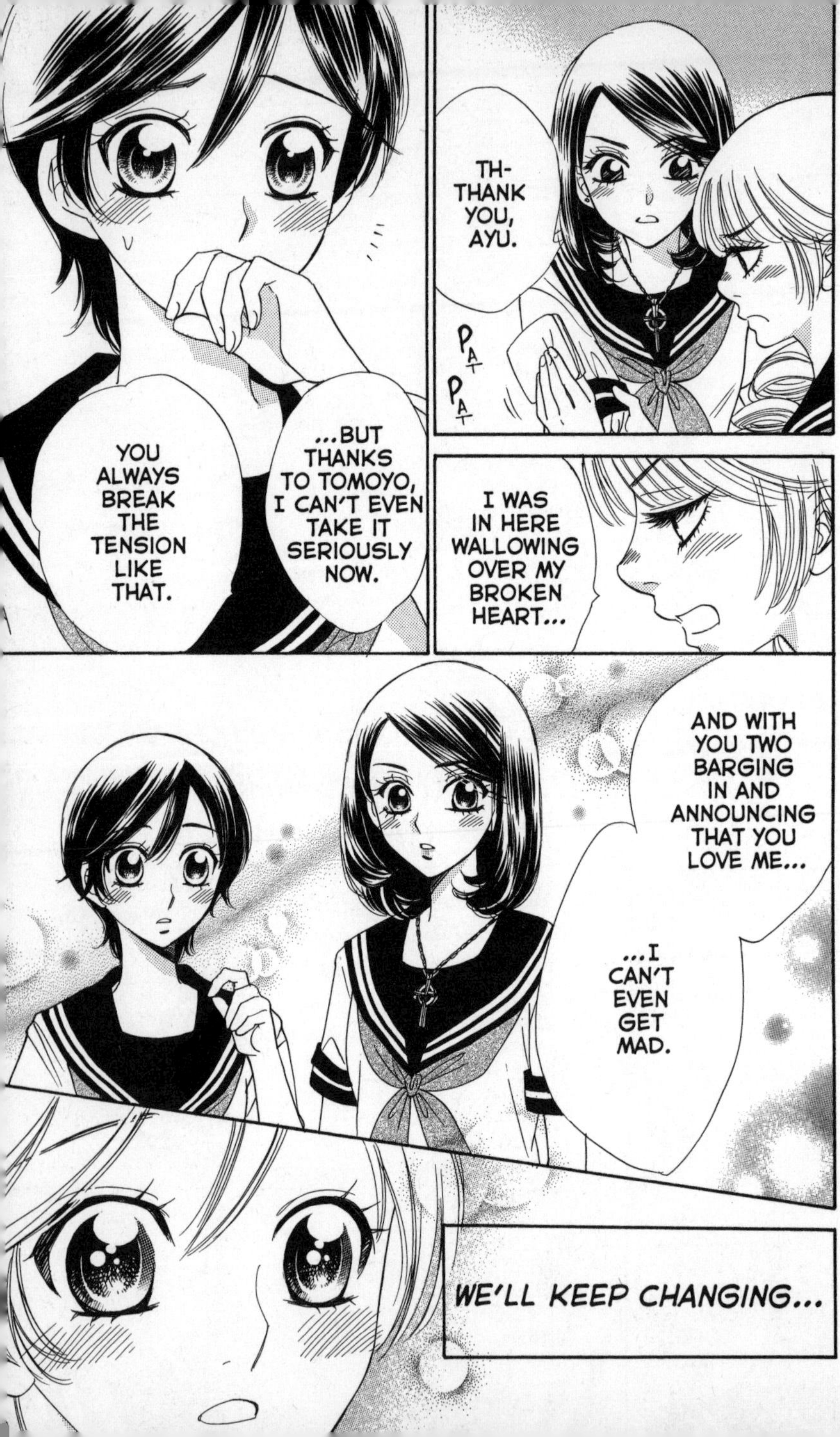
TH-THANK YOU, AYU.
PAT
PAT
I WAS IN HERE WALLOWING OVER MY BROKEN HEART...
...BUT THANKS TO TOMOYO, I CAN'T EVEN TAKE IT SERIOUSLY NOW.
YOU ALWAYS BREAK THE TENSION LIKE THAT.
AND WITH YOU TWO BARGING IN AND ANNOUNCING THAT YOU LOVE ME...
...I CAN'T EVEN GET MAD.
WE'LL KEEP CHANGING...

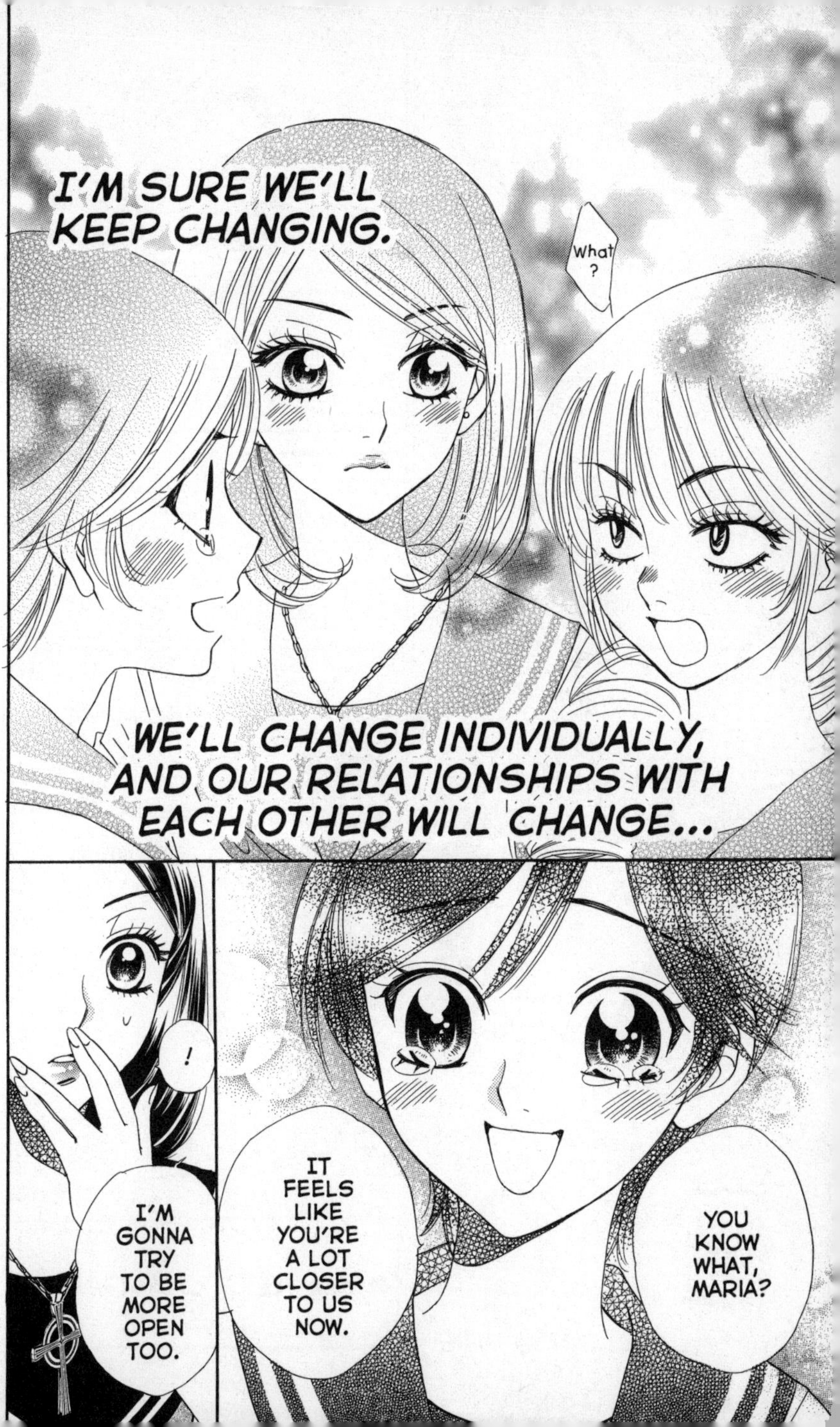
I'M SURE WE'LL KEEP CHANGING.
What?
WE'LL CHANGE INDIVIDUALLY, AND OUR RELATIONSHIPS WITH EACH OTHER WILL CHANGE...
YOU KNOW WHAT, MARIA?
IT FEELS LIKE YOU'RE A LOT CLOSER TO US NOW.
!
I'M GONNA TRY TO BE MORE OPEN TOO.

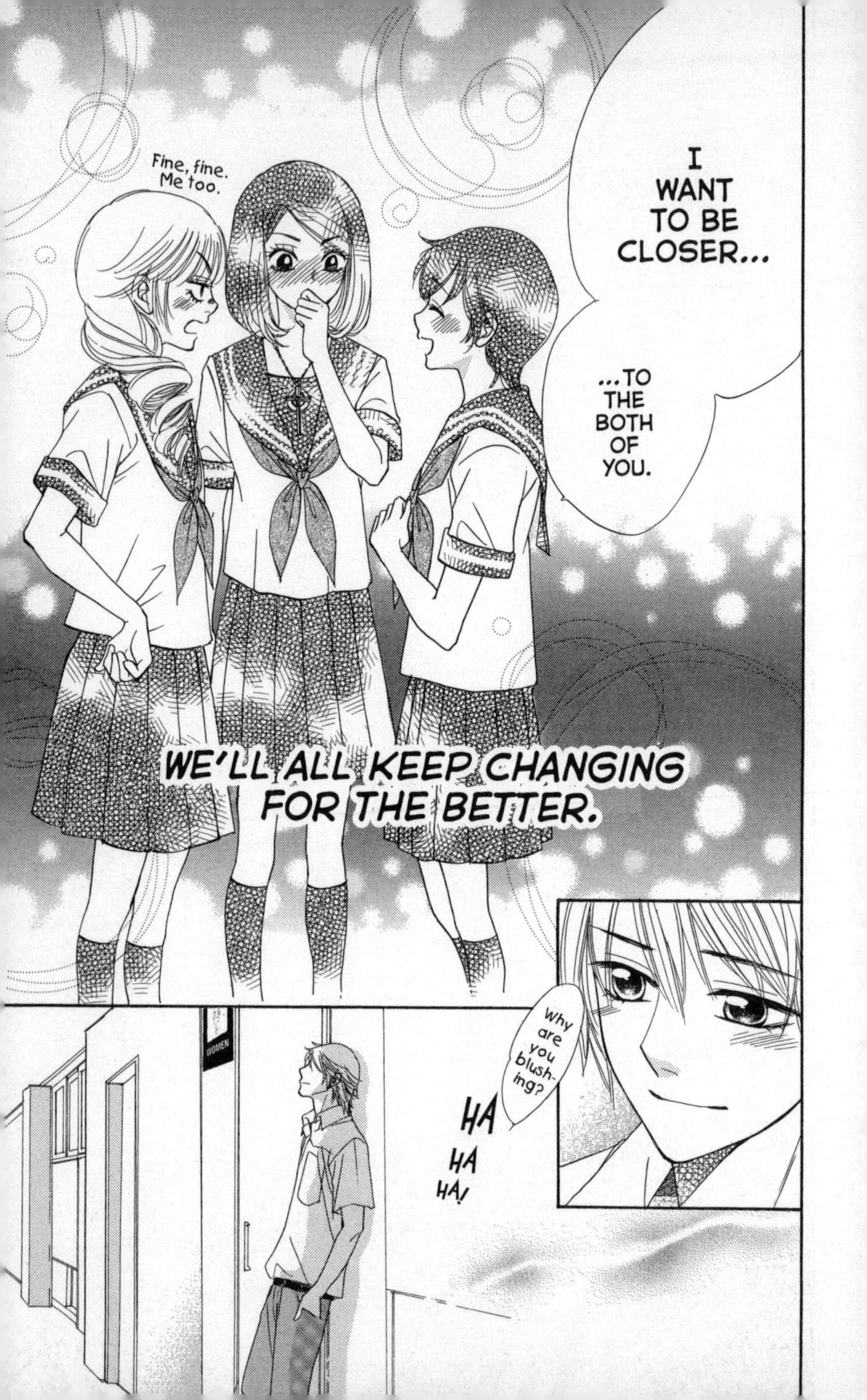
I WANT TO BE CLOSER...
...TO THE BOTH OF YOU.
Fine, fine. Me too.
WE'LL ALL KEEP CHANGING FOR THE BETTER.
Why are you blush-ing?
HA HA HA!
WOMEN

A Devil and Her Love Song

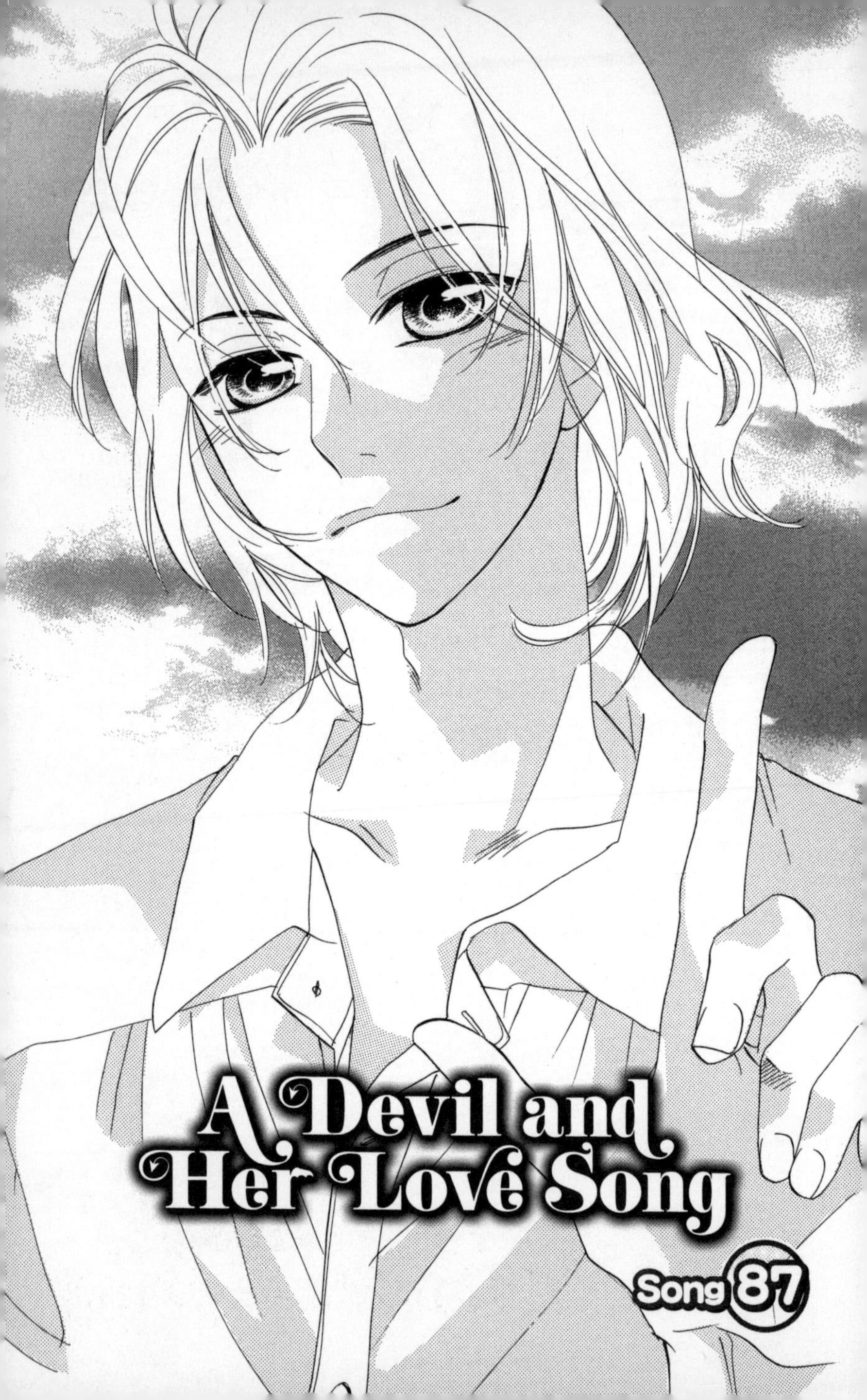
A Devil and Her Love Song
Song 87

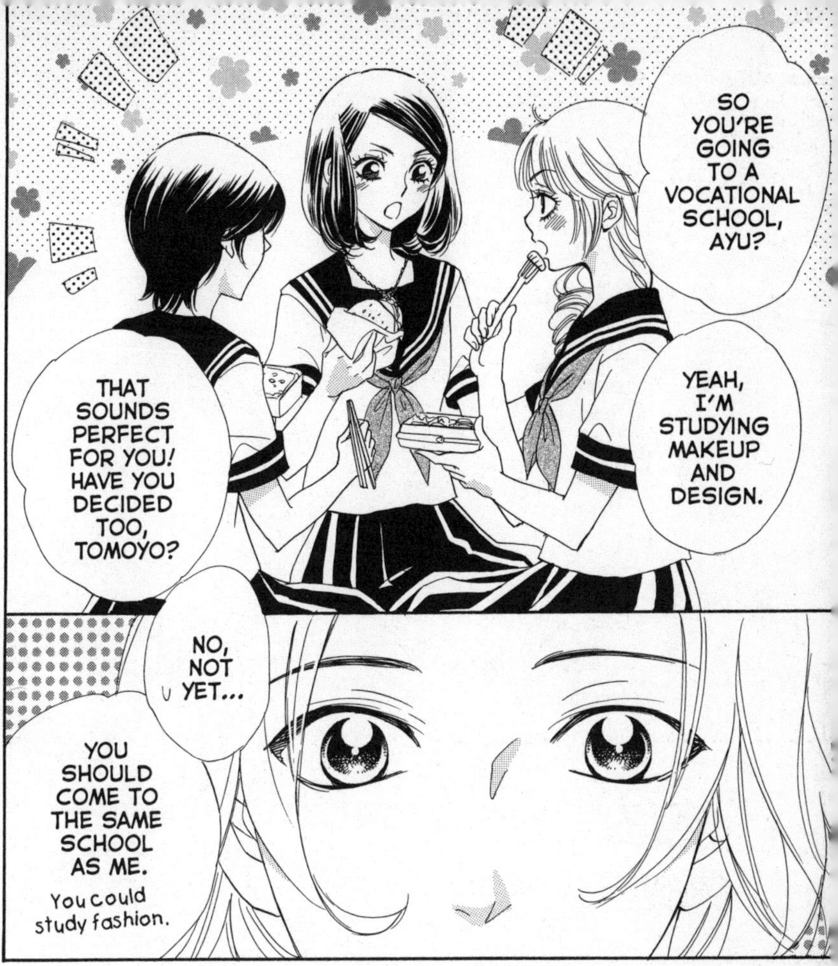
SO YOU'RE GOING TO A VOCATIONAL SCHOOL, AYU?
YEAH, I'M STUDYING MAKEUP AND DESIGN.
THAT SOUNDS PERFECT FOR YOU! HAVE YOU DECIDED TOO, TOMOYO?
NO, NOT YET...
YOU SHOULD COME TO THE SAME SCHOOL AS ME.
You could study fashion.

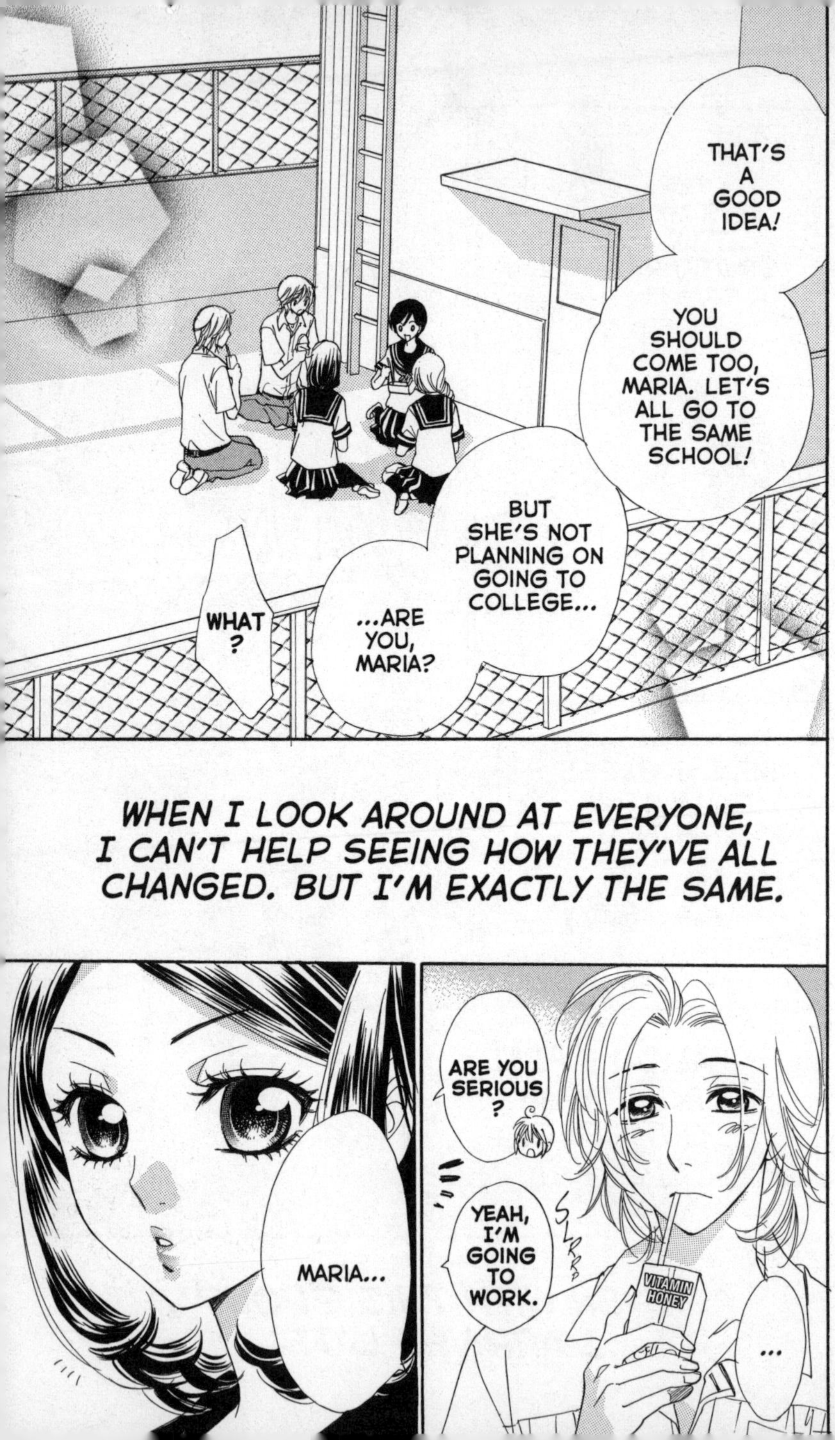
THAT'S A GOOD IDEA!
YOU SHOULD COME TOO, MARIA. LET'S ALL GO TO THE SAME SCHOOL!
BUT SHE'S NOT PLANNING ON GOING TO COLLEGE...
...ARE YOU, MARIA?
WHAT?
WHEN I LOOK AROUND AT EVERYONE, I CAN'T HELP SEEING HOW THEY'VE ALL CHANGED. BUT I'M EXACTLY THE SAME.
ARE YOU SERIOUS?
YEAH, I'M GOING TO WORK.
VITAMIN HONEY
...
MARIA...

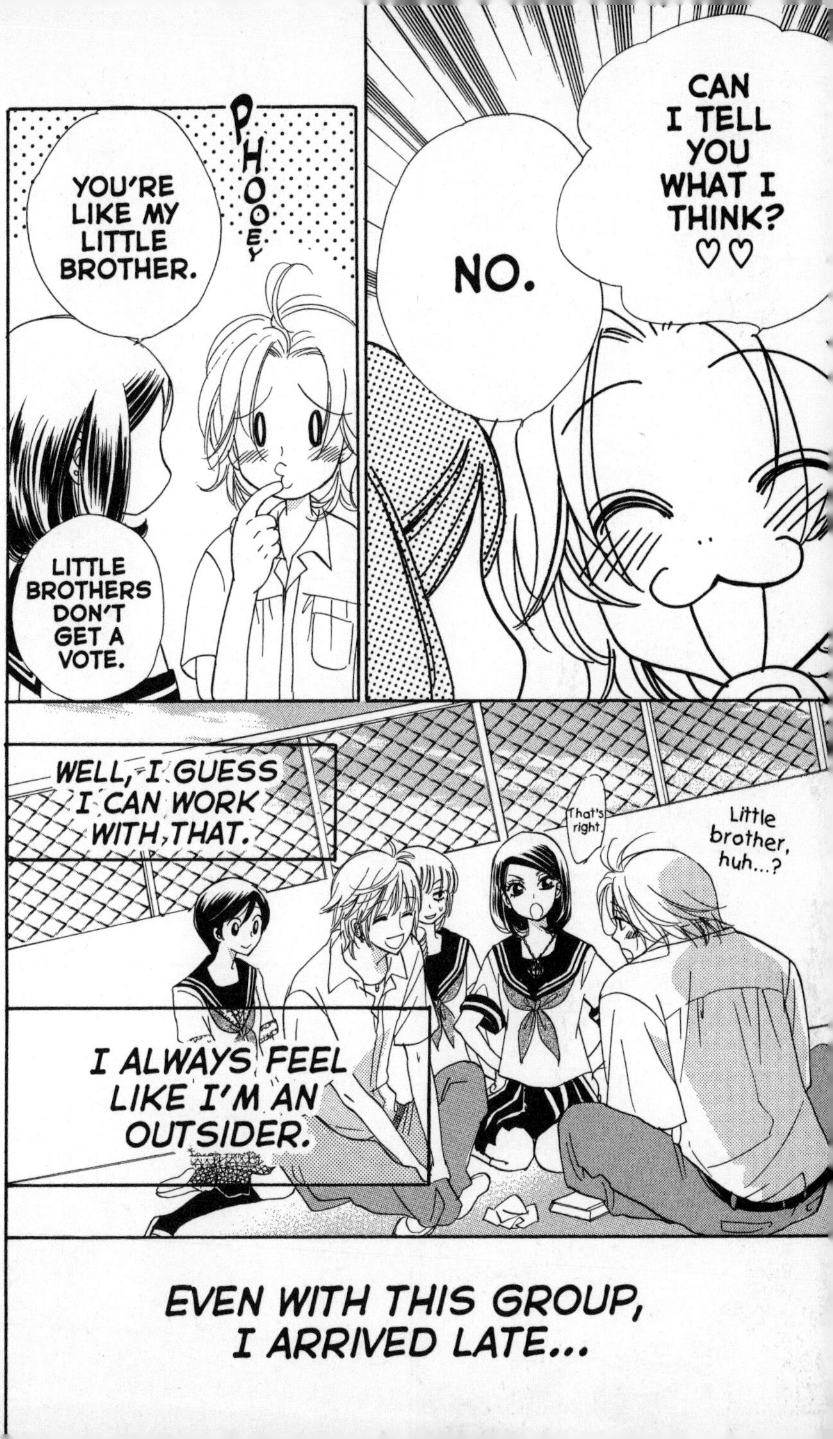
CAN I TELL YOU WHAT I THINK? ♡♡
NO.
YOU'RE LIKE MY LITTLE BROTHER.
PHOOEY
LITTLE BROTHERS DON'T GET A VOTE.
WELL, I GUESS I CAN WORK WITH THAT.
Little brother, huh...?
That's right.
I ALWAYS FEEL LIKE I'M AN OUTSIDER.
EVEN WITH THIS GROUP, I ARRIVED LATE...

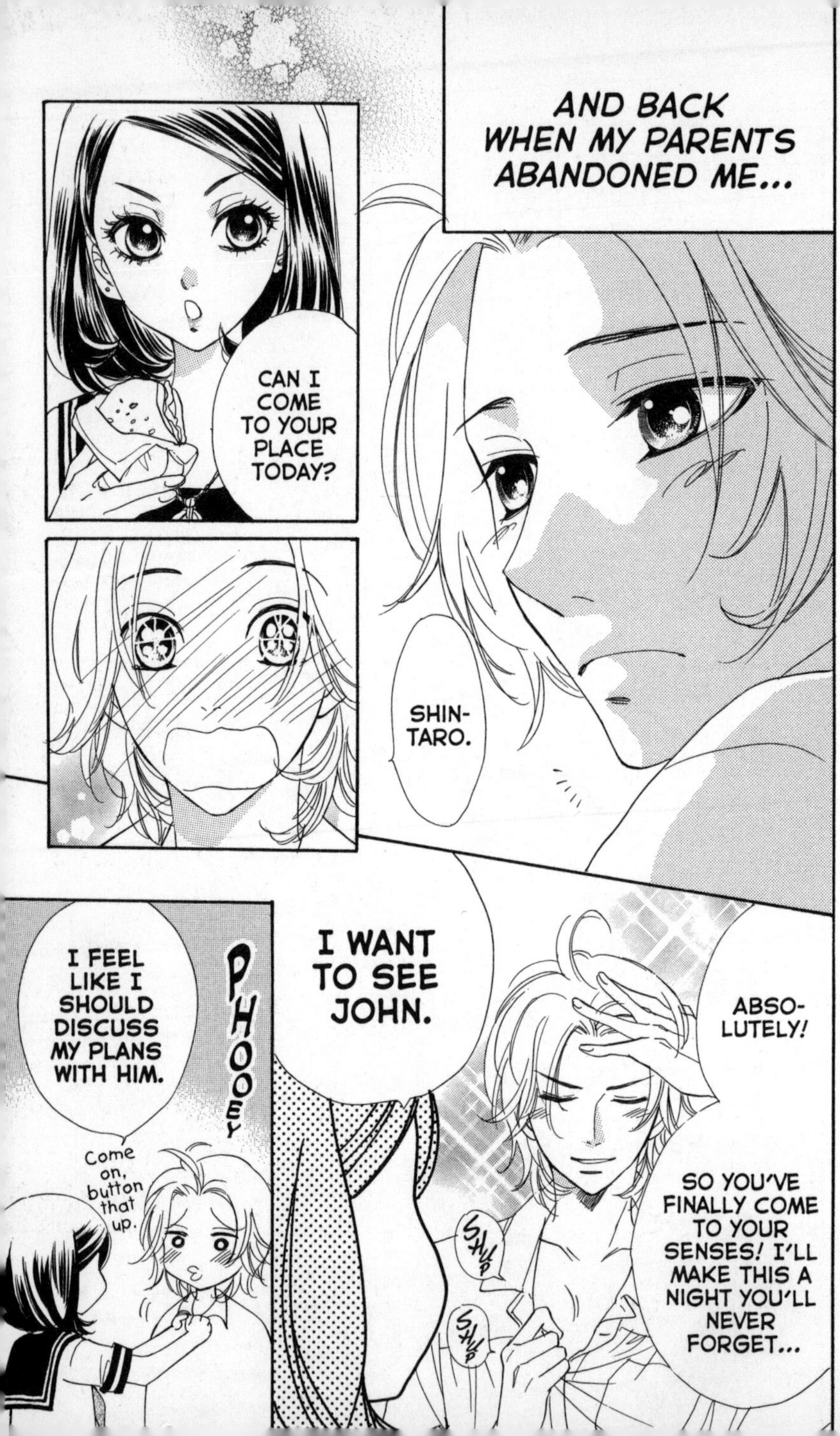
AND BACK WHEN MY PARENTS ABANDONED ME...
SHIN-TARO.
CAN I COME TO YOUR PLACE TODAY?
I WANT TO SEE JOHN.
ABSO-LUTELY!
SO YOU'VE FINALLY COME TO YOUR SENSES! I'LL MAKE THIS A NIGHT YOU'LL NEVER FORGET...
SHUP
SHUP
I FEEL LIKE I SHOULD DISCUSS MY PLANS WITH HIM.
PHOOEY
Come on, button that up.

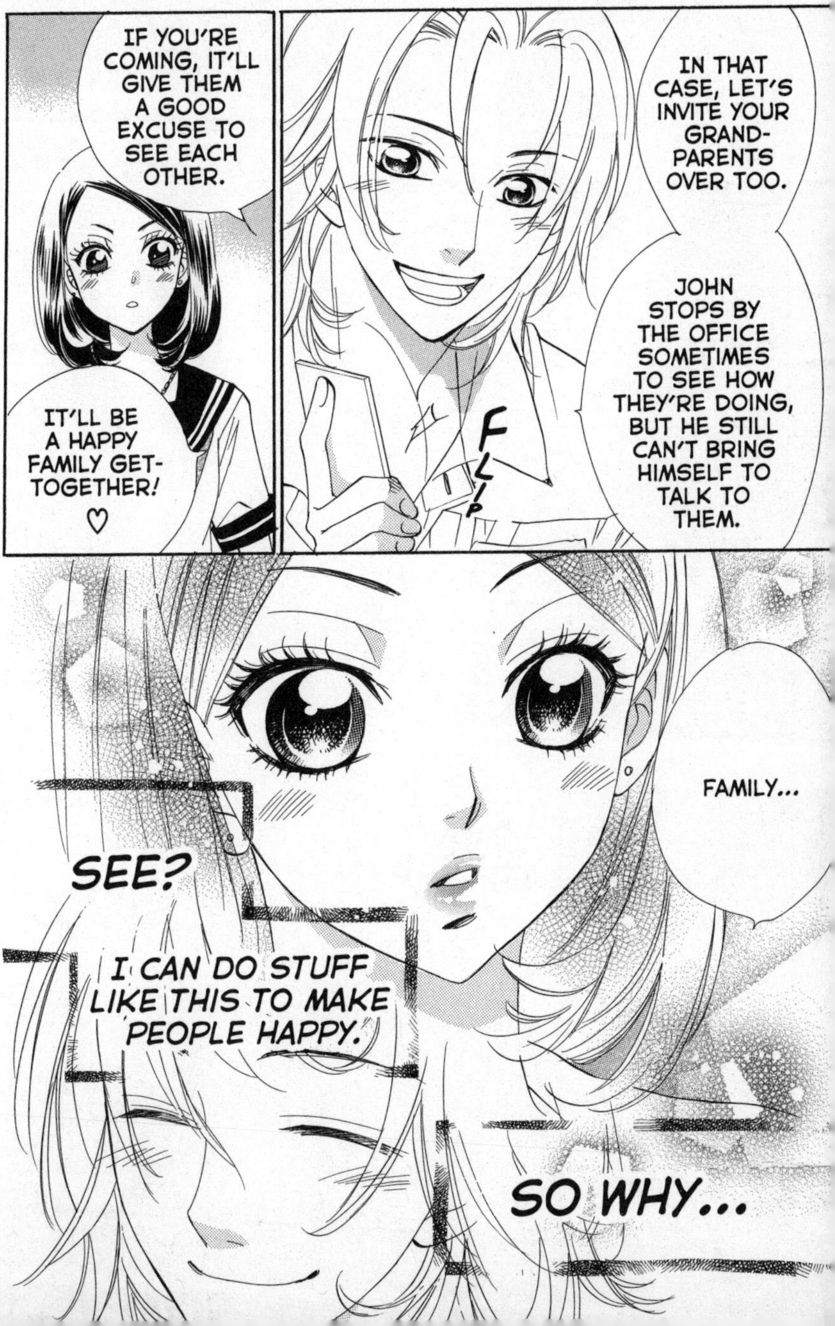
IN THAT CASE, LET'S INVITE YOUR GRAND-PARENTS OVER TOO.
JOHN STOPS BY THE OFFICE SOMETIMES TO SEE HOW THEY'RE DOING, BUT HE STILL CAN'T BRING HIMSELF TO TALK TO THEM.
FLIP
IF YOU'RE COMING, IT'LL GIVE THEM A GOOD EXCUSE TO SEE EACH OTHER.
IT'LL BE A HAPPY FAMILY GET-TOGETHER! ♡
FAMILY...
SEE?
I CAN DO STUFF LIKE THIS TO MAKE PEOPLE HAPPY.
SO WHY...

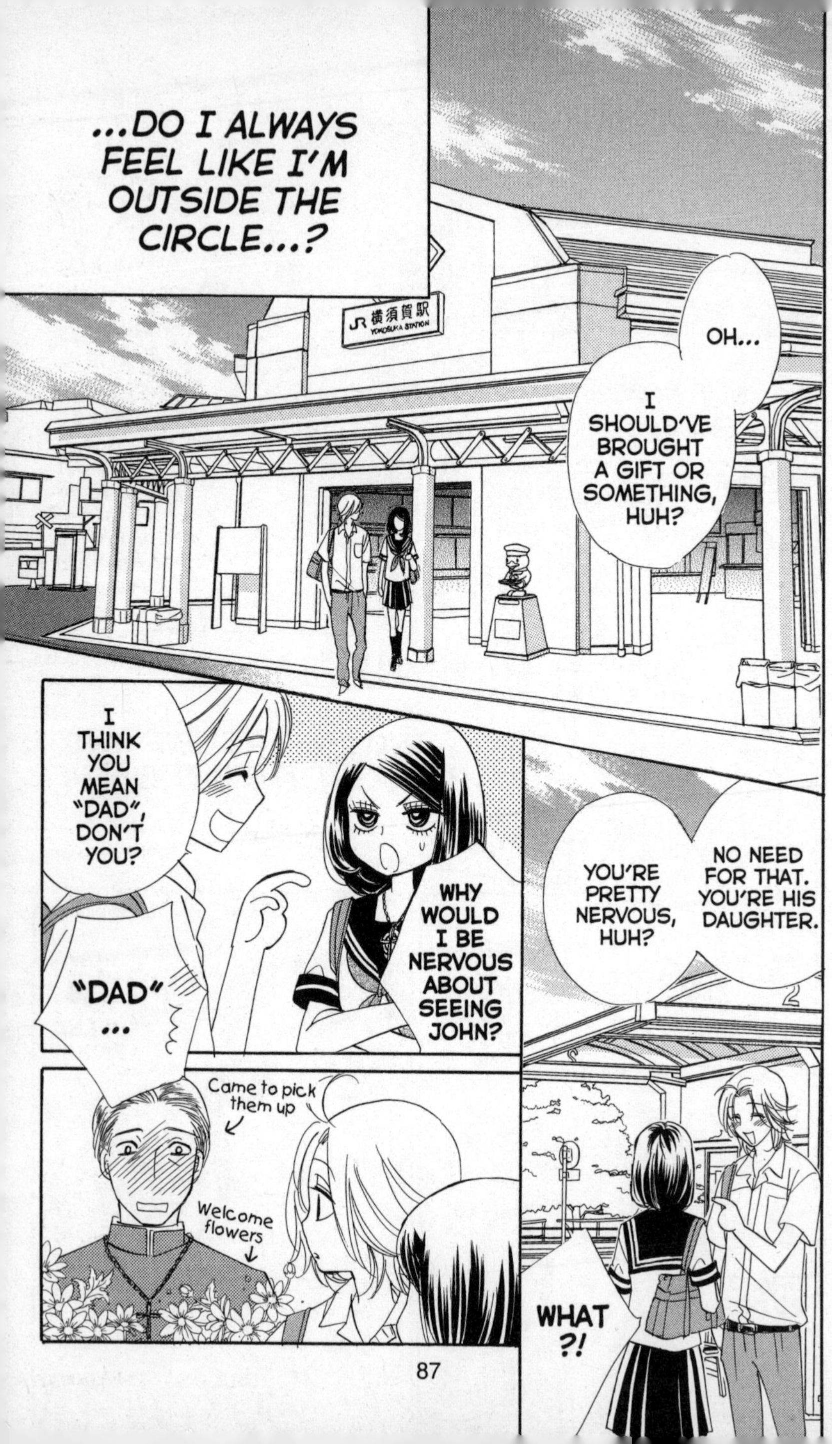
...DO I ALWAYS FEEL LIKE I'M OUTSIDE THE CIRCLE...?
JR 横須賀駅 YOKOSUKA STATION
OH...
I SHOULD'VE BROUGHT A GIFT OR SOMETHING, HUH?
NO NEED FOR THAT. YOU'RE HIS DAUGHTER.
YOU'RE PRETTY NERVOUS, HUH?
WHAT?!
WHY WOULD I BE NERVOUS ABOUT SEEING JOHN?
I THINK YOU MEAN "DAD", DON'T YOU?
"DAD"...
Came to pick them up
Welcome flowers

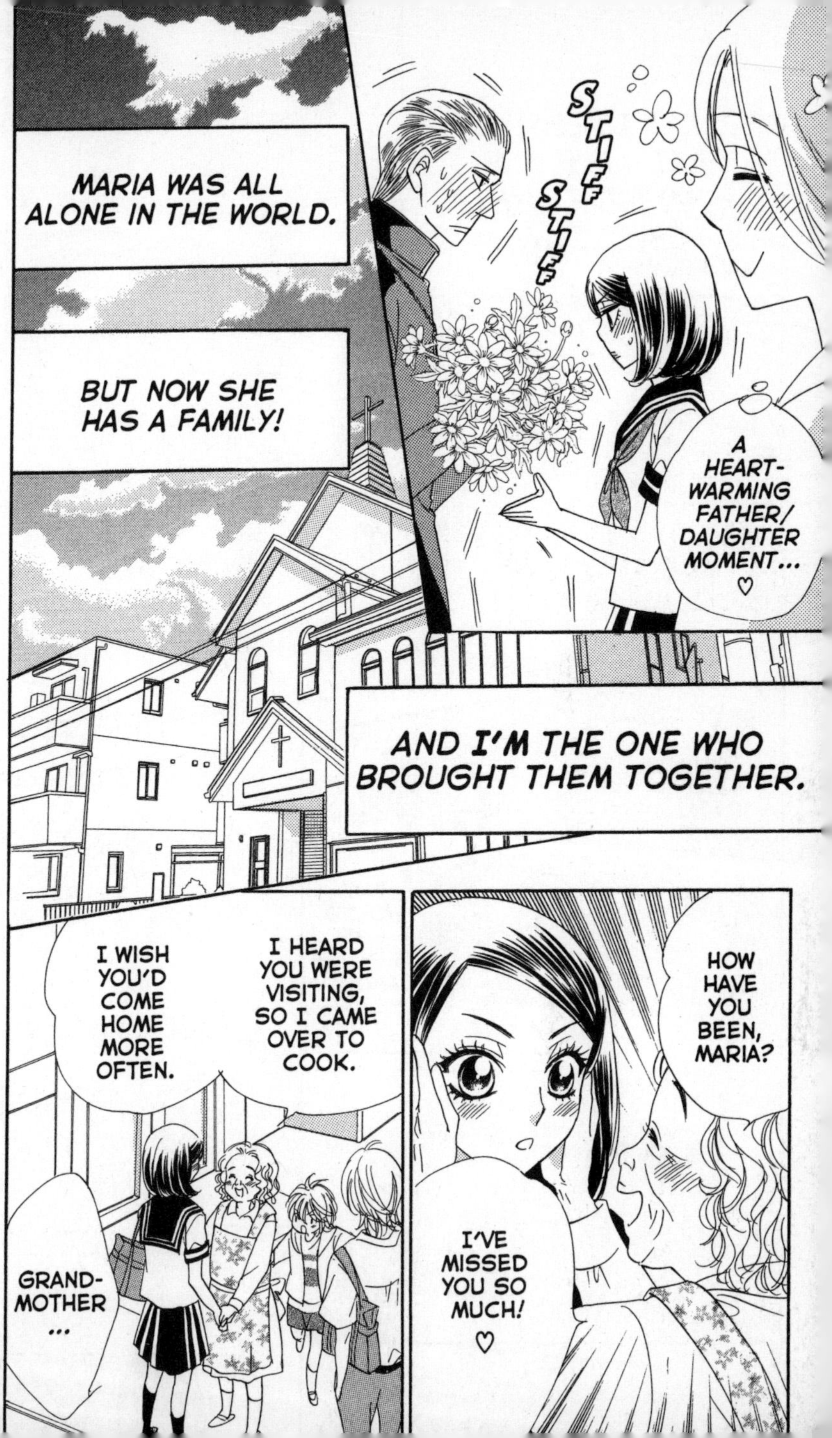
STIFF STIFF
A HEART-WARMING FATHER/DAUGHTER MOMENT... ♡
MARIA WAS ALL ALONE IN THE WORLD.
BUT NOW SHE HAS A FAMILY!
AND I'M THE ONE WHO BROUGHT THEM TOGETHER.
HOW HAVE YOU BEEN, MARIA?
I'VE MISSED YOU SO MUCH! ♡
I HEARD YOU WERE VISITING, SO I CAME OVER TO COOK.
I WISH YOU'D COME HOME MORE OFTEN.
GRAND-MOTHER...

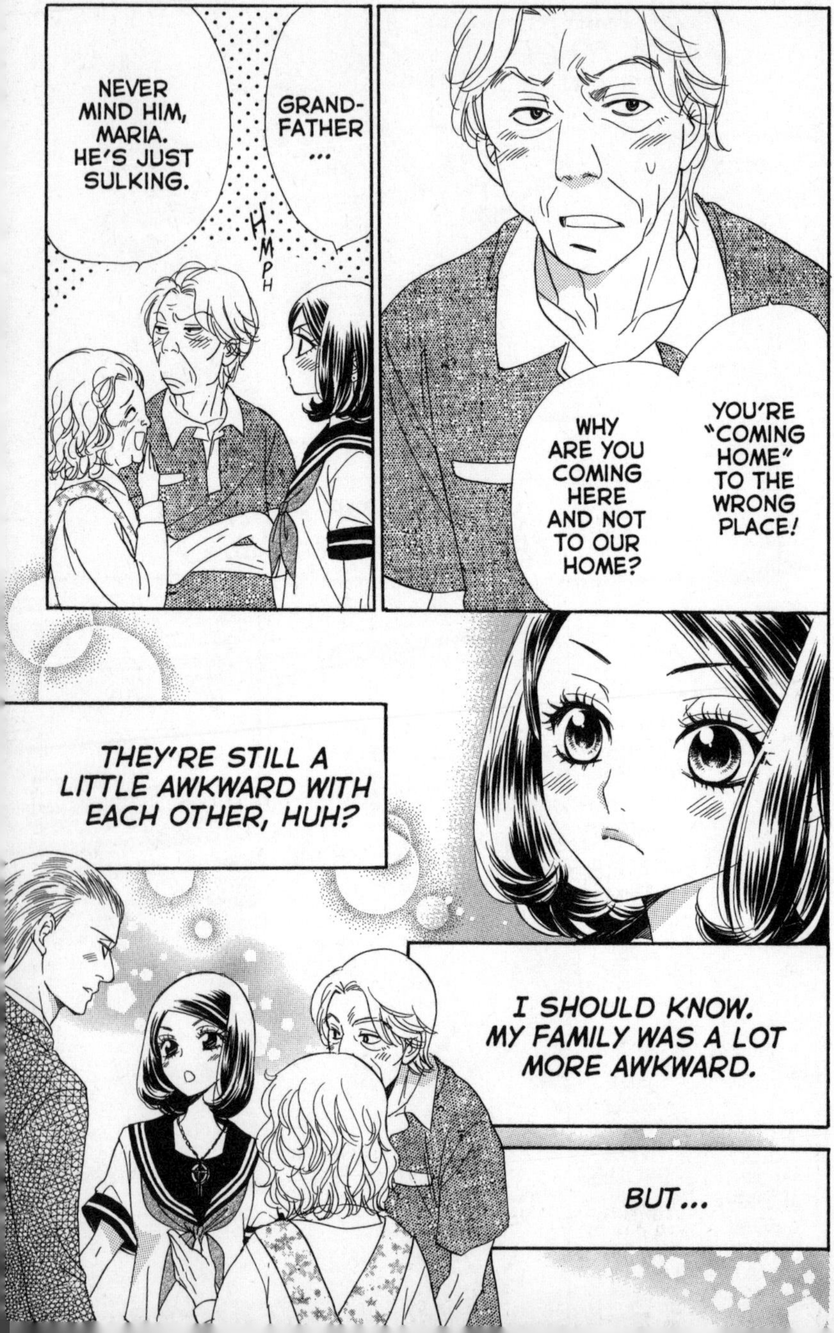
YOU'RE "COMING HOME" TO THE WRONG PLACE!
WHY ARE YOU COMING HERE AND NOT TO OUR HOME?
GRAND-FATHER ...
HMPH
NEVER MIND HIM, MARIA. HE'S JUST SULKING.
THEY'RE STILL A LITTLE AWKWARD WITH EACH OTHER, HUH?
I SHOULD KNOW. MY FAMILY WAS A LOT MORE AWKWARD.
BUT...

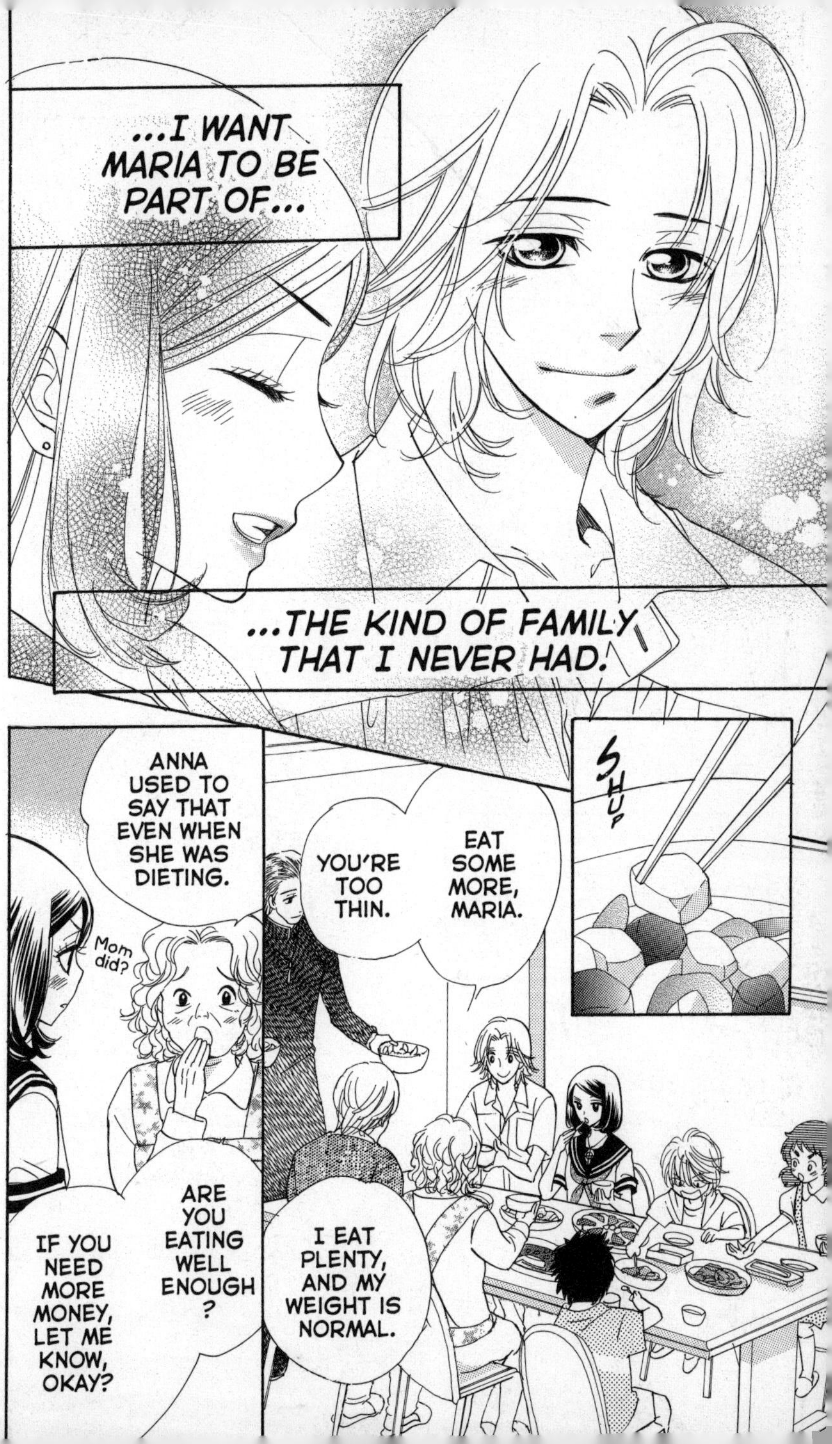
...I WANT MARIA TO BE PART OF...
...THE KIND OF FAMILY THAT I NEVER HAD.
SHUP
EAT SOME MORE, MARIA.
YOU'RE TOO THIN.
I EAT PLENTY, AND MY WEIGHT IS NORMAL.
ANNA USED TO SAY THAT EVEN WHEN SHE WAS DIETING.
Mom did?
ARE YOU EATING WELL ENOUGH?
IF YOU NEED MORE MONEY, LET ME KNOW, OKAY?

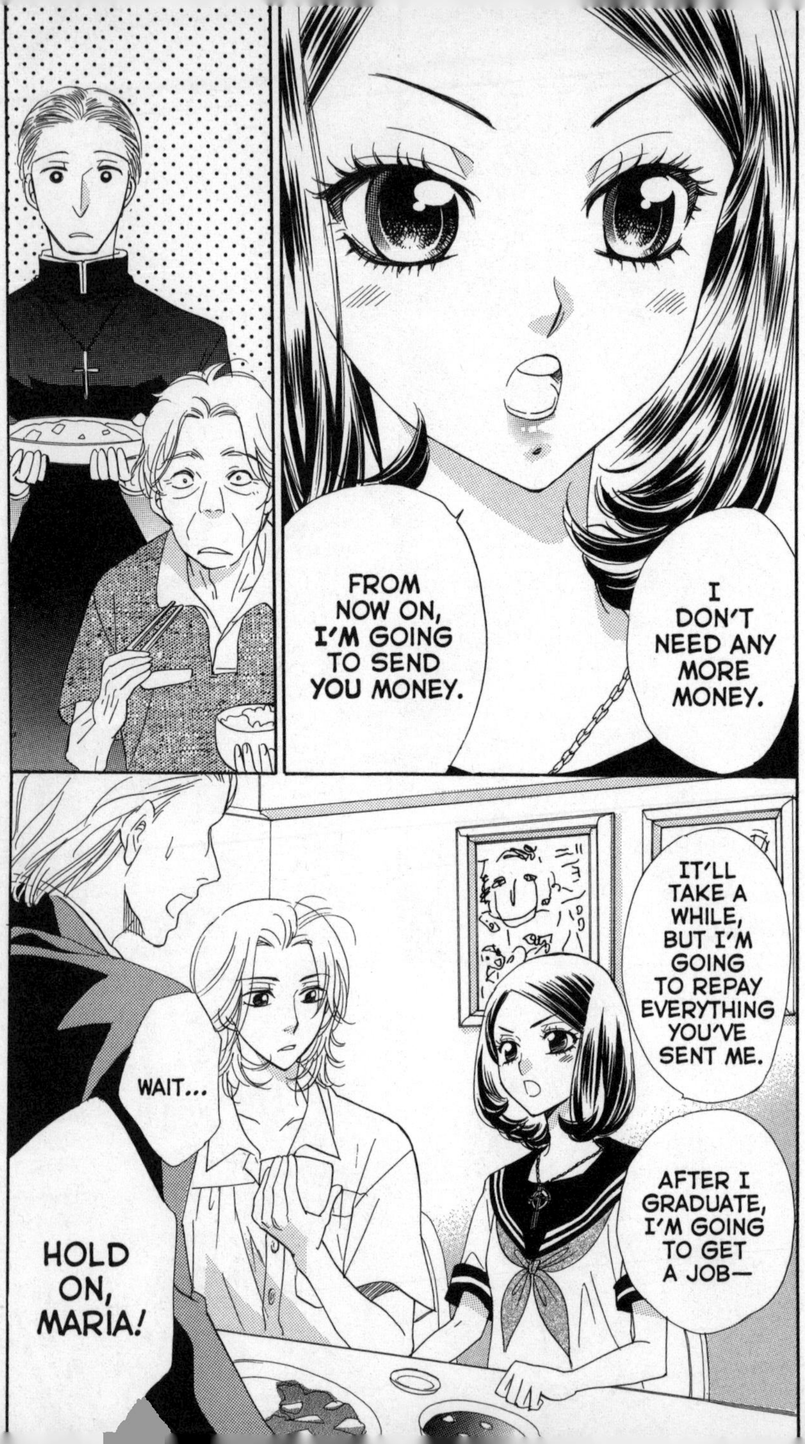
I DON'T NEED ANY MORE MONEY.
FROM NOW ON, I'M GOING TO SEND YOU MONEY.
IT'LL TAKE A WHILE, BUT I'M GOING TO REPAY EVERYTHING YOU'VE SENT ME.
AFTER I GRADUATE, I'M GOING TO GET A JOB—
WAIT...
HOLD ON, MARIA!

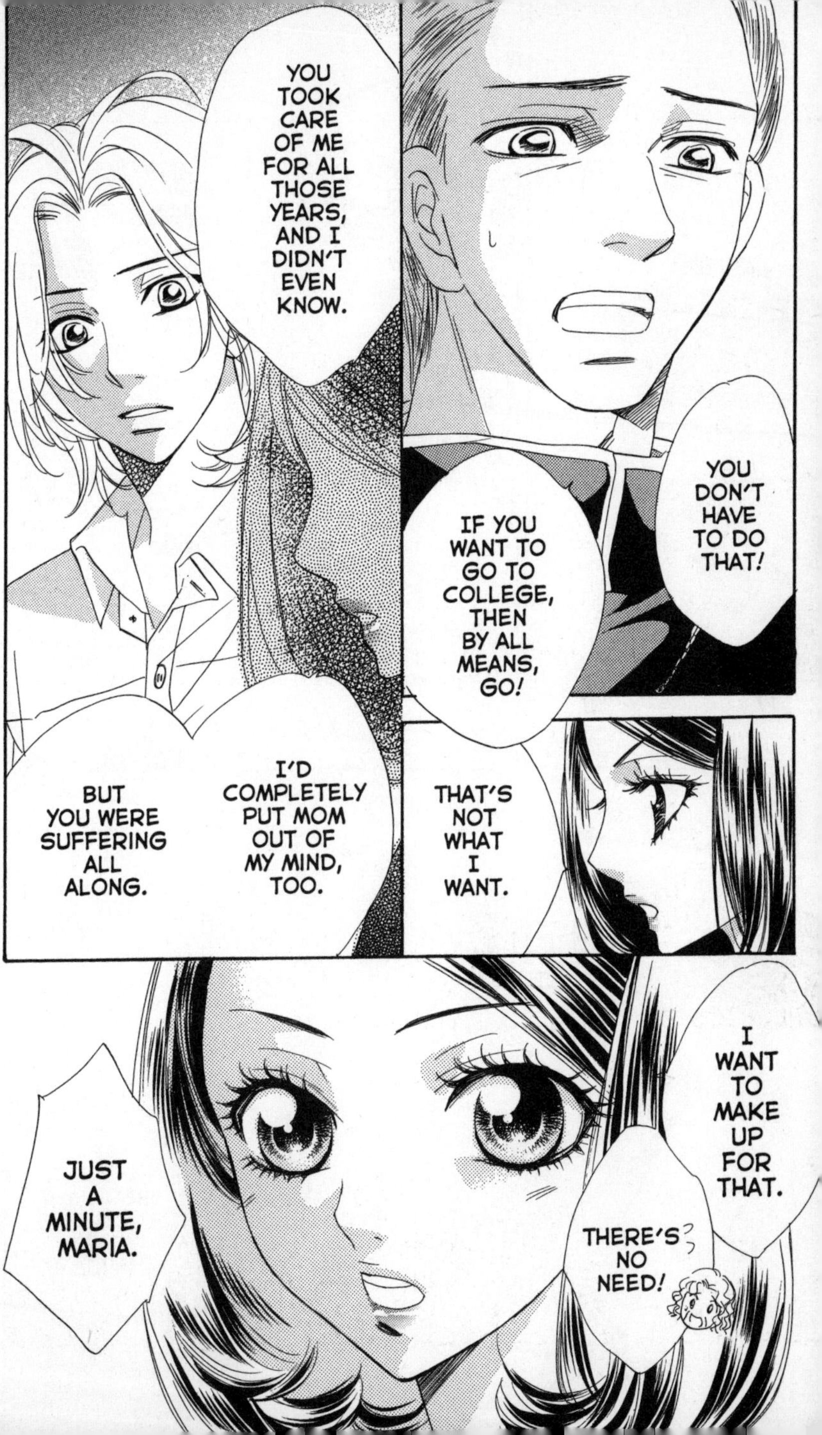
YOU DON'T HAVE TO DO THAT!
IF YOU WANT TO GO TO COLLEGE, THEN BY ALL MEANS, GO!
THAT'S NOT WHAT I WANT.
YOU TOOK CARE OF ME FOR ALL THOSE YEARS, AND I DIDN'T EVEN KNOW.
I'D COMPLETELY PUT MOM OUT OF MY MIND, TOO.
BUT YOU WERE SUFFERING ALL ALONG.
I WANT TO MAKE UP FOR THAT.
THERE'S NO NEED!
JUST A MINUTE, MARIA.

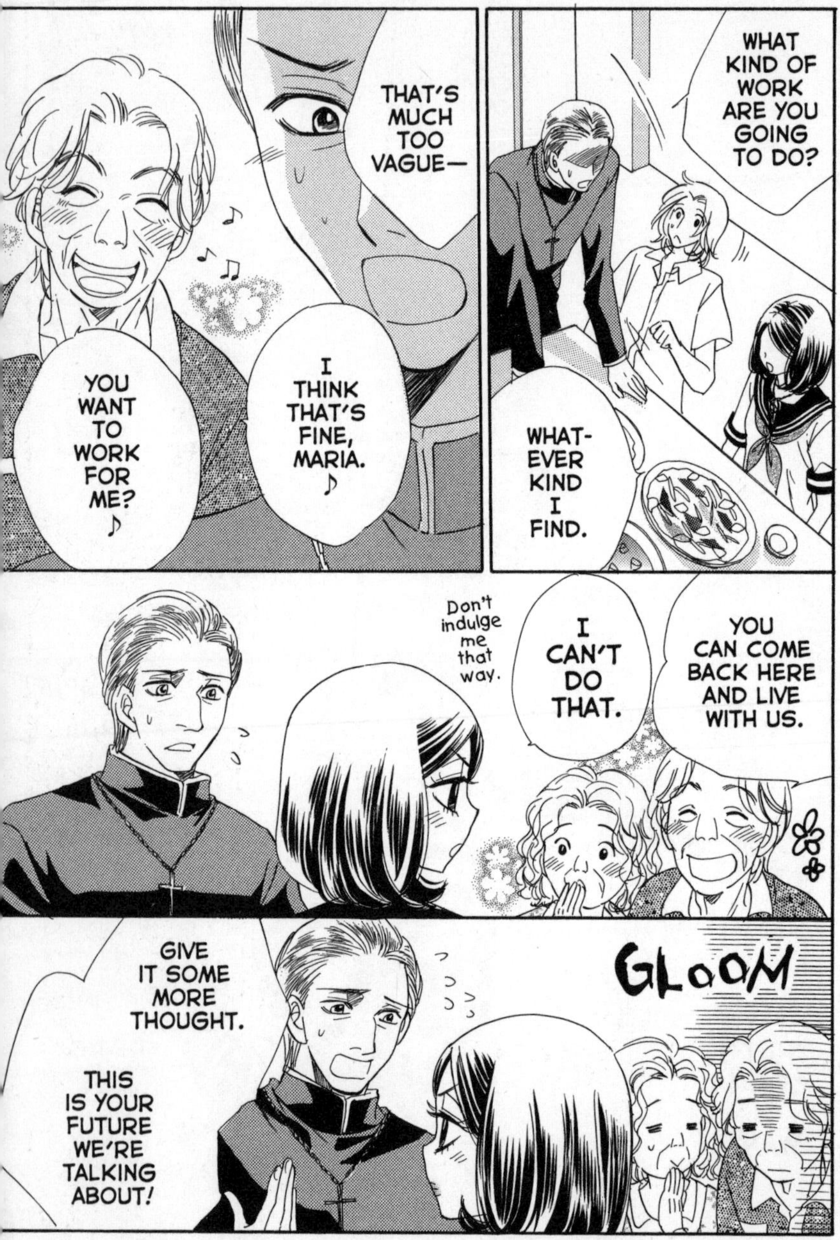
WHAT KIND OF WORK ARE YOU GOING TO DO?
WHAT-EVER KIND I FIND.
THAT'S MUCH TOO VAGUE—
I THINK THAT'S FINE, MARIA. ♪
YOU WANT TO WORK FOR ME? ♪
YOU CAN COME BACK HERE AND LIVE WITH US.
I CAN'T DO THAT.
Don't indulge me that way.
GLOOM
GIVE IT SOME MORE THOUGHT.
THIS IS YOUR FUTURE WE'RE TALKING ABOUT!

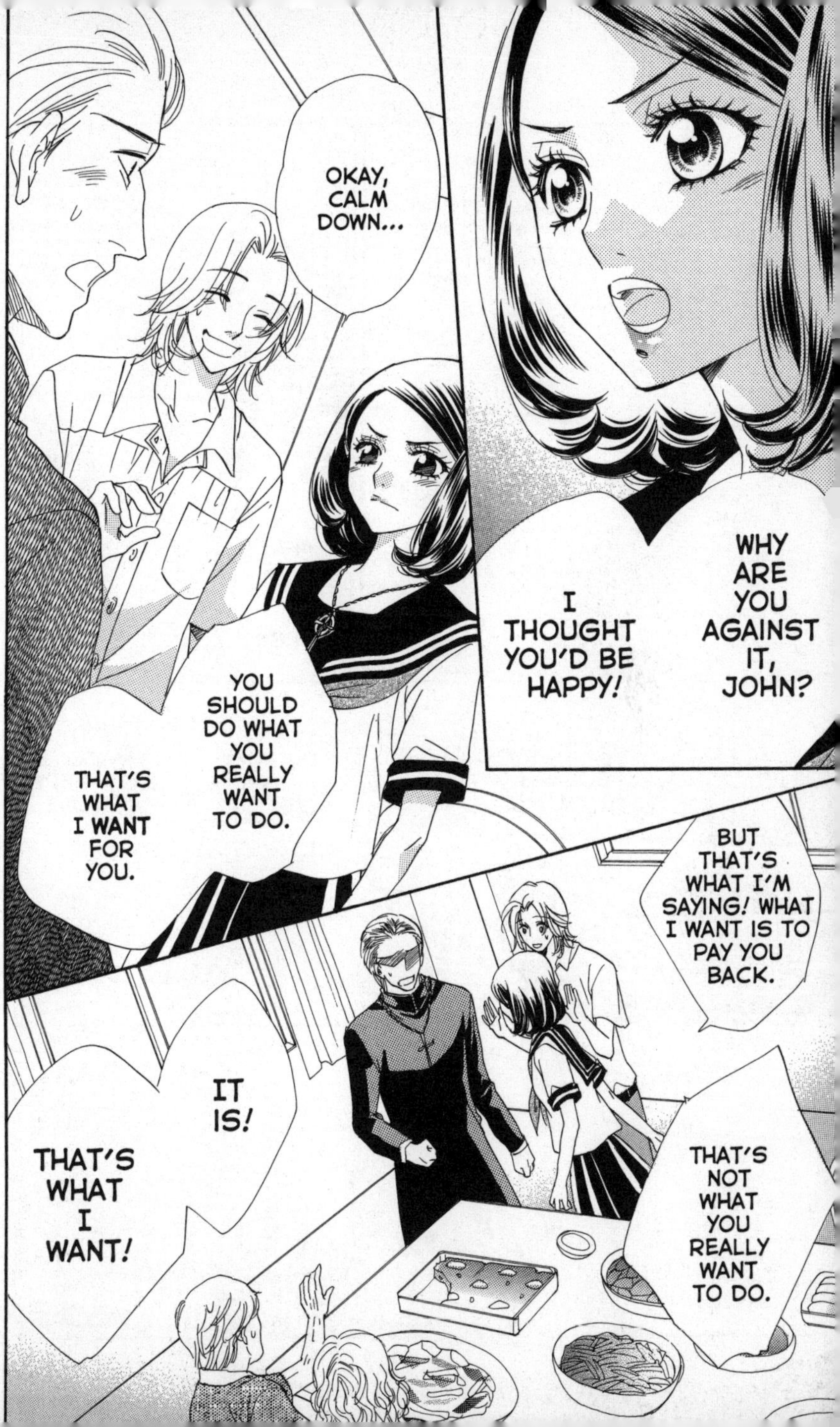

WHY ARE YOU AGAINST IT, JOHN?
I THOUGHT YOU'D BE HAPPY!
OKAY, CALM DOWN...
YOU SHOULD DO WHAT YOU REALLY WANT TO DO.
THAT'S WHAT I WANT FOR YOU.
BUT THAT'S WHAT I'M SAYING! WHAT I WANT IS TO PAY YOU BACK.
THAT'S NOT WHAT YOU REALLY WANT TO DO.
IT IS!
THAT'S WHAT I WANT!

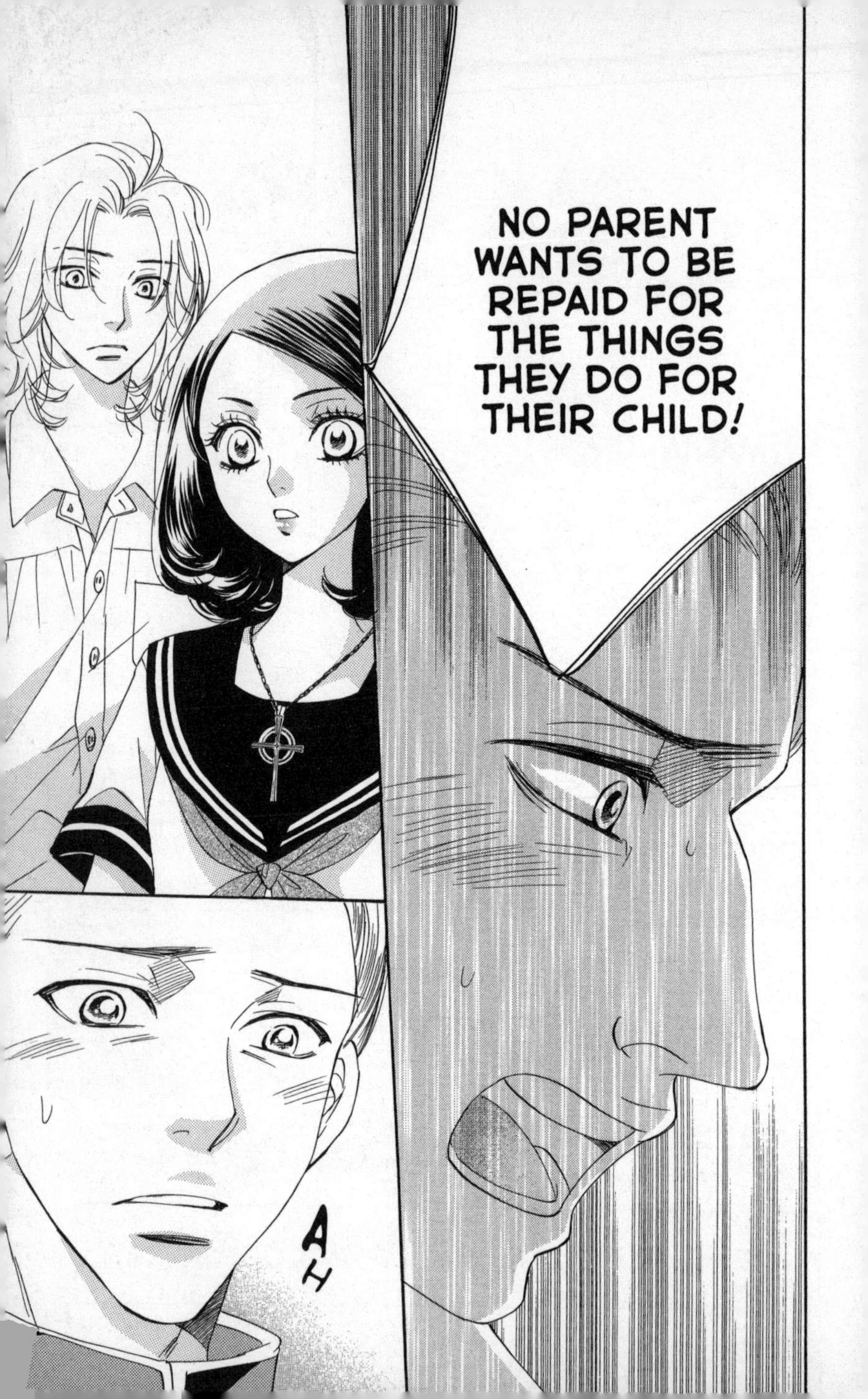
NO PARENT WANTS TO BE REPAID FOR THE THINGS THEY DO FOR THEIR CHILD!
AH

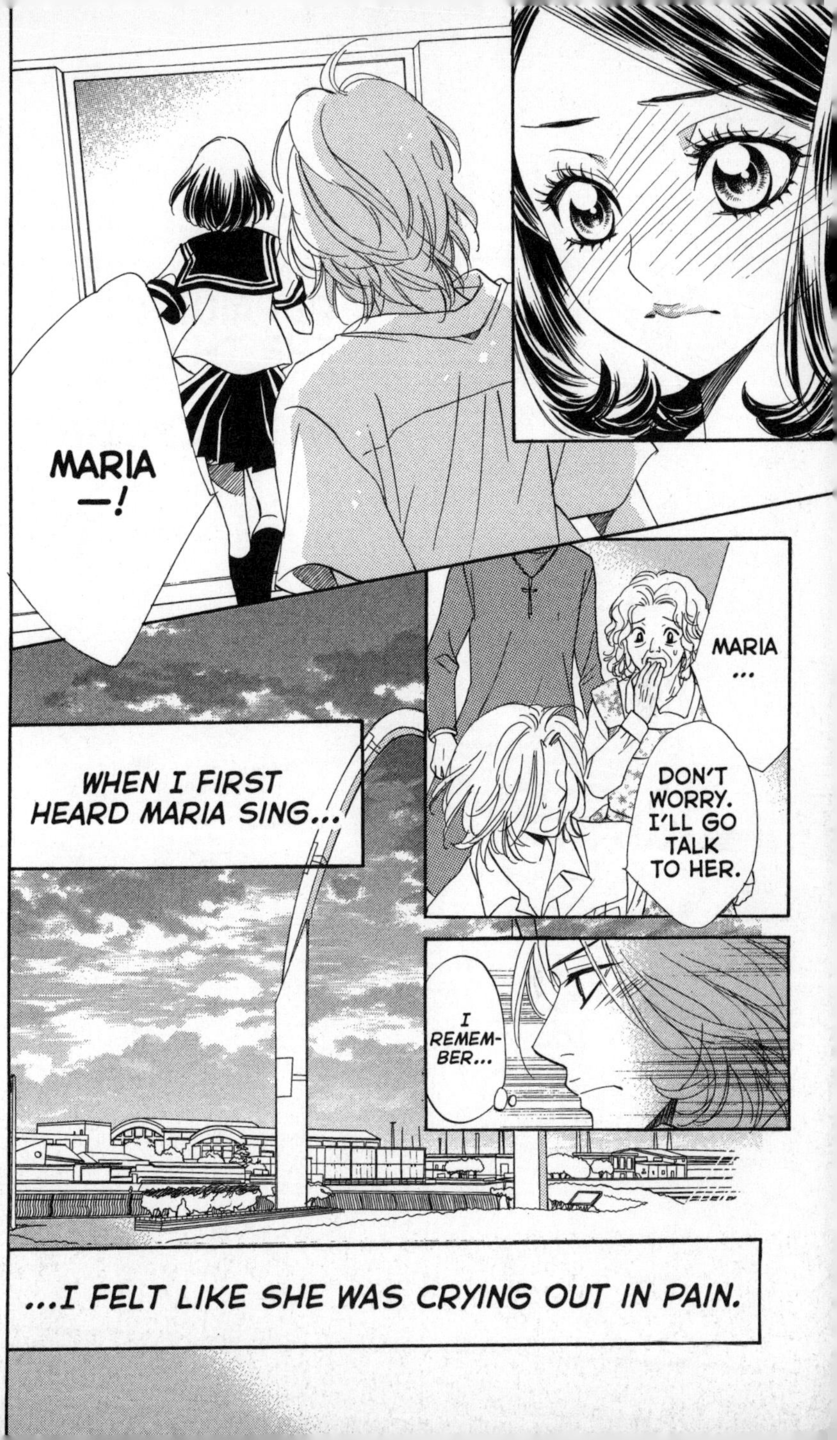
MARIA —!
MARIA ...
DON'T WORRY. I'LL GO TALK TO HER.
I REMEMBER...
WHEN I FIRST HEARD MARIA SING...
...I FELT LIKE SHE WAS CRYING OUT IN PAIN.

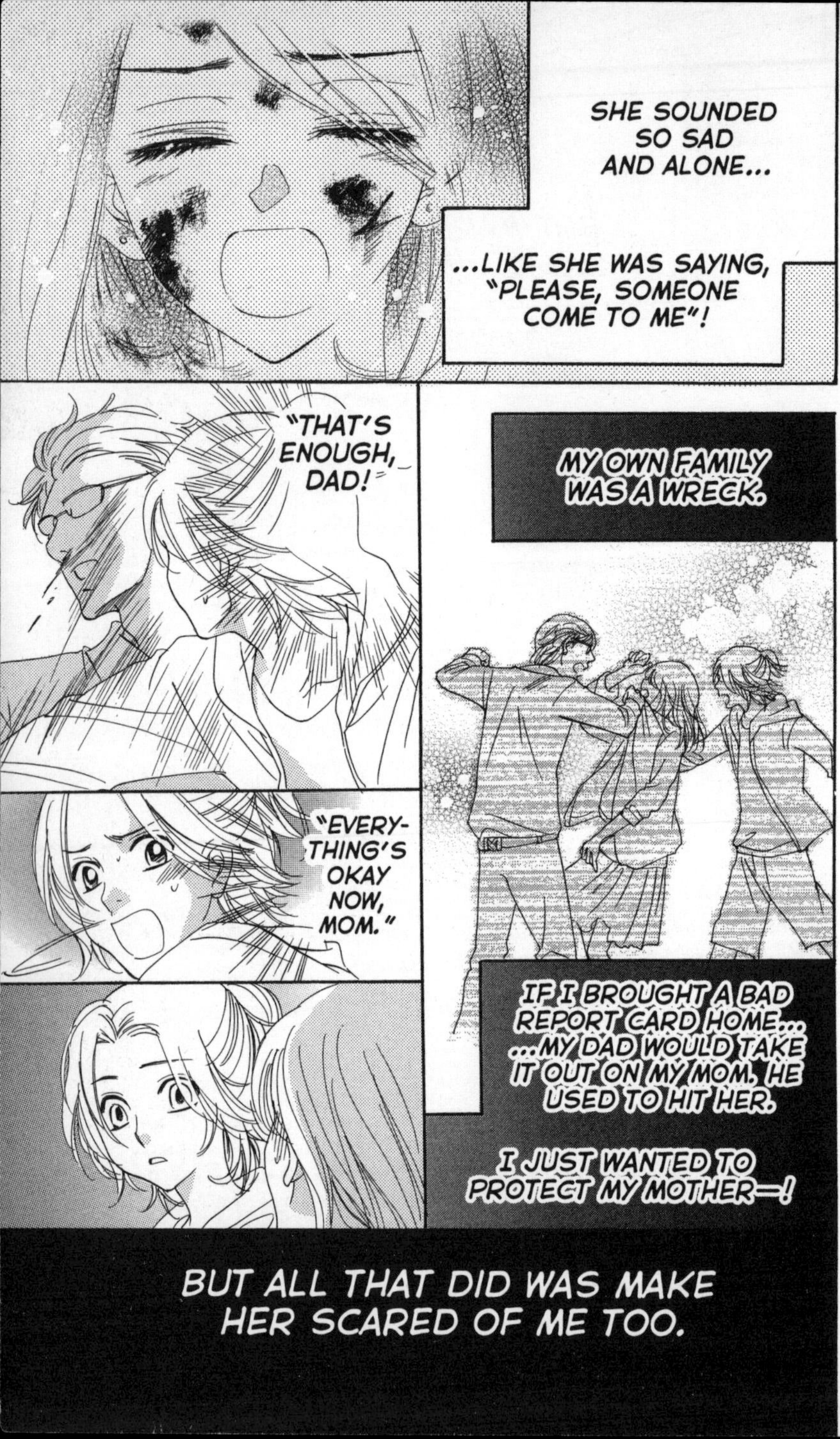
SHE SOUNDED SO SAD AND ALONE...
...LIKE SHE WAS SAYING, "PLEASE, SOMEONE COME TO ME"!
MY OWN FAMILY WAS A WRECK.
IF I BROUGHT A BAD REPORT CARD HOME... ...MY DAD WOULD TAKE IT OUT ON MY MOM. HE USED TO HIT HER.
I JUST WANTED TO PROTECT MY MOTHER—!
"THAT'S ENOUGH, DAD!
"EVERY-THING'S OKAY NOW, MOM."
BUT ALL THAT DID WAS MAKE HER SCARED OF ME TOO.

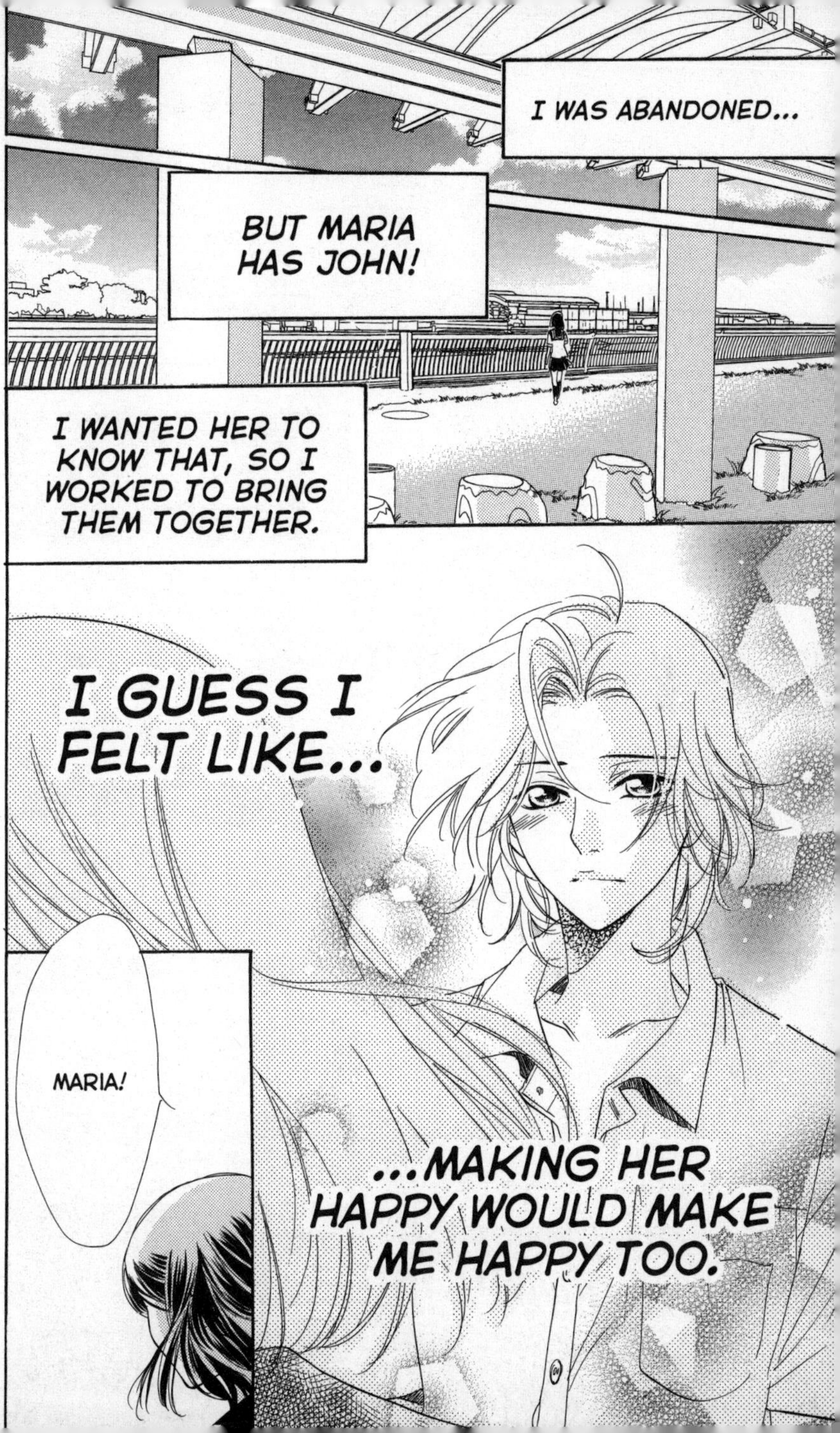
I WAS ABANDONED...
BUT MARIA HAS JOHN!
I WANTED HER TO KNOW THAT, SO I WORKED TO BRING THEM TOGETHER.
I GUESS I FELT LIKE...
...MAKING HER HAPPY WOULD MAKE ME HAPPY TOO.
MARIA!

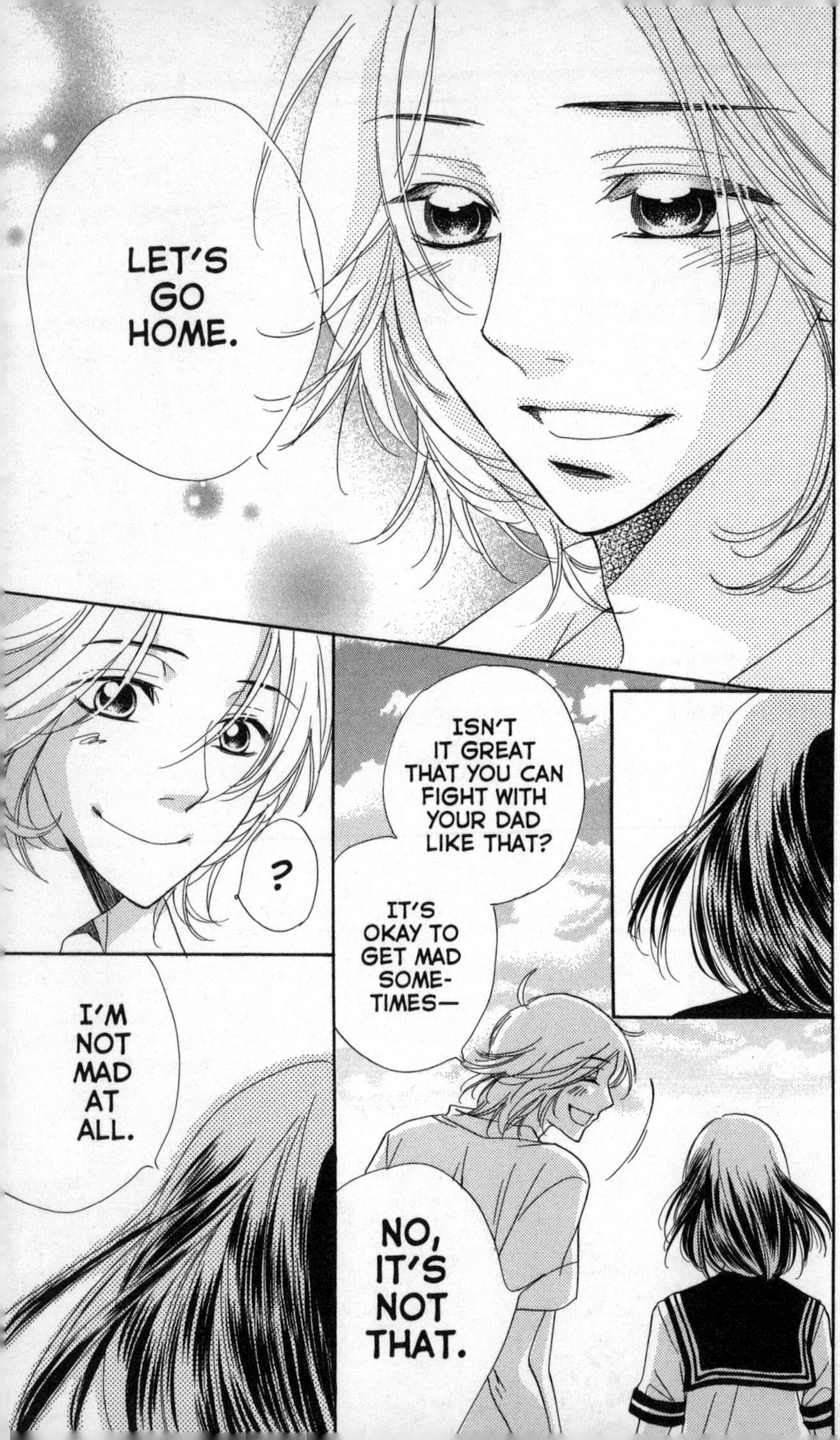
LET'S GO HOME.
ISN'T IT GREAT THAT YOU CAN FIGHT WITH YOUR DAD LIKE THAT?
IT'S OKAY TO GET MAD SOME-TIMES—
NO, IT'S NOT THAT.
?
I'M NOT MAD AT ALL.

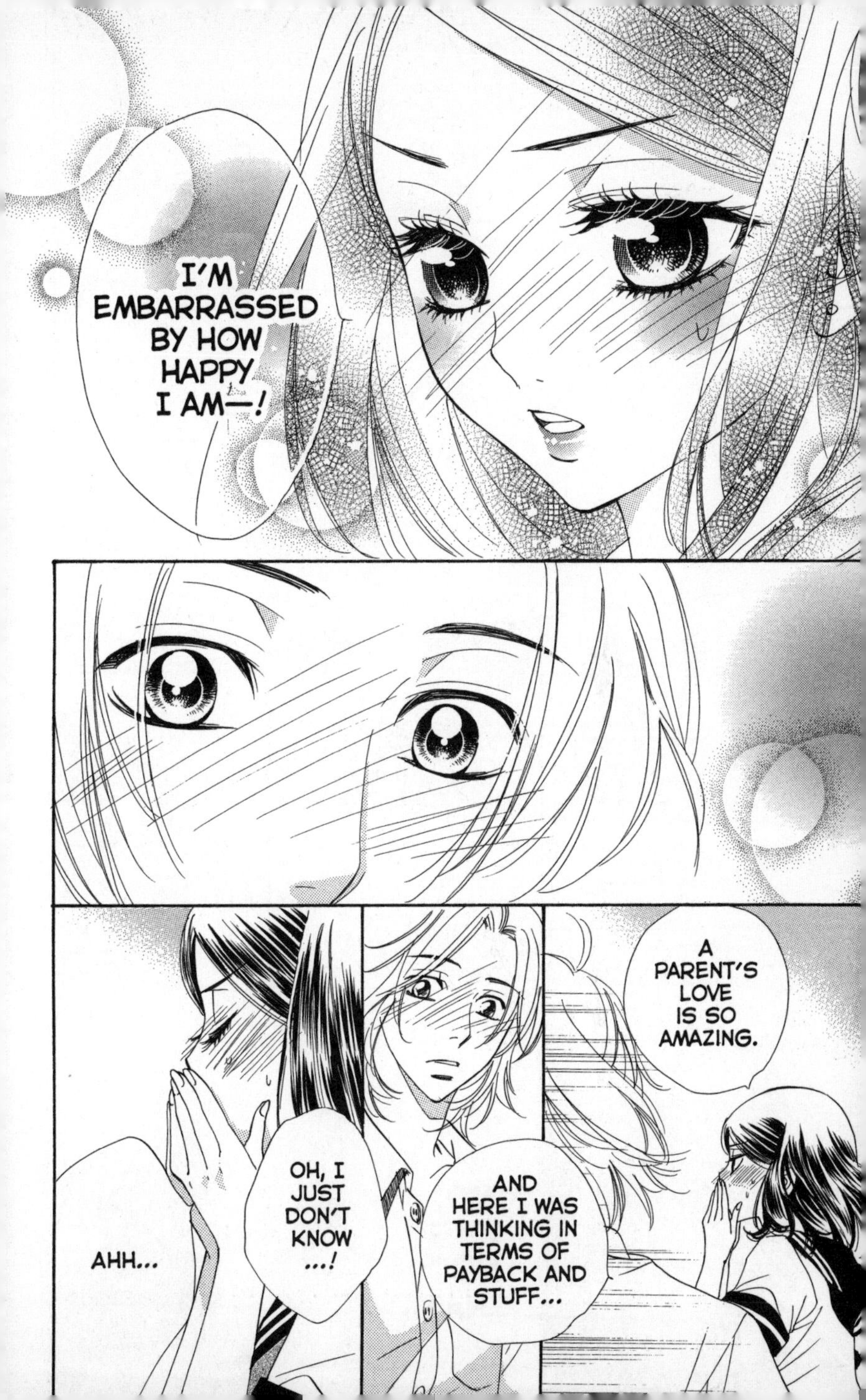
I'M EMBARRASSED BY HOW HAPPY I AM—!
A PARENT'S LOVE IS SO AMAZING.
AND HERE I WAS THINKING IN TERMS OF PAYBACK AND STUFF...
OH, I JUST DON'T KNOW ...!
AHH...

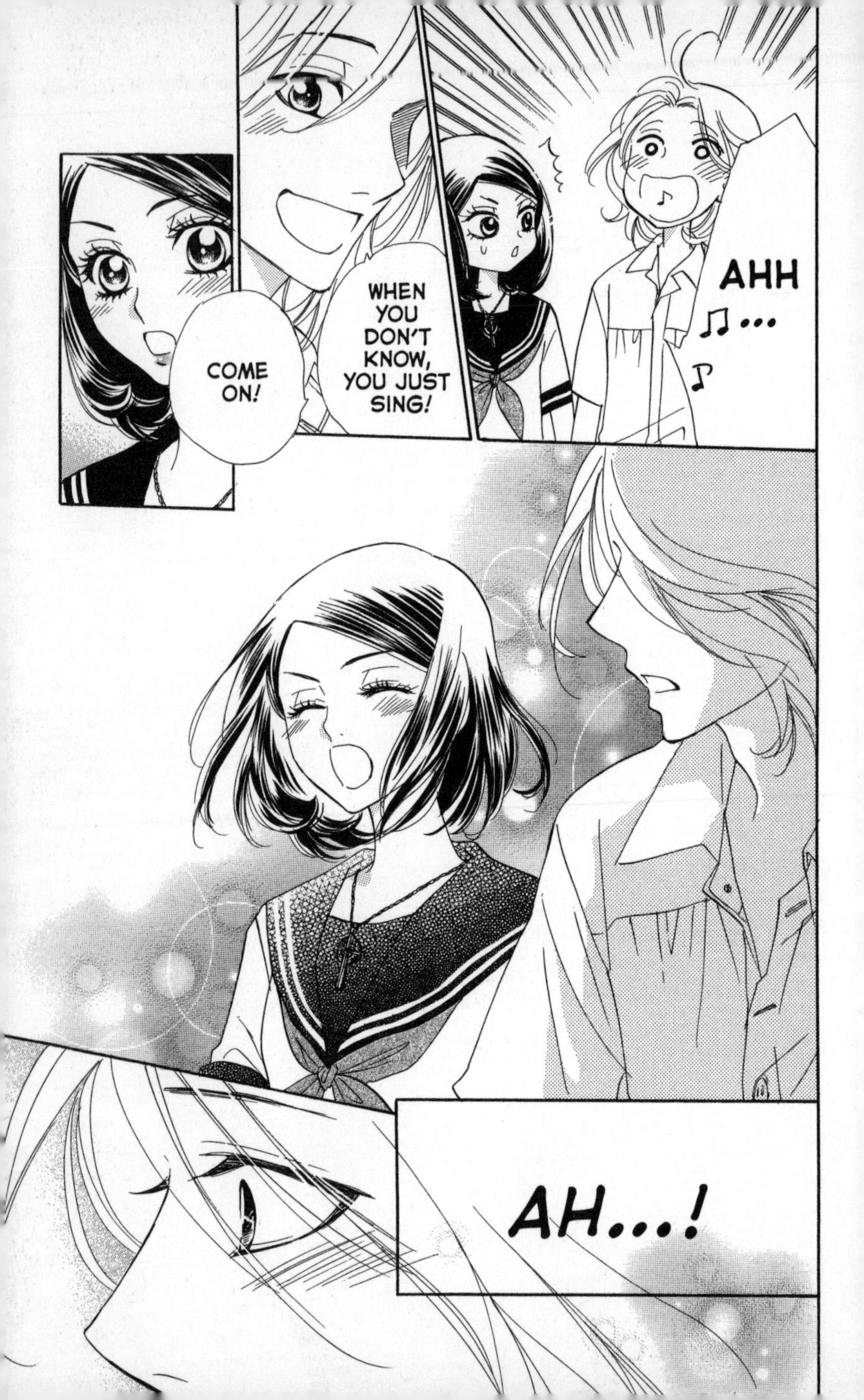
AHH ♫...
♪
WHEN YOU DON'T KNOW, YOU JUST SING!
COME ON!
AH...!

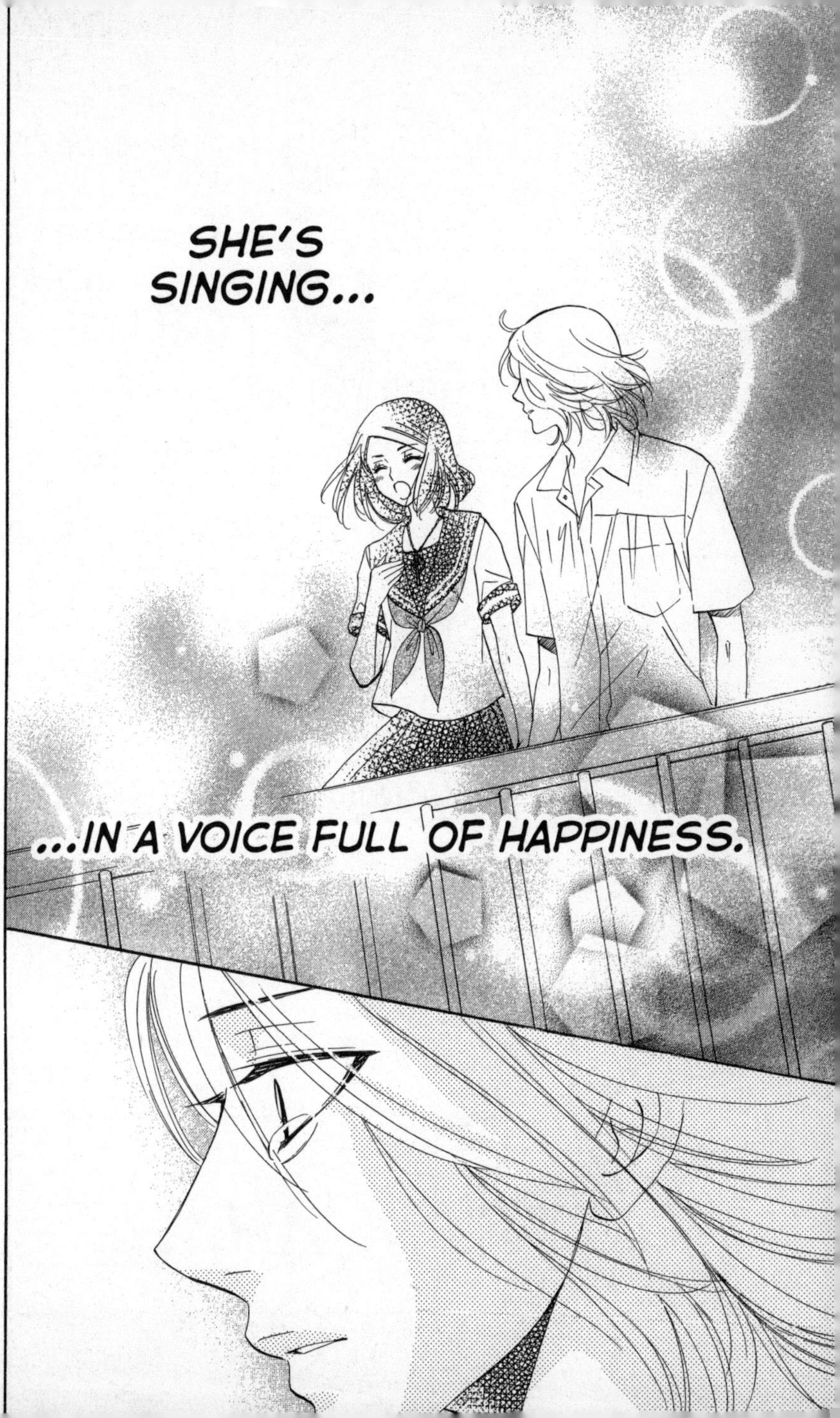
SHE'S SINGING...
...IN A VOICE FULL OF HAPPINESS.

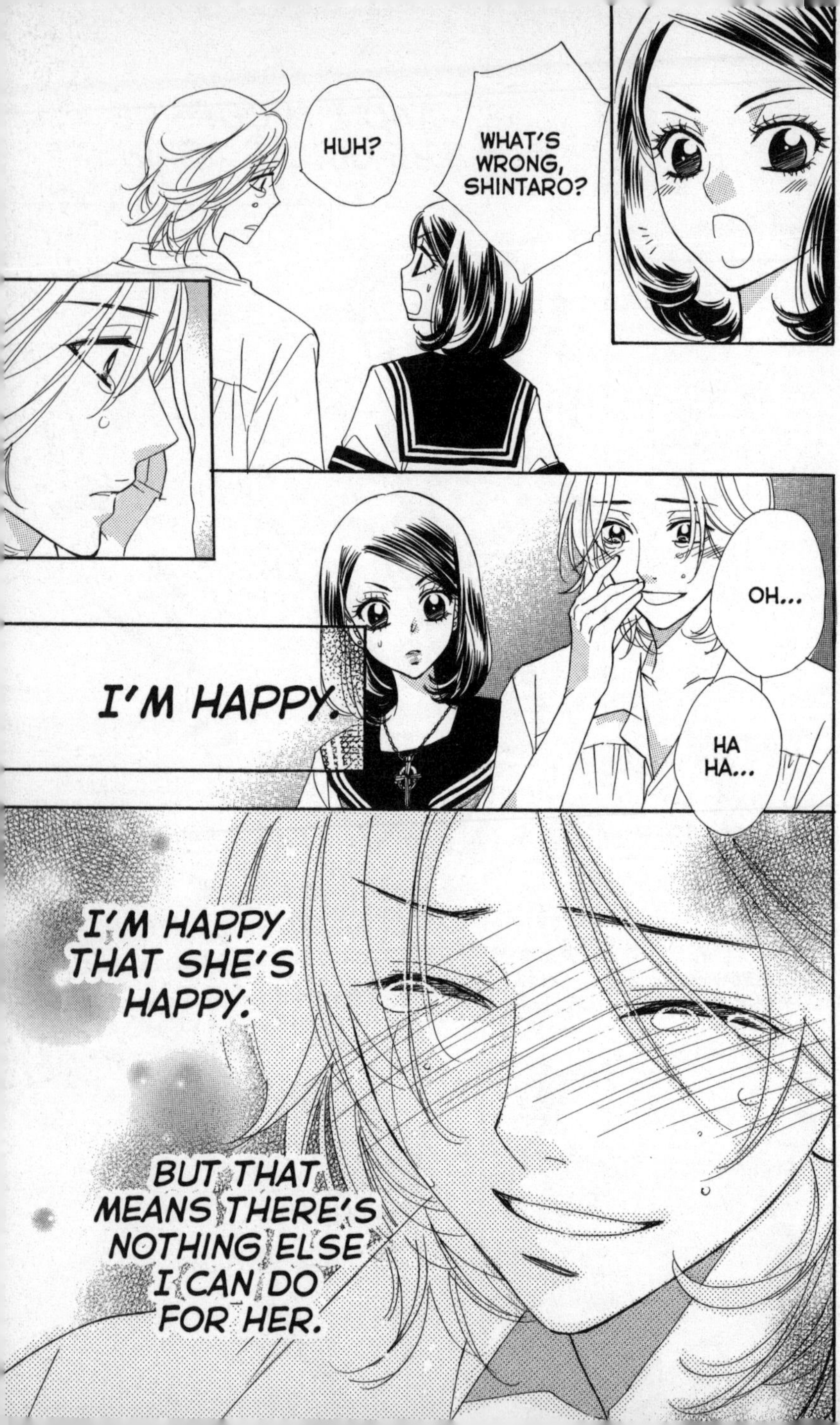
WHAT'S WRONG, SHINTARO?
HUH?
OH...
HA HA...
I'M HAPPY.
I'M HAPPY THAT SHE'S HAPPY.
BUT THAT MEANS THERE'S NOTHING ELSE I CAN DO FOR HER.

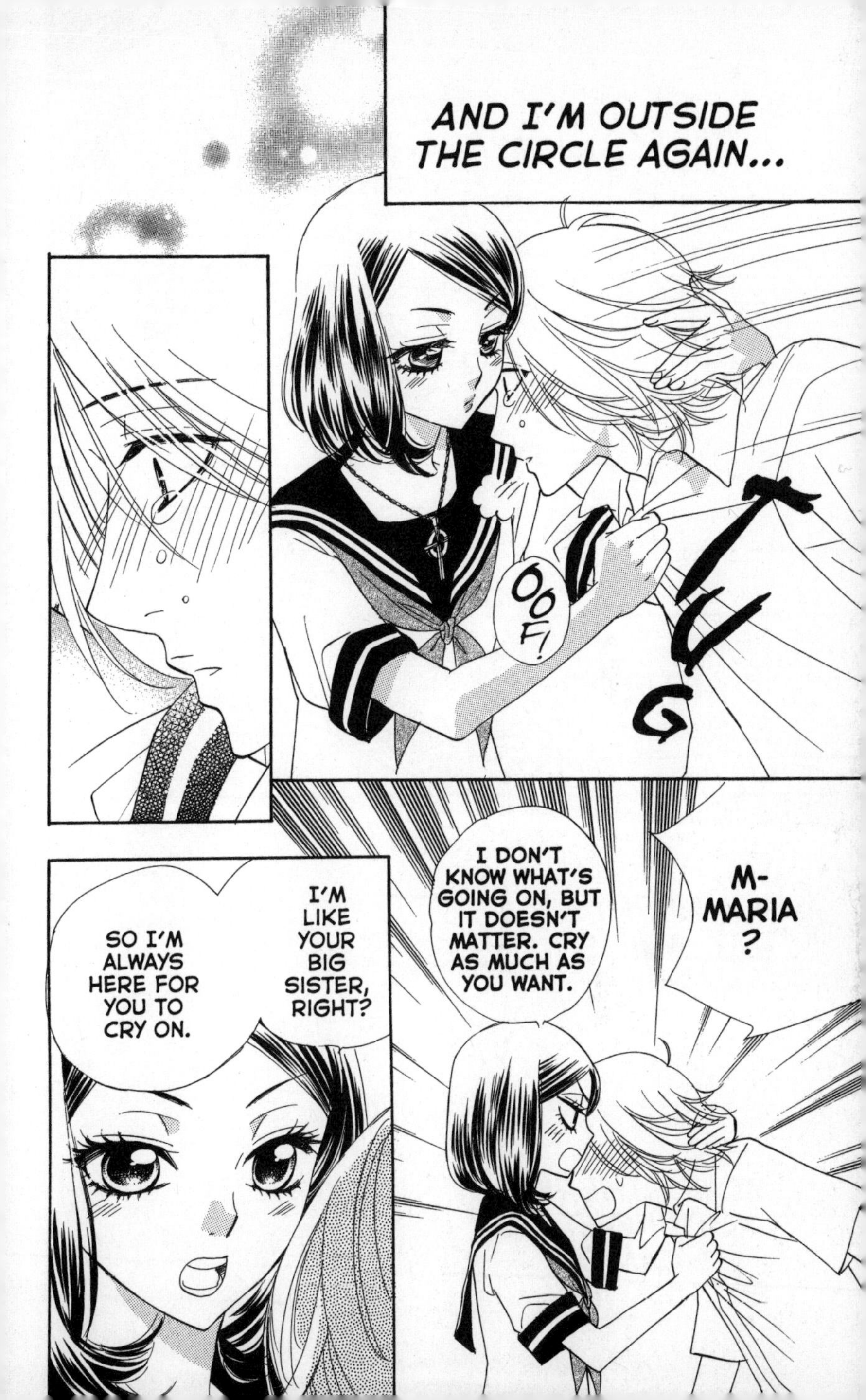
AND I'M OUTSIDE THE CIRCLE AGAIN...
TUG
OOF!
M-MARIA?
I DON'T KNOW WHAT'S GOING ON, BUT IT DOESN'T MATTER. CRY AS MUCH AS YOU WANT.
I'M LIKE YOUR BIG SISTER, RIGHT?
SO I'M ALWAYS HERE FOR YOU TO CRY ON.

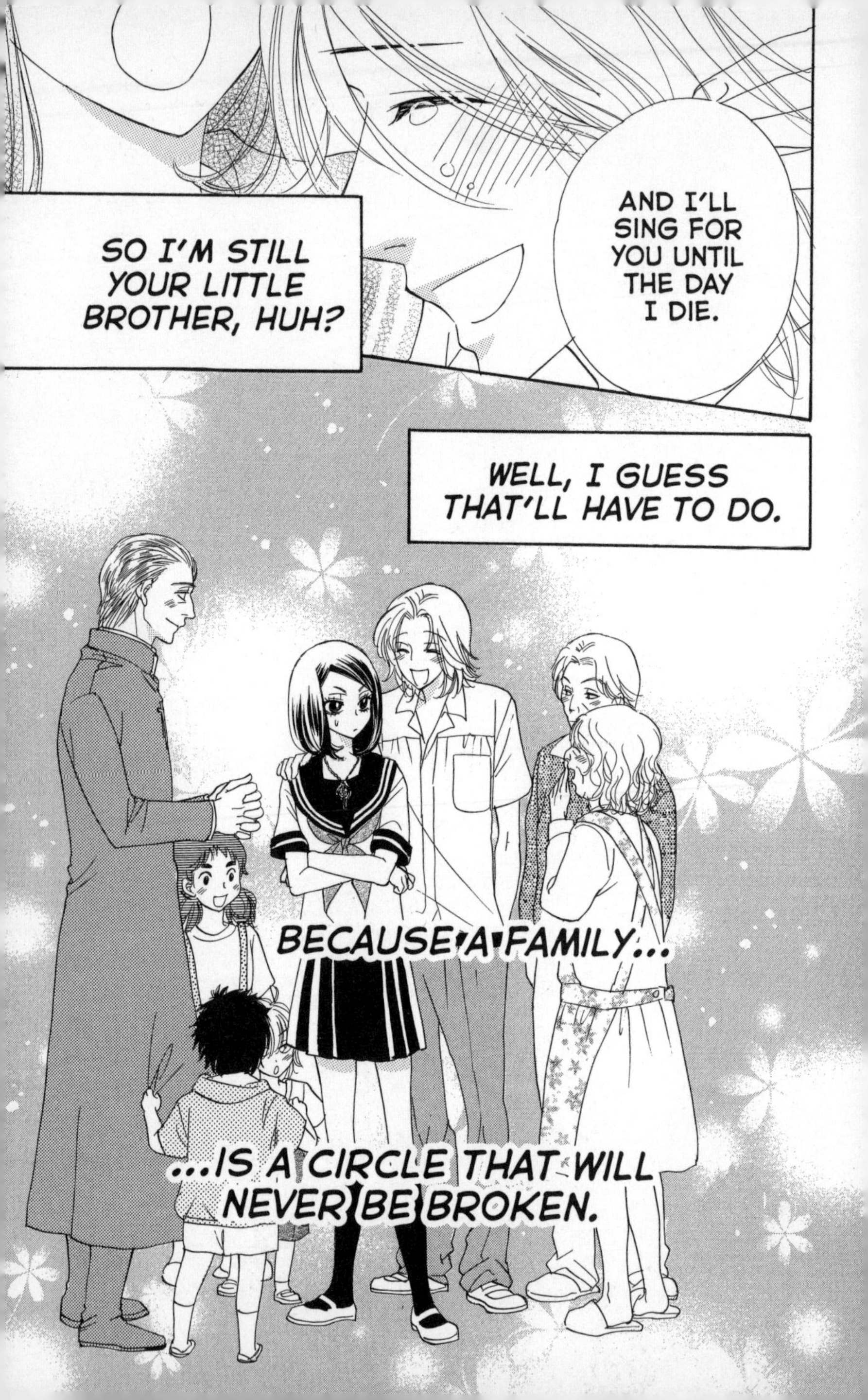
AND I'LL SING FOR YOU UNTIL THE DAY I DIE.
SO I'M STILL YOUR LITTLE BROTHER, HUH?
WELL, I GUESS THAT'LL HAVE TO DO.
BECAUSE A FAMILY...
...IS A CIRCLE THAT WILL NEVER BE BROKEN.

A Devil and
Her Love Song

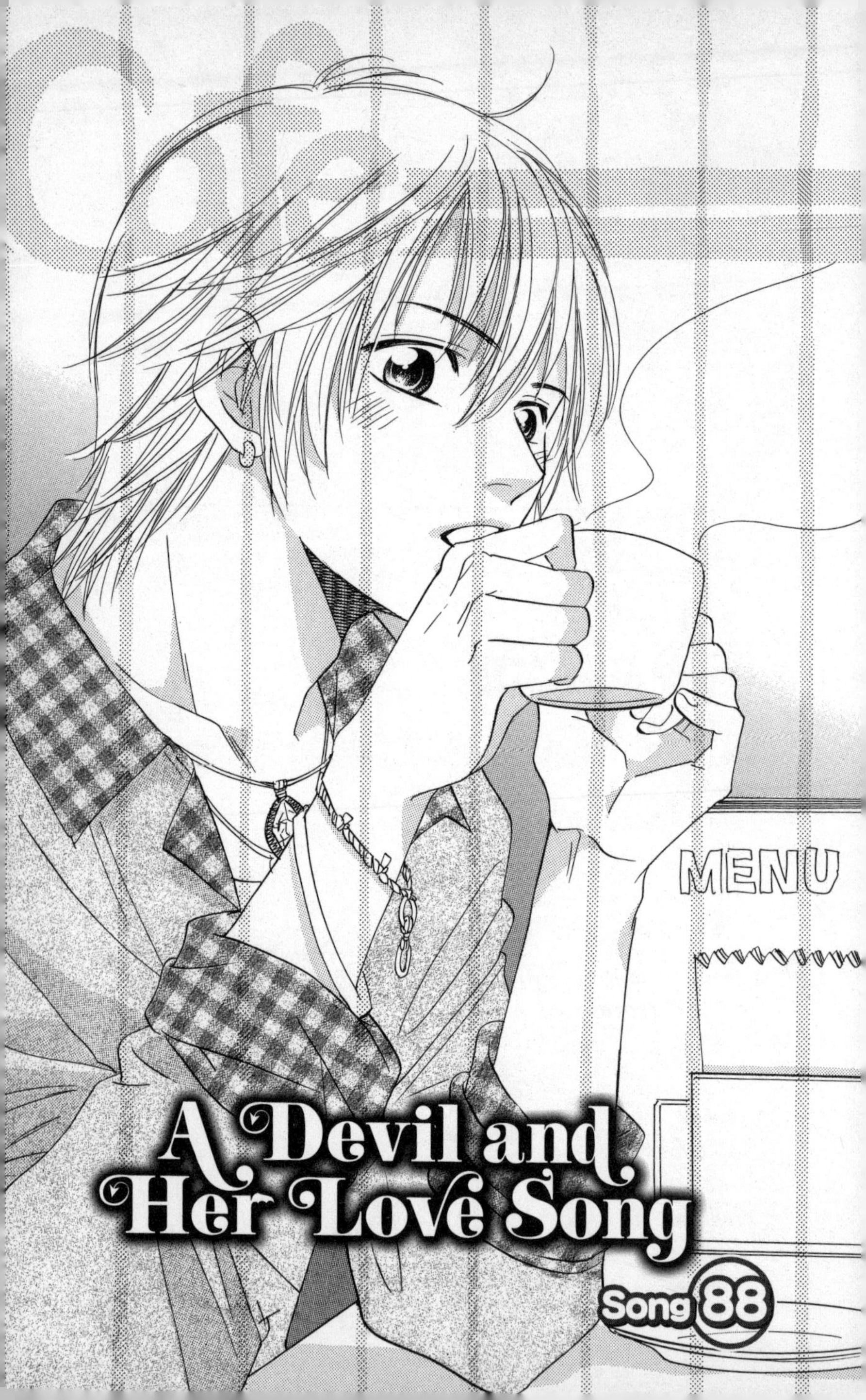
MENU
A Devil and Her Love Song
Song 88

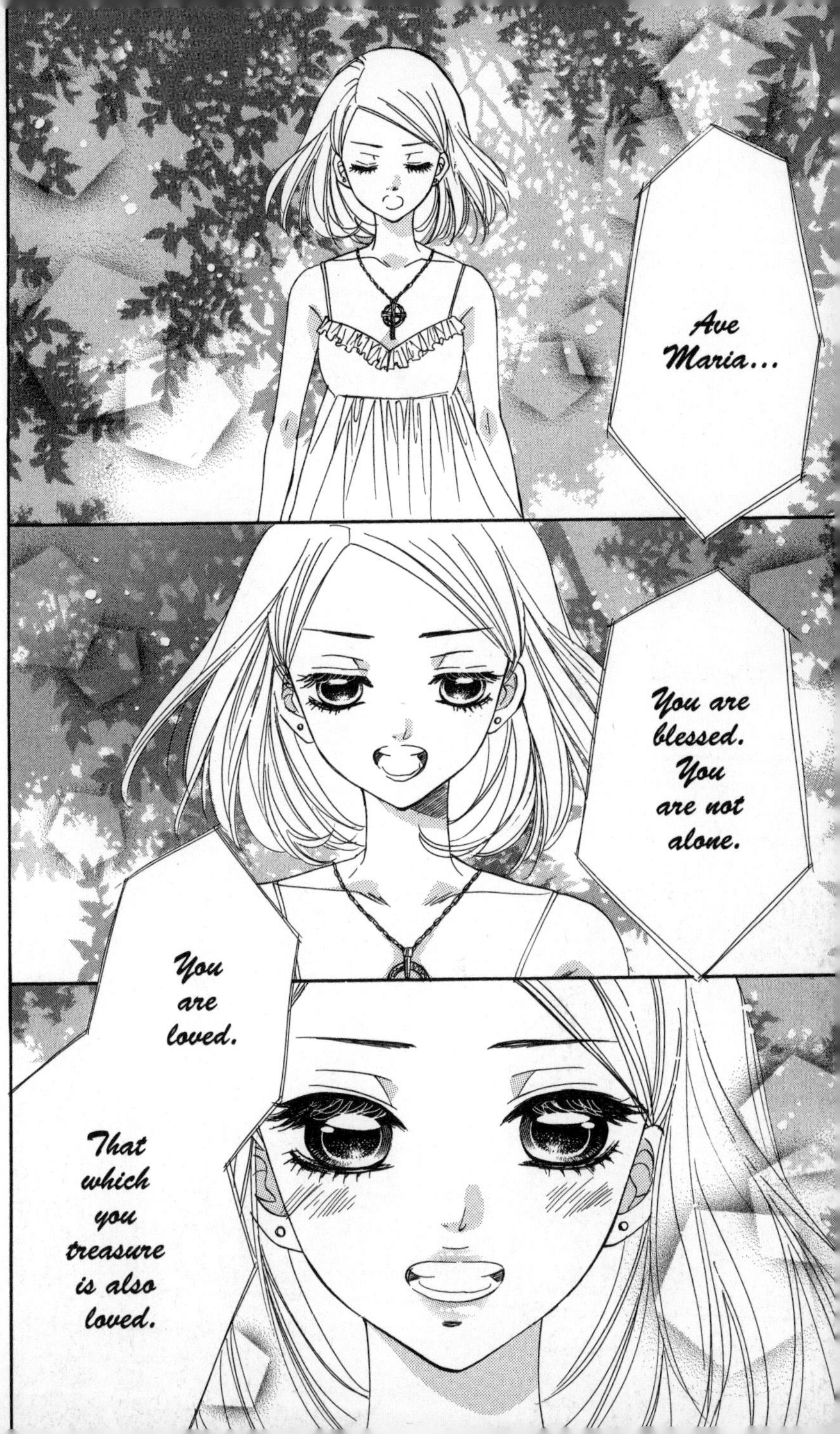
Ave Maria...
You are blessed. You are not alone.
You are loved.
That which you treasure is also loved.

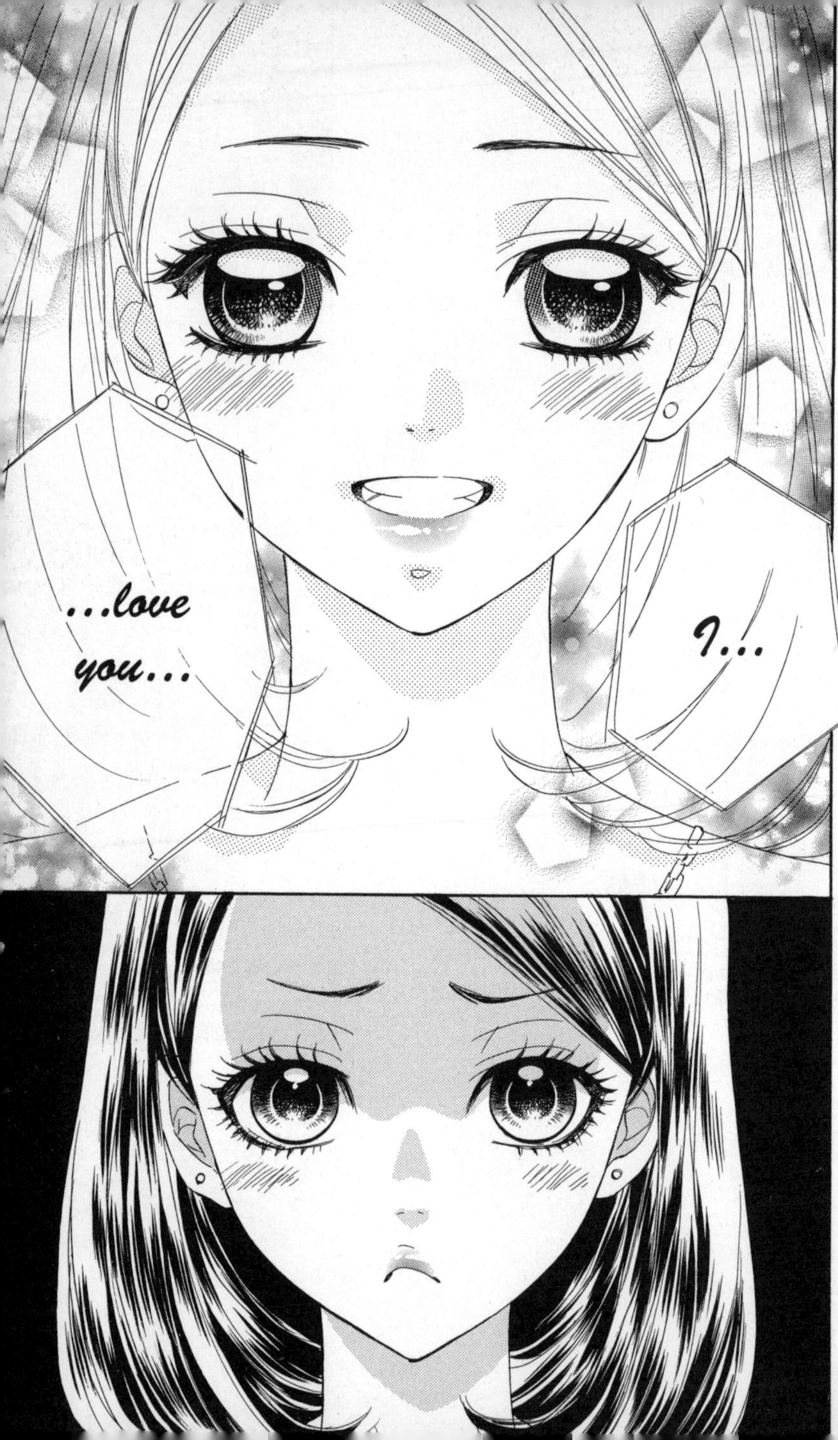
I...
...love you...

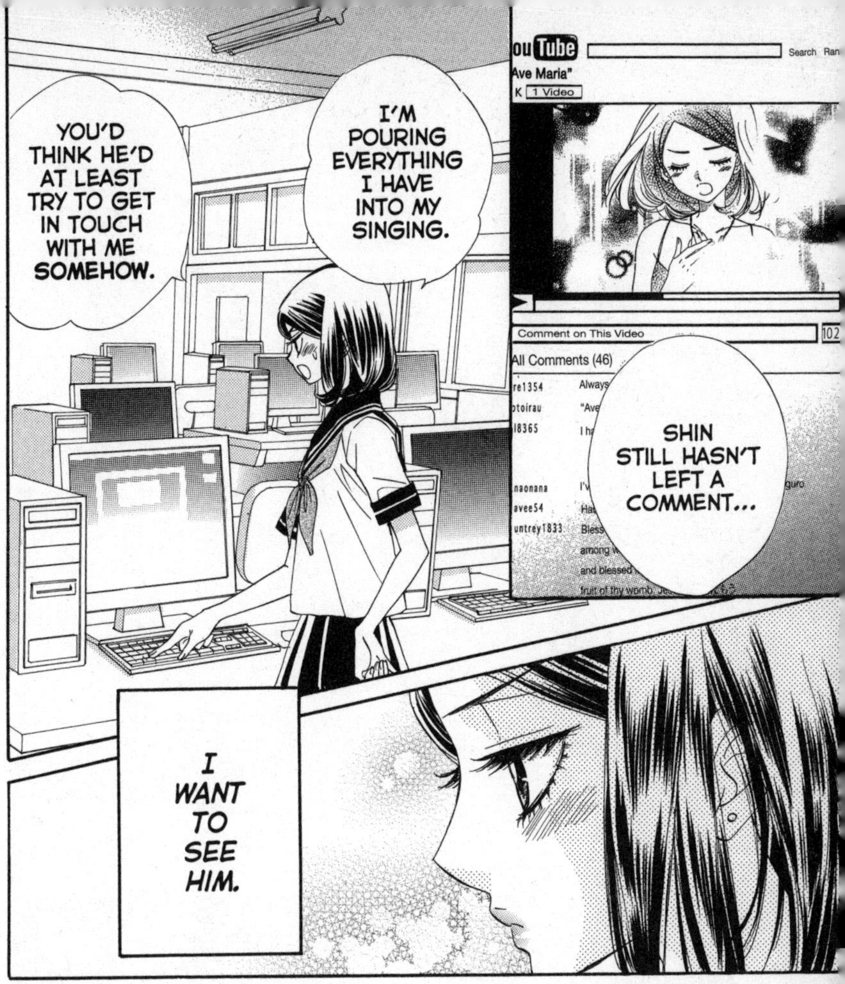
ouTube
Search
"Ave Maria"
K 1 Video
Comment on This Video
102
All Comments (46)
re1354 Always
otoirau "Ave
naonana
avee54
untrey1833 Bless
among
and blessed
fruit of thy womb,
SHIN STILL HASN'T LEFT A COMMENT...
I'M POURING EVERYTHING I HAVE INTO MY SINGING.
YOU'D THINK HE'D AT LEAST TRY TO GET IN TOUCH WITH ME SOMEHOW.
I WANT TO SEE HIM.

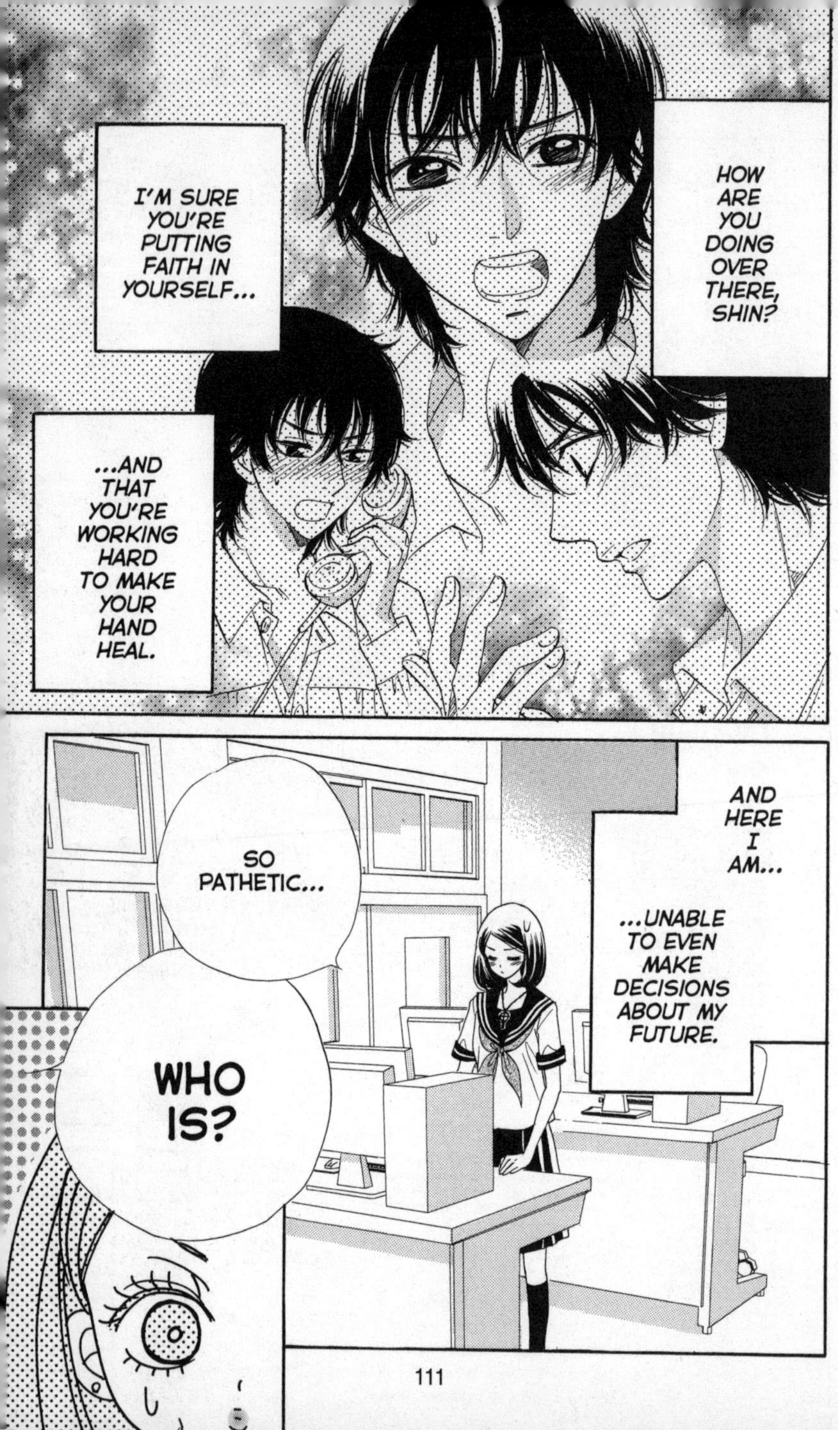
HOW ARE YOU DOING OVER THERE, SHIN?
I'M SURE YOU'RE PUTTING FAITH IN YOURSELF...
...AND THAT YOU'RE WORKING HARD TO MAKE YOUR HAND HEAL.
AND HERE I AM...
...UNABLE TO EVEN MAKE DECISIONS ABOUT MY FUTURE.
SO PATHETIC...
WHO IS?

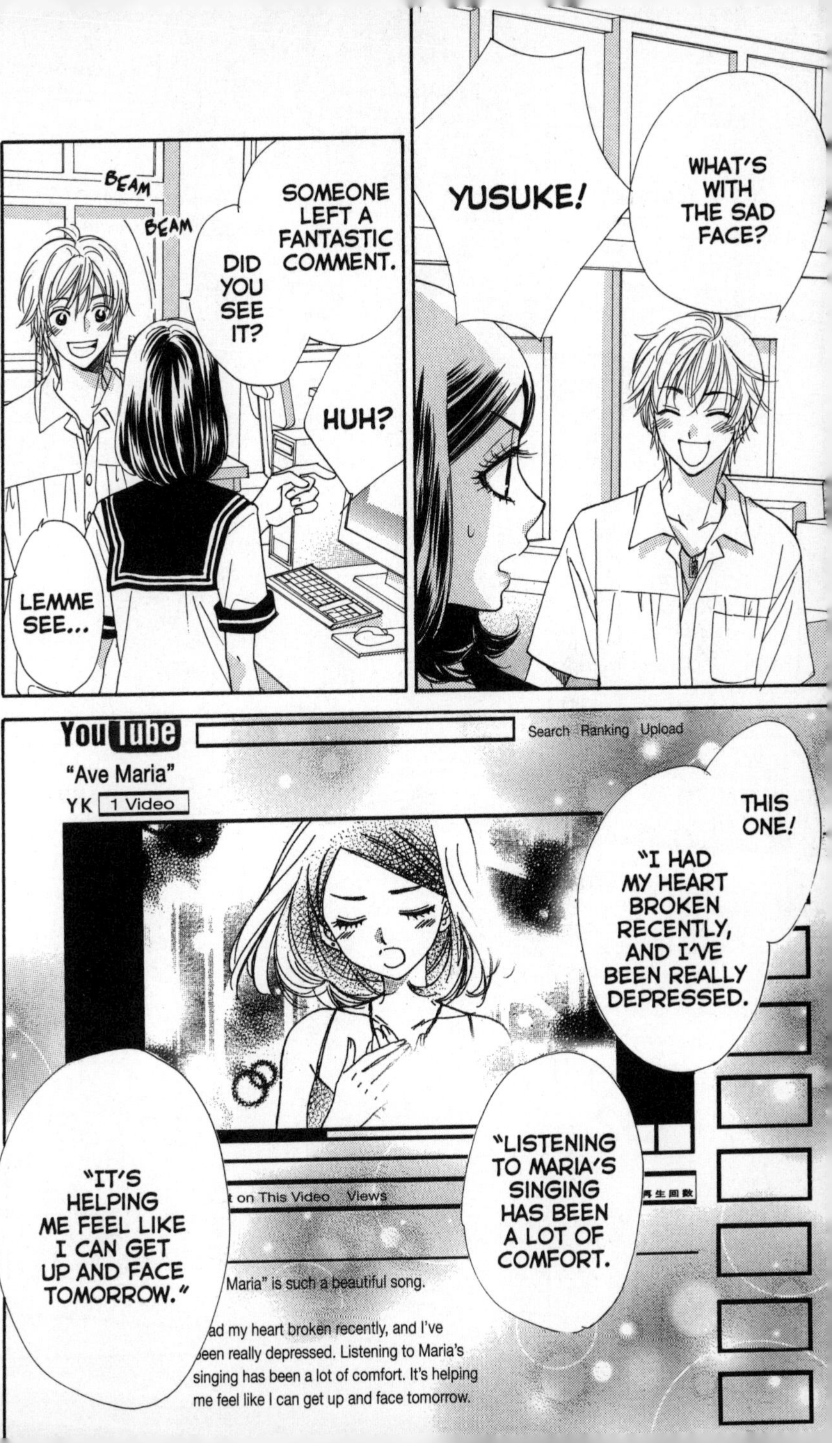
YUSUKE!
WHAT'S WITH THE SAD FACE?
SOMEONE LEFT A FANTASTIC COMMENT.
DID YOU SEE IT?
BEAM
BEAM
HUH?
LEMME SEE...
YouTube
Search Ranking Upload
"Ave Maria"
YK 1 Video
THIS ONE!
"I HAD MY HEART BROKEN RECENTLY, AND I'VE BEEN REALLY DEPRESSED.
"LISTENING TO MARIA'S SINGING HAS BEEN A LOT OF COMFORT.
"IT'S HELPING ME FEEL LIKE I CAN GET UP AND FACE TOMORROW."
t on This Video Views
再生回数
Maria" is such a beautiful song.
ad my heart broken recently, and I've
een really depressed. Listening to Maria's
singing has been a lot of comfort. It's helping
me feel like I can get up and face tomorrow.

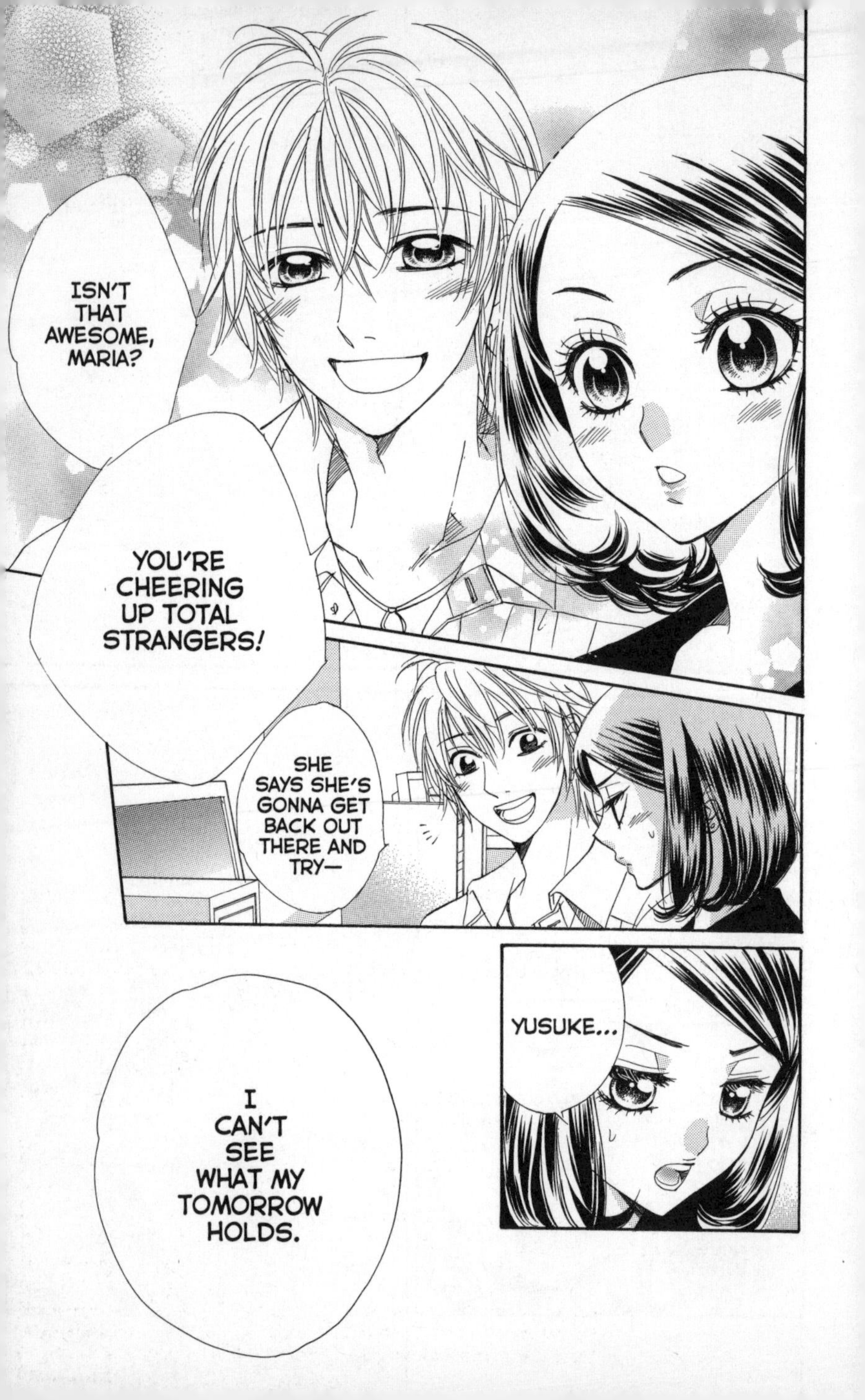
ISN'T THAT AWESOME, MARIA?
YOU'RE CHEERING UP TOTAL STRANGERS!
SHE SAYS SHE'S GONNA GET BACK OUT THERE AND TRY—
YUSUKE...
I CAN'T SEE WHAT MY TOMORROW HOLDS.

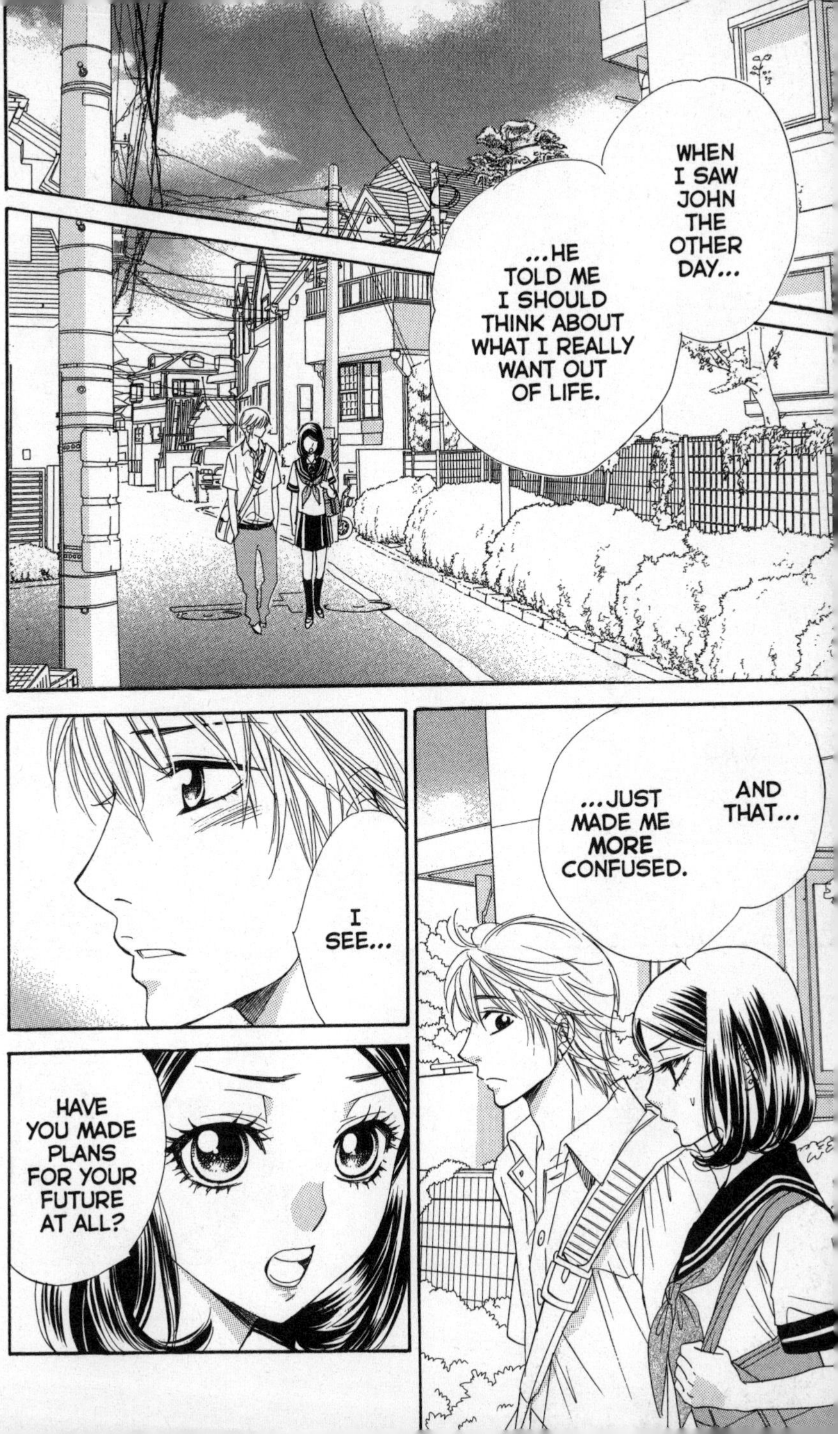
WHEN I SAW JOHN THE OTHER DAY...
...HE TOLD ME I SHOULD THINK ABOUT WHAT I REALLY WANT OUT OF LIFE.
AND THAT...
...JUST MADE ME MORE CONFUSED.
I SEE...
HAVE YOU MADE PLANS FOR YOUR FUTURE AT ALL?

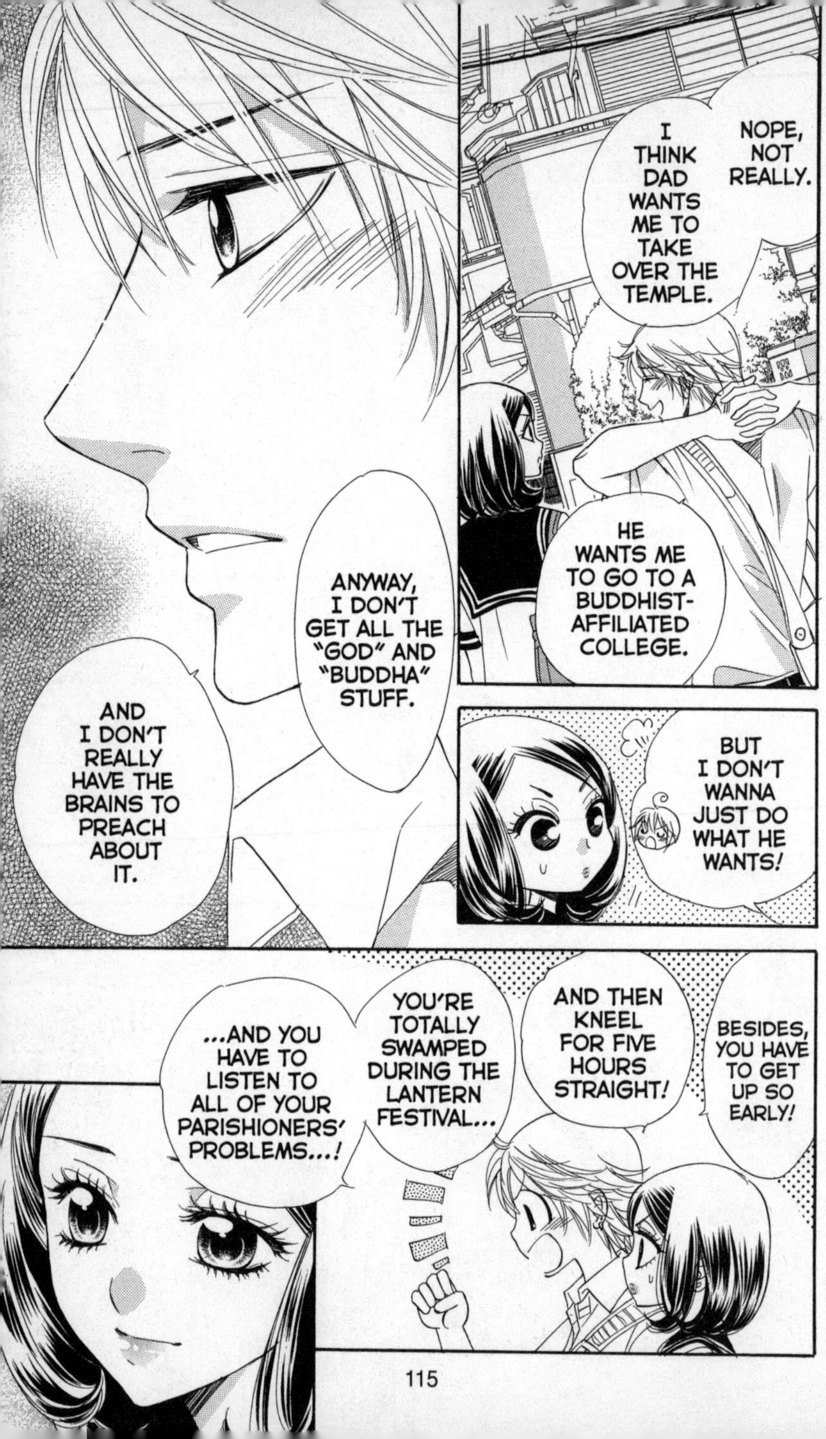
NOPE, NOT REALLY.
I THINK DAD WANTS ME TO TAKE OVER THE TEMPLE.
HE WANTS ME TO GO TO A BUDDHIST-AFFILIATED COLLEGE.
BUT I DON'T WANNA JUST DO WHAT HE WANTS!
ANYWAY, I DON'T GET ALL THE "GOD" AND "BUDDHA" STUFF.
AND I DON'T REALLY HAVE THE BRAINS TO PREACH ABOUT IT.
BESIDES, YOU HAVE TO GET UP SO EARLY!
AND THEN KNEEL FOR FIVE HOURS STRAIGHT!
YOU'RE TOTALLY SWAMPED DURING THE LANTERN FESTIVAL...
...AND YOU HAVE TO LISTEN TO ALL OF YOUR PARISHIONERS' PROBLEMS...!

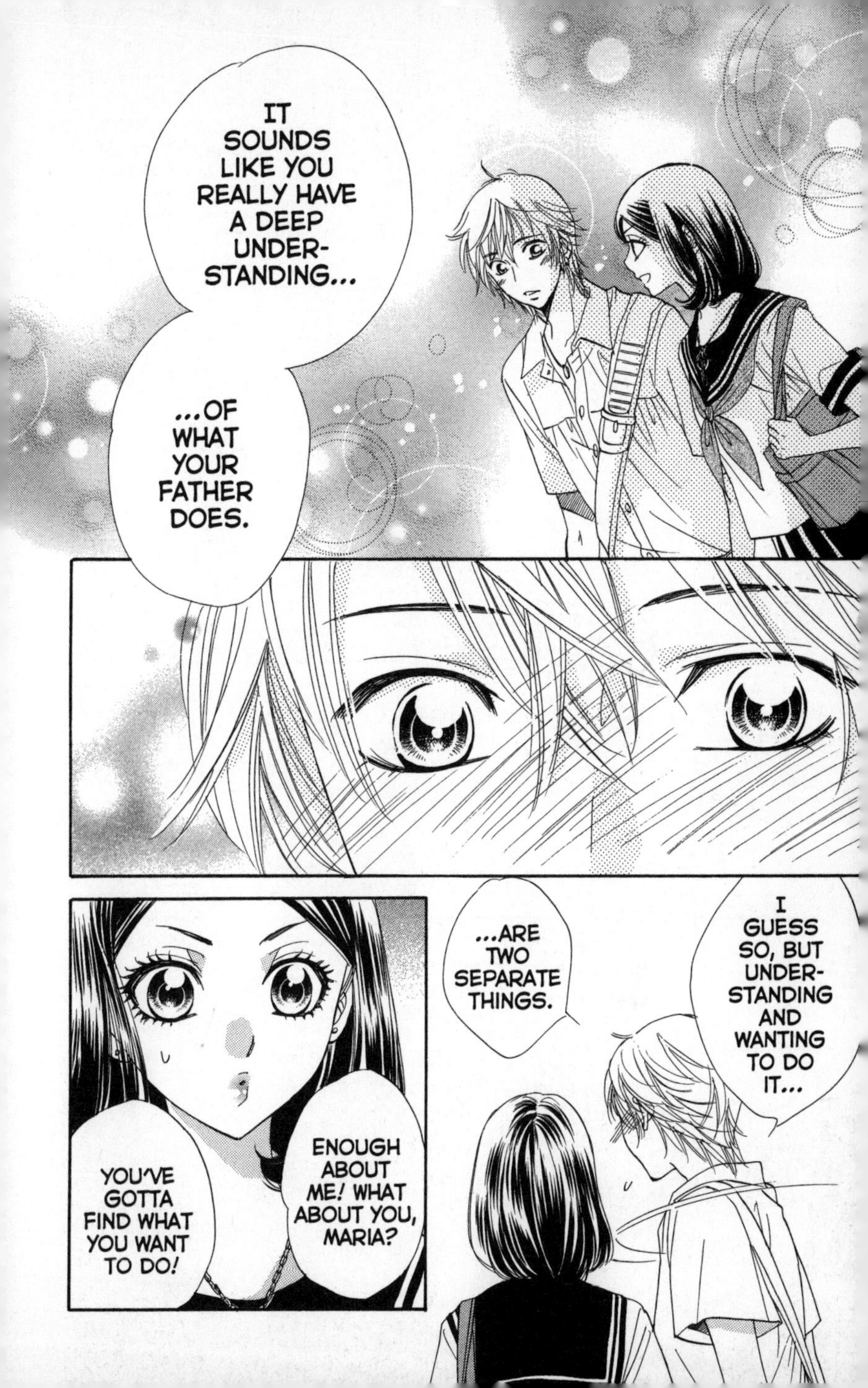
IT SOUNDS LIKE YOU REALLY HAVE A DEEP UNDER-STANDING...
...OF WHAT YOUR FATHER DOES.
I GUESS SO, BUT UNDER-STANDING AND WANTING TO DO IT...
...ARE TWO SEPARATE THINGS.
ENOUGH ABOUT ME! WHAT ABOUT YOU, MARIA?
YOU'VE GOTTA FIND WHAT YOU WANT TO DO!

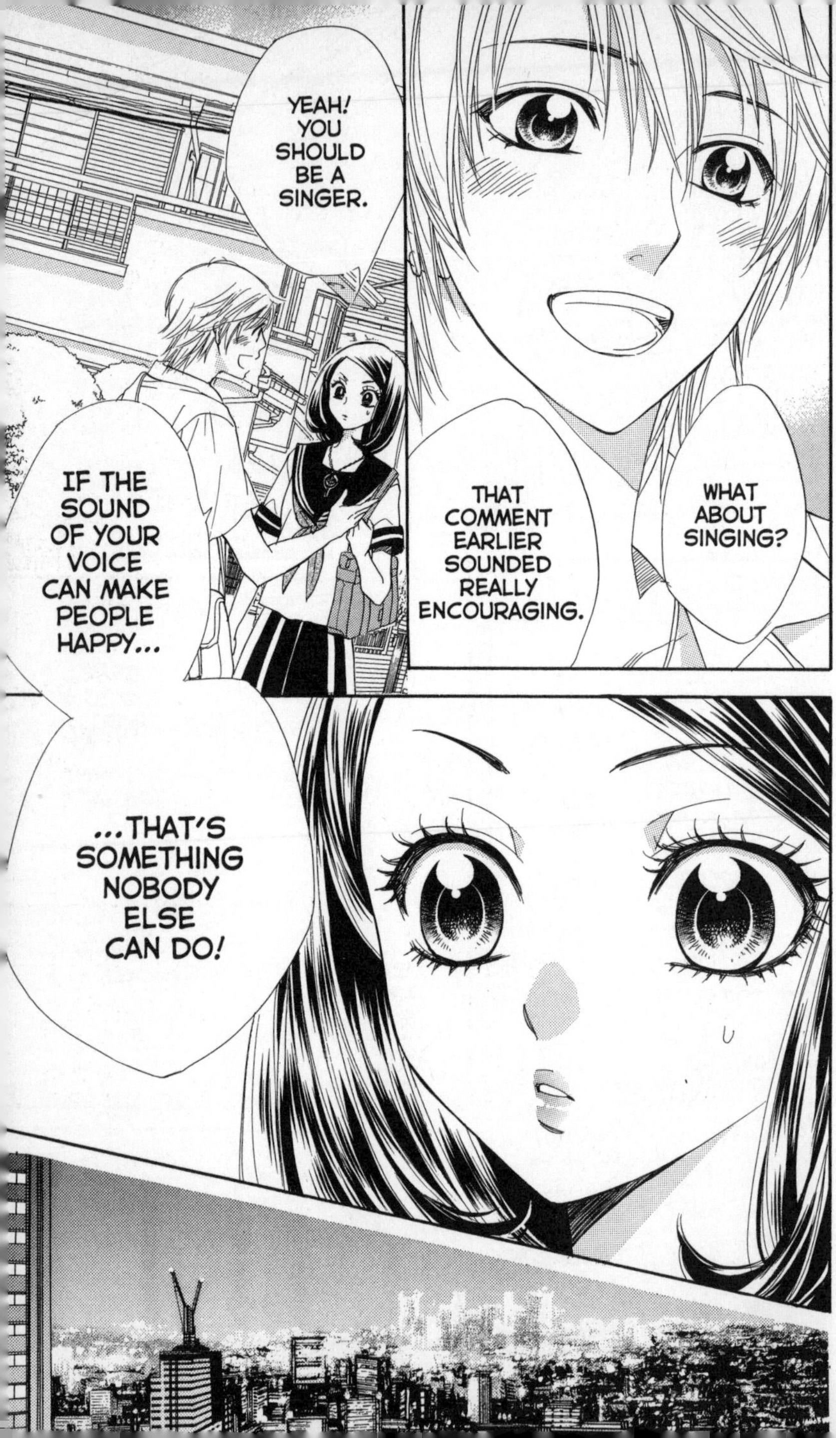
WHAT ABOUT SINGING?
THAT COMMENT EARLIER SOUNDED REALLY ENCOURAGING.
YEAH! YOU SHOULD BE A SINGER.
IF THE SOUND OF YOUR VOICE CAN MAKE PEOPLE HAPPY...
...THAT'S SOMETHING NOBODY ELSE CAN DO!

SINGING, MAKING THE LEAP!

SINGI...

SO YOU WANT TO BE A ...
THIS IS THE ULTIMATE ...K!
–YOU ARE NOT MISTAKEN...
VOICE TRAINING

A SINGER...

STEP 1.
GO TO AN
AUDITION.

SEND
IN A
DEMO
TAPE.

A
DEMO
TAPE...
SO A
MUSIC
VIDEO
WON'T
CUT IT?

I
DON'T
KNOW
FOR
SURE
YET...

...BUT
WHEN
I HEARD
YUSUKE
SAY THE
WORD
"SINGER"
OUT
LOUD...

I THINK
YUSUKE GAVE
ME SOME
INFORMATION
...

YOKOHAMA MUSIC OFFICE

SHK

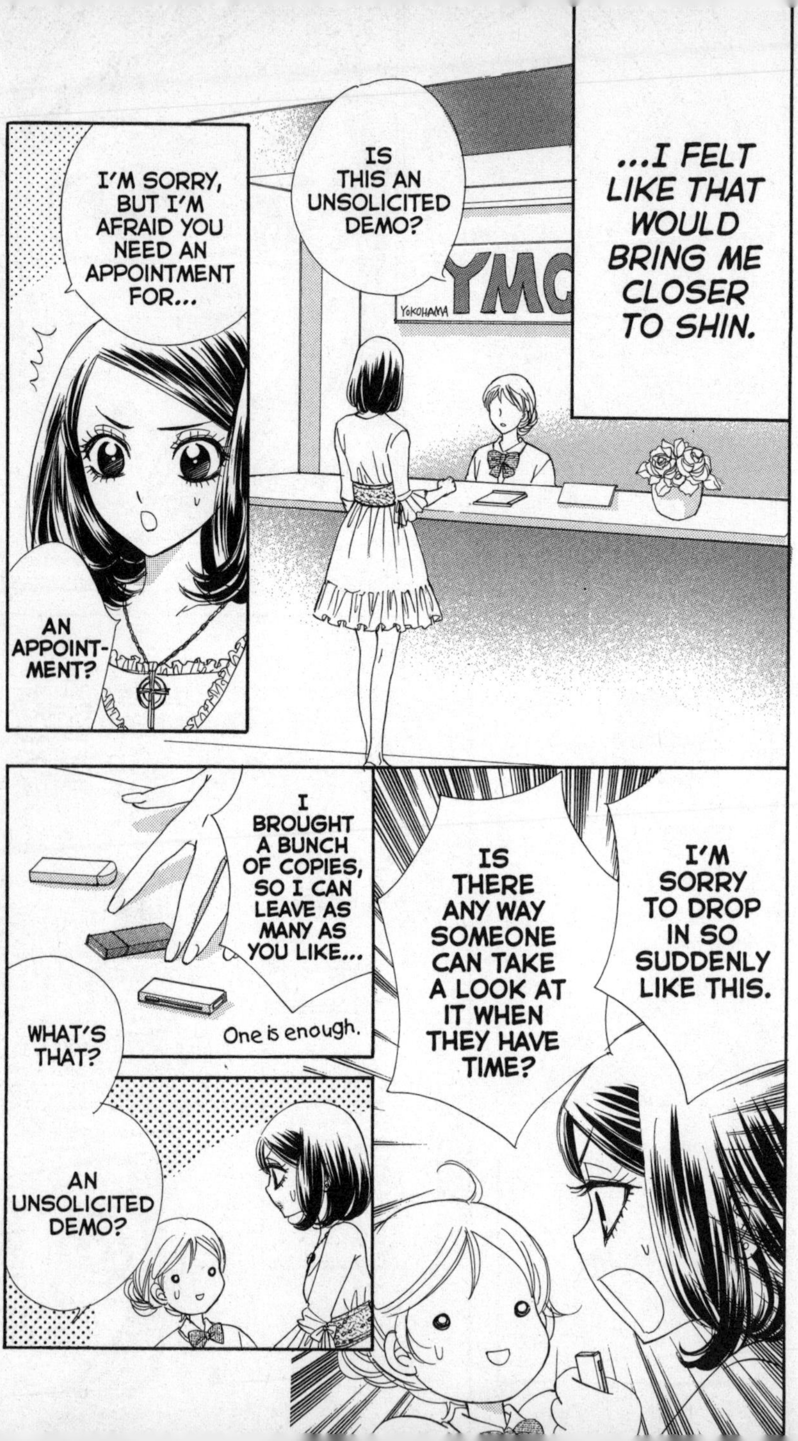
...I FELT LIKE THAT WOULD BRING ME CLOSER TO SHIN.
IS THIS AN UNSOLICITED DEMO?
YOKOHAMA
I'M SORRY, BUT I'M AFRAID YOU NEED AN APPOINTMENT FOR...
AN APPOINTMENT?
I'M SORRY TO DROP IN SO SUDDENLY LIKE THIS.
IS THERE ANY WAY SOMEONE CAN TAKE A LOOK AT IT WHEN THEY HAVE TIME?
I BROUGHT A BUNCH OF COPIES, SO I CAN LEAVE AS MANY AS YOU LIKE...
One is enough.
WHAT'S THAT?
AN UNSOLICITED DEMO?

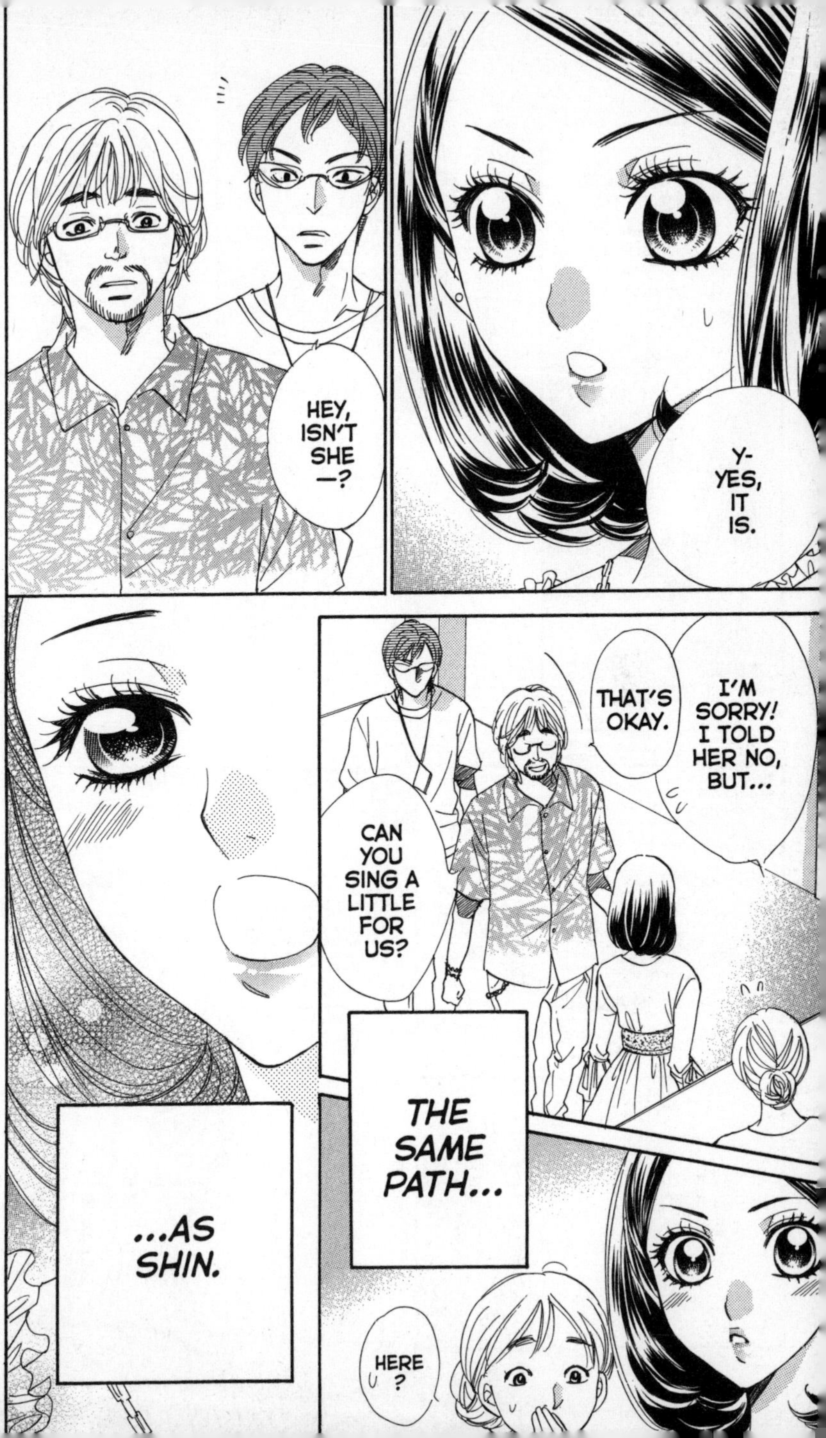
Y-YES, IT IS.
HEY, ISN'T SHE—?
I'M SORRY! I TOLD HER NO, BUT...
THAT'S OKAY.
CAN YOU SING A LITTLE FOR US?
HERE?
THE SAME PATH...
...AS SHIN.

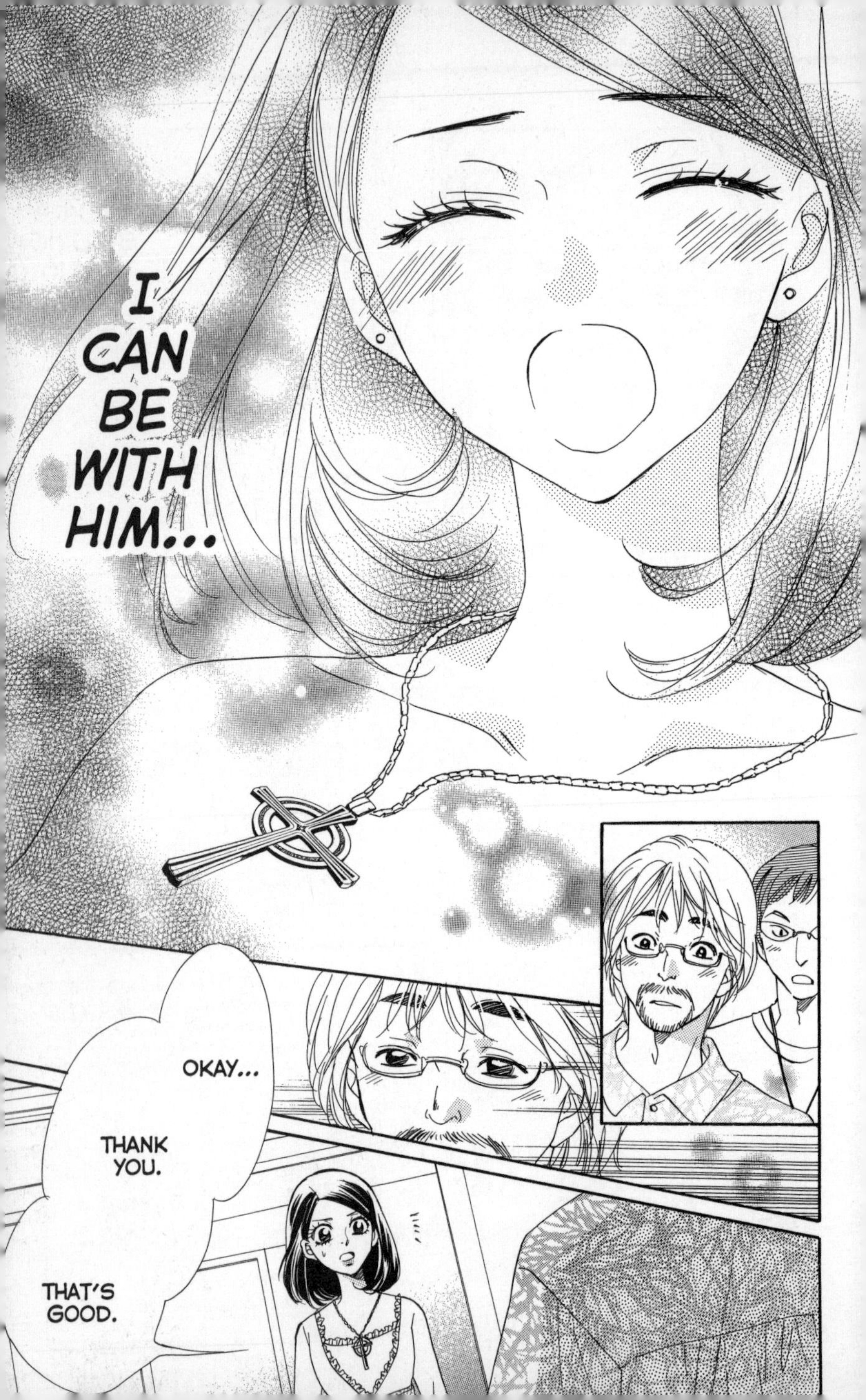
I CAN BE WITH HIM...
OKAY...
THANK YOU.
THAT'S GOOD.

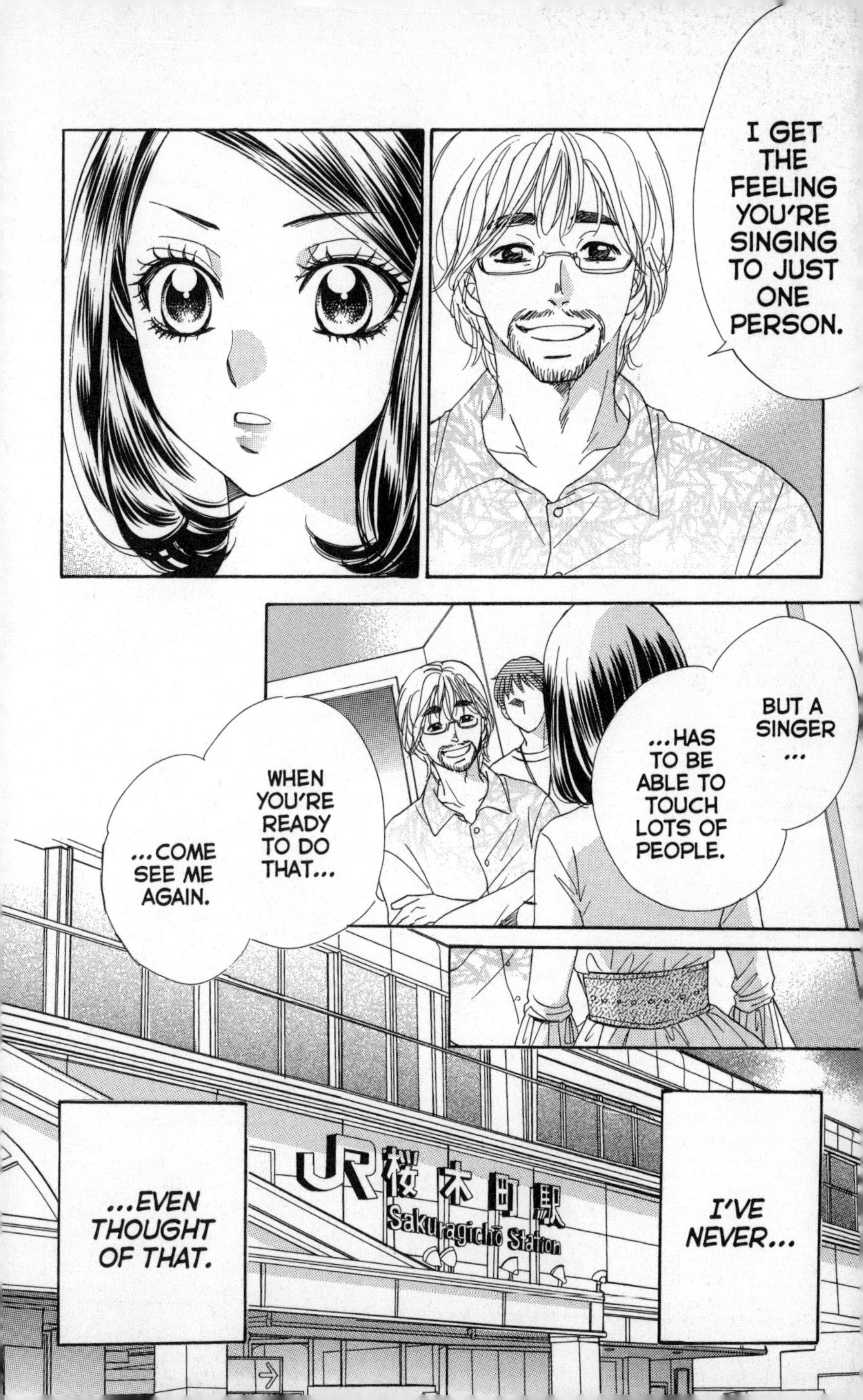
I GET THE FEELING YOU'RE SINGING TO JUST ONE PERSON.
BUT A SINGER ...
...HAS TO BE ABLE TO TOUCH LOTS OF PEOPLE.
WHEN YOU'RE READY TO DO THAT...
...COME SEE ME AGAIN.
JR 桜木町駅
Sakuragichō Station
I'VE NEVER...
...EVEN THOUGHT OF THAT.

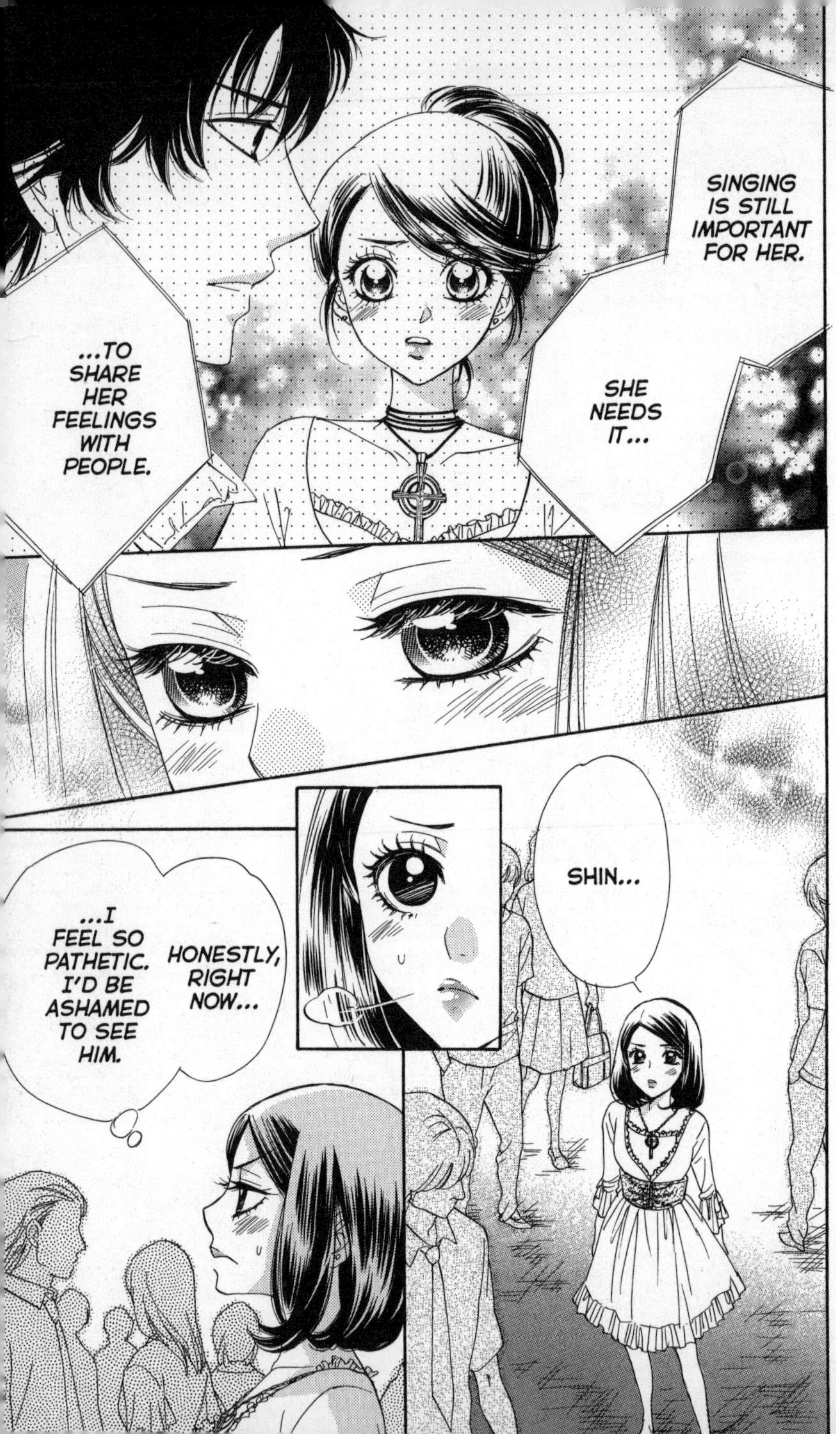
SINGING IS STILL IMPORTANT FOR HER.
SHE NEEDS IT...
...TO SHARE HER FEELINGS WITH PEOPLE.
SHIN...
HONESTLY, RIGHT NOW...
...I FEEL SO PATHETIC. I'D BE ASHAMED TO SEE HIM.

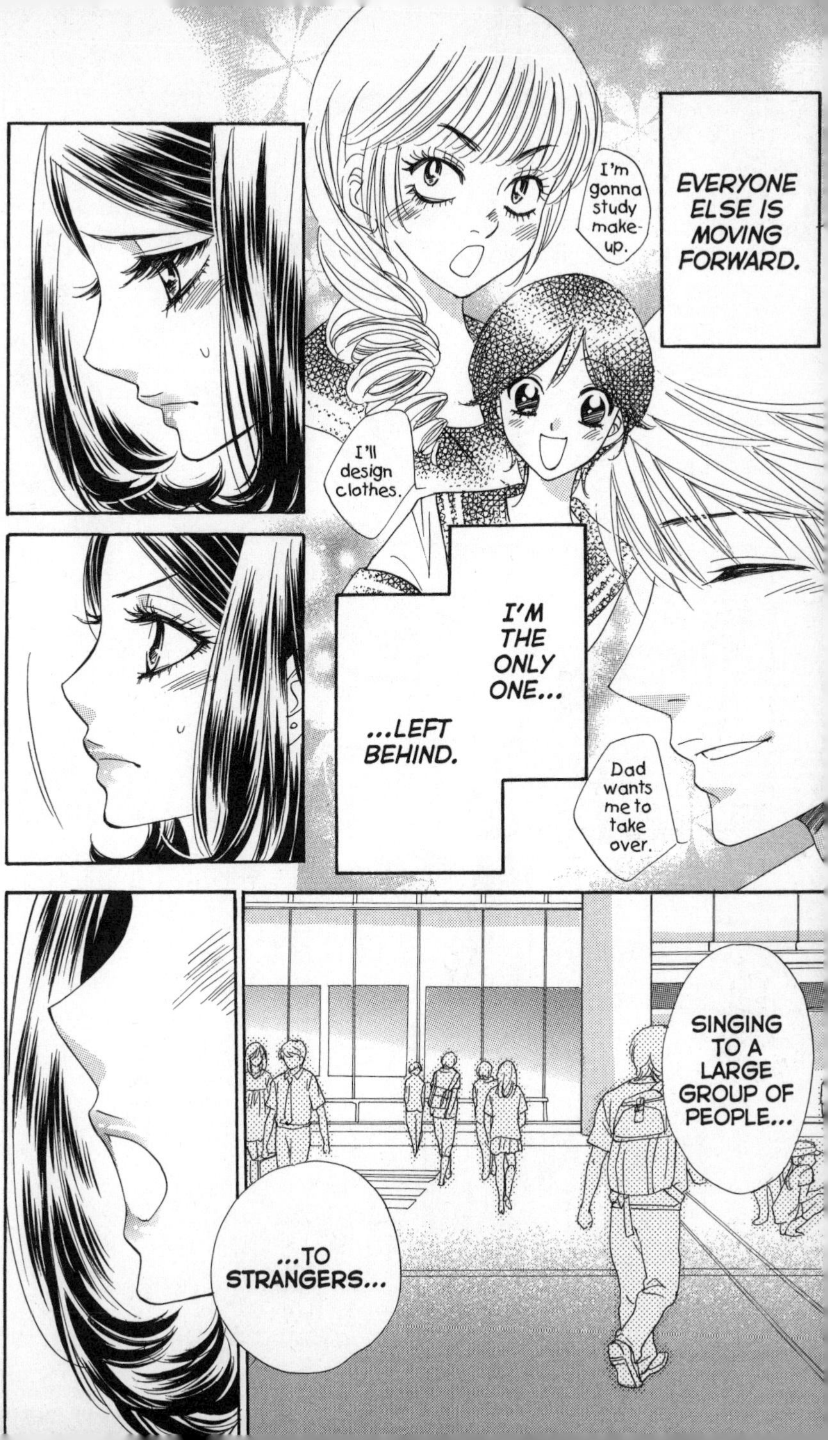
EVERYONE ELSE IS MOVING FORWARD.
I'm gonna study make-up.
I'll design clothes.
Dad wants me to take over.
I'M THE ONLY ONE...
...LEFT BEHIND.
SINGING TO A LARGE GROUP OF PEOPLE...
...TO STRANGERS...

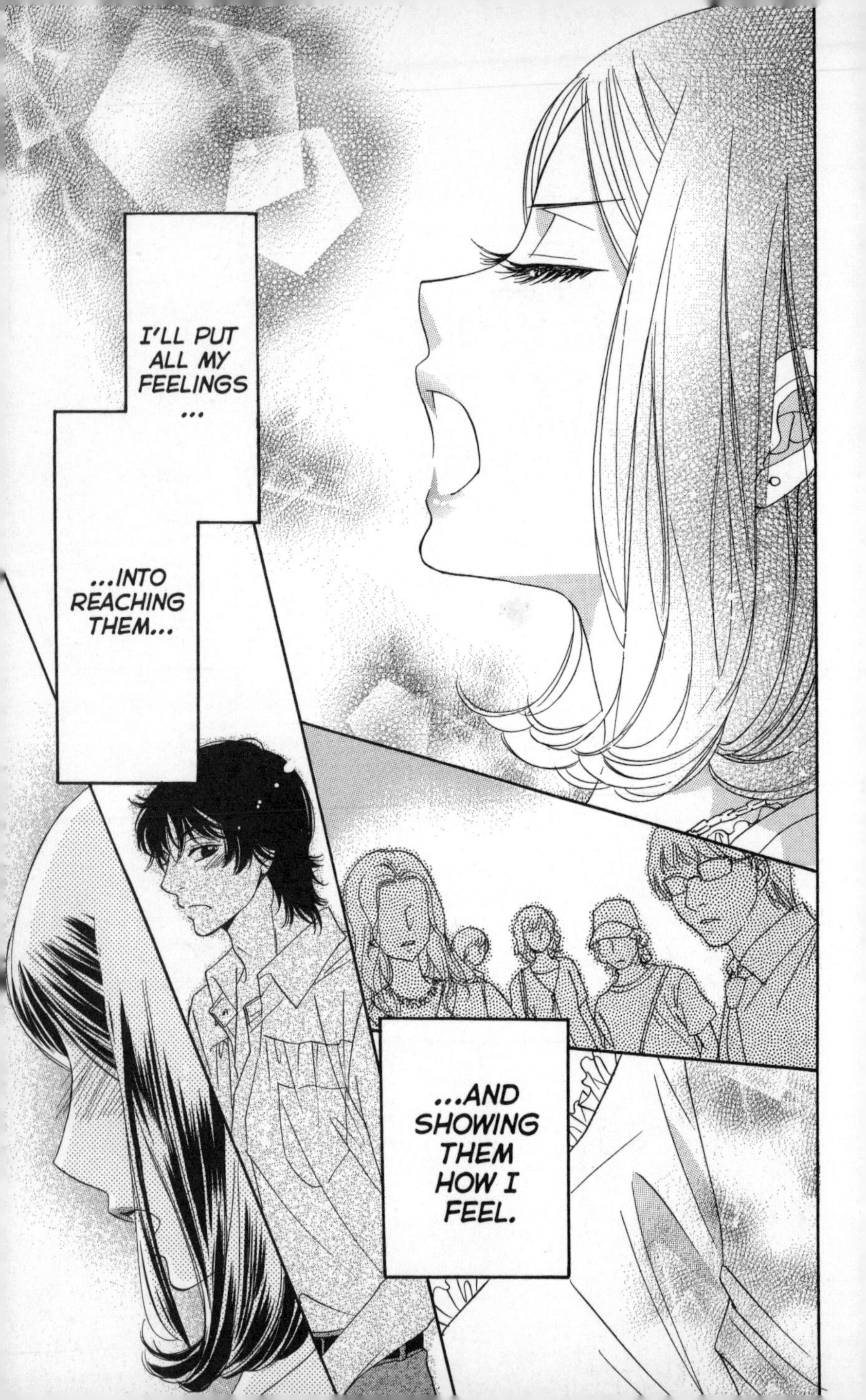
I'LL PUT ALL MY FEELINGS ...
...INTO REACHING THEM...
...AND SHOWING THEM HOW I FEEL.

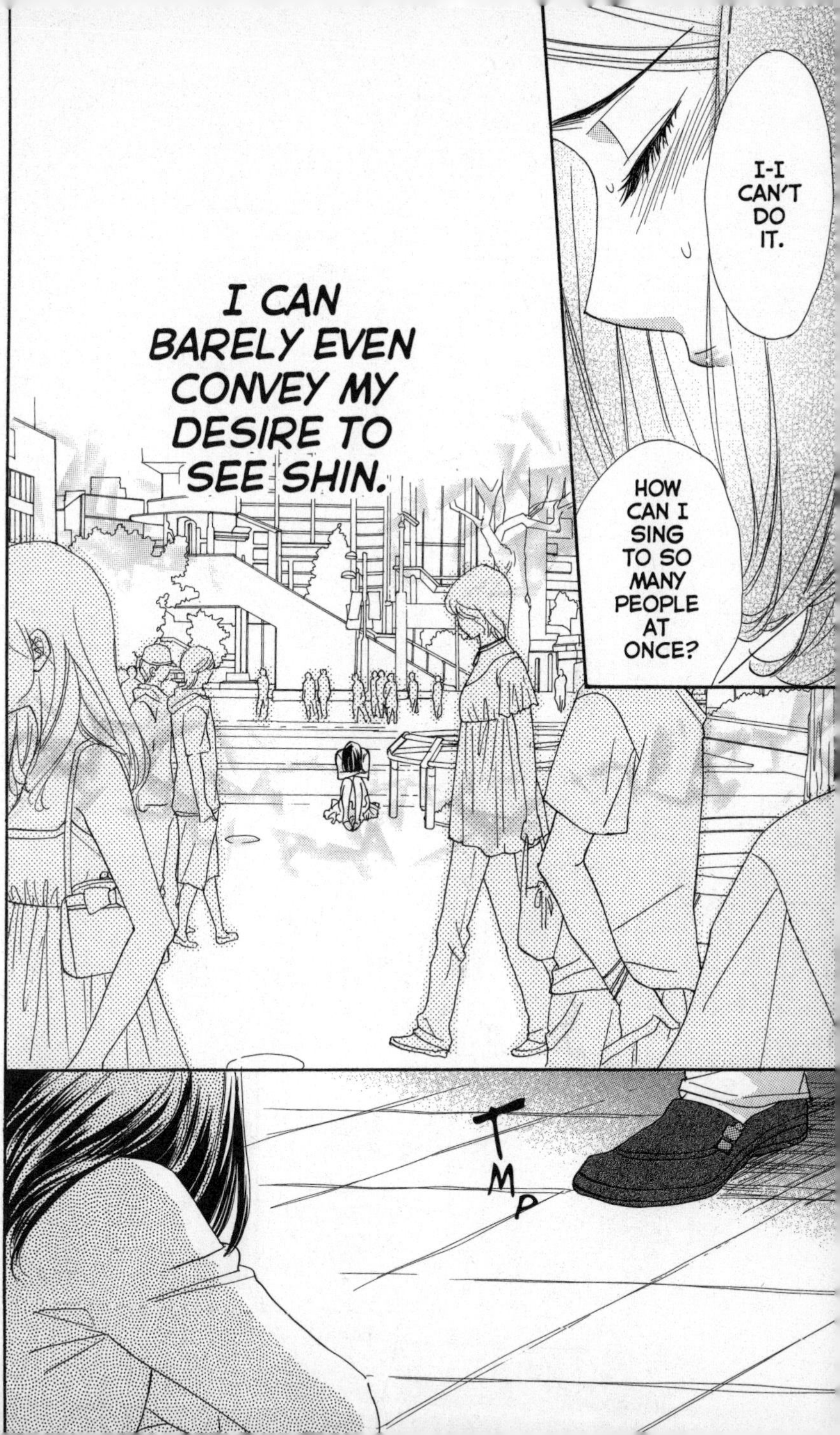
I-I CAN'T DO IT.
HOW CAN I SING TO SO MANY PEOPLE AT ONCE?
I CAN BARELY EVEN CONVEY MY DESIRE TO SEE SHIN.
TMP

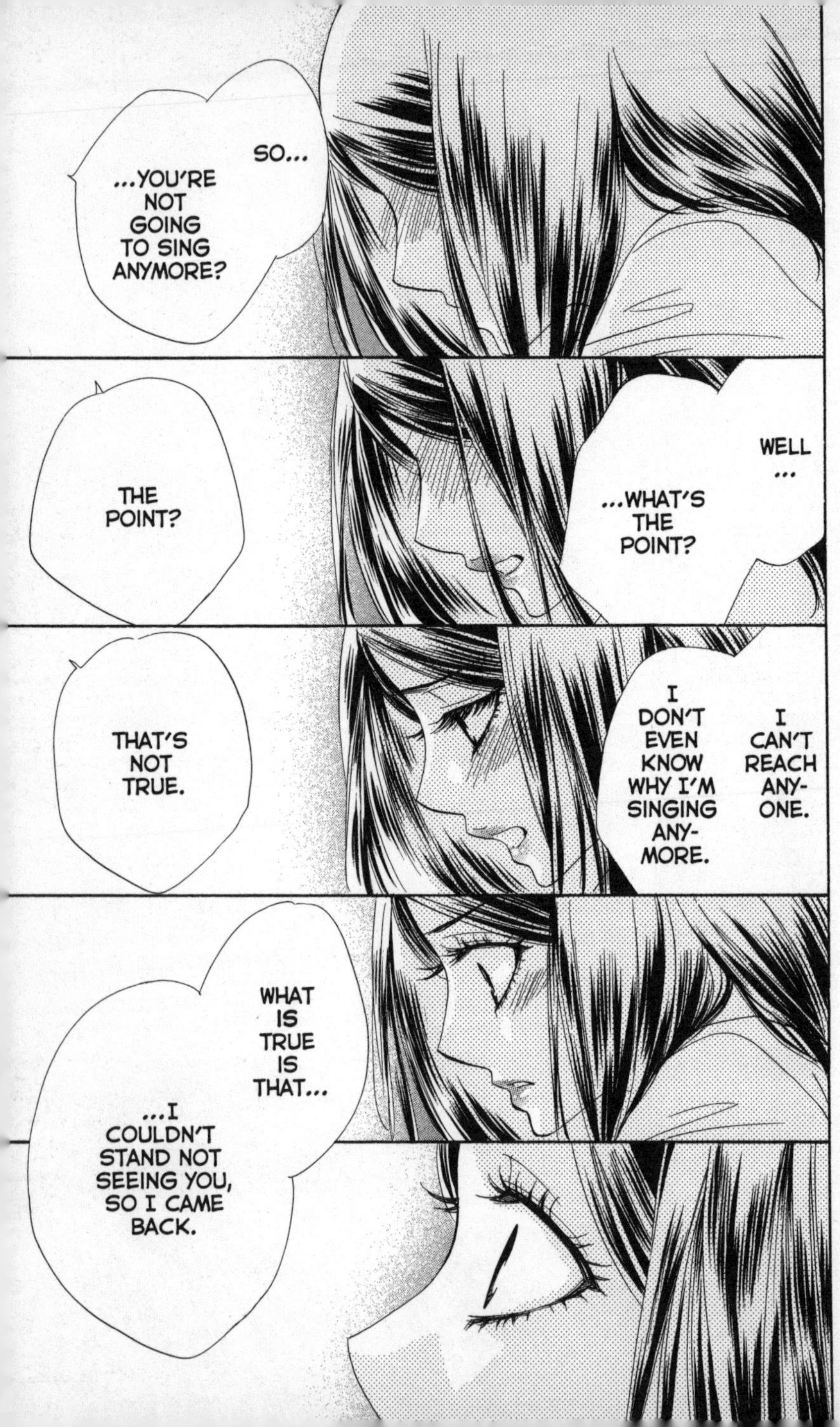
SO... ...YOU'RE NOT GOING TO SING ANYMORE?
WELL ... ...WHAT'S THE POINT?
THE POINT?
I CAN'T REACH ANY-ONE.
I DON'T EVEN KNOW WHY I'M SINGING ANY-MORE.
THAT'S NOT TRUE.
WHAT IS TRUE IS THAT... ...I COULDN'T STAND NOT SEEING YOU, SO I CAME BACK.

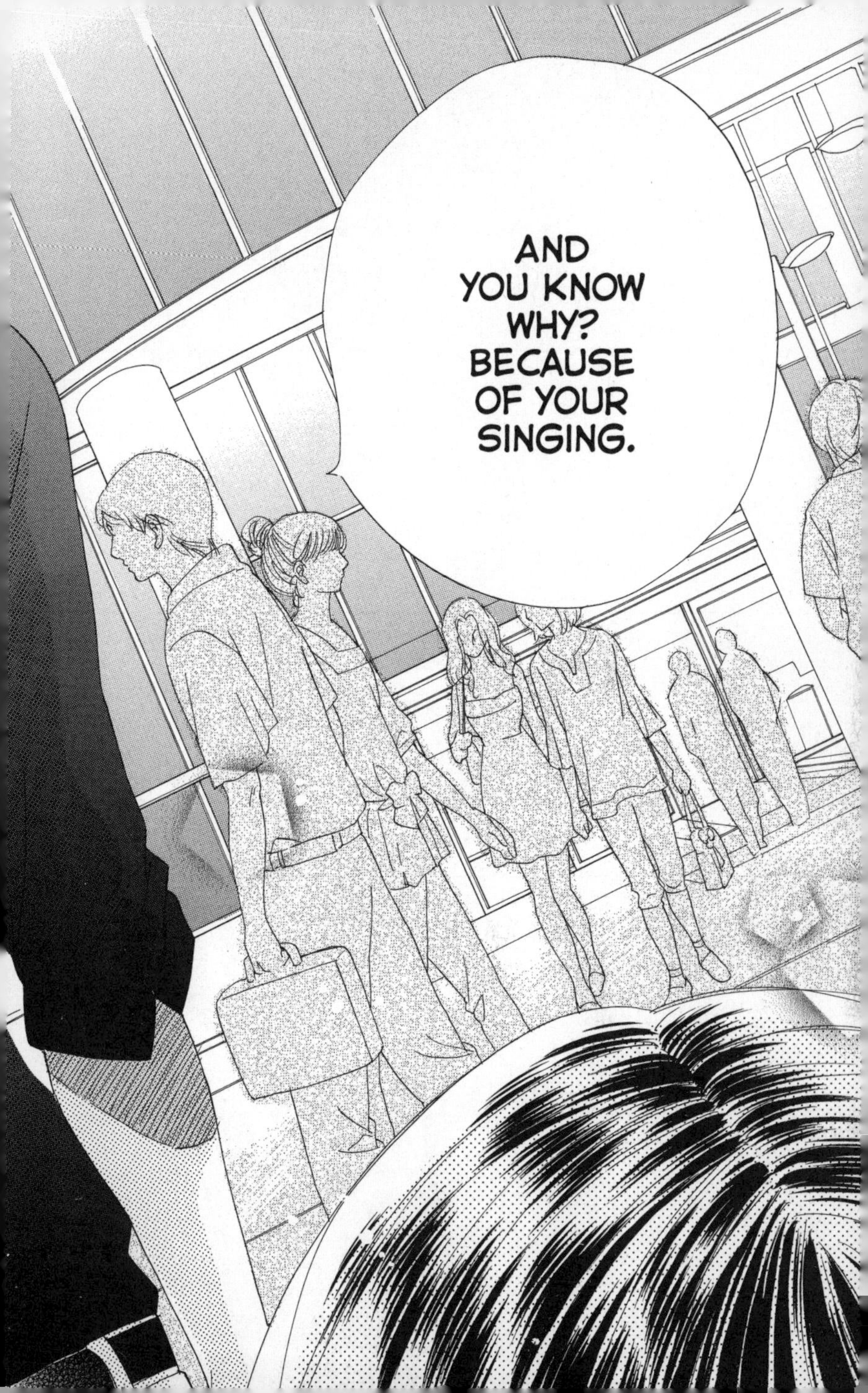
AND YOU KNOW WHY? BECAUSE OF YOUR SINGING.

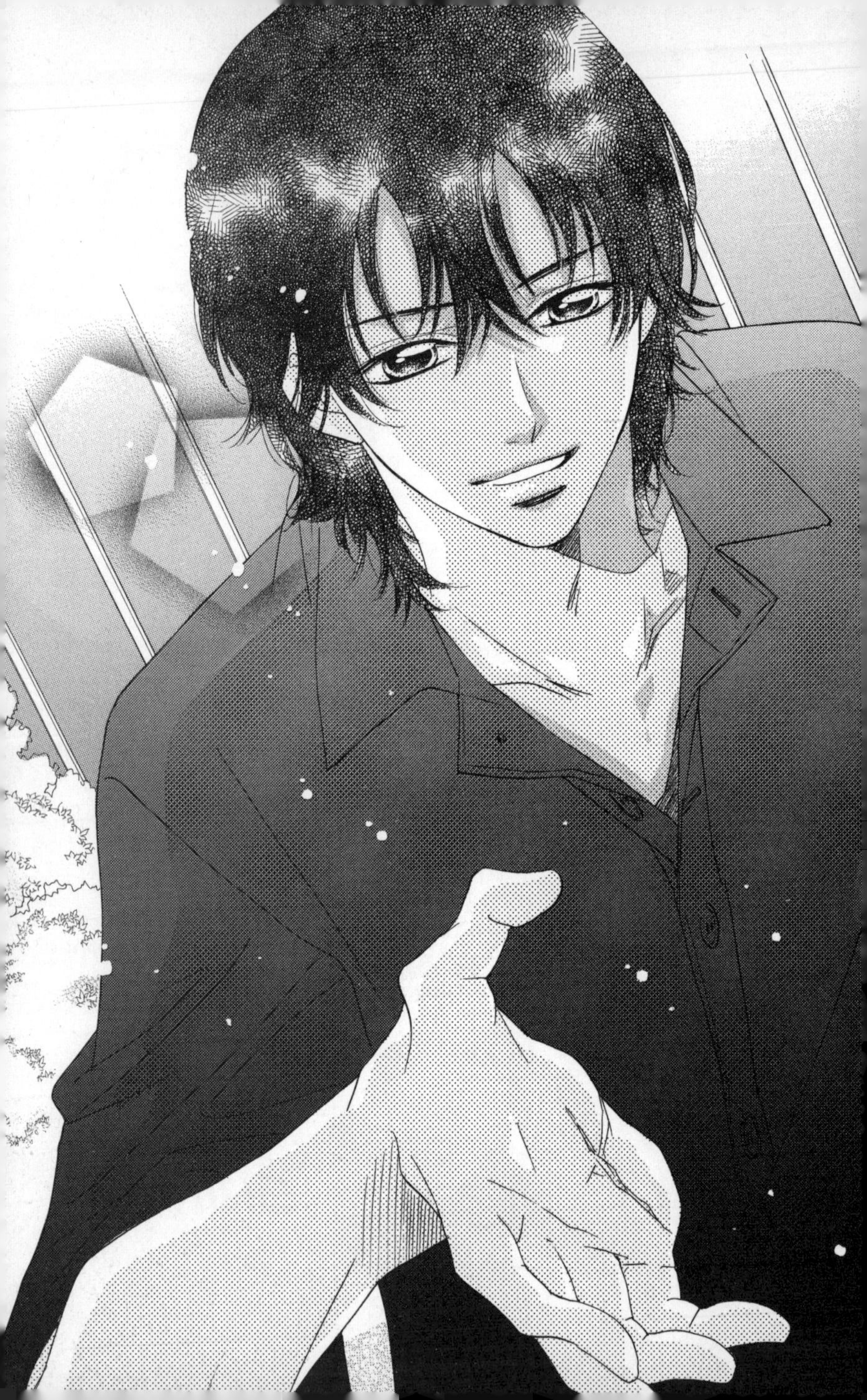

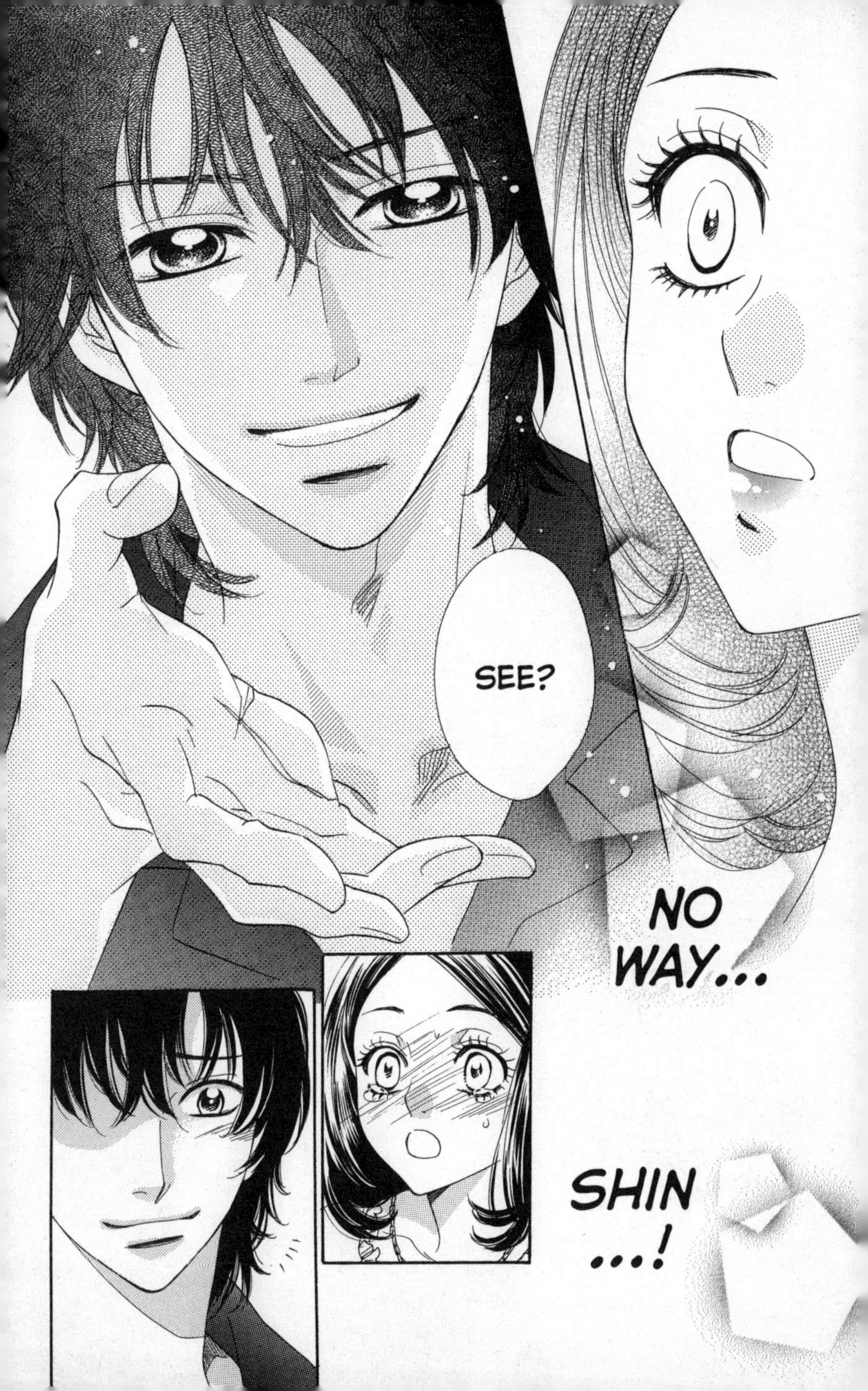
SEE?
NO WAY...
SHIN ...!

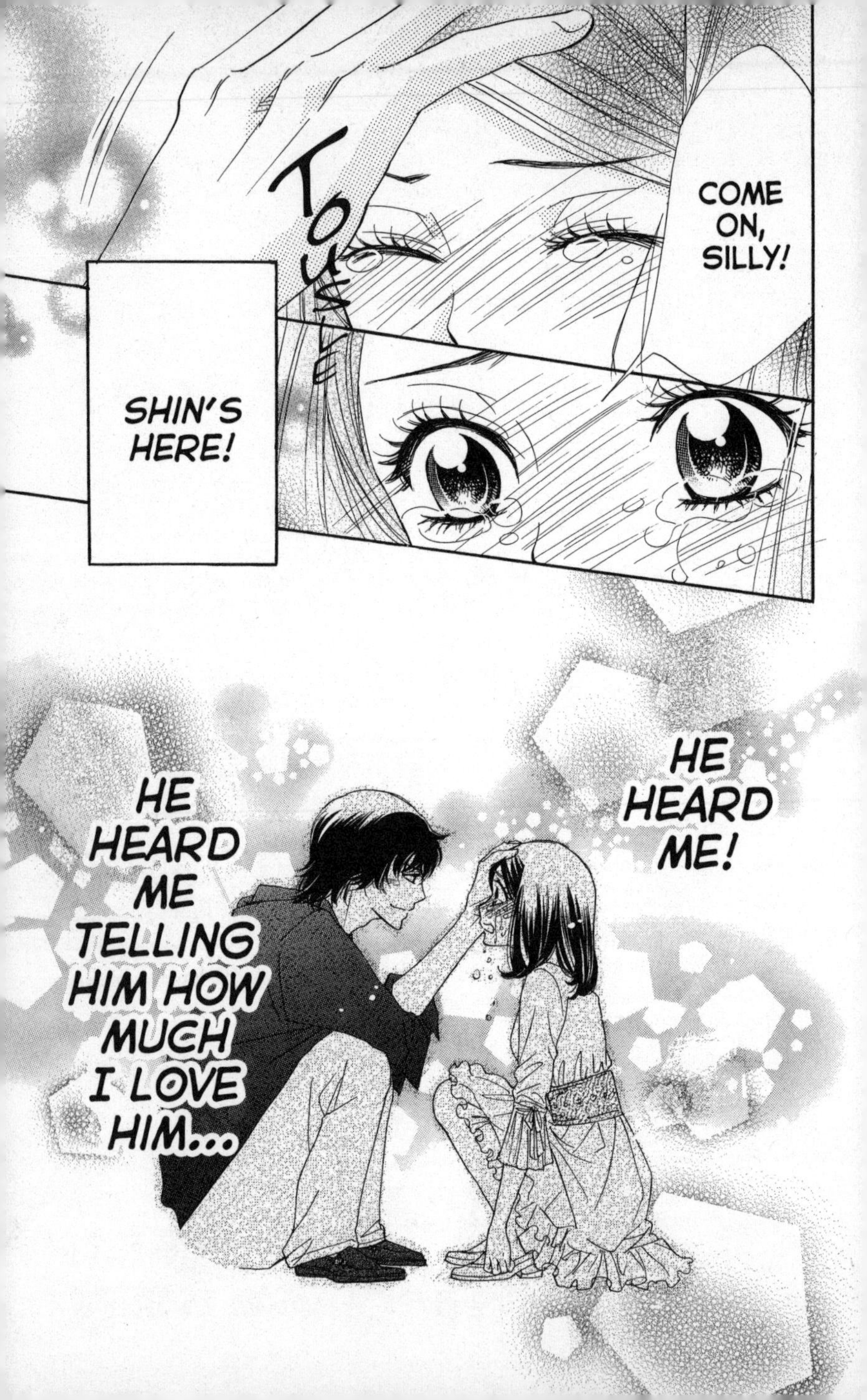
COME ON, SILLY!
TOUSLE
SHIN'S HERE!
HE HEARD ME!
HE HEARD ME TELLING HIM HOW MUCH I LOVE HIM...

A Devil and Her Love Song

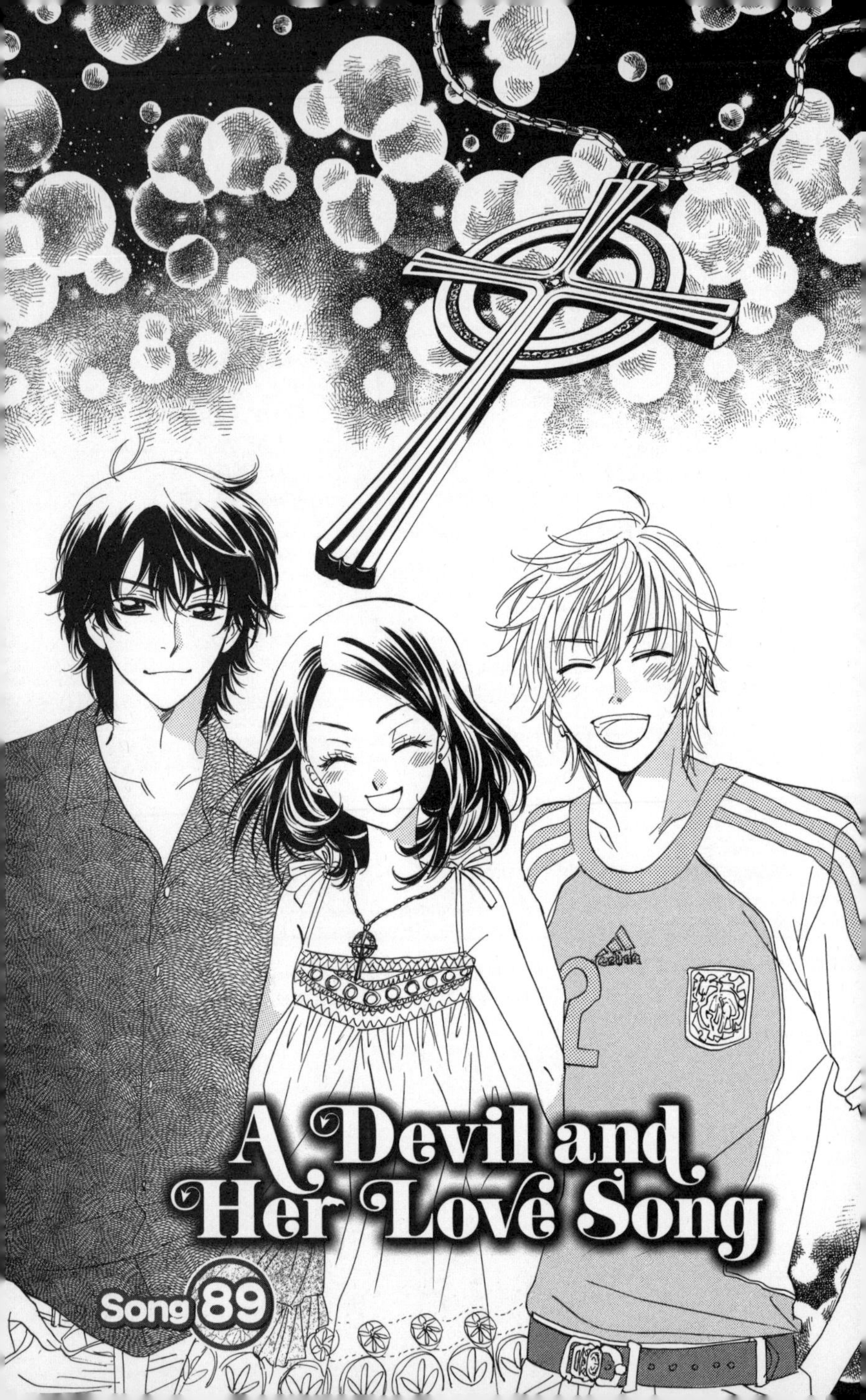
A Devil and Her Love Song
Song 89

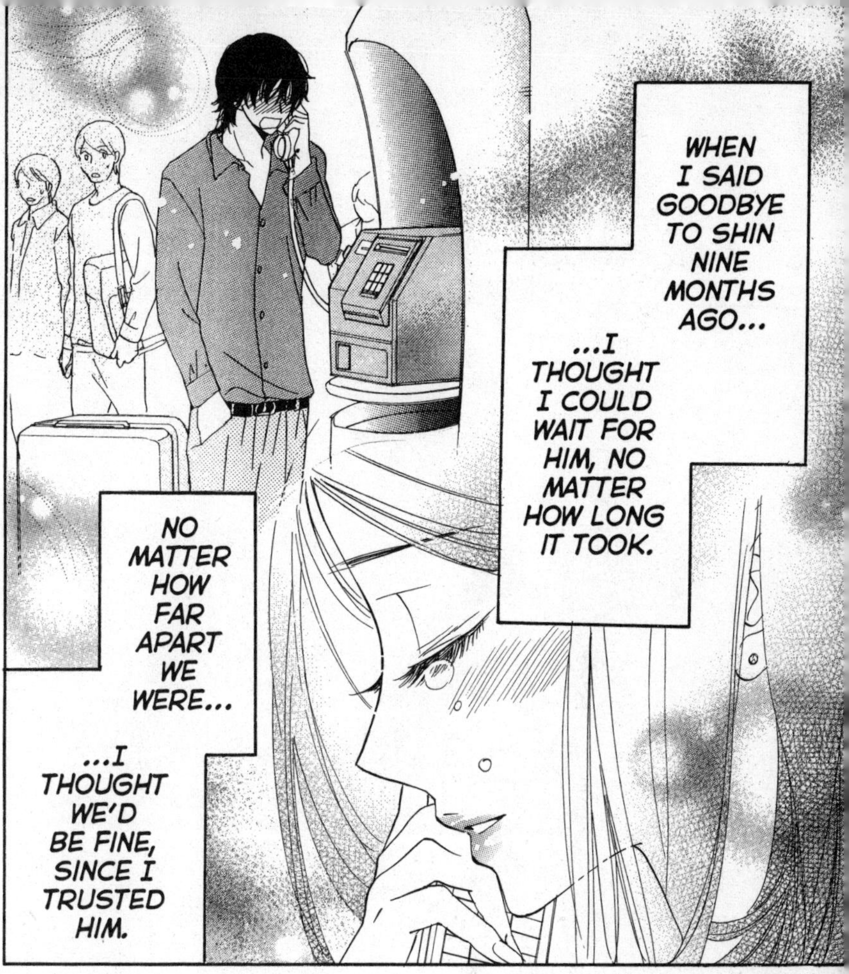
WHEN I SAID GOODBYE TO SHIN NINE MONTHS AGO...
...I THOUGHT I COULD WAIT FOR HIM, NO MATTER HOW LONG IT TOOK.
NO MATTER HOW FAR APART WE WERE...
...I THOUGHT WE'D BE FINE, SINCE I TRUSTED HIM.

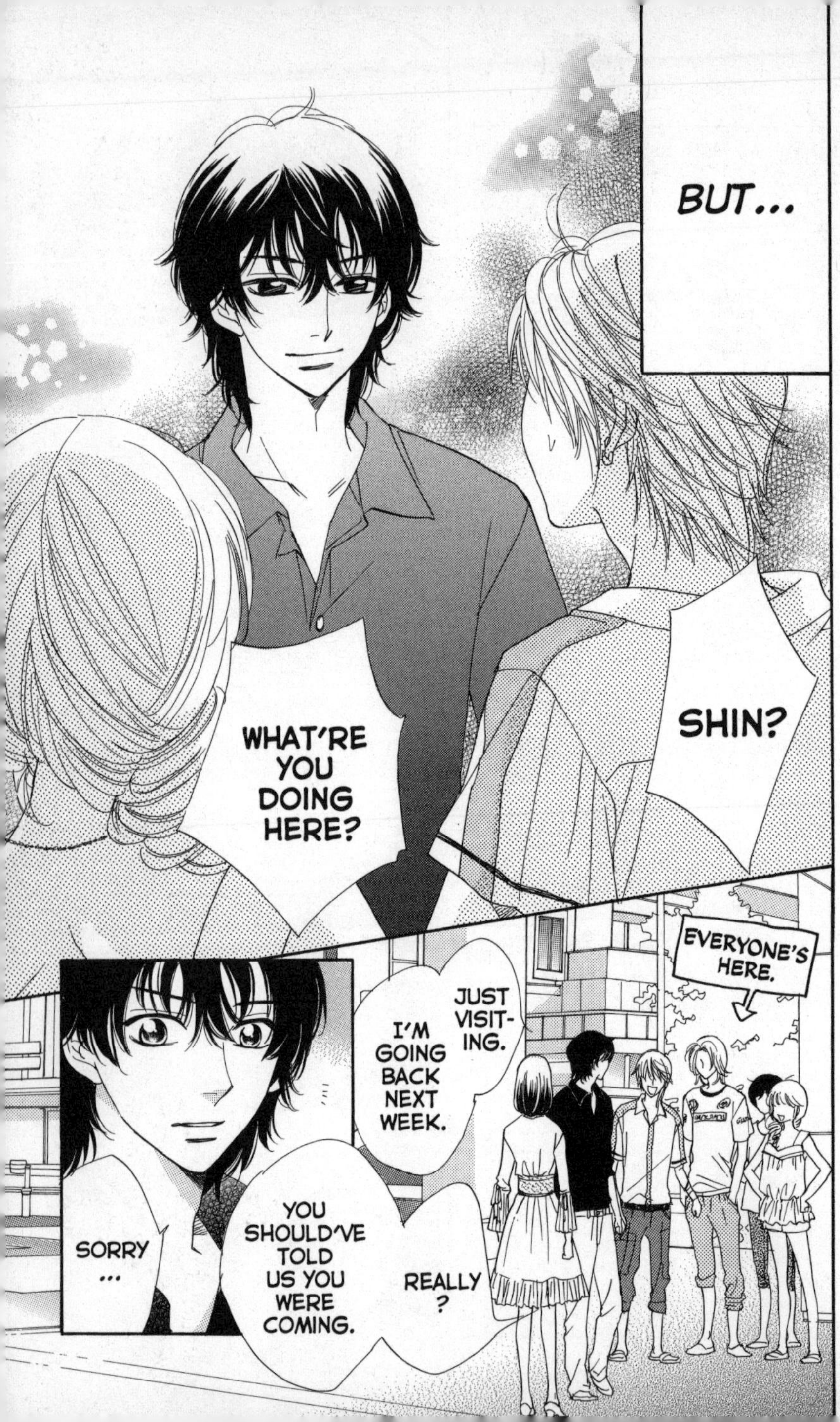
BUT...
SHIN?
WHAT'RE YOU DOING HERE?
EVERYONE'S HERE.
JUST VISITING.
I'M GOING BACK NEXT WEEK.
REALLY?
YOU SHOULD'VE TOLD US YOU WERE COMING.
SORRY...

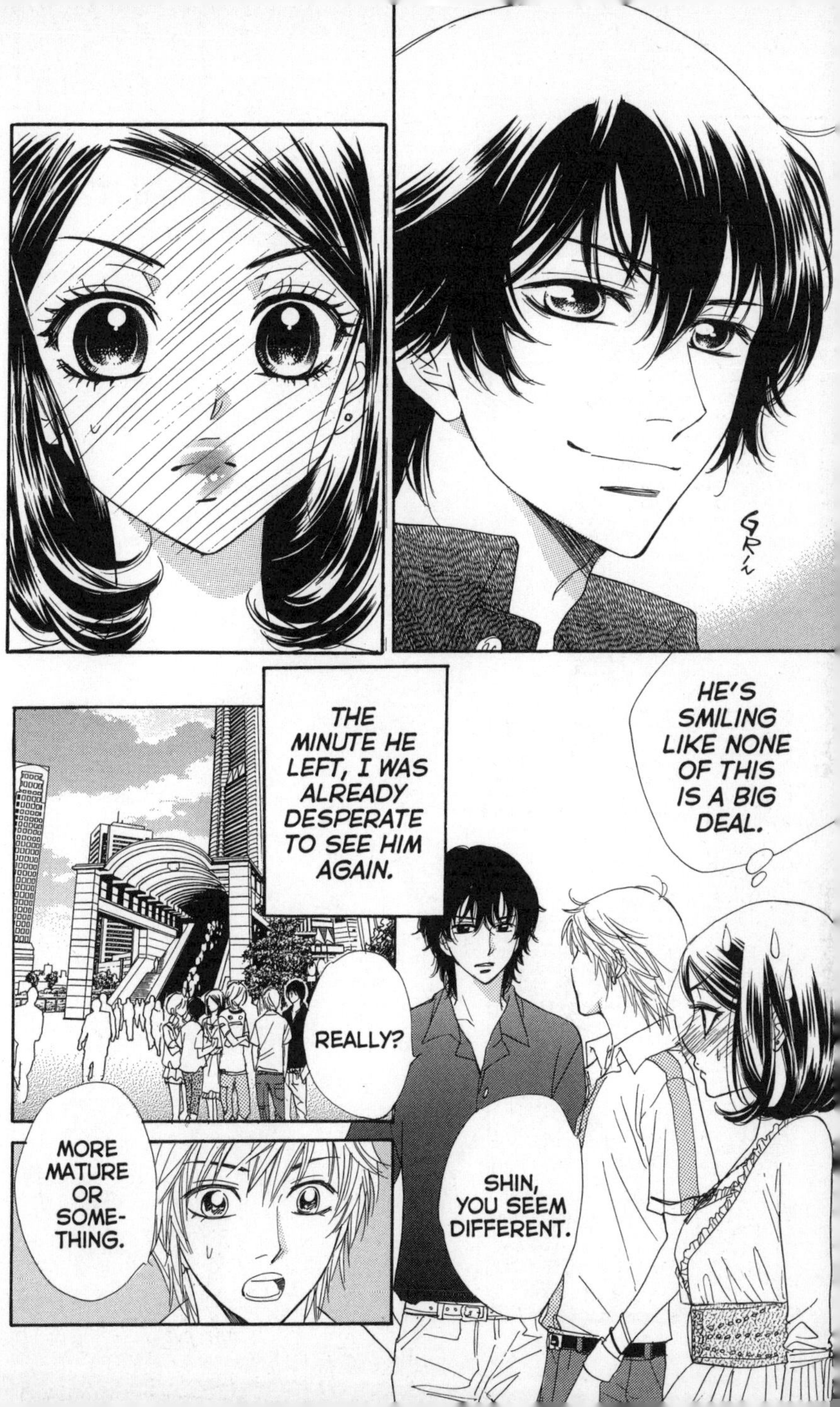
GRIN
HE'S SMILING LIKE NONE OF THIS IS A BIG DEAL.
THE MINUTE HE LEFT, I WAS ALREADY DESPERATE TO SEE HIM AGAIN.
SHIN, YOU SEEM DIFFERENT.
MORE MATURE OR SOME-THING.
REALLY?

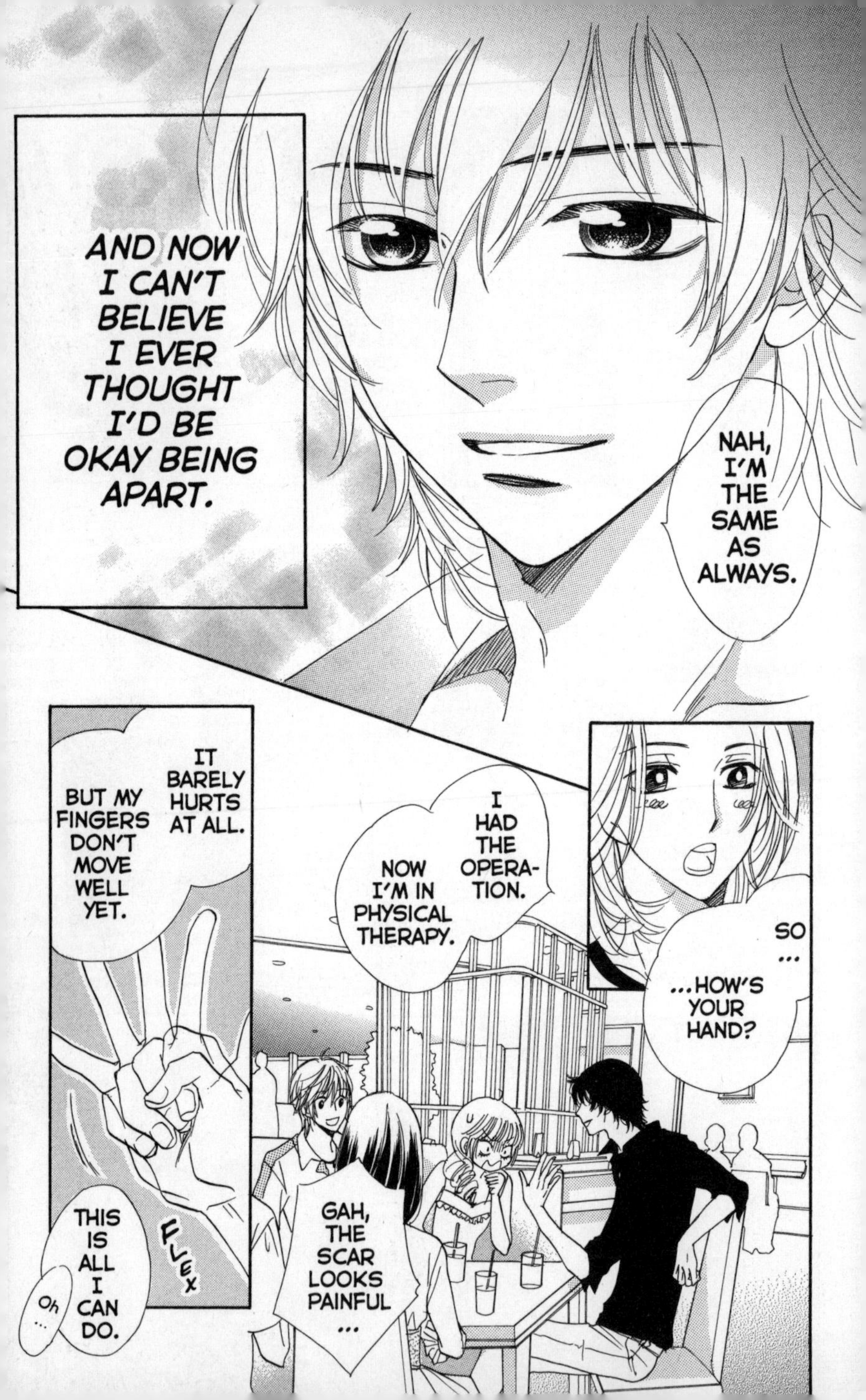
NAH, I'M THE SAME AS ALWAYS.
AND NOW I CAN'T BELIEVE I EVER THOUGHT I'D BE OKAY BEING APART.
SO ...
...HOW'S YOUR HAND?
I HAD THE OPERATION.
NOW I'M IN PHYSICAL THERAPY.
GAH, THE SCAR LOOKS PAINFUL ...
IT BARELY HURTS AT ALL.
BUT MY FINGERS DON'T MOVE WELL YET.
FLEX
THIS IS ALL I CAN DO.
Oh ...

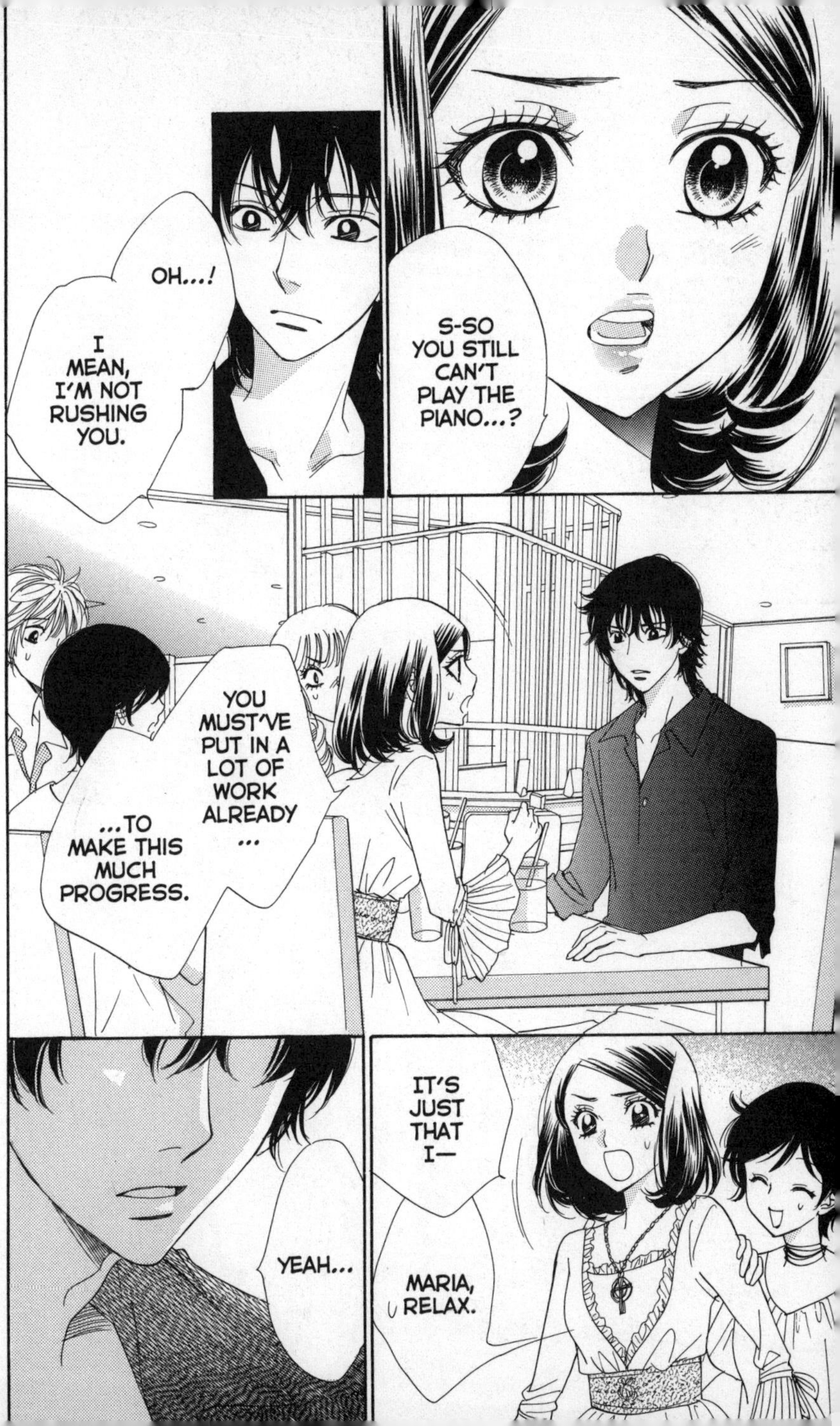
S-SO YOU STILL CAN'T PLAY THE PIANO...?
OH...!
I MEAN, I'M NOT RUSHING YOU.
YOU MUST'VE PUT IN A LOT OF WORK ALREADY...
...TO MAKE THIS MUCH PROGRESS.
IT'S JUST THAT I—
MARIA, RELAX.
YEAH...

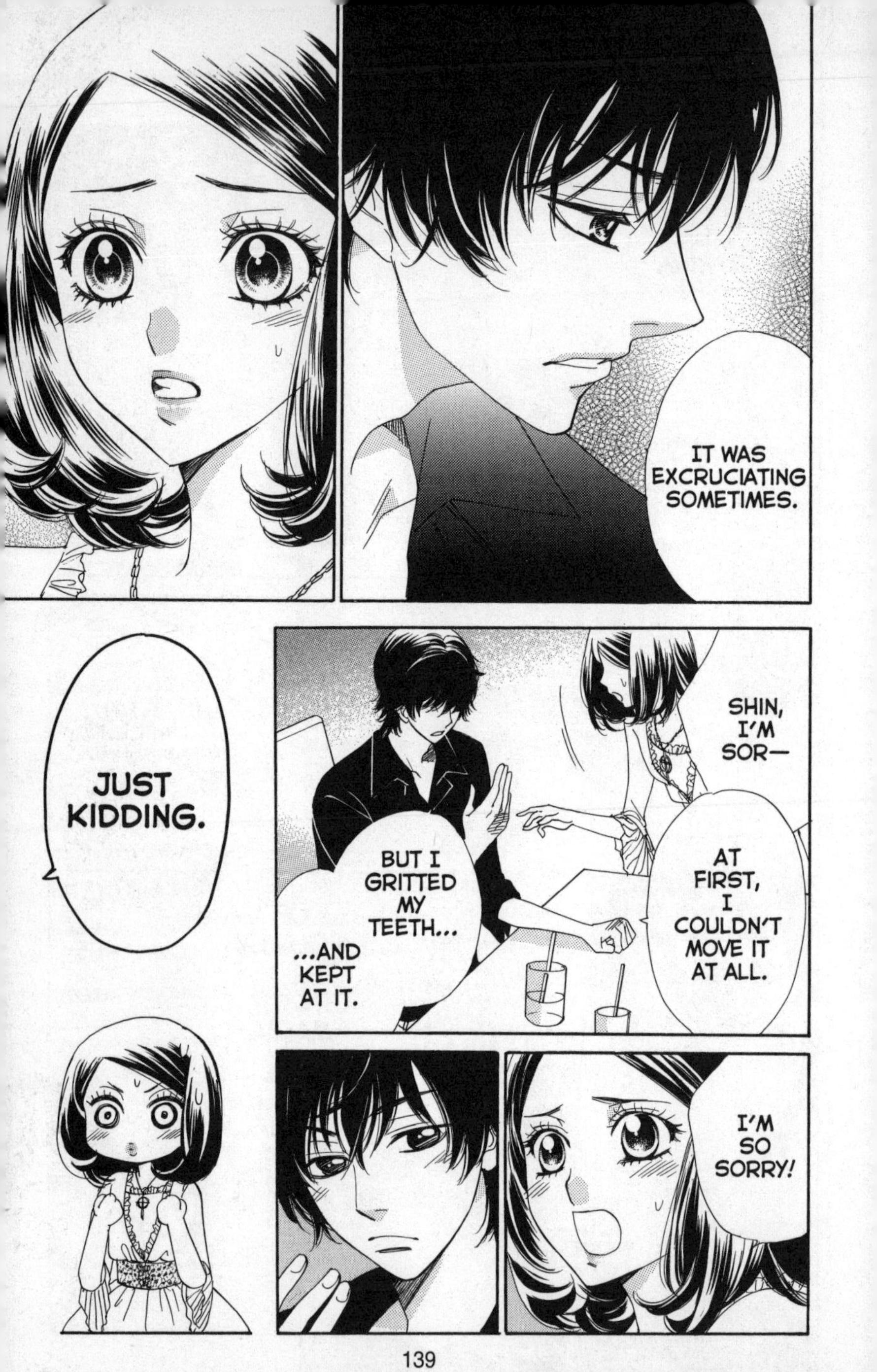
IT WAS EXCRUCIATING SOMETIMES.
SHIN, I'M SOR—
AT FIRST, I COULDN'T MOVE IT AT ALL.
BUT I GRITTED MY TEETH...
...AND KEPT AT IT.
I'M SO SORRY!
JUST KIDDING.

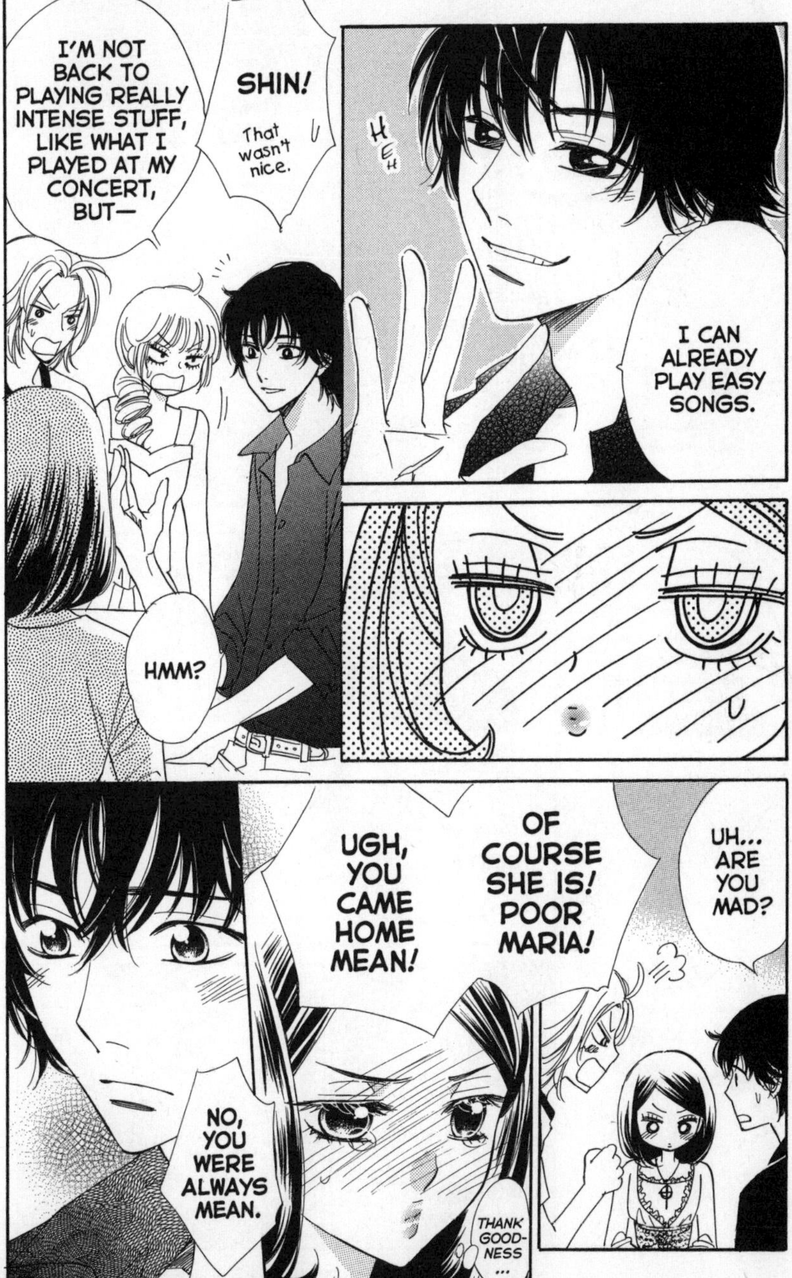
HEH
I CAN ALREADY PLAY EASY SONGS.
SHIN!
That wasn't nice.
I'M NOT BACK TO PLAYING REALLY INTENSE STUFF, LIKE WHAT I PLAYED AT MY CONCERT, BUT—
HMM?
UH... ARE YOU MAD?
OF COURSE SHE IS! POOR MARIA!
UGH, YOU CAME HOME MEAN!
NO, YOU WERE ALWAYS MEAN.
THANK GOOD-NESS ...

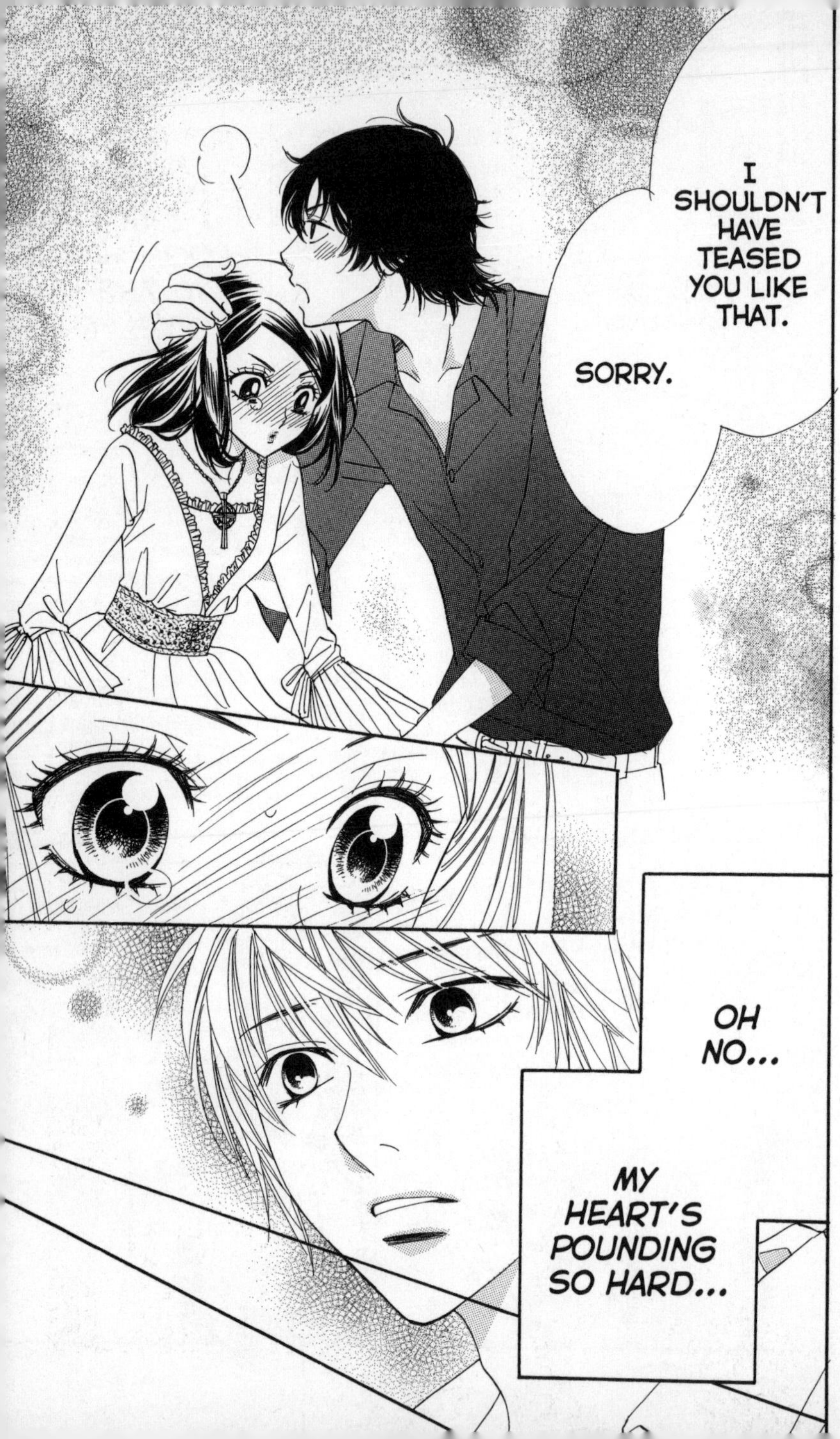
I SHOULDN'T HAVE TEASED YOU LIKE THAT.
SORRY.
OH NO...
MY HEART'S POUNDING SO HARD...

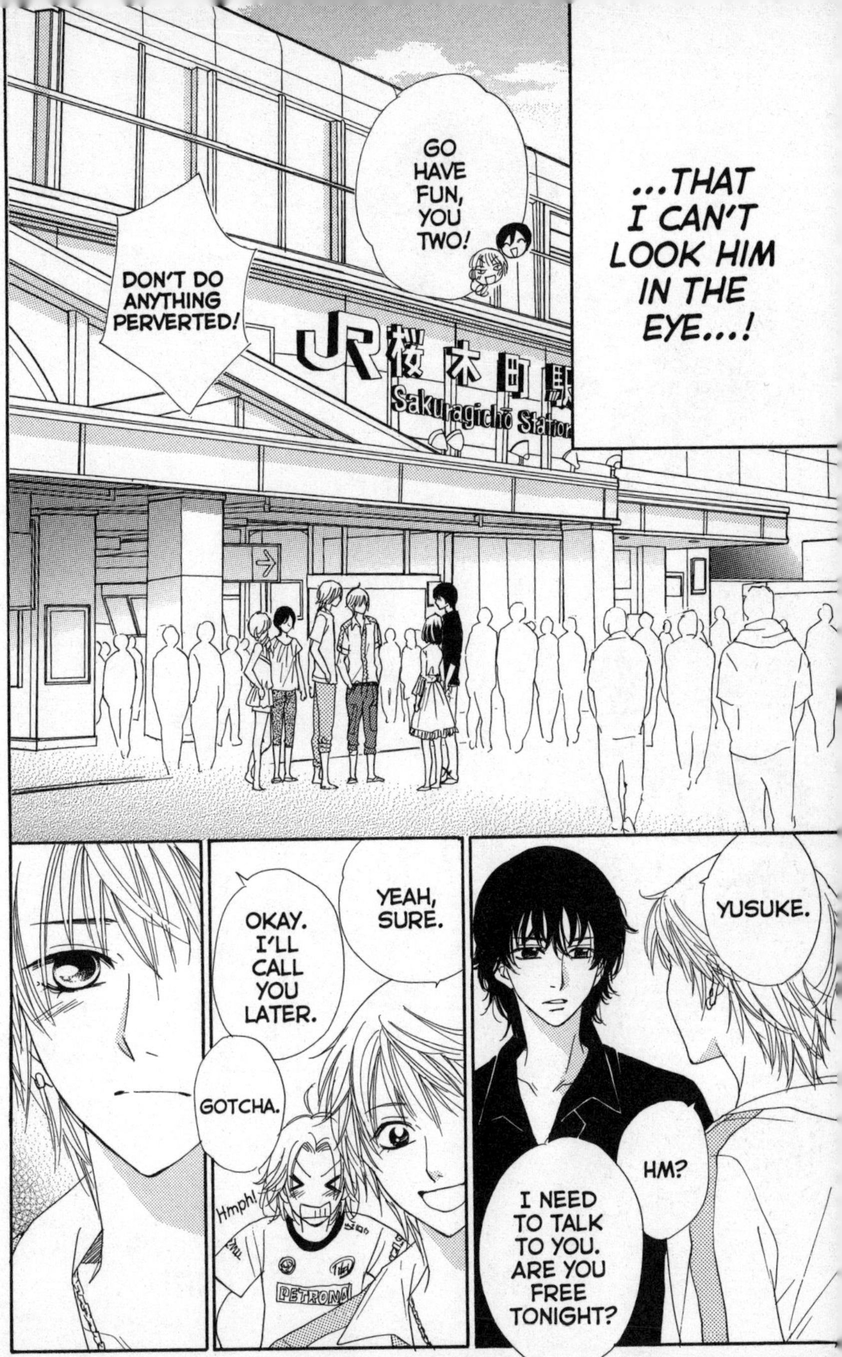
...THAT I CAN'T LOOK HIM IN THE EYE...!
GO HAVE FUN, YOU TWO!
DON'T DO ANYTHING PERVERTED!
YUSUKE.
HM?
I NEED TO TALK TO YOU. ARE YOU FREE TONIGHT?
YEAH, SURE.
OKAY. I'LL CALL YOU LATER.
GOTCHA.
Hmph!

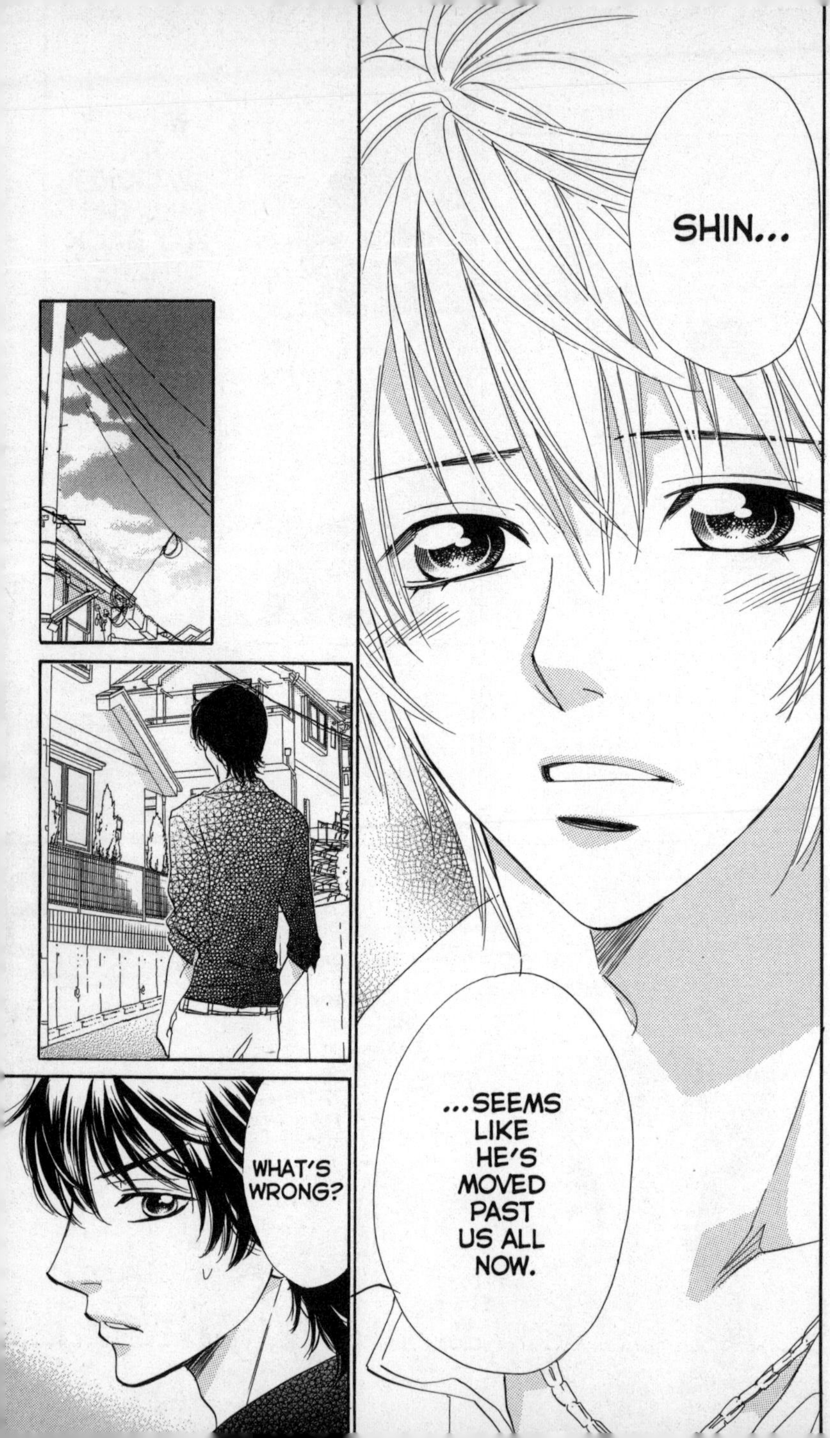
SHIN...
...SEEMS LIKE HE'S MOVED PAST US ALL NOW.
WHAT'S WRONG?

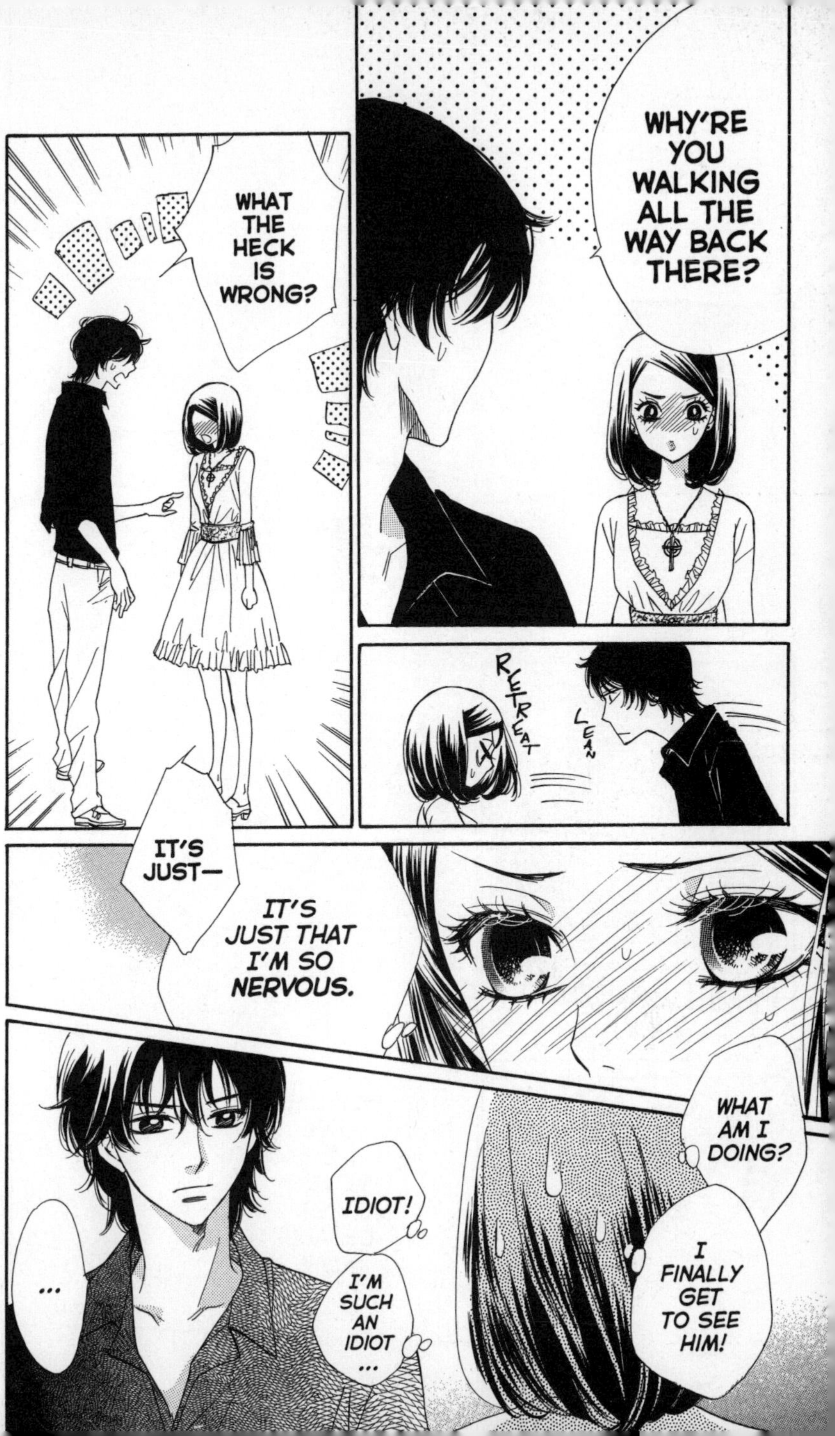
WHY'RE YOU WALKING ALL THE WAY BACK THERE?
RETREAT
LEAN
WHAT THE HECK IS WRONG?
IT'S JUST—
IT'S JUST THAT I'M SO NERVOUS.
WHAT AM I DOING?
I FINALLY GET TO SEE HIM!
IDIOT!
I'M SUCH AN IDIOT...
...

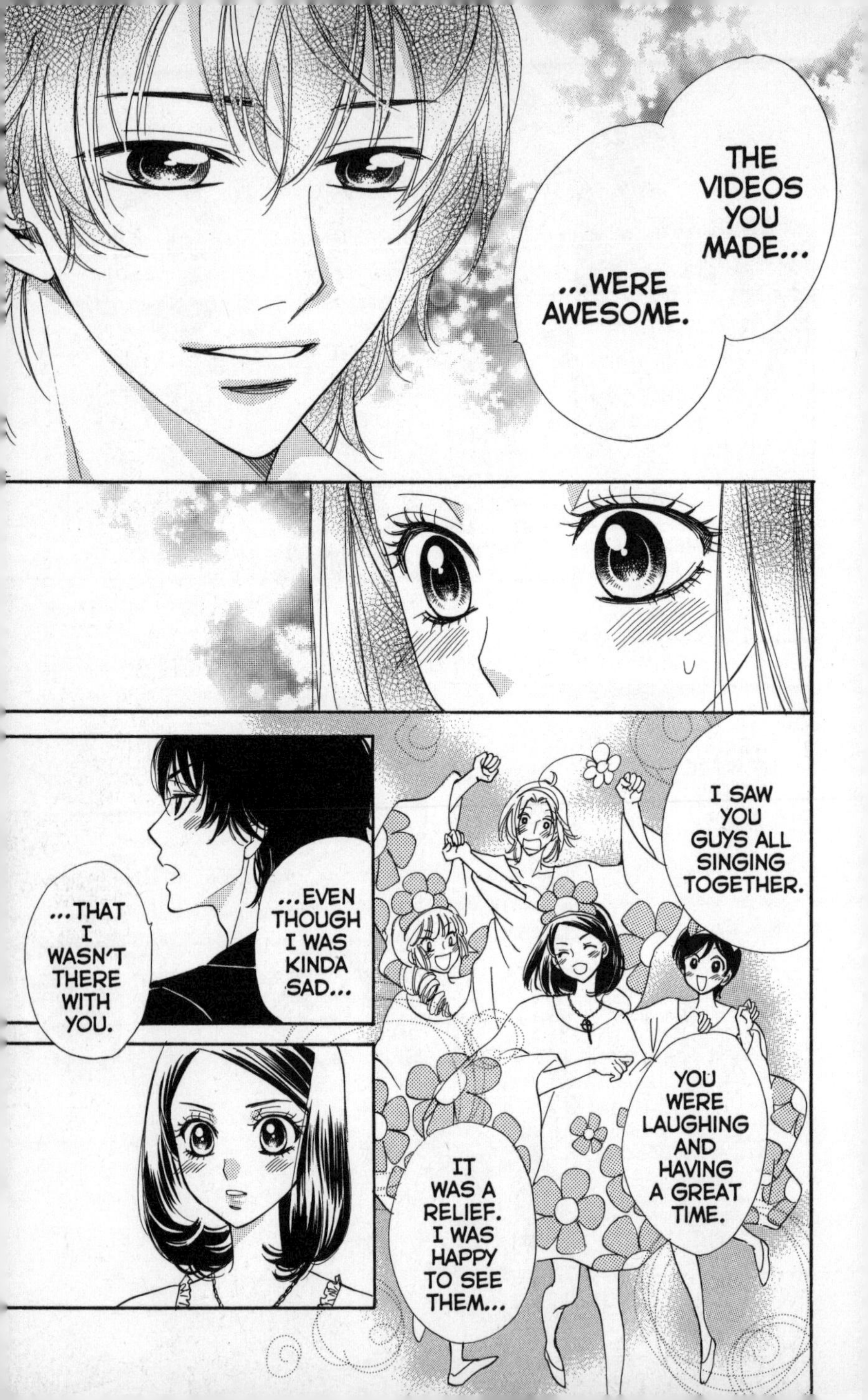
THE VIDEOS YOU MADE...
...WERE AWESOME.
I SAW YOU GUYS ALL SINGING TOGETHER.
YOU WERE LAUGHING AND HAVING A GREAT TIME.
IT WAS A RELIEF. I WAS HAPPY TO SEE THEM...
...EVEN THOUGH I WAS KINDA SAD...
...THAT I WASN'T THERE WITH YOU.

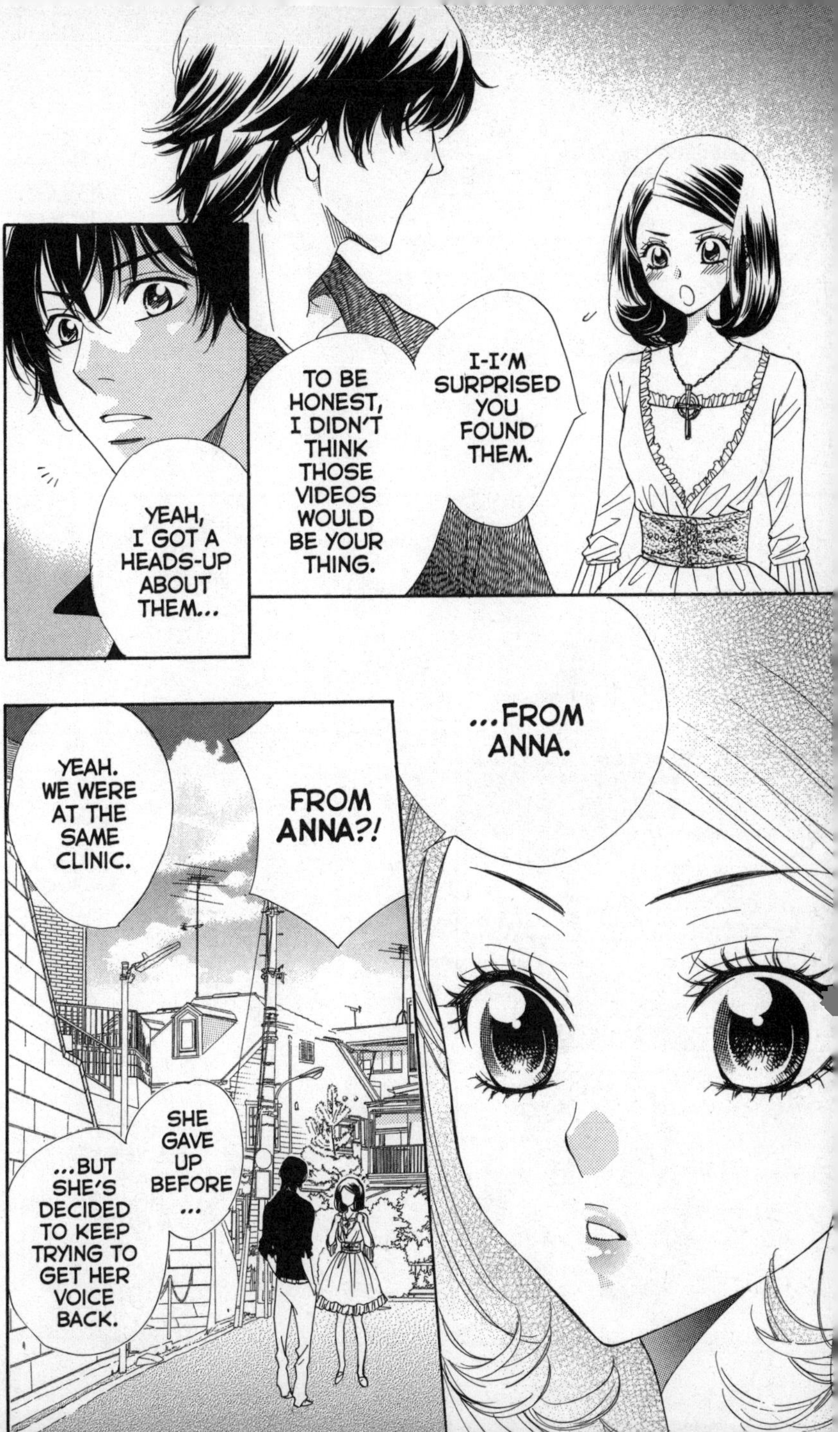
I-I'M SURPRISED YOU FOUND THEM.
TO BE HONEST, I DIDN'T THINK THOSE VIDEOS WOULD BE YOUR THING.
YEAH, I GOT A HEADS-UP ABOUT THEM...
...FROM ANNA.
FROM ANNA?!
YEAH. WE WERE AT THE SAME CLINIC.
SHE GAVE UP BEFORE...
...BUT SHE'S DECIDED TO KEEP TRYING TO GET HER VOICE BACK.

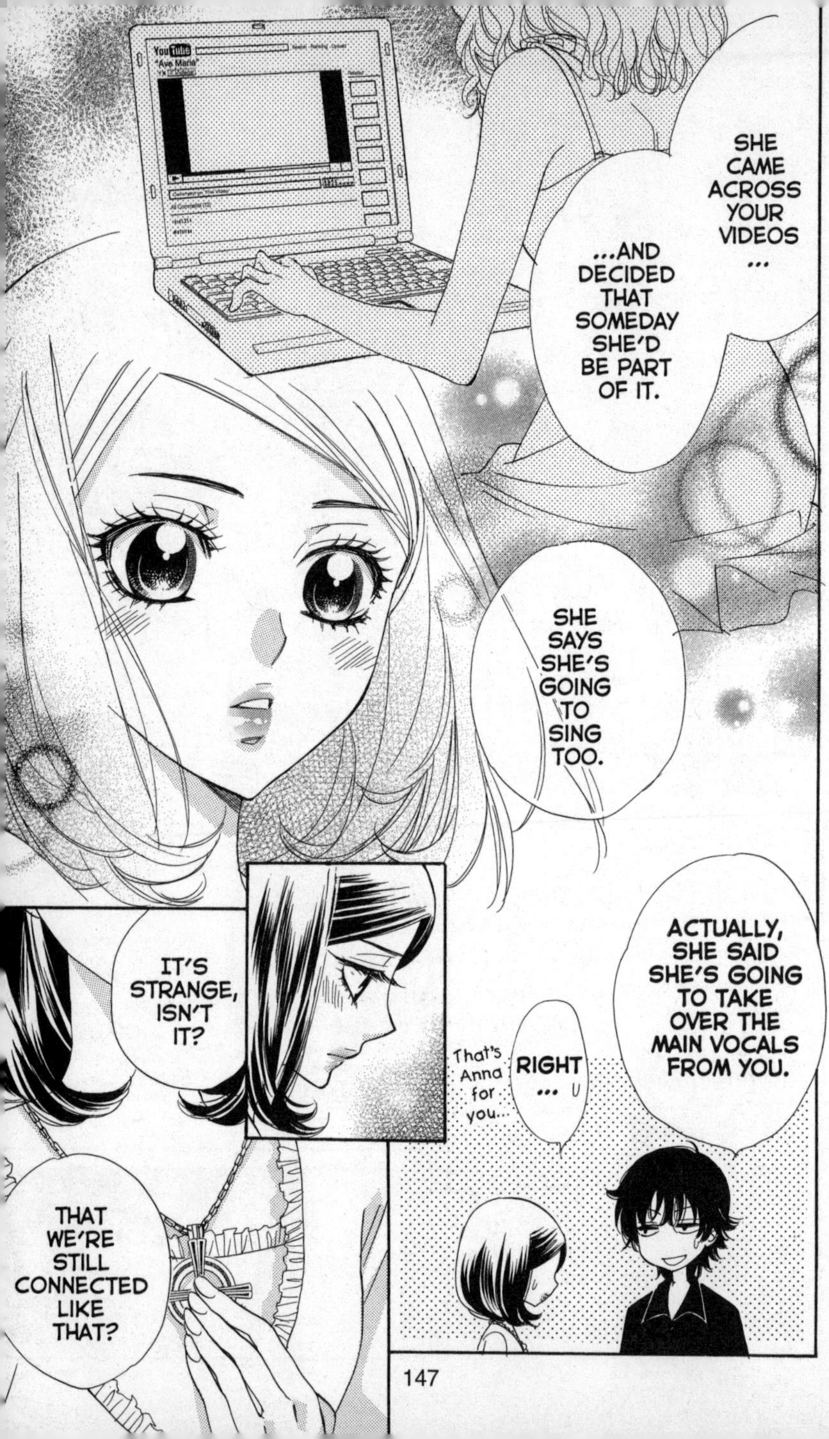
YouTube
"Ave Maria"
SHE CAME ACROSS YOUR VIDEOS...
...AND DECIDED THAT SOMEDAY SHE'D BE PART OF IT.
SHE SAYS SHE'S GOING TO SING TOO.
ACTUALLY, SHE SAID SHE'S GOING TO TAKE OVER THE MAIN VOCALS FROM YOU.
RIGHT...
That's Anna for you...
IT'S STRANGE, ISN'T IT?
THAT WE'RE STILL CONNECTED LIKE THAT?

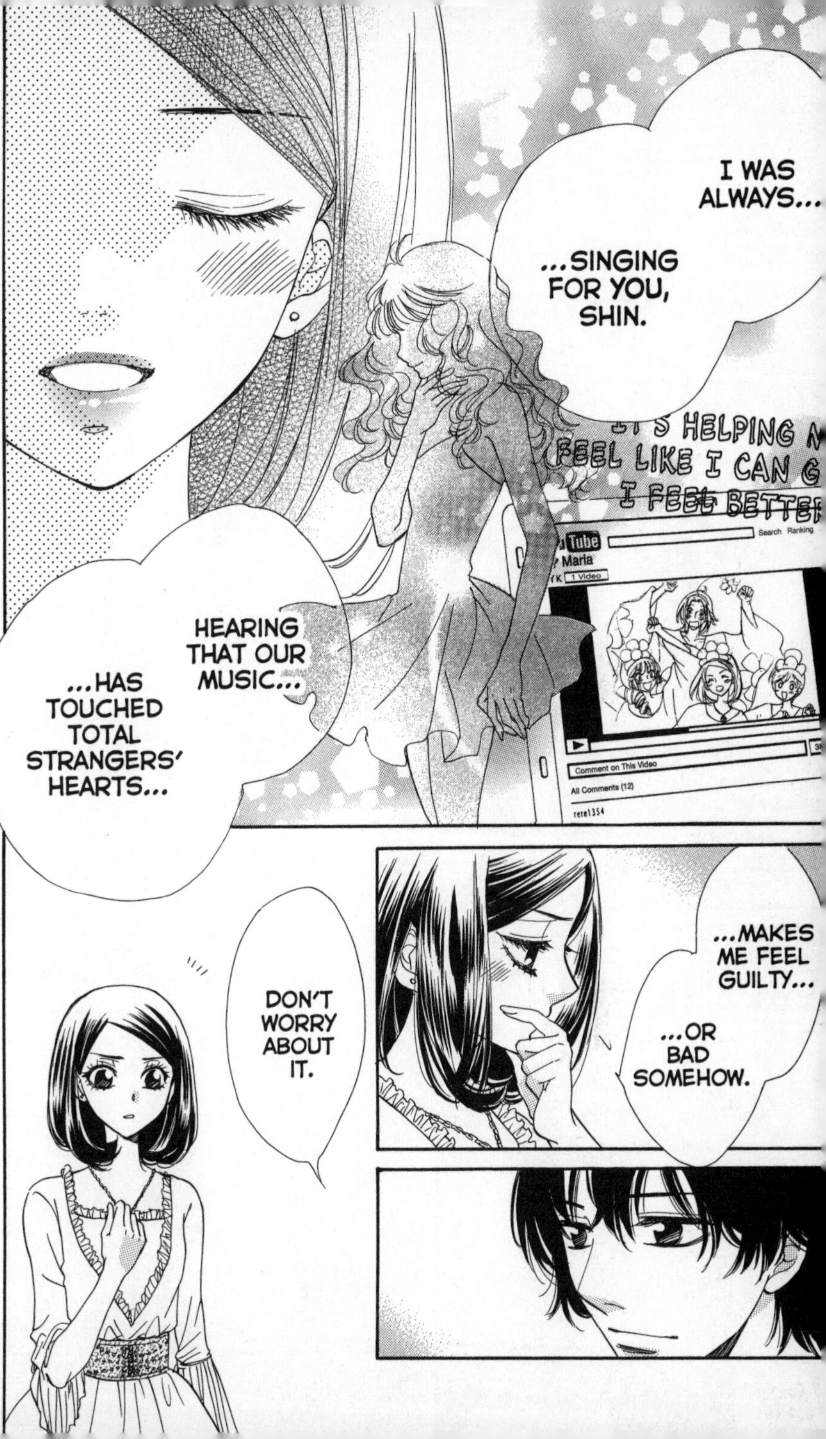
I WAS ALWAYS...
...SINGING FOR YOU, SHIN.
FEEL LIKE I CAN
Search Ranking
Maria
1 Video
Comment on This Video
All Comments (12)
rere1354
HEARING THAT OUR MUSIC...
...HAS TOUCHED TOTAL STRANGERS' HEARTS...
...MAKES ME FEEL GUILTY...
...OR BAD SOMEHOW.
DON'T WORRY ABOUT IT.

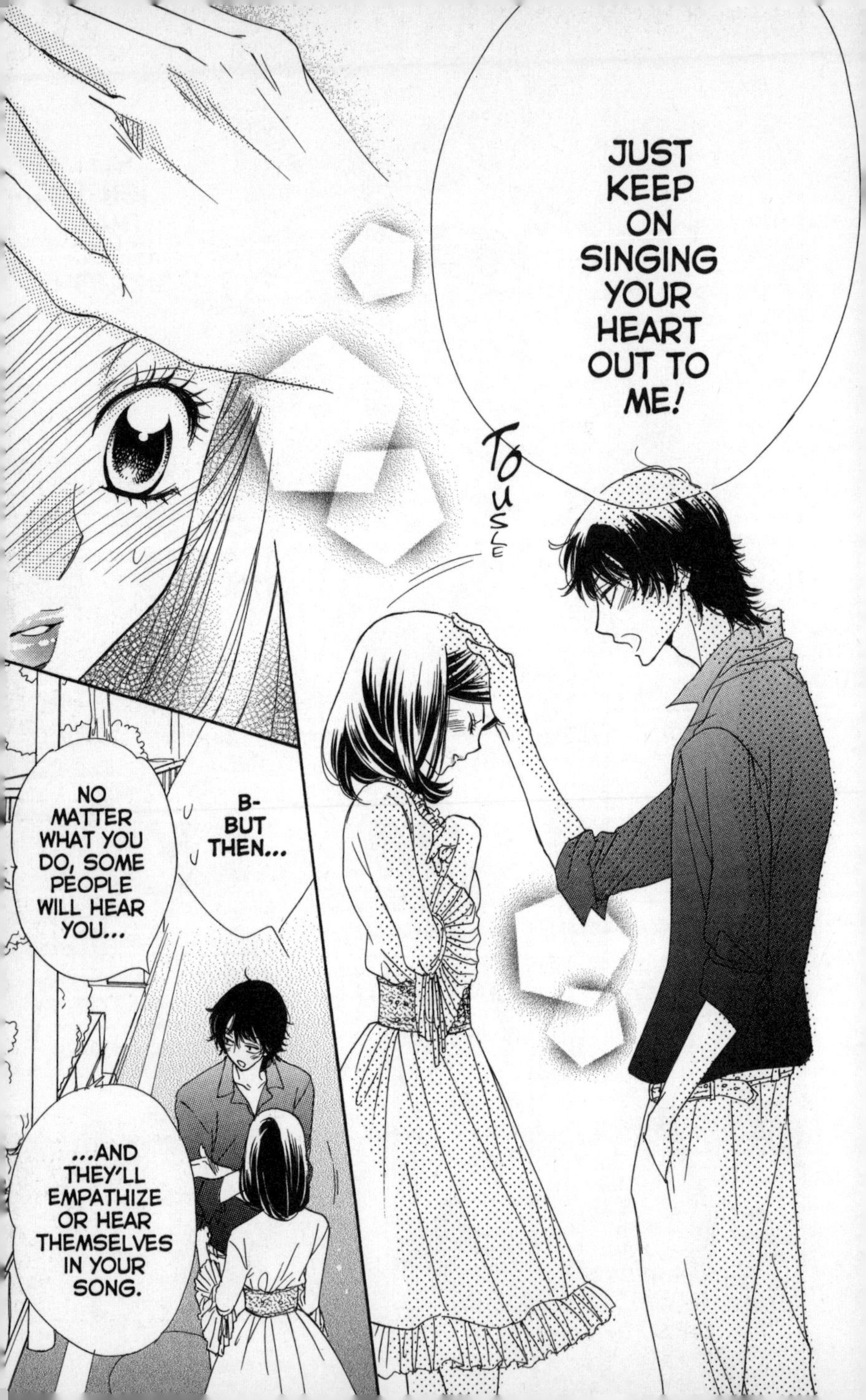
JUST KEEP ON SINGING YOUR HEART OUT TO ME!
TOUSLE
B-BUT THEN...
NO MATTER WHAT YOU DO, SOME PEOPLE WILL HEAR YOU...
...AND THEY'LL EMPATHIZE OR HEAR THEMSELVES IN YOUR SONG.

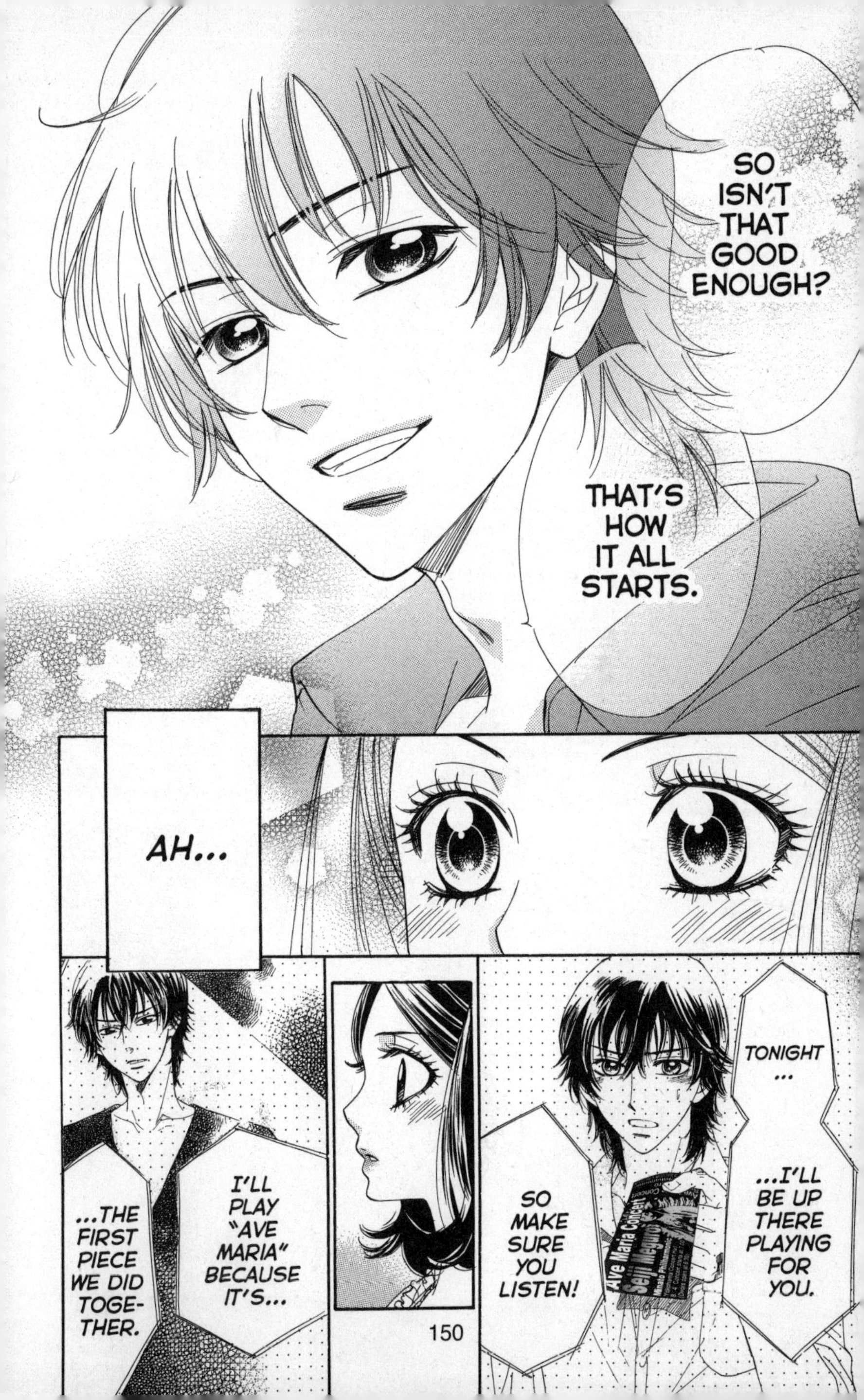
SO ISN'T THAT GOOD ENOUGH?
THAT'S HOW IT ALL STARTS.
AH...
TONIGHT...
...I'LL BE UP THERE PLAYING FOR YOU.
SO MAKE SURE YOU LISTEN!
Ave Maria Concert
Seiji Meguro
I'LL PLAY "AVE MARIA" BECAUSE IT'S...
...THE FIRST PIECE WE DID TOGE-THER.

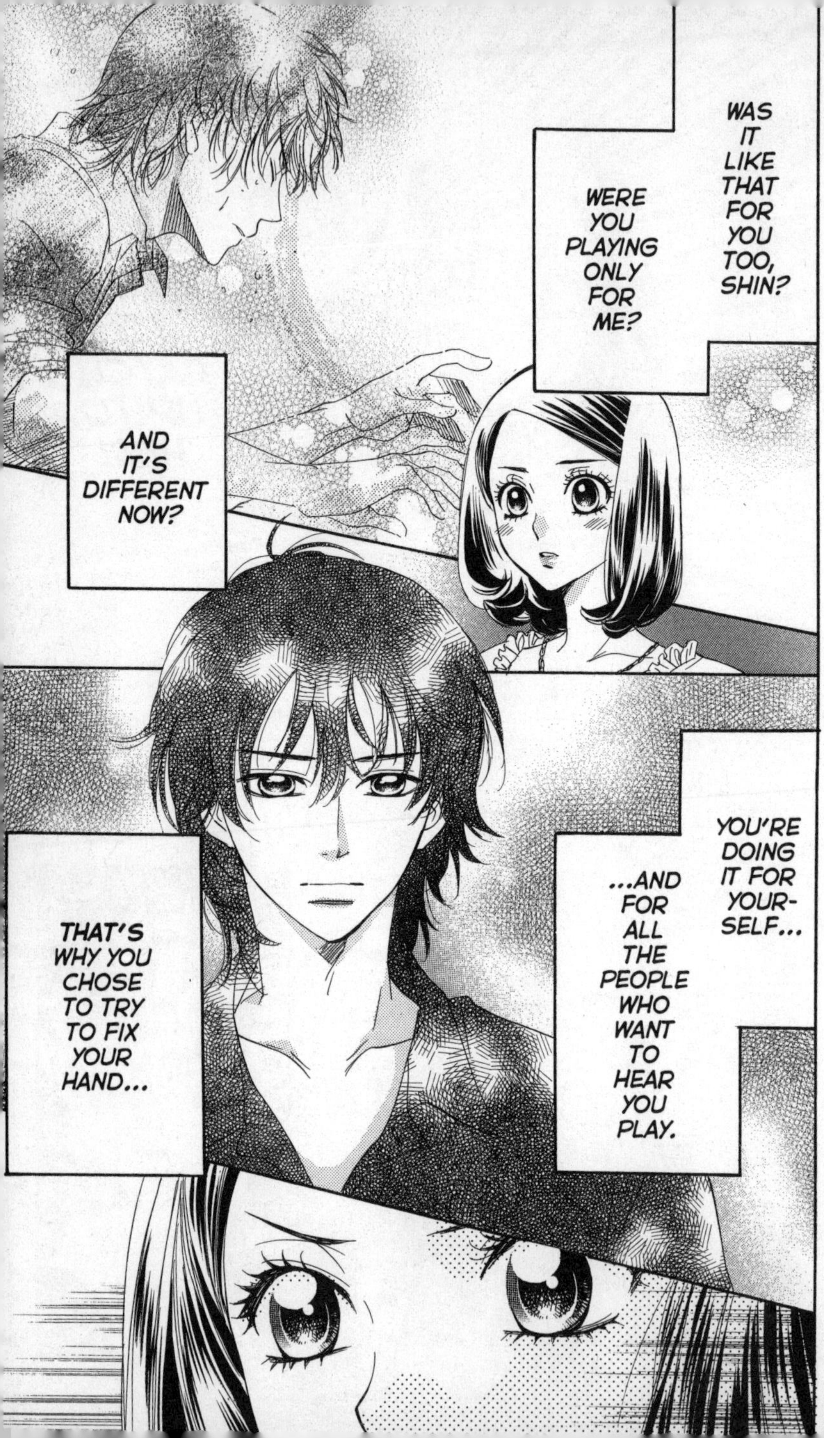
WAS IT LIKE THAT FOR YOU TOO, SHIN?
WERE YOU PLAYING ONLY FOR ME?
AND IT'S DIFFERENT NOW?
YOU'RE DOING IT FOR YOUR-SELF...
...AND FOR ALL THE PEOPLE WHO WANT TO HEAR YOU PLAY.
THAT'S WHY YOU CHOSE TO TRY TO FIX YOUR HAND...

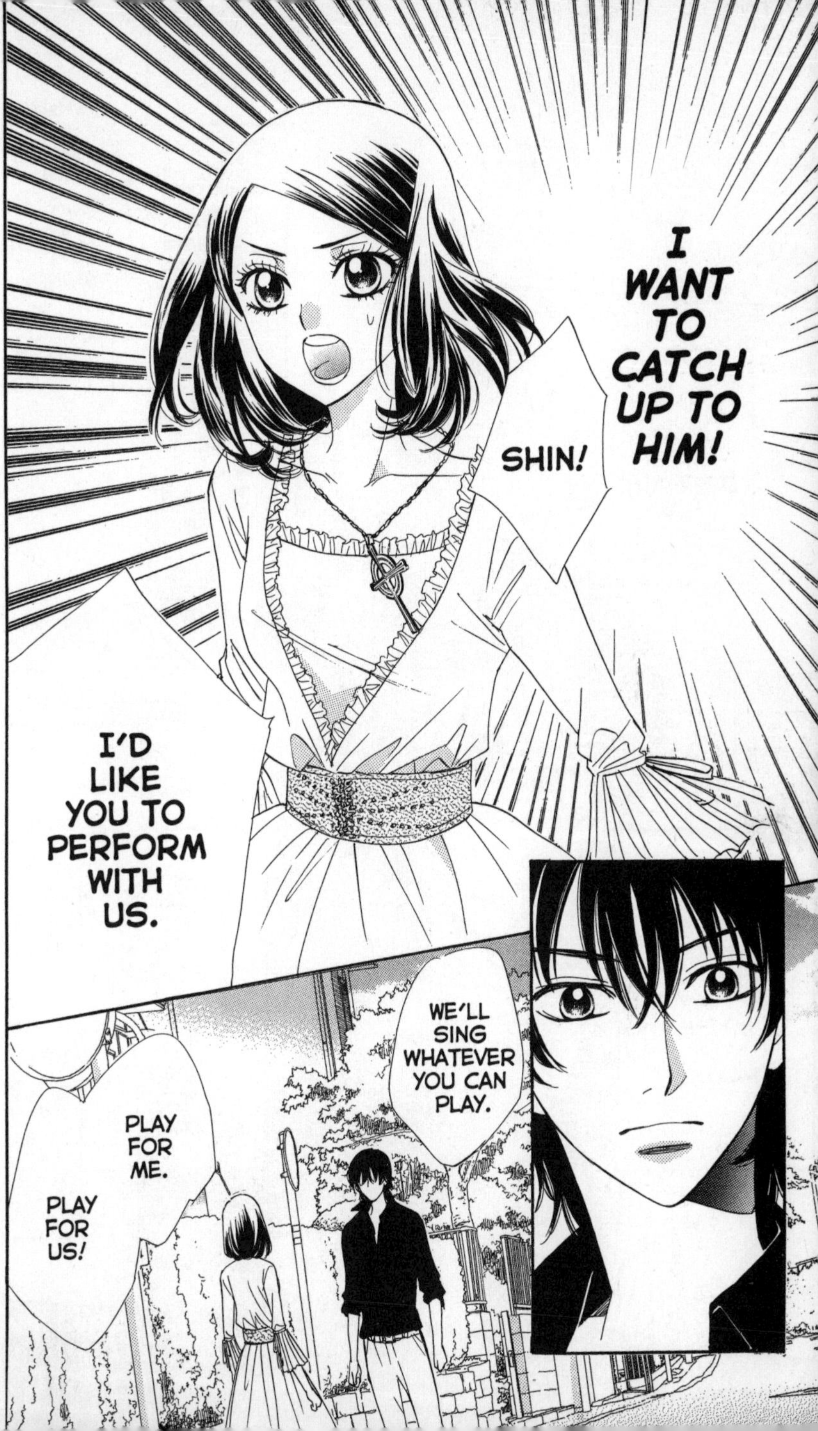
I WANT TO CATCH UP TO HIM!
SHIN!
I'D LIKE YOU TO PERFORM WITH US.
WE'LL SING WHATEVER YOU CAN PLAY.
PLAY FOR ME.
PLAY FOR US!

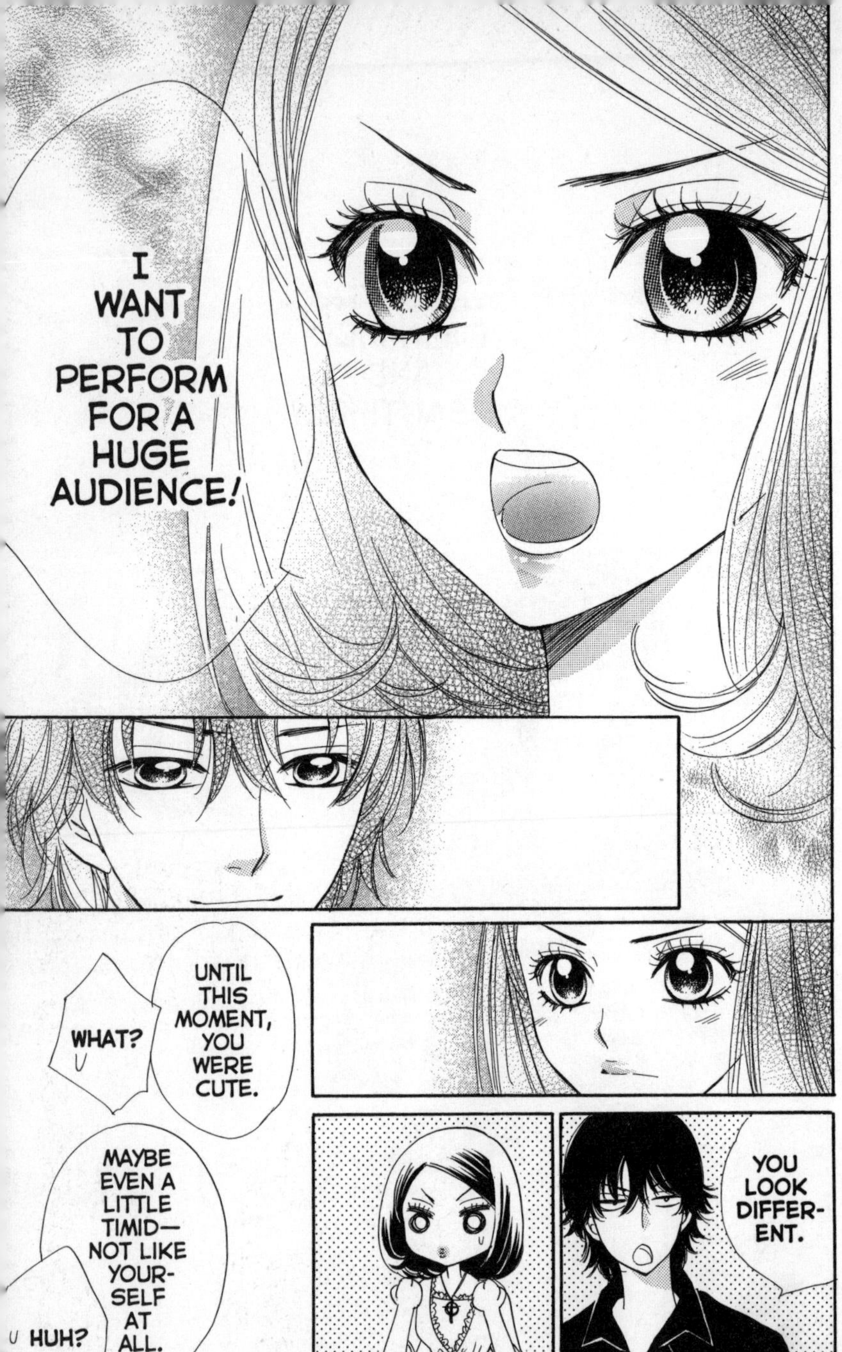
I WANT TO PERFORM FOR A HUGE AUDIENCE!
YOU LOOK DIFFER-ENT.
UNTIL THIS MOMENT, YOU WERE CUTE.
WHAT?
MAYBE EVEN A LITTLE TIMID— NOT LIKE YOUR-SELF AT ALL.
HUH?

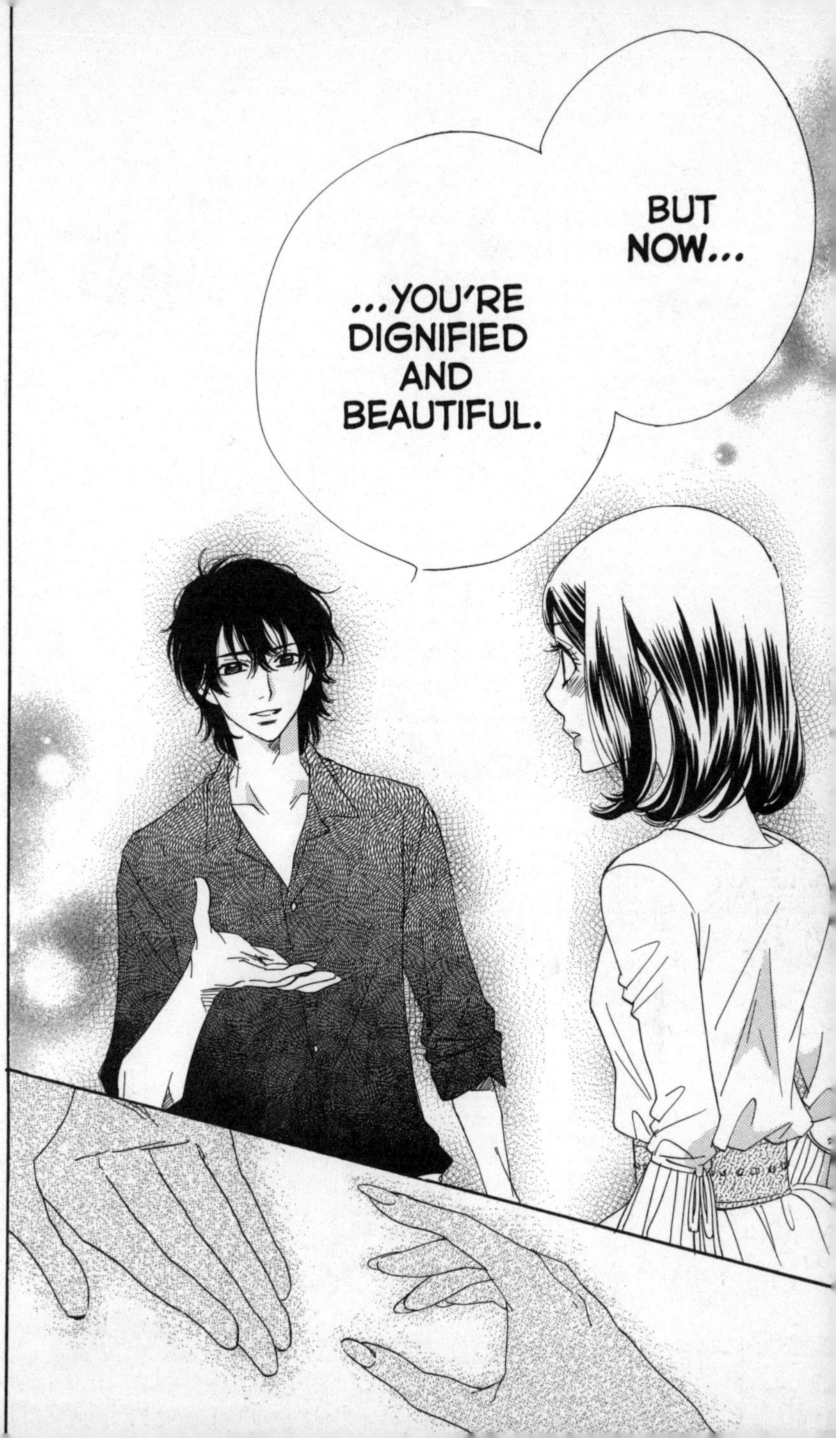
BUT NOW...
...YOU'RE DIGNIFIED AND BEAUTIFUL.

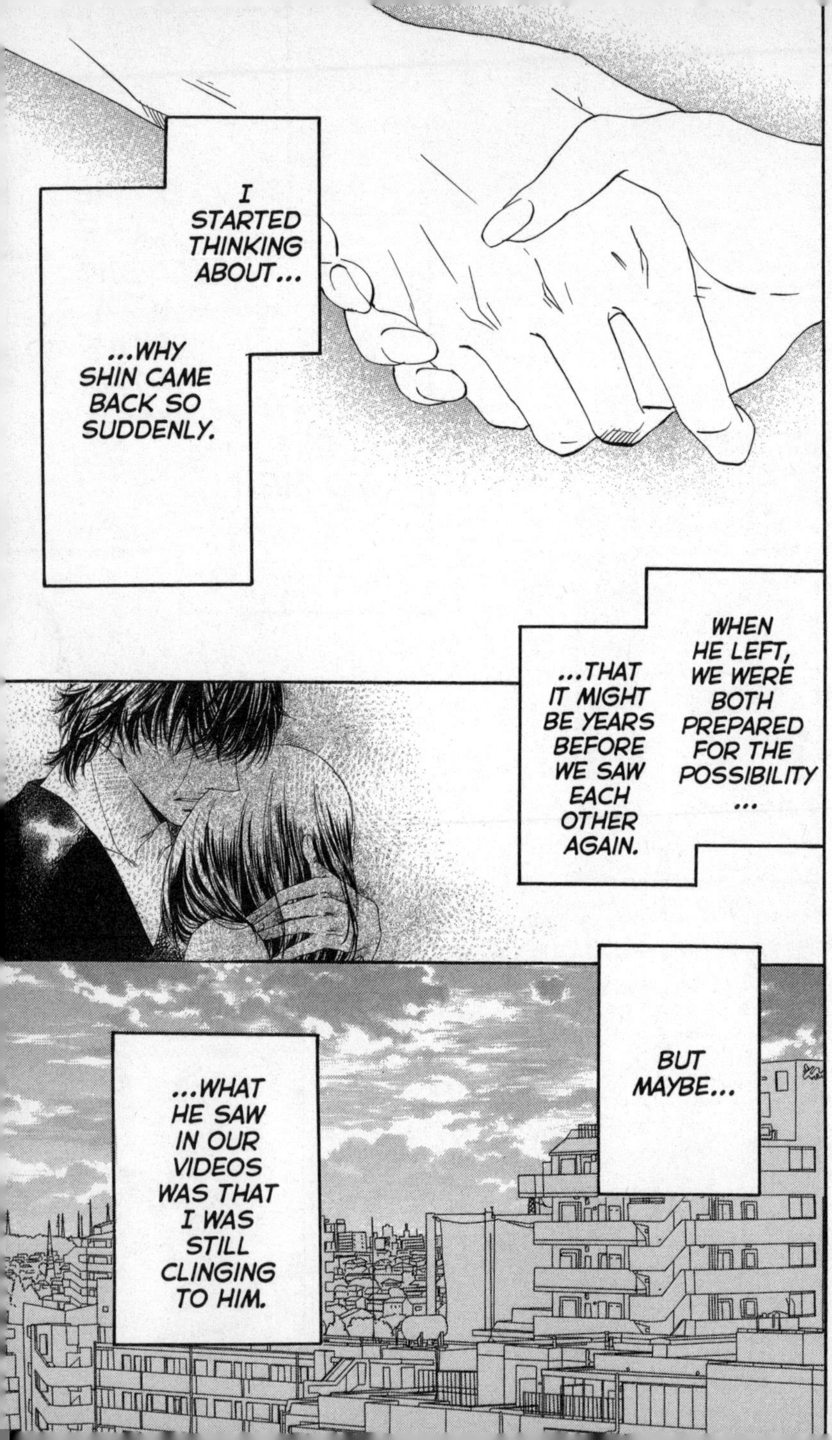
I STARTED THINKING ABOUT...
...WHY SHIN CAME BACK SO SUDDENLY.
WHEN HE LEFT, WE WERE BOTH PREPARED FOR THE POSSIBILITY...
...THAT IT MIGHT BE YEARS BEFORE WE SAW EACH OTHER AGAIN.
BUT MAYBE...
...WHAT HE SAW IN OUR VIDEOS WAS THAT I WAS STILL CLINGING TO HIM.

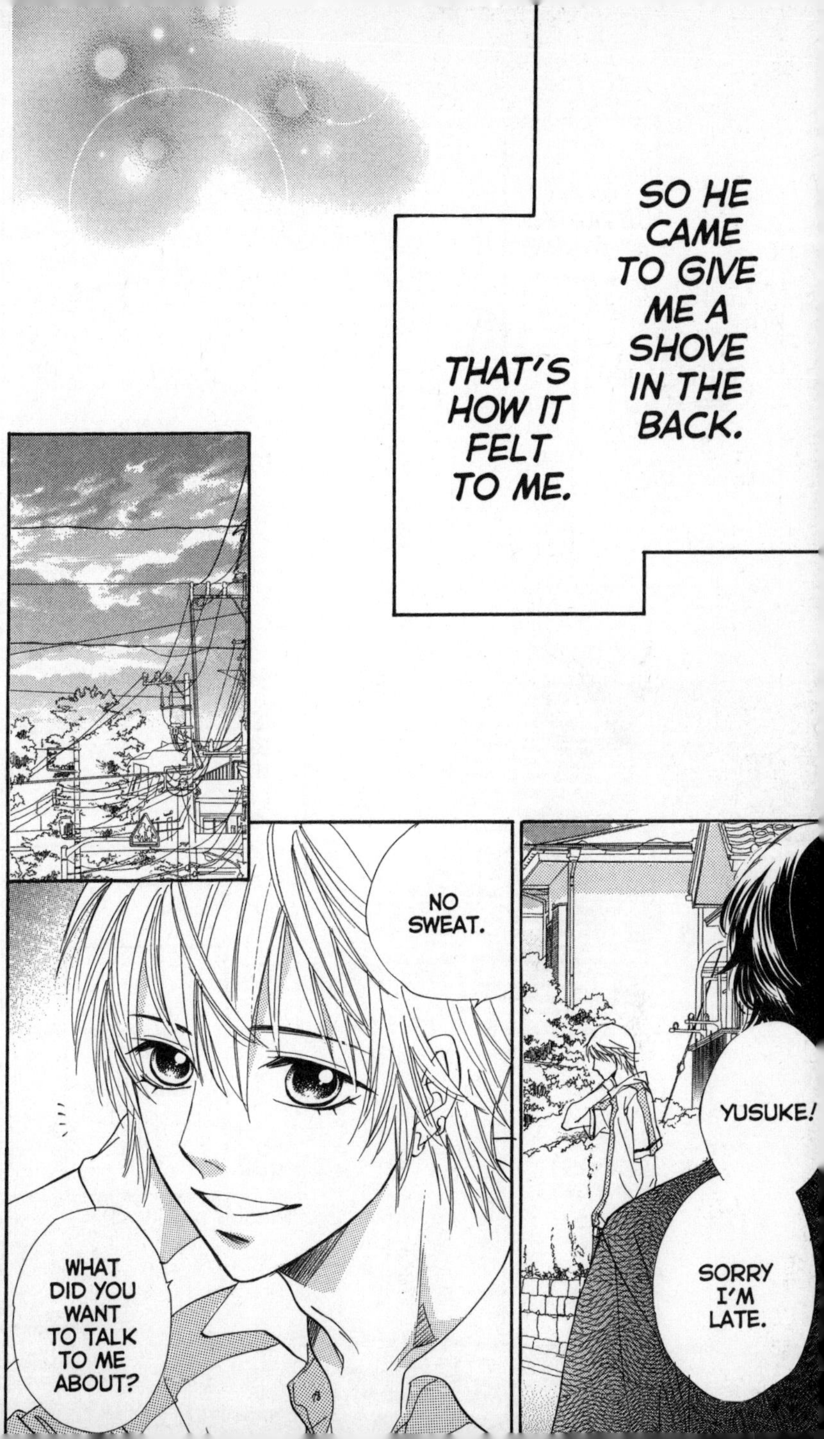
SO HE CAME TO GIVE ME A SHOVE IN THE BACK.
THAT'S HOW IT FELT TO ME.
YUSUKE!
SORRY I'M LATE.
NO SWEAT.
WHAT DID YOU WANT TO TALK TO ME ABOUT?

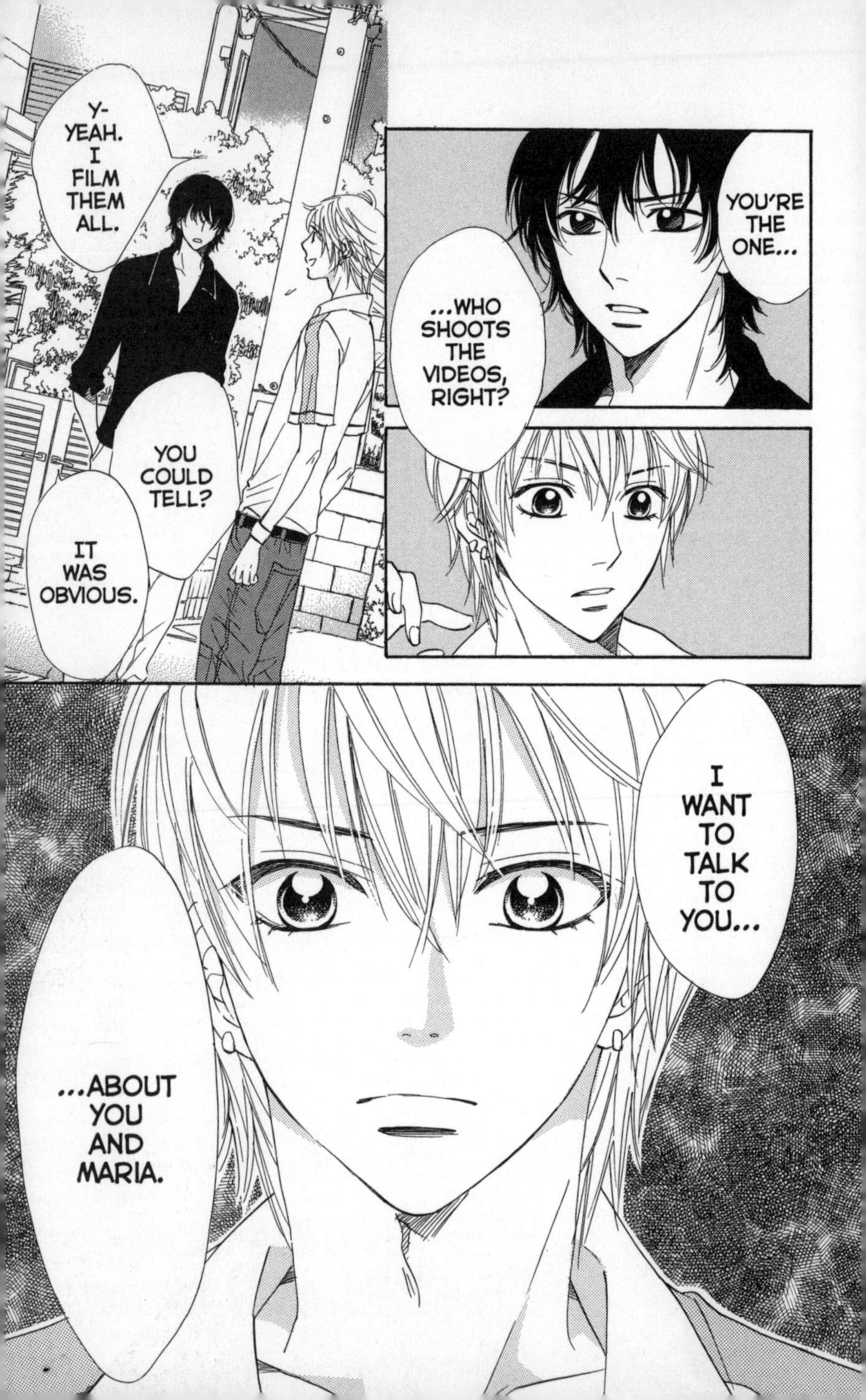
YOU'RE THE ONE...
...WHO SHOOTS THE VIDEOS, RIGHT?
Y-YEAH. I FILM THEM ALL.
YOU COULD TELL?
IT WAS OBVIOUS.
I WANT TO TALK TO YOU...
...ABOUT YOU AND MARIA.

A Devil and
Her Love Song

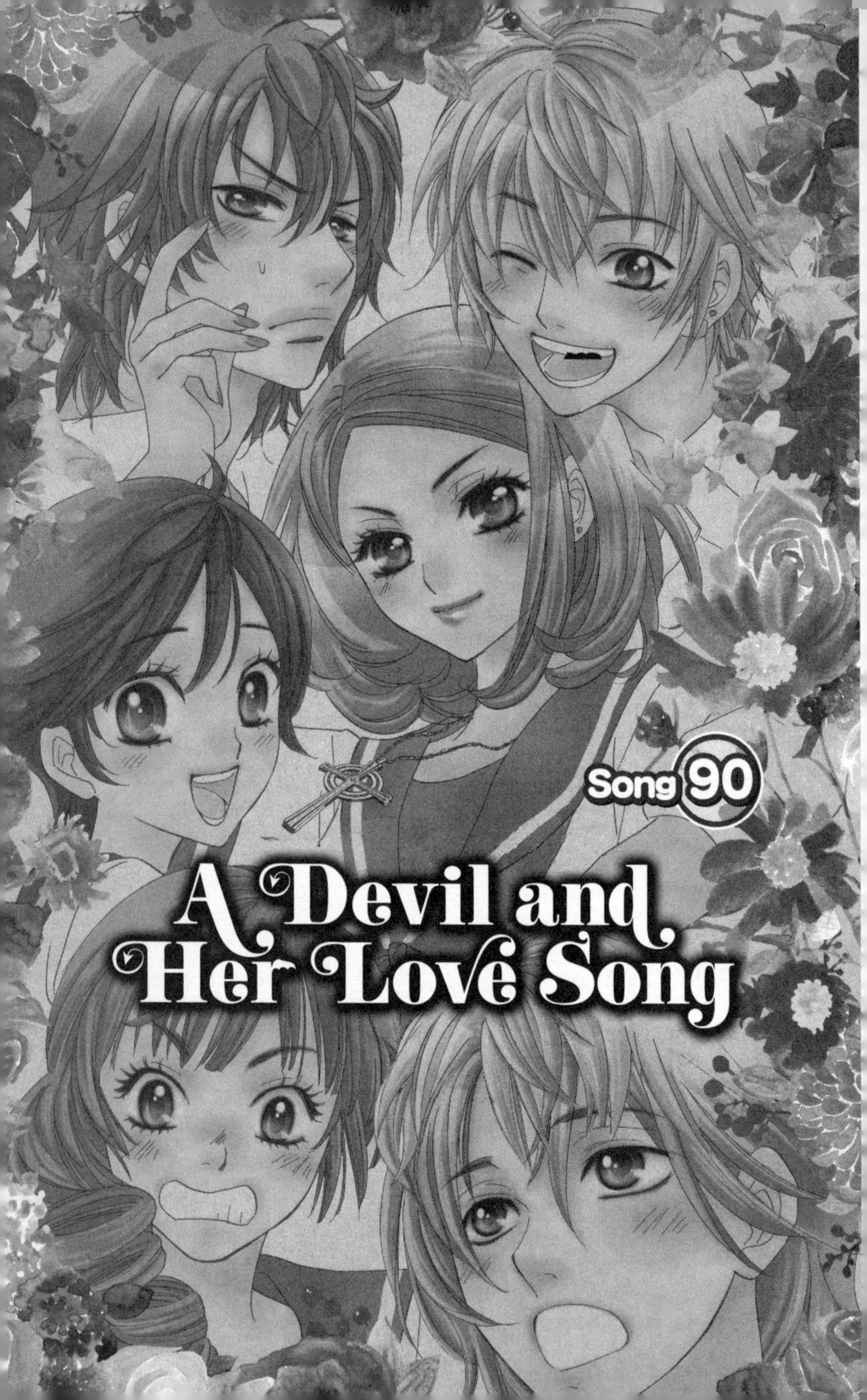
Song 90
A Devil and Her Love Song

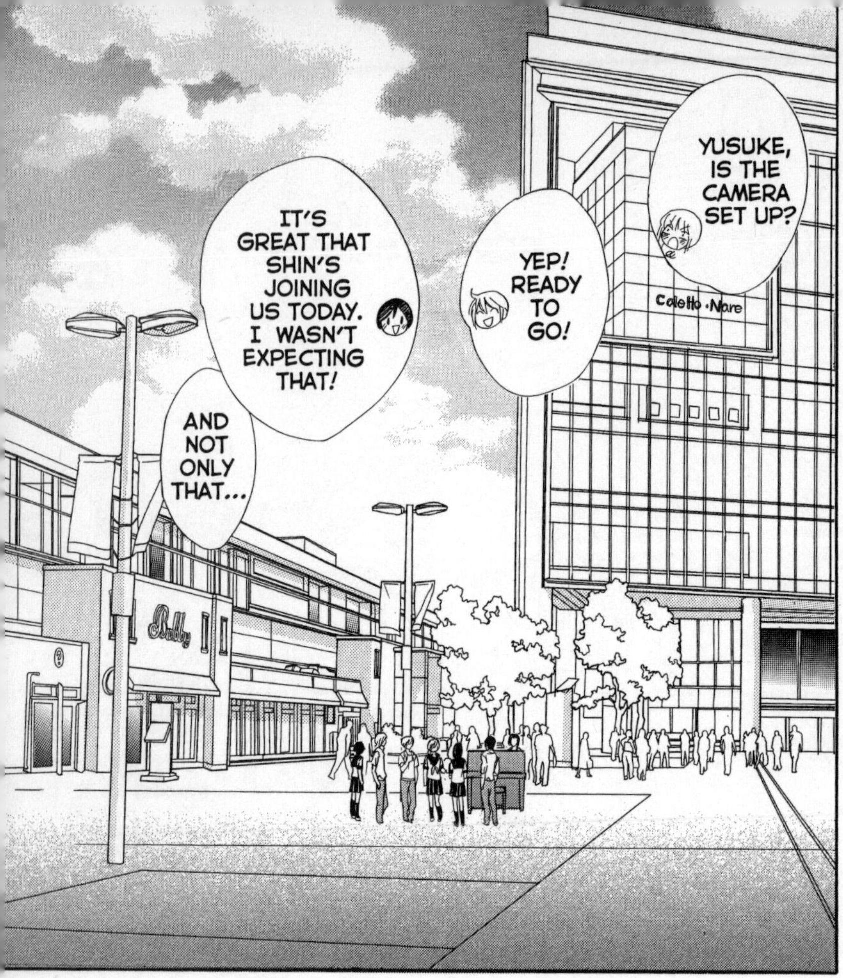
YUSUKE, IS THE CAMERA SET UP?
YEP! READY TO GO!
IT'S GREAT THAT SHIN'S JOINING US TODAY. I WASN'T EXPECTING THAT!
AND NOT ONLY THAT...

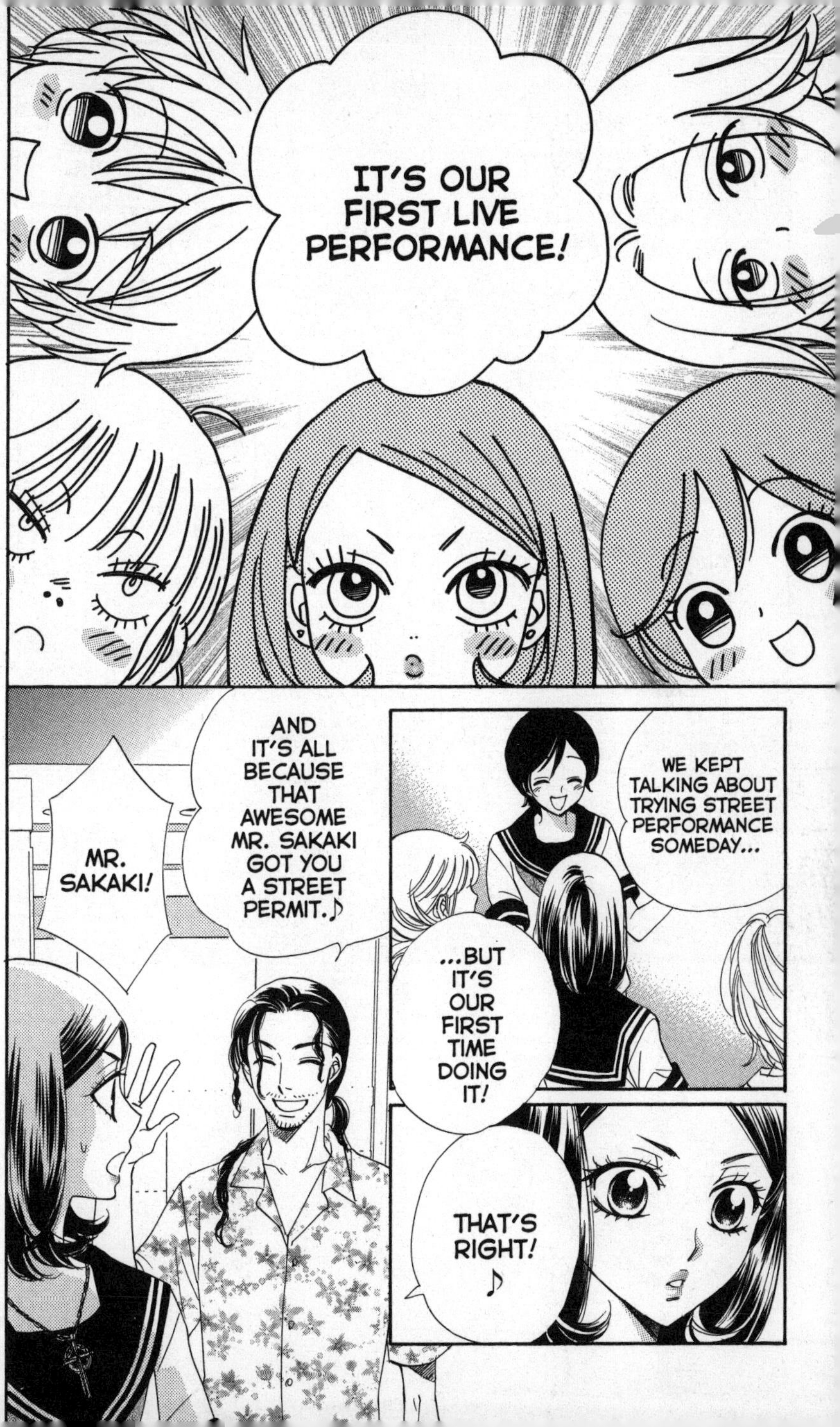

IT'S OUR FIRST LIVE PERFORMANCE!
WE KEPT TALKING ABOUT TRYING STREET PERFORMANCE SOMEDAY...
...BUT IT'S OUR FIRST TIME DOING IT!
THAT'S RIGHT! ♪
AND IT'S ALL BECAUSE THAT AWESOME MR. SAKAKI GOT YOU A STREET PERMIT. ♪
MR. SAKAKI!

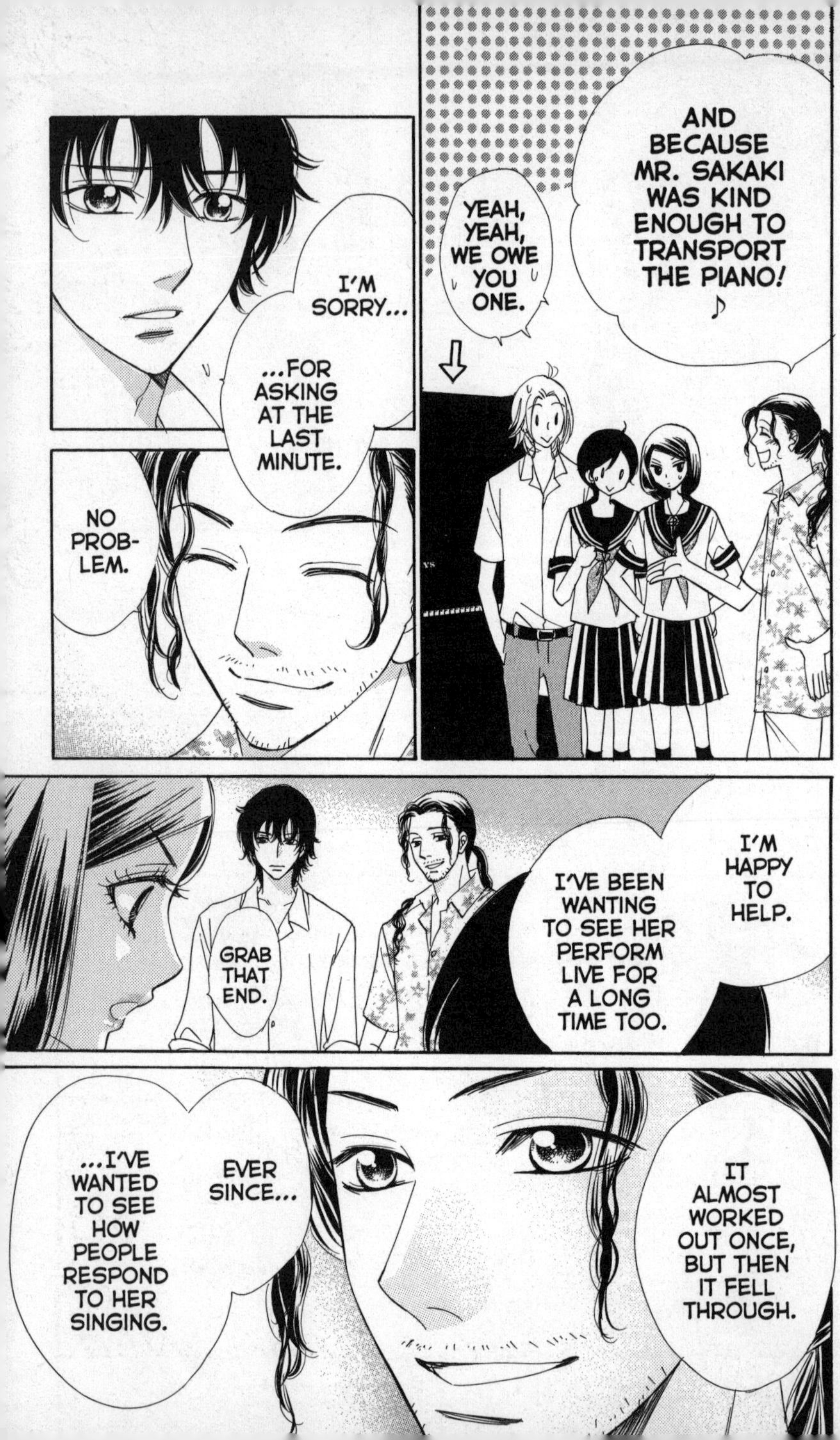
AND BECAUSE MR. SAKAKI WAS KIND ENOUGH TO TRANSPORT THE PIANO! ♪
YEAH, YEAH, WE OWE YOU ONE.
I'M SORRY...
...FOR ASKING AT THE LAST MINUTE.
NO PROB-LEM.
I'M HAPPY TO HELP.
I'VE BEEN WANTING TO SEE HER PERFORM LIVE FOR A LONG TIME TOO.
GRAB THAT END.
IT ALMOST WORKED OUT ONCE, BUT THEN IT FELL THROUGH.
EVER SINCE...
...I'VE WANTED TO SEE HOW PEOPLE RESPOND TO HER SINGING.

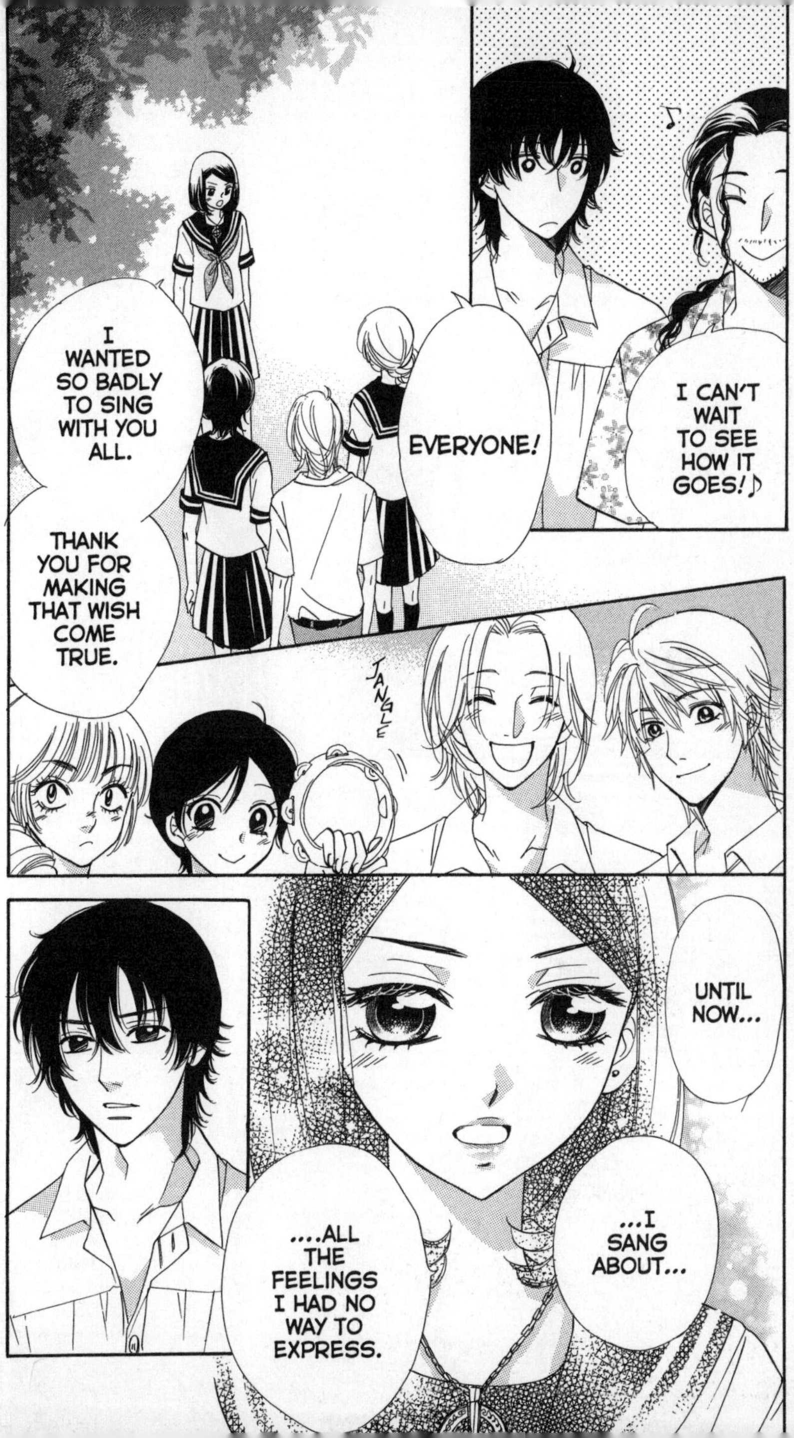

I CAN'T WAIT TO SEE HOW IT GOES!♪
EVERYONE!
I WANTED SO BADLY TO SING WITH YOU ALL.
THANK YOU FOR MAKING THAT WISH COME TRUE.
JANGLE
UNTIL NOW...
...I SANG ABOUT...
....ALL THE FEELINGS I HAD NO WAY TO EXPRESS.

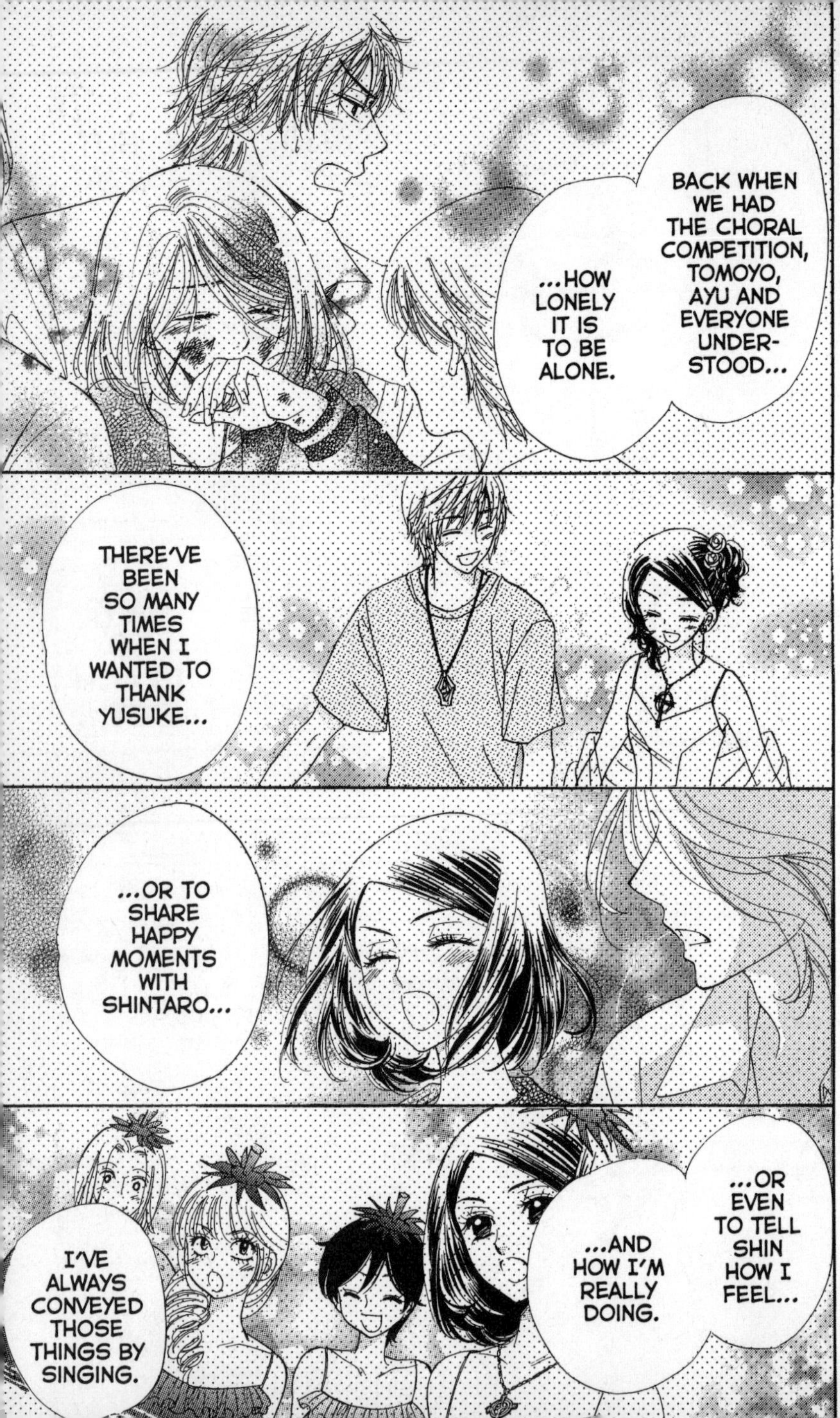
BACK WHEN WE HAD THE CHORAL COMPETITION, TOMOYO, AYU AND EVERYONE UNDER-STOOD...
...HOW LONELY IT IS TO BE ALONE.
THERE'VE BEEN SO MANY TIMES WHEN I WANTED TO THANK YUSUKE...
...OR TO SHARE HAPPY MOMENTS WITH SHINTARO...
...OR EVEN TO TELL SHIN HOW I FEEL...
...AND HOW I'M REALLY DOING.
I'VE ALWAYS CONVEYED THOSE THINGS BY SINGING.

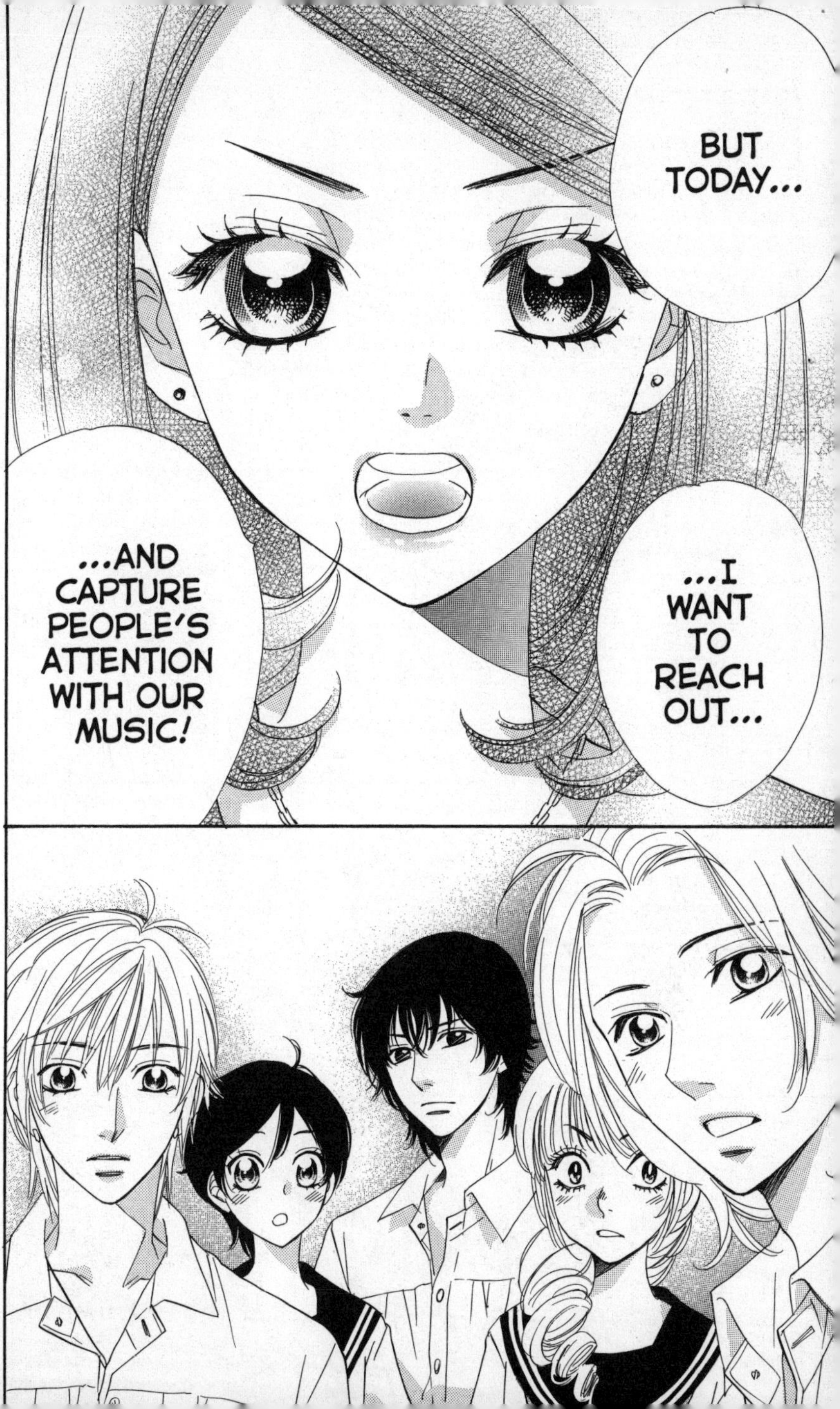
BUT TODAY...
...I WANT TO REACH OUT...
...AND CAPTURE PEOPLE'S ATTENTION WITH OUR MUSIC!

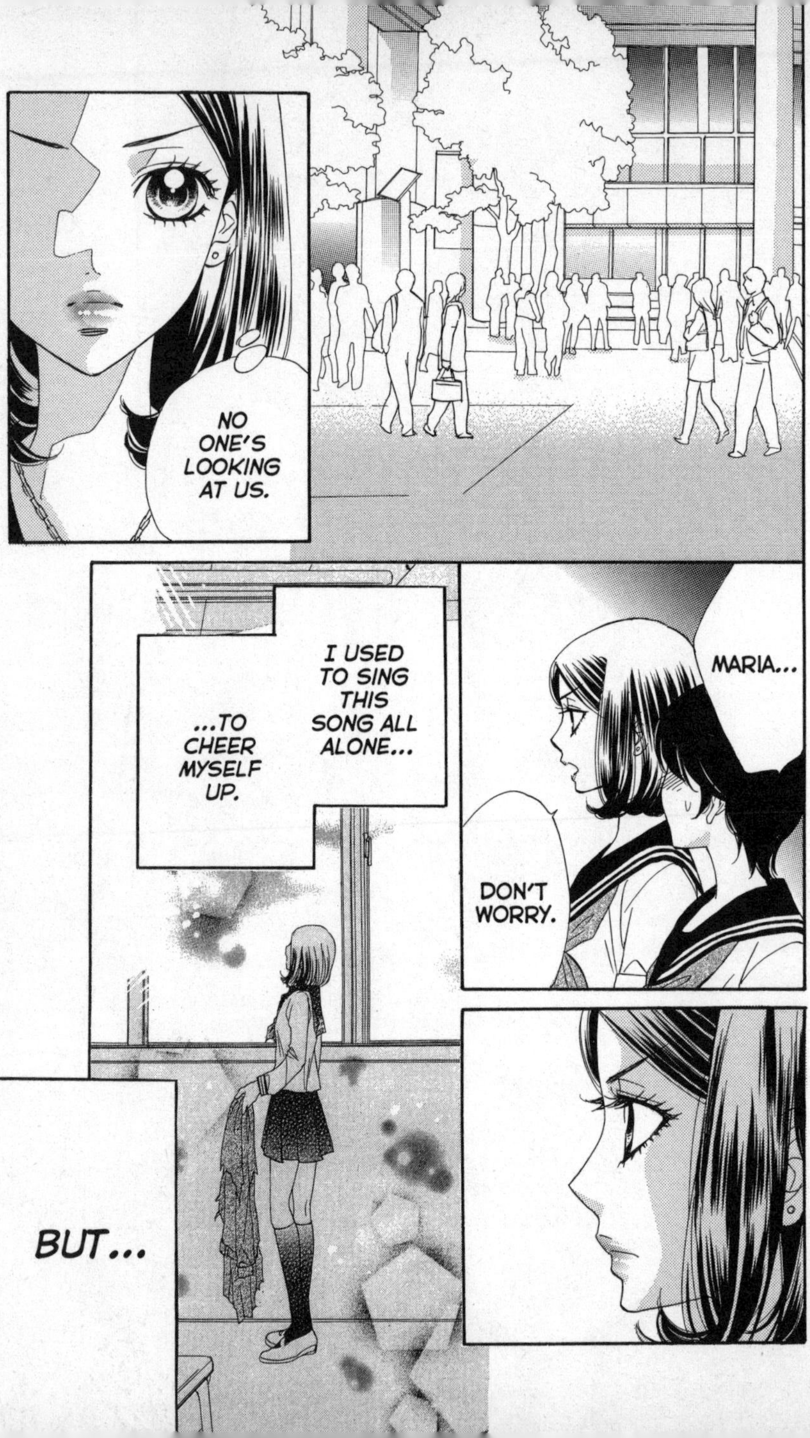
NO ONE'S LOOKING AT US.
MARIA...
DON'T WORRY.
I USED TO SING THIS SONG ALL ALONE...
...TO CHEER MYSELF UP.
BUT...

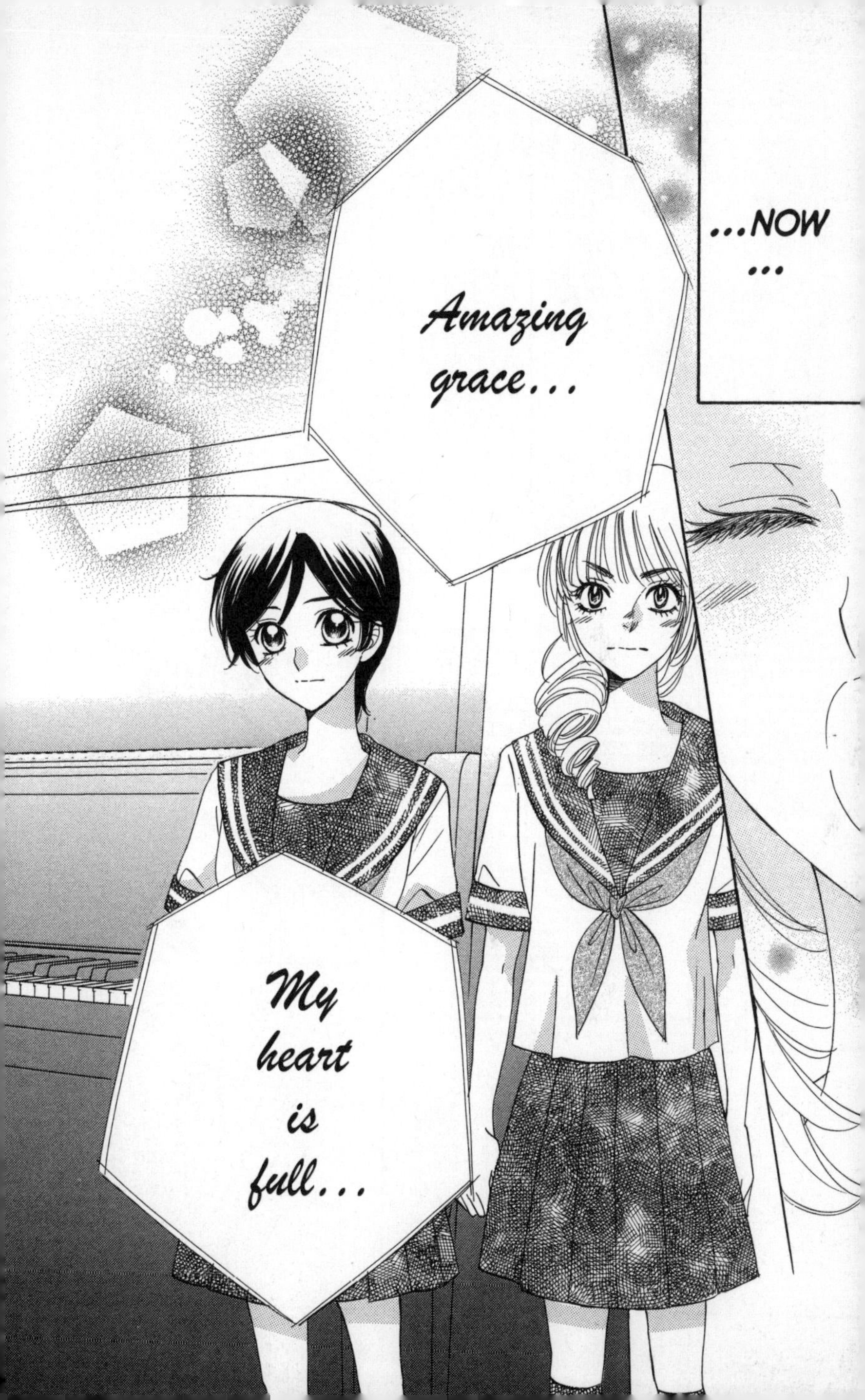
...NOW ...
Amazing grace...
My heart is full...

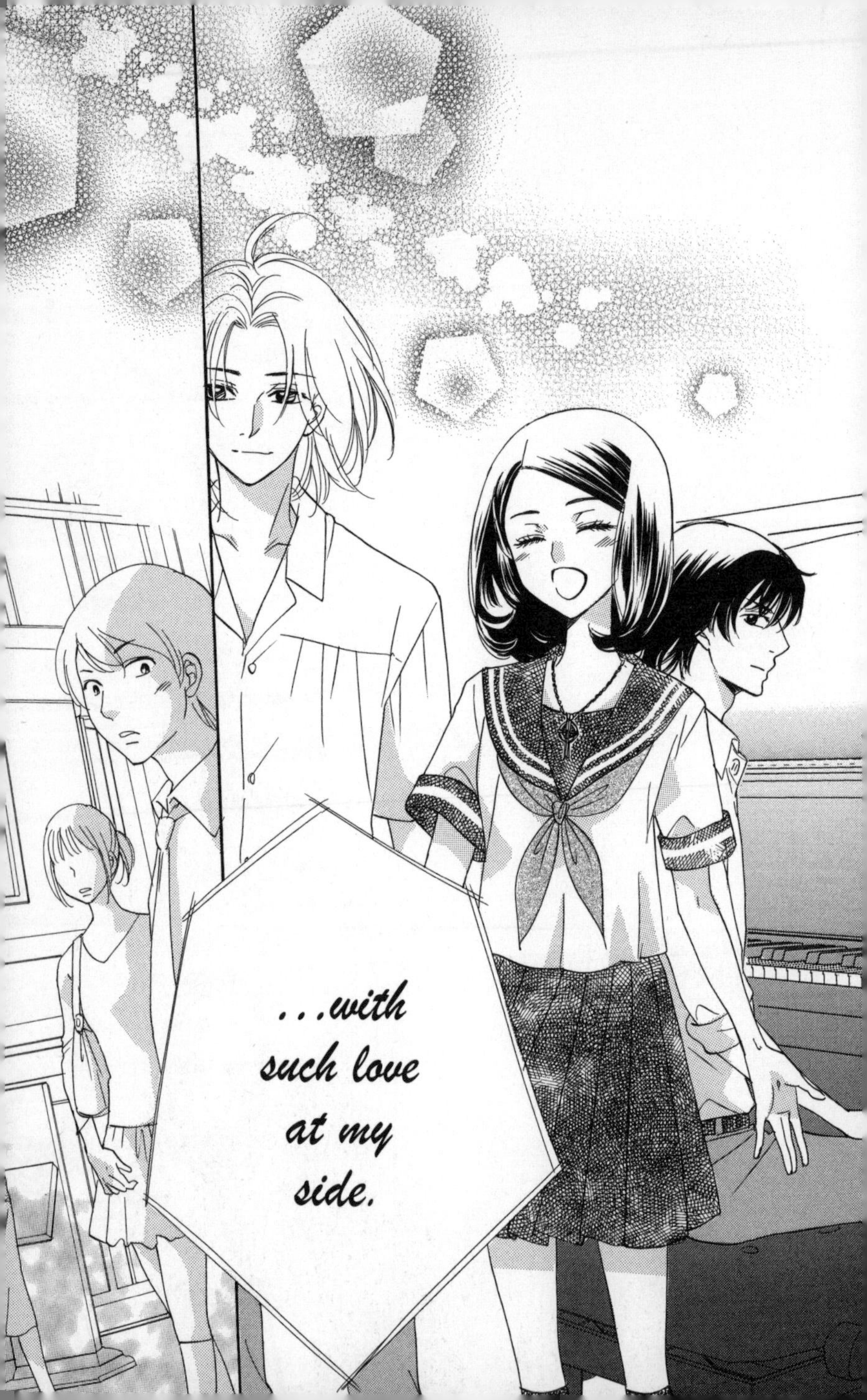
...with such love at my side.

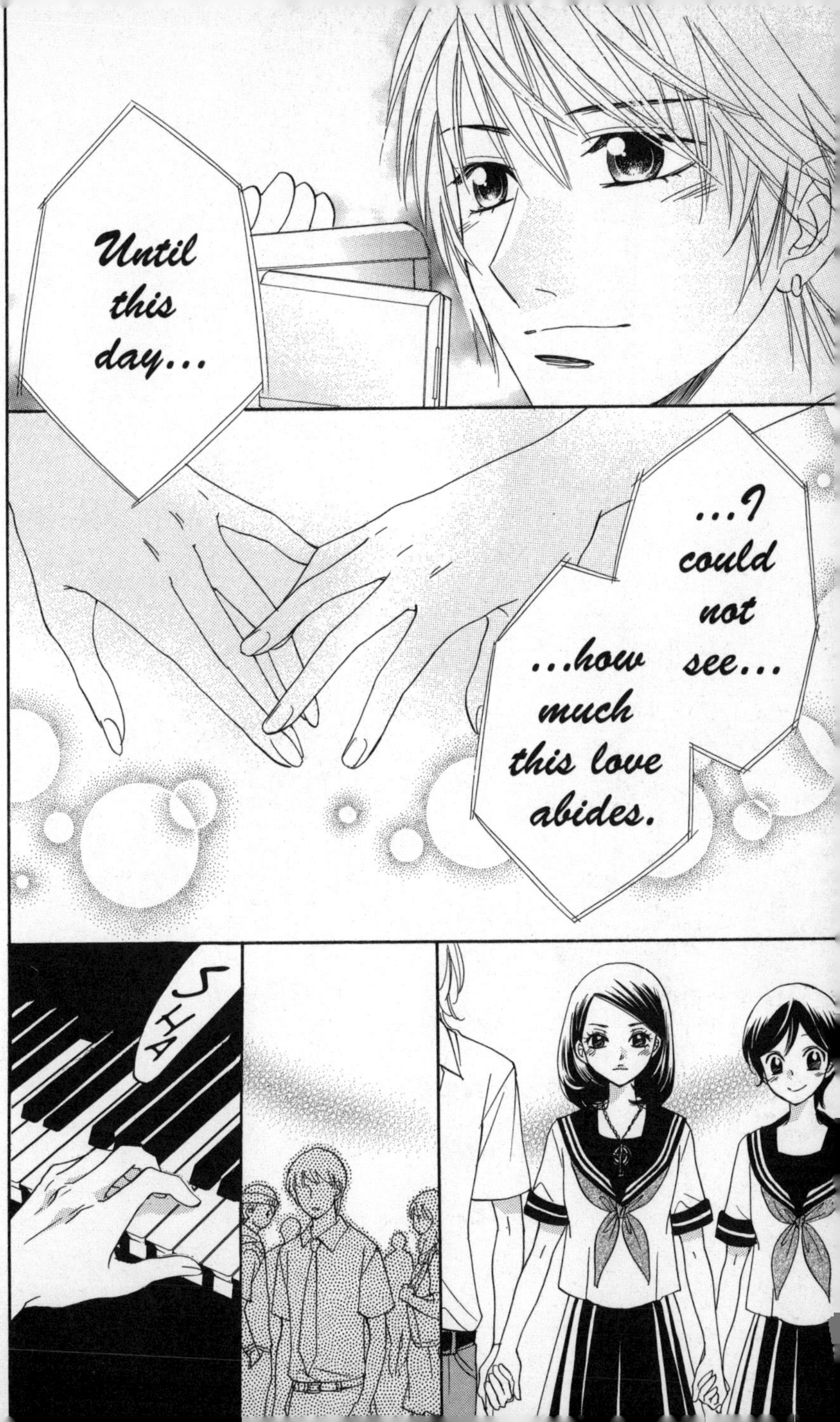
Until this day...
...I could not see...
...how much this love abides.
SHA

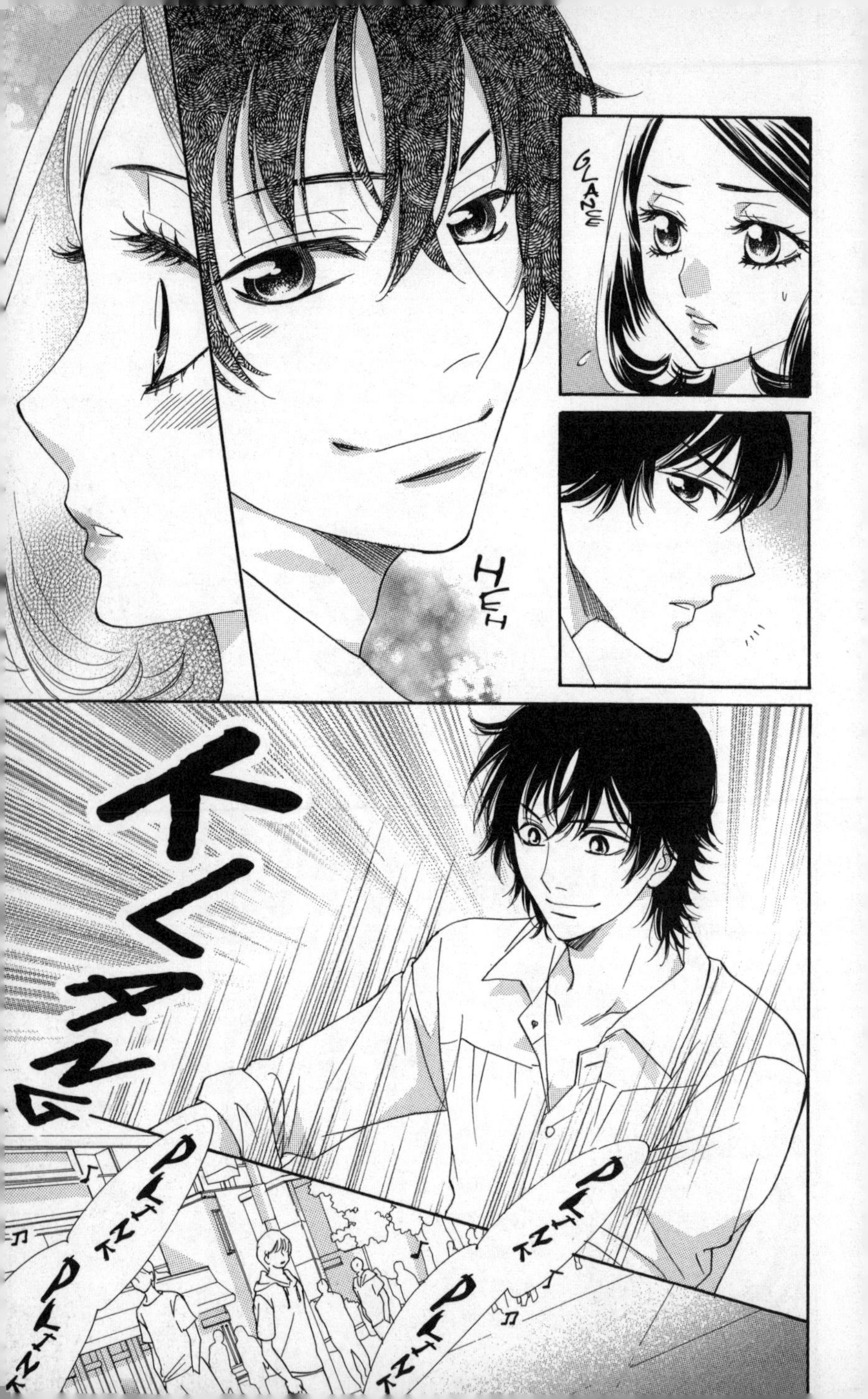
GLANCE
HEH
KLANG
PITTINK
PITTINK
PITTINK
PITTINK

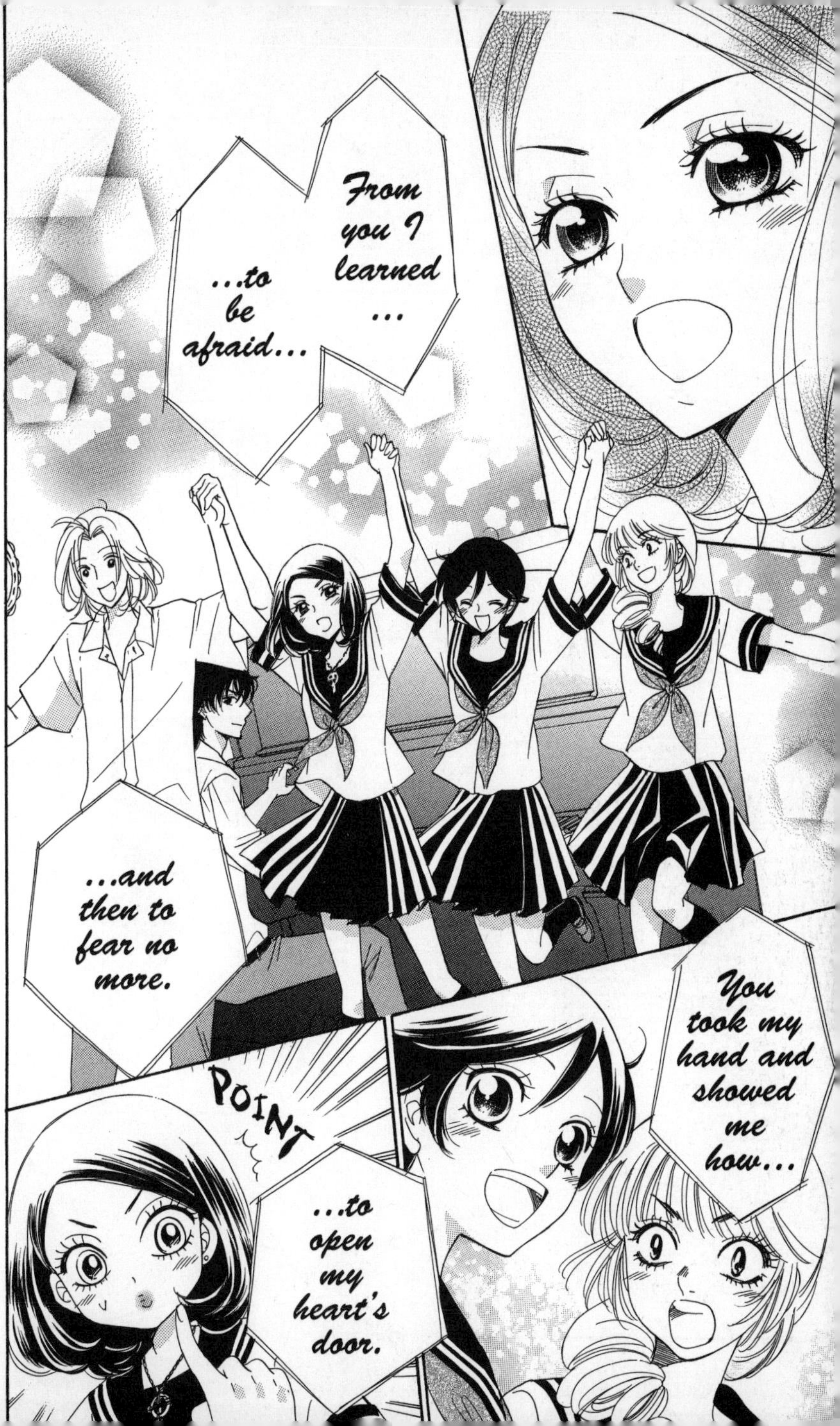
From you I learned...
...to be afraid...
...and then to fear no more.
You took my hand and showed me how...
POINT
...to open my heart's door.

We have gone through...
HA HA HA?
...many dark days...
...and doubtless shall...
...face more.
But walking with...
...your hand in mine...
...I've faith we shall endure.
OHHHH, NO.

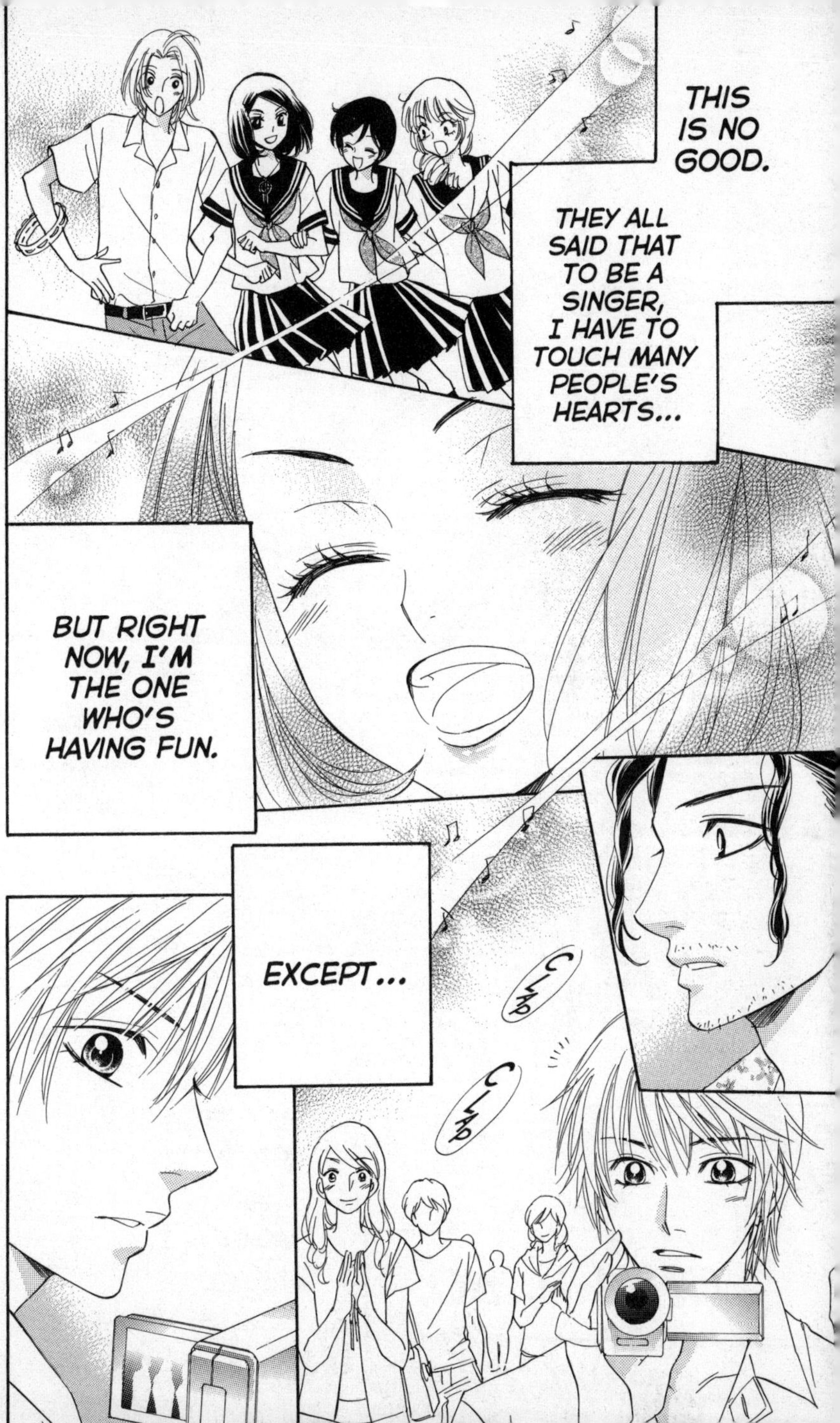
THIS IS NO GOOD.
THEY ALL SAID THAT TO BE A SINGER, I HAVE TO TOUCH MANY PEOPLE'S HEARTS...
BUT RIGHT NOW, I'M THE ONE WHO'S HAVING FUN.
EXCEPT...
CLAP
CLAP

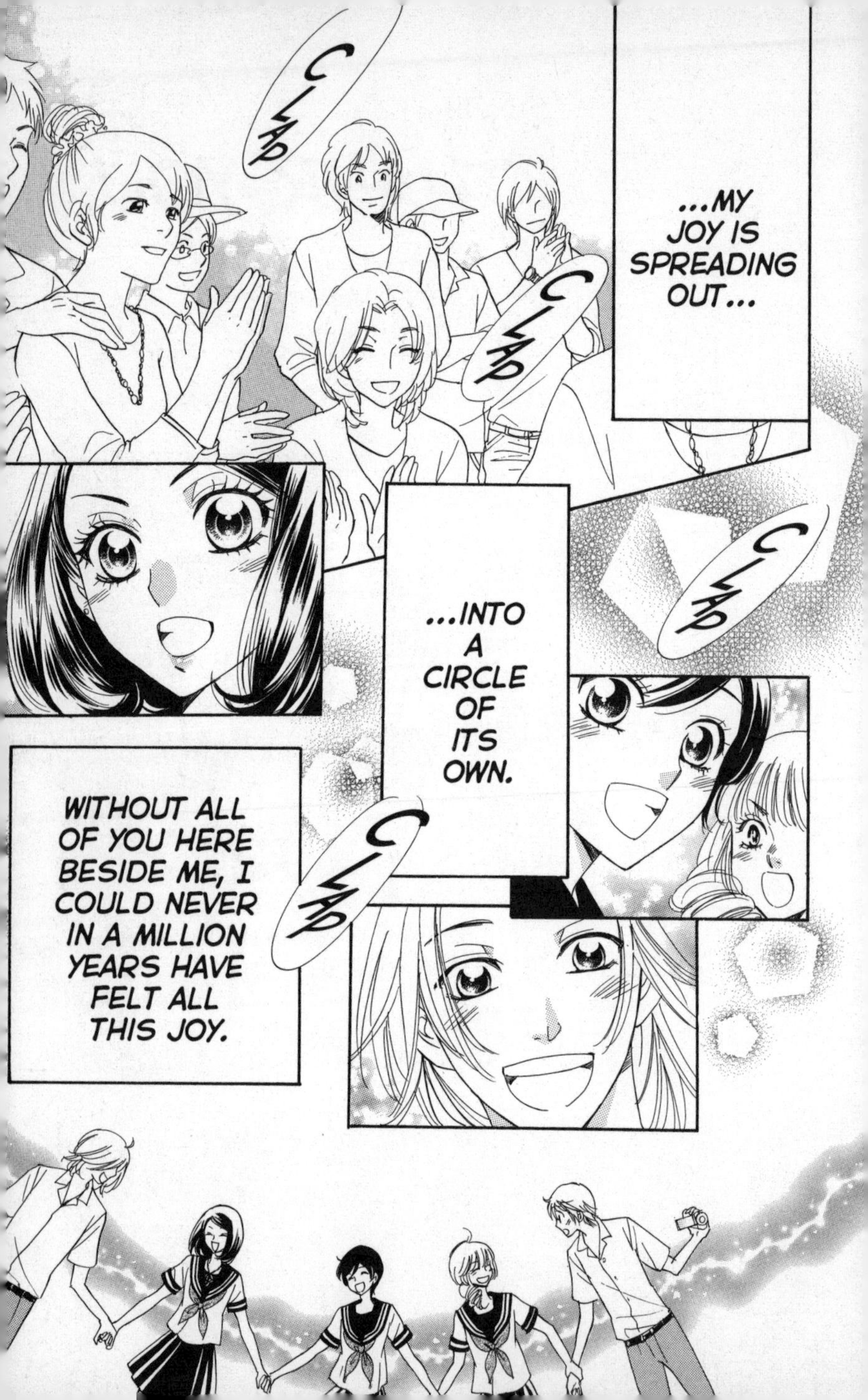
...MY JOY IS SPREADING OUT...
CLAP
CLAP
CLAP
...INTO A CIRCLE OF ITS OWN.
CLAP
WITHOUT ALL OF YOU HERE BESIDE ME, I COULD NEVER IN A MILLION YEARS HAVE FELT ALL THIS JOY.

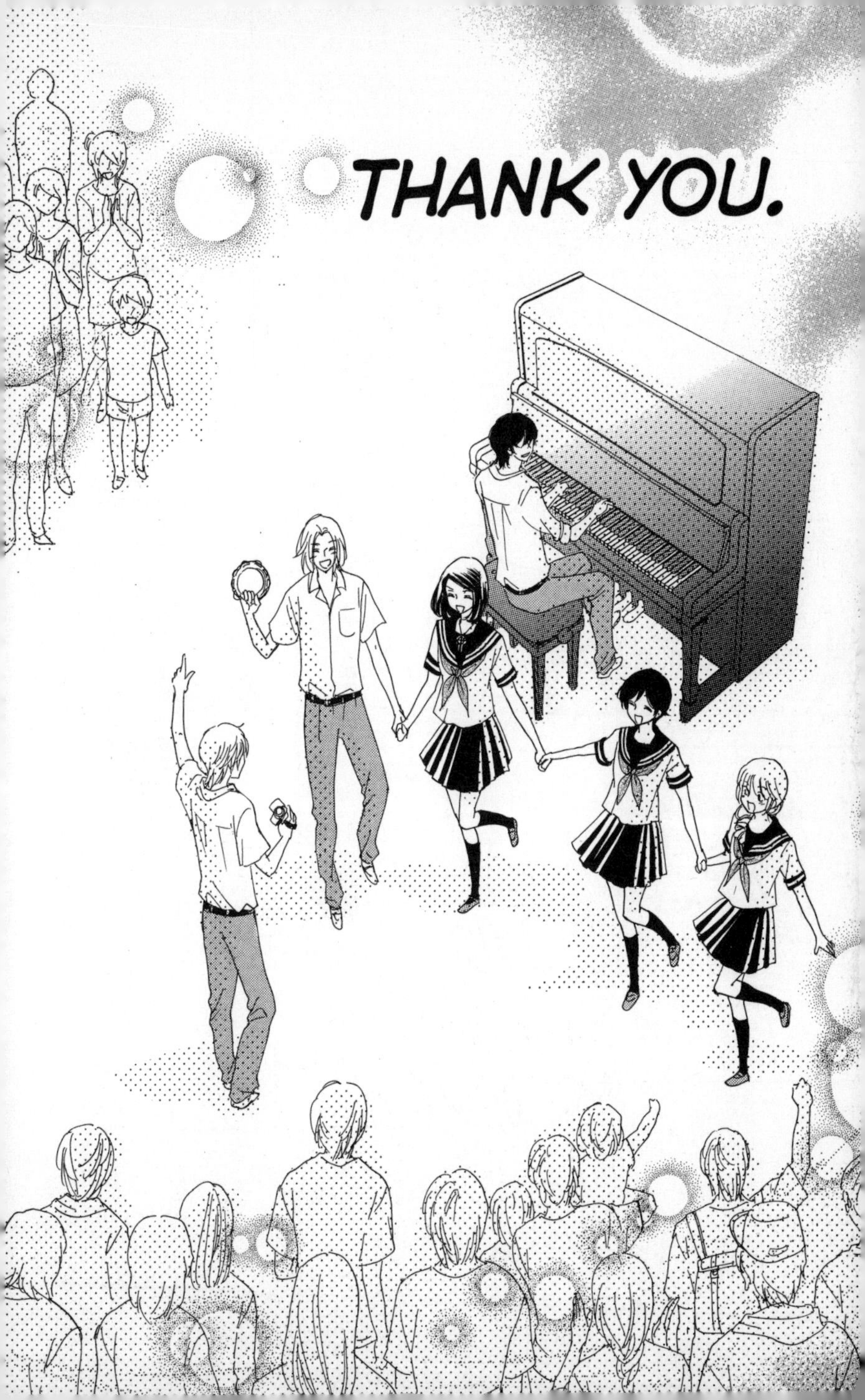
THANK YOU.

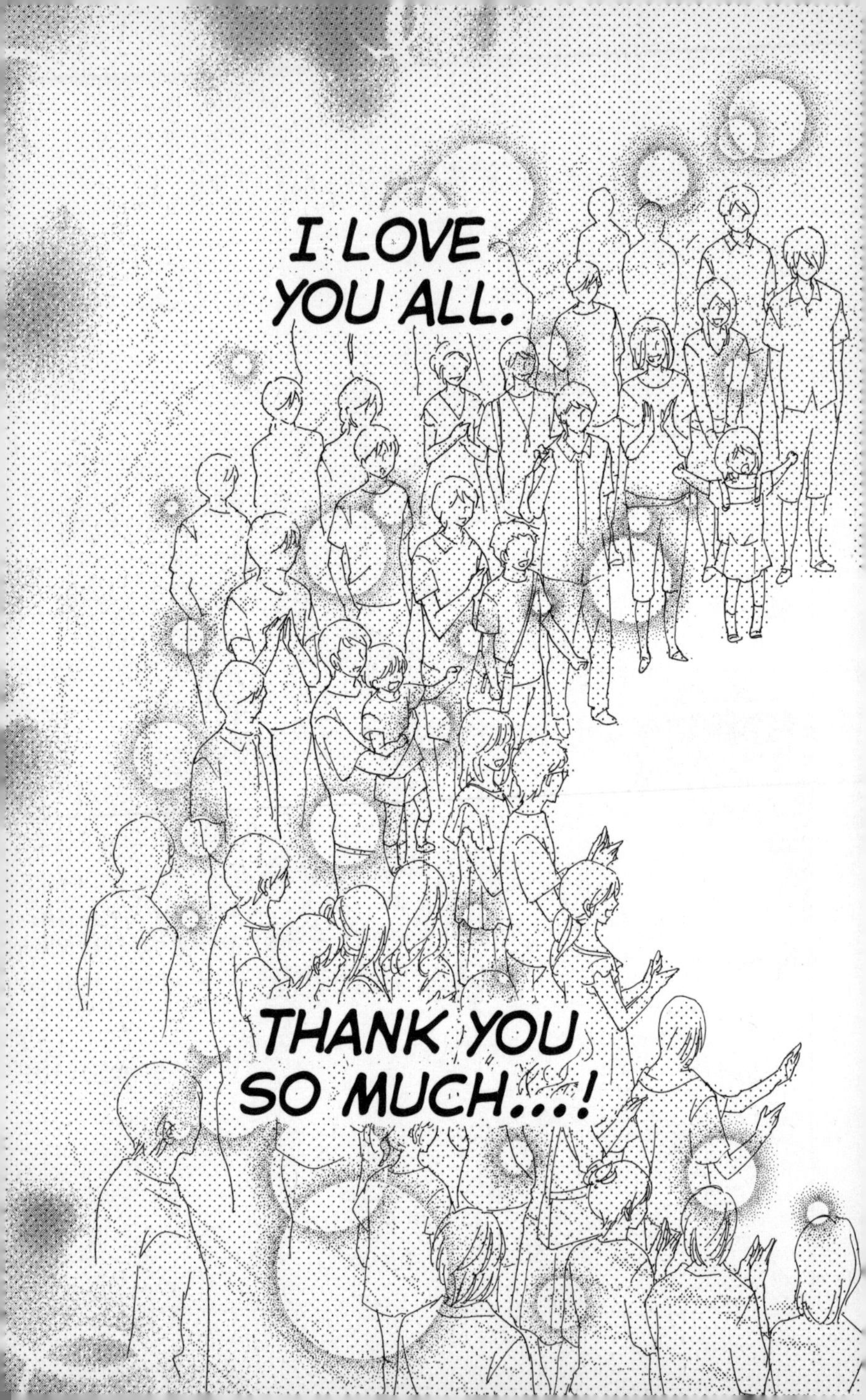
I LOVE YOU ALL.
THANK YOU SO MUCH...!

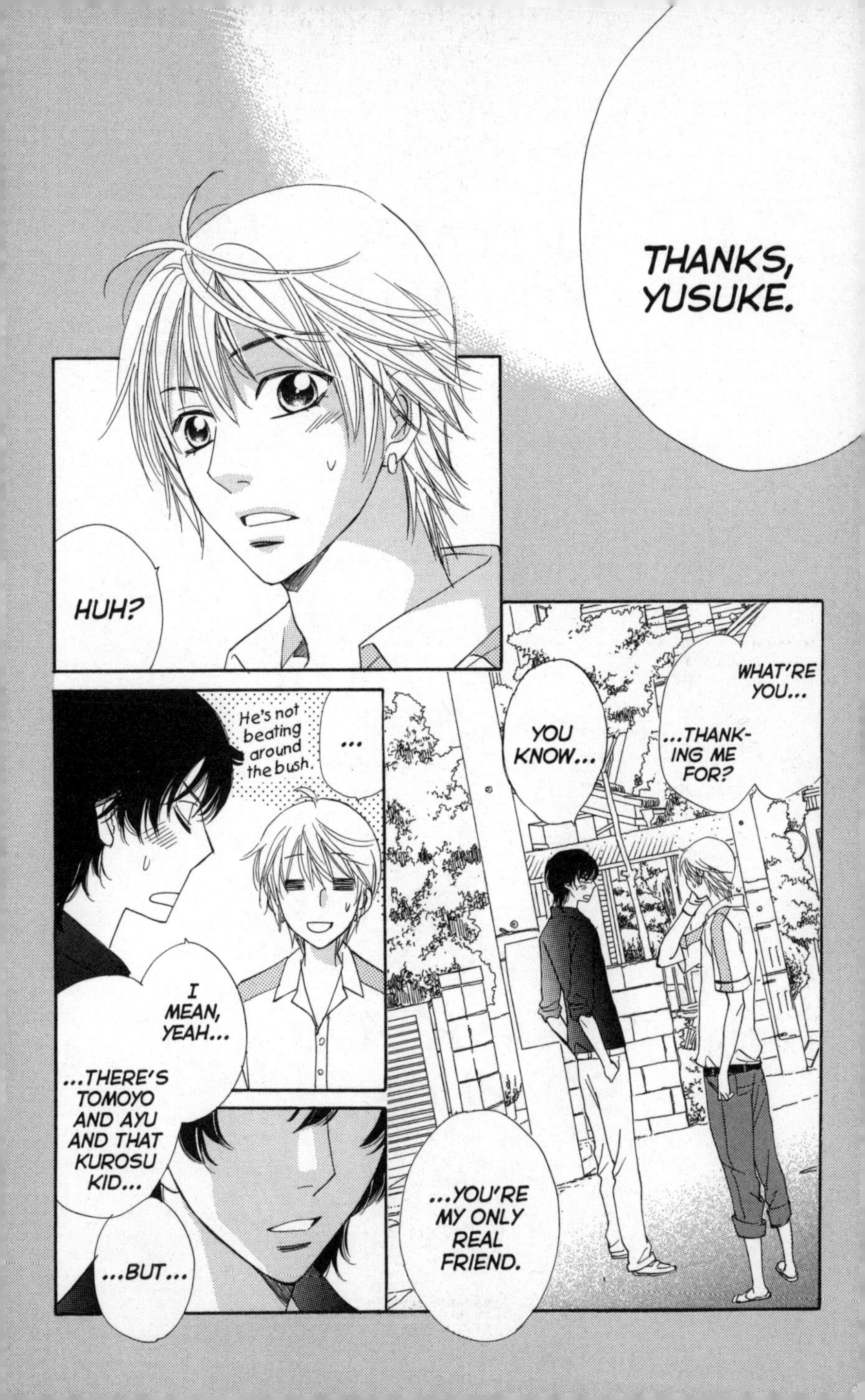
THANKS, YUSUKE.
HUH?
WHAT'RE YOU...
...THANKING ME FOR?
YOU KNOW...
...
He's not beating around the bush.
I MEAN, YEAH...
...THERE'S TOMOYO AND AYU AND THAT KUROSU KID...
...BUT...
...YOU'RE MY ONLY REAL FRIEND.

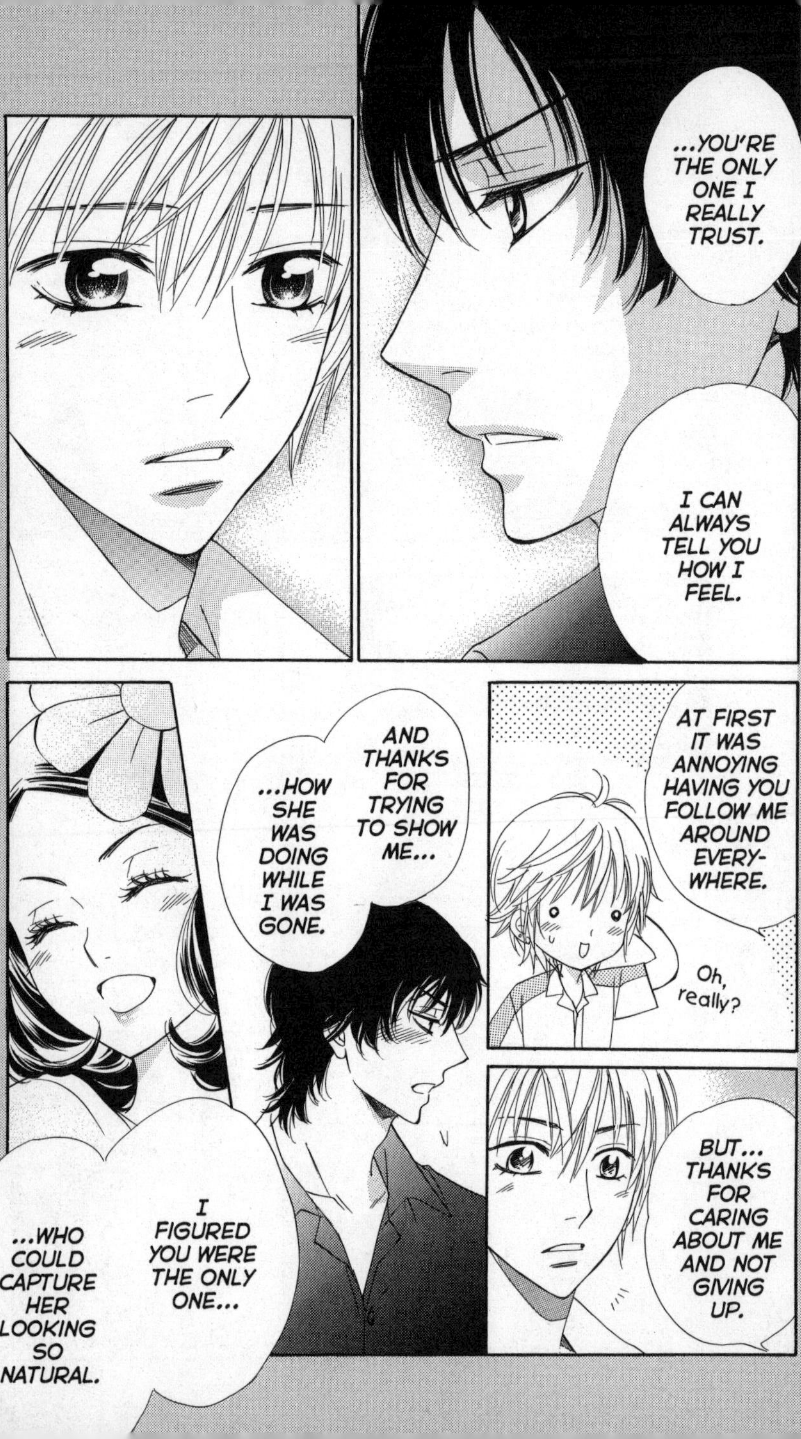
...YOU'RE THE ONLY ONE I REALLY TRUST.
I CAN ALWAYS TELL YOU HOW I FEEL.
AT FIRST IT WAS ANNOYING HAVING YOU FOLLOW ME AROUND EVERY-WHERE.
Oh, really?
BUT... THANKS FOR CARING ABOUT ME AND NOT GIVING UP.
AND THANKS FOR TRYING TO SHOW ME...
...HOW SHE WAS DOING WHILE I WAS GONE.
I FIGURED YOU WERE THE ONLY ONE...
...WHO COULD CAPTURE HER LOOKING SO NATURAL.

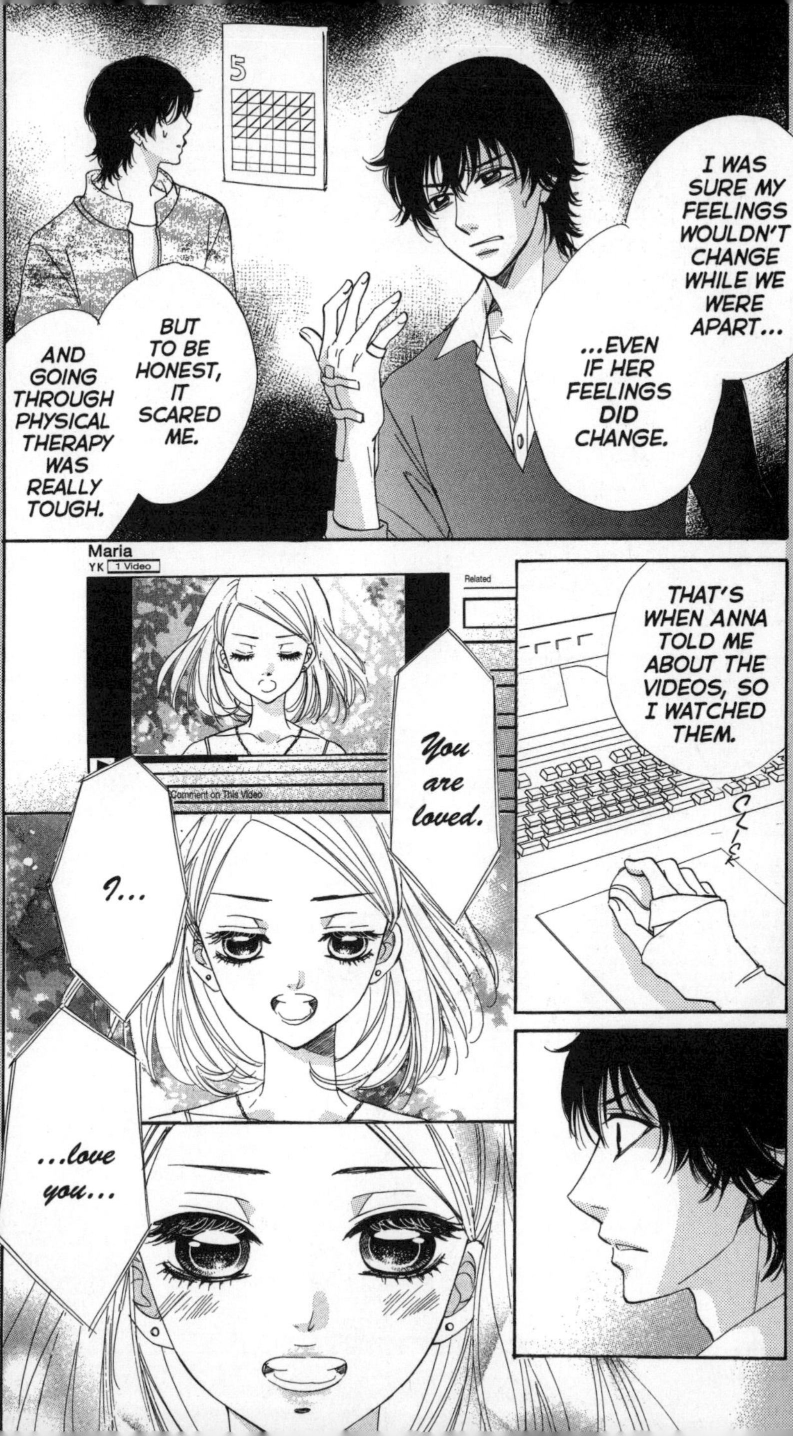
I WAS SURE MY FEELINGS WOULDN'T CHANGE WHILE WE WERE APART...
...EVEN IF HER FEELINGS DID CHANGE.
BUT TO BE HONEST, IT SCARED ME.
AND GOING THROUGH PHYSICAL THERAPY WAS REALLY TOUGH.
THAT'S WHEN ANNA TOLD ME ABOUT THE VIDEOS, SO I WATCHED THEM.
CLICK
Maria
YK 1 Video
Related
Comment on This Video
You are loved.
I...
...love you...

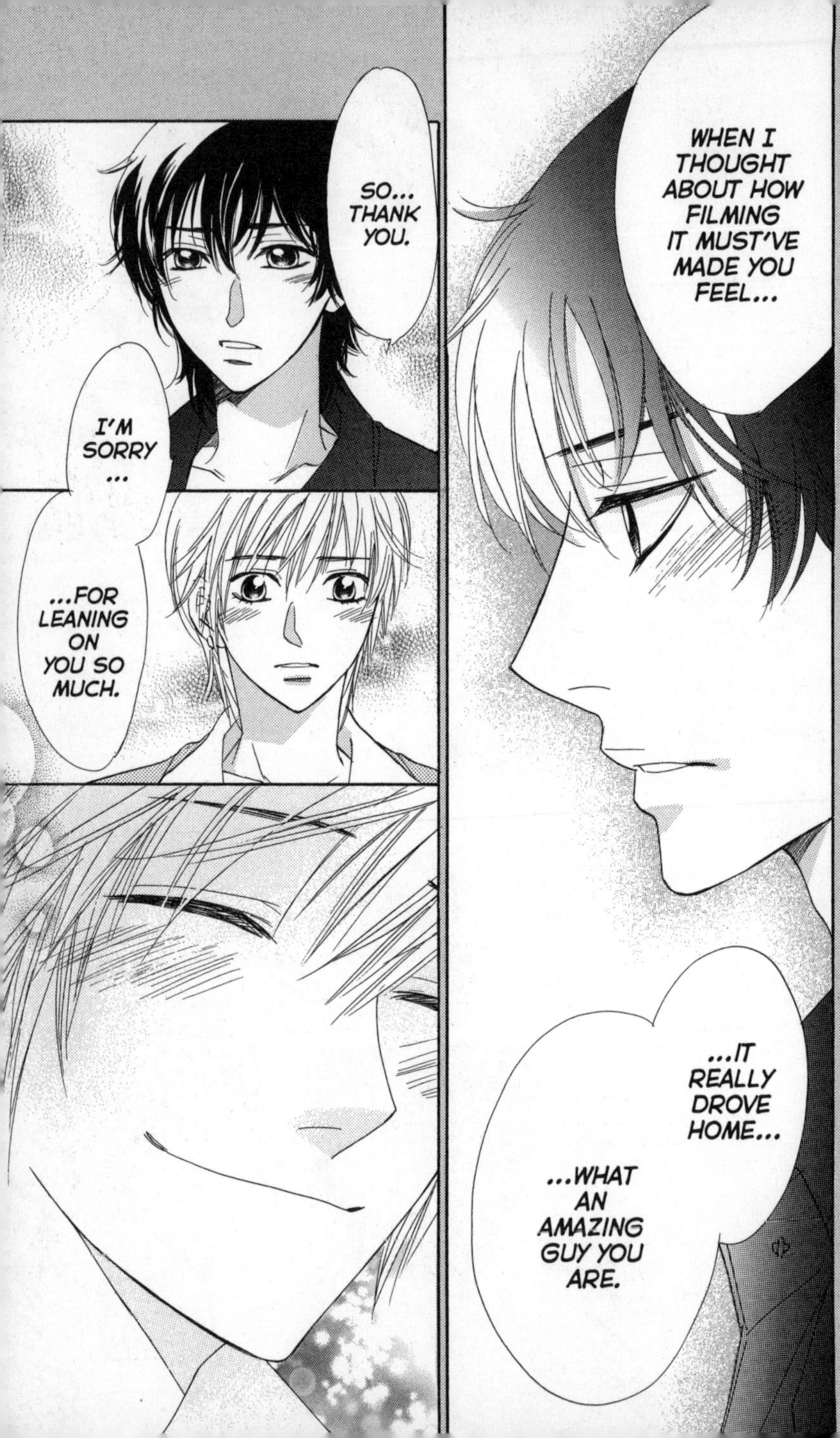
WHEN I THOUGHT ABOUT HOW FILMING IT MUST'VE MADE YOU FEEL...
...IT REALLY DROVE HOME...
...WHAT AN AMAZING GUY YOU ARE.
SO... THANK YOU.
I'M SORRY...
...FOR LEANING ON YOU SO MUCH.

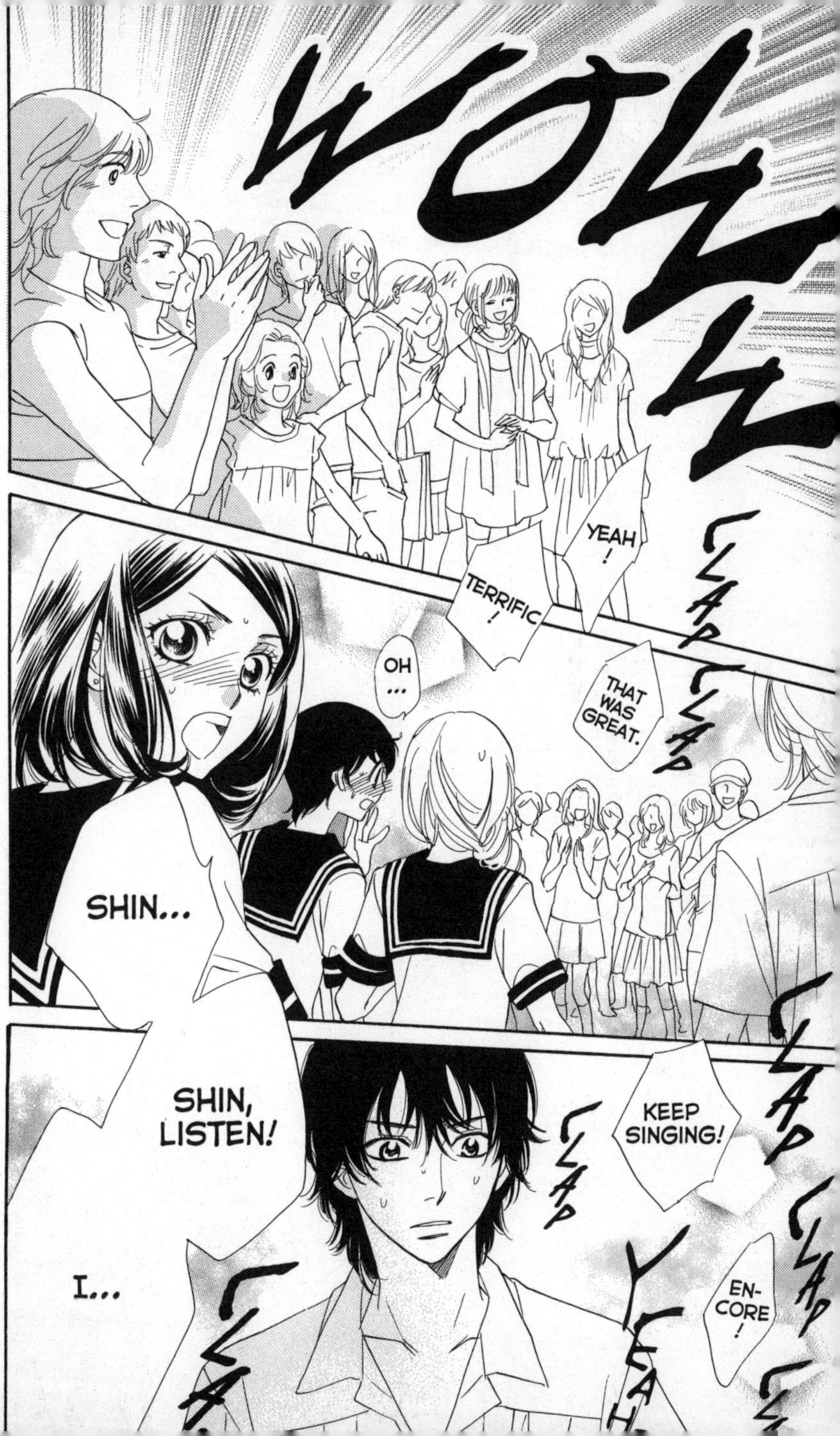
WOW
YEAH!
TERRIFIC!
CLAP CLAP CLAP
THAT WAS GREAT.
OH...
SHIN...
CLAP CLAP
KEEP SINGING!
CLAP
SHIN, LISTEN!
EN-CORE!
YEAH
CLAP
I...

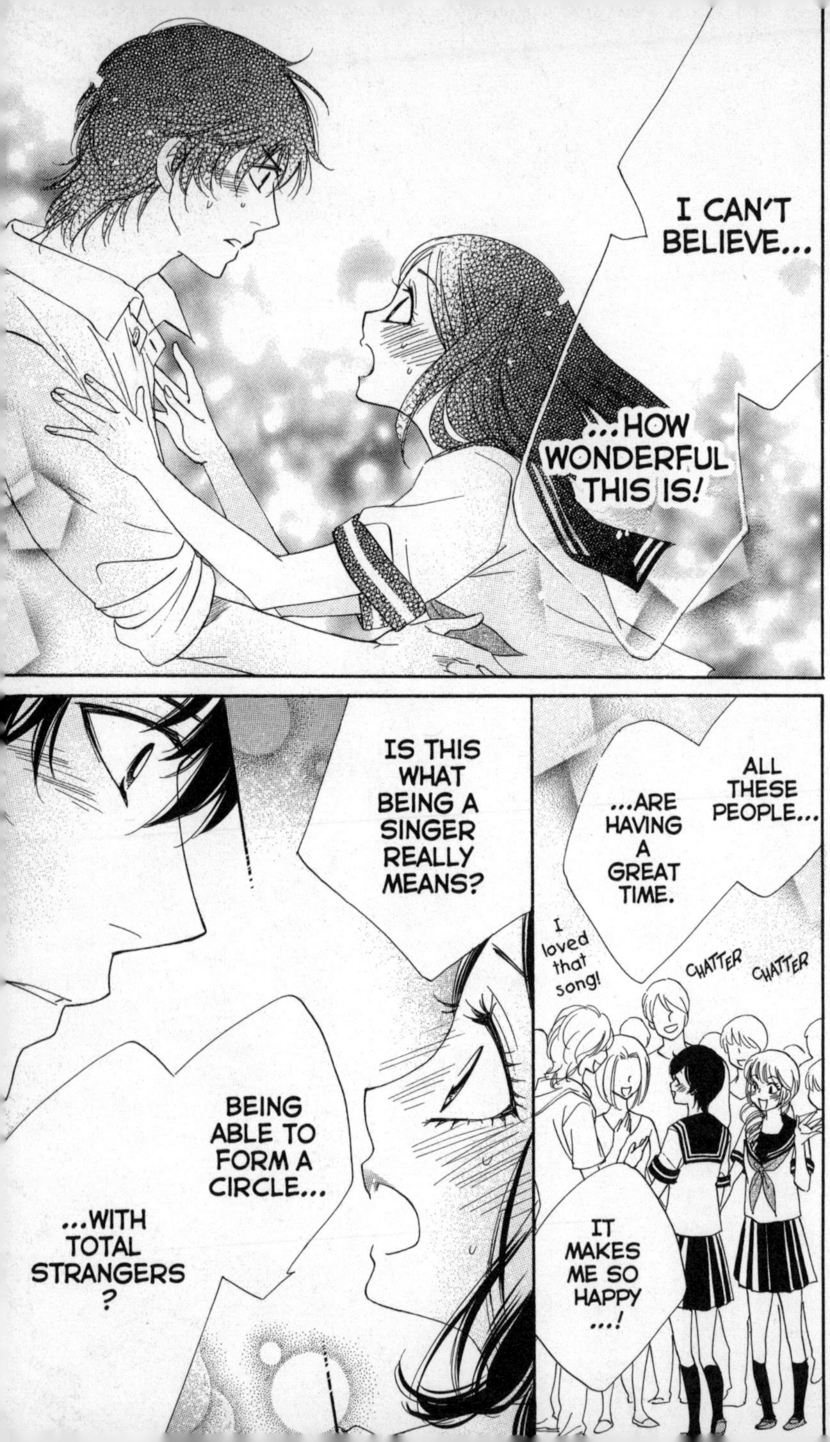
I CAN'T BELIEVE...
...HOW WONDERFUL THIS IS!
ALL THESE PEOPLE...
...ARE HAVING A GREAT TIME.
I loved that song!
CHATTER
CHATTER
IT MAKES ME SO HAPPY ...!
IS THIS WHAT BEING A SINGER REALLY MEANS?
BEING ABLE TO FORM A CIRCLE...
...WITH TOTAL STRANGERS ?

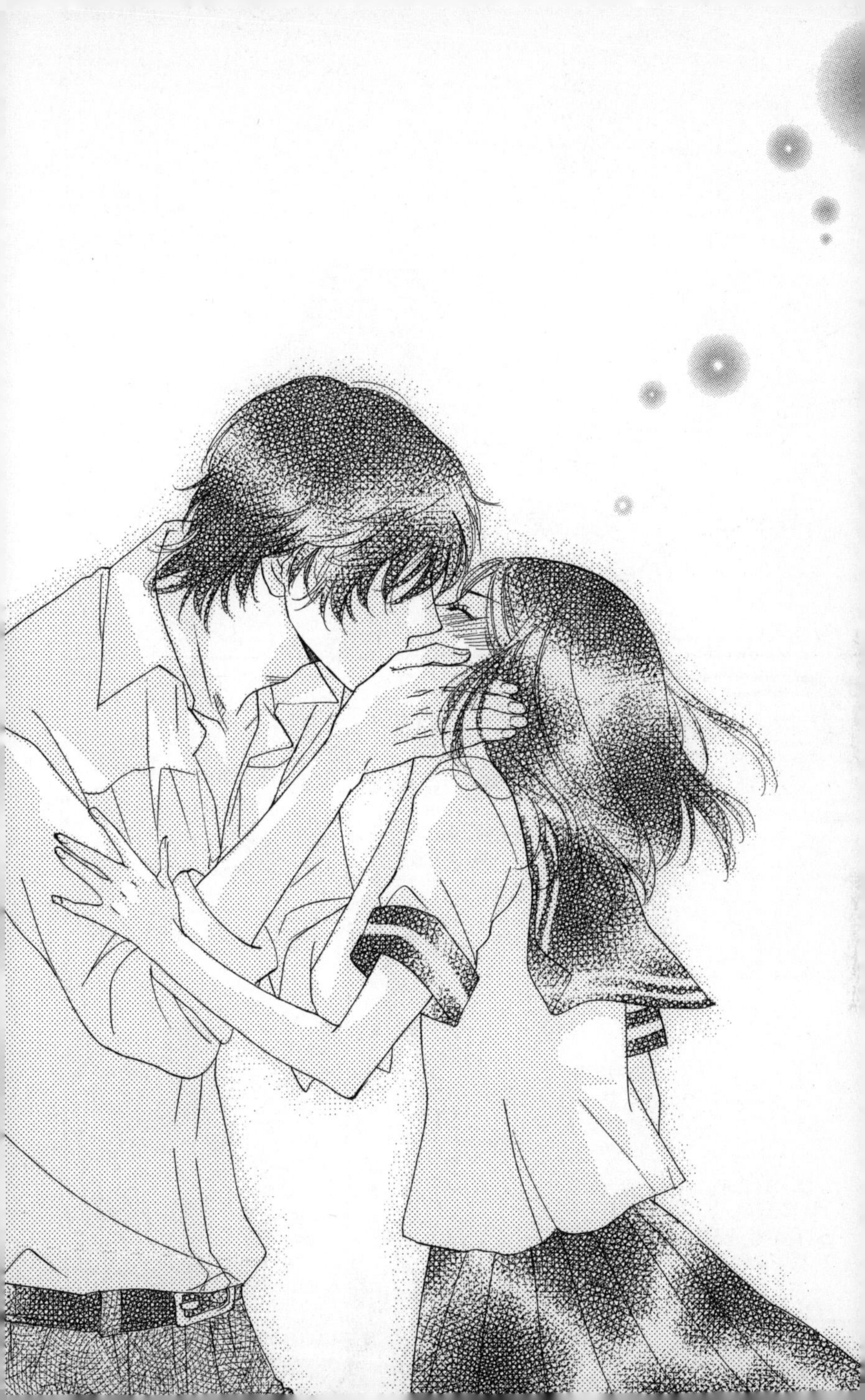

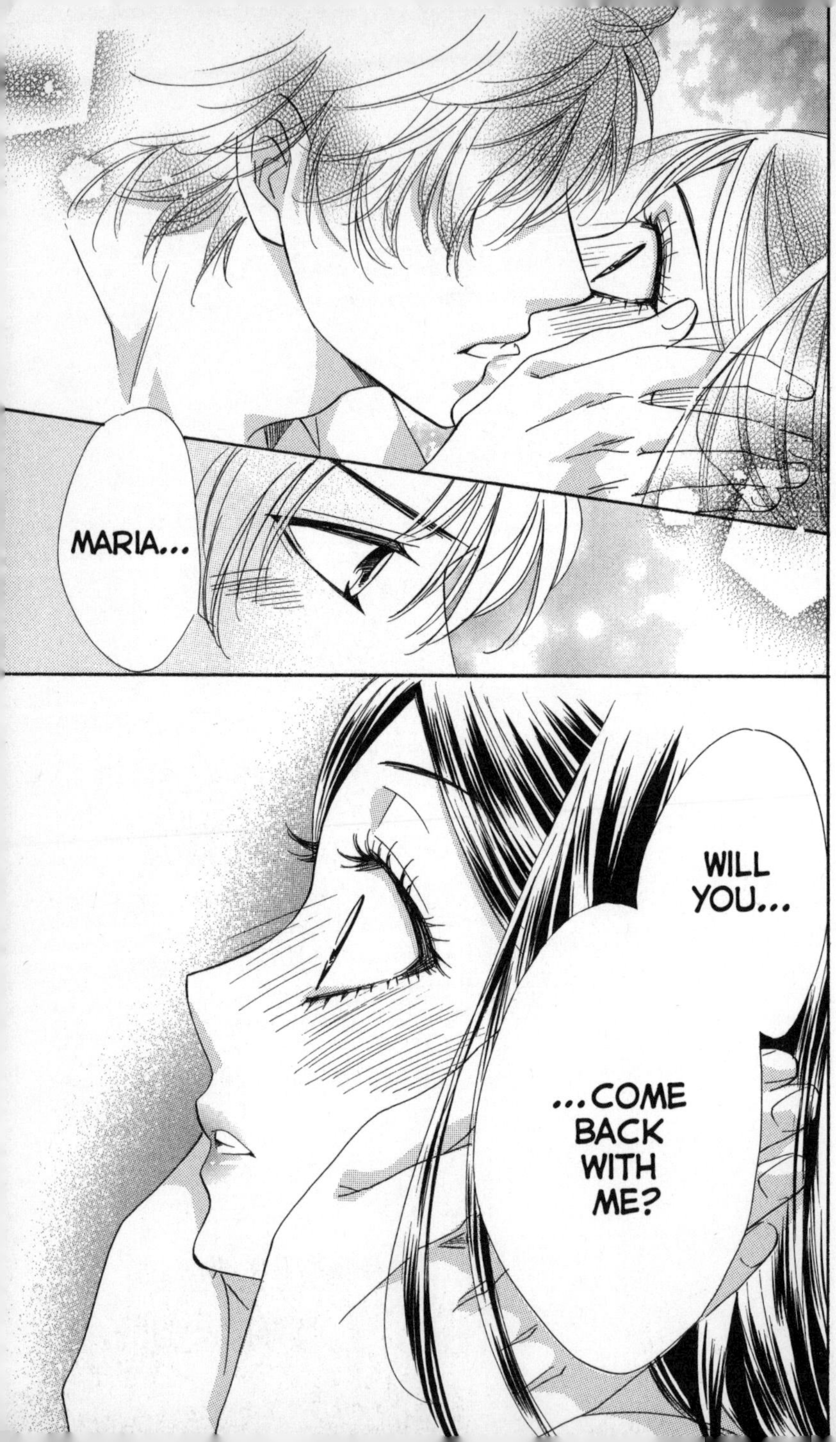
MARIA...
WILL YOU...
...COME BACK WITH ME?

A Devil and Her Love Song

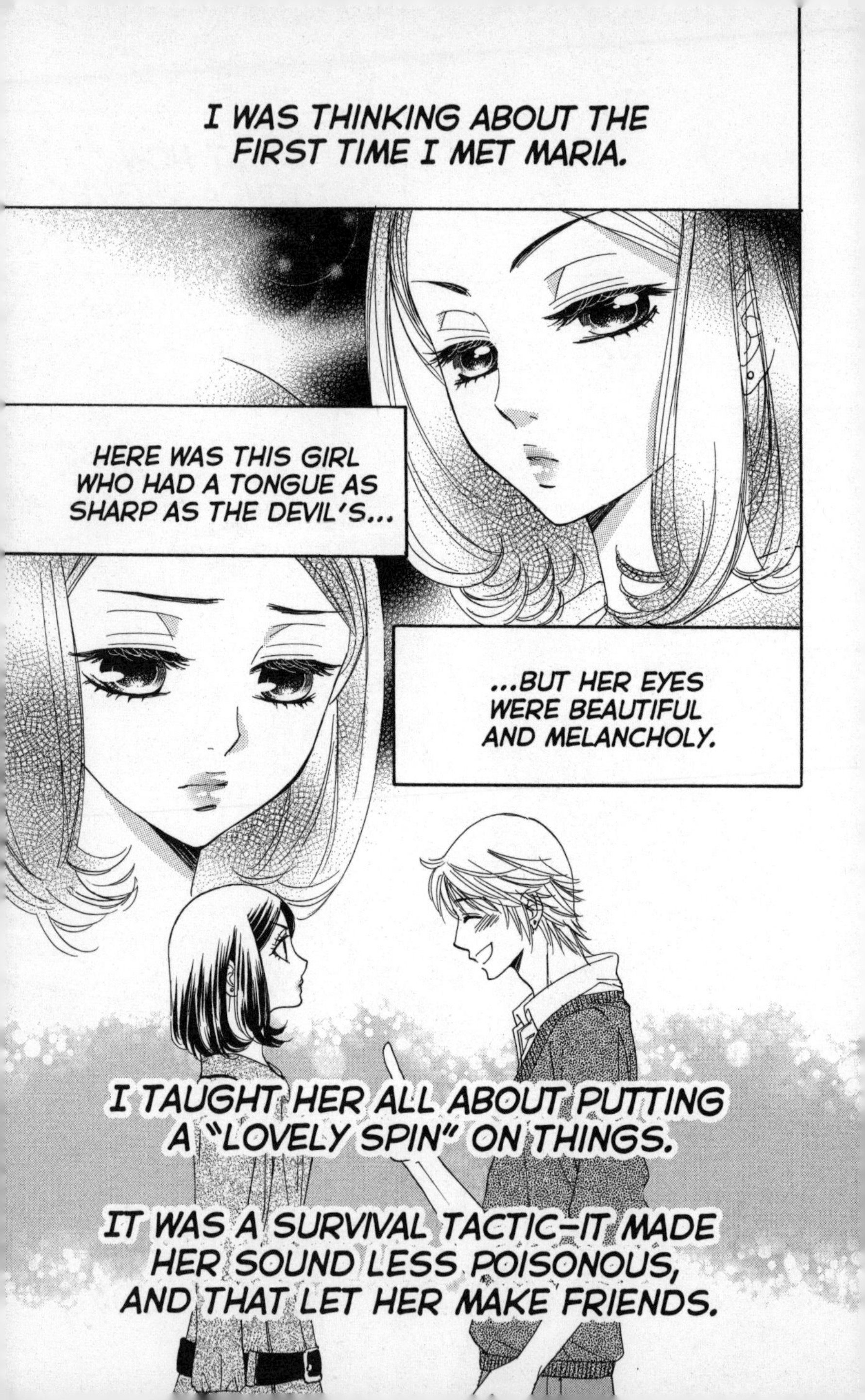

I WAS THINKING ABOUT THE FIRST TIME I MET MARIA.
HERE WAS THIS GIRL WHO HAD A TONGUE AS SHARP AS THE DEVIL'S...
...BUT HER EYES WERE BEAUTIFUL AND MELANCHOLY.
I TAUGHT HER ALL ABOUT PUTTING A "LOVELY SPIN" ON THINGS.
IT WAS A SURVIVAL TACTIC—IT MADE HER SOUND LESS POISONOUS, AND THAT LET HER MAKE FRIENDS.

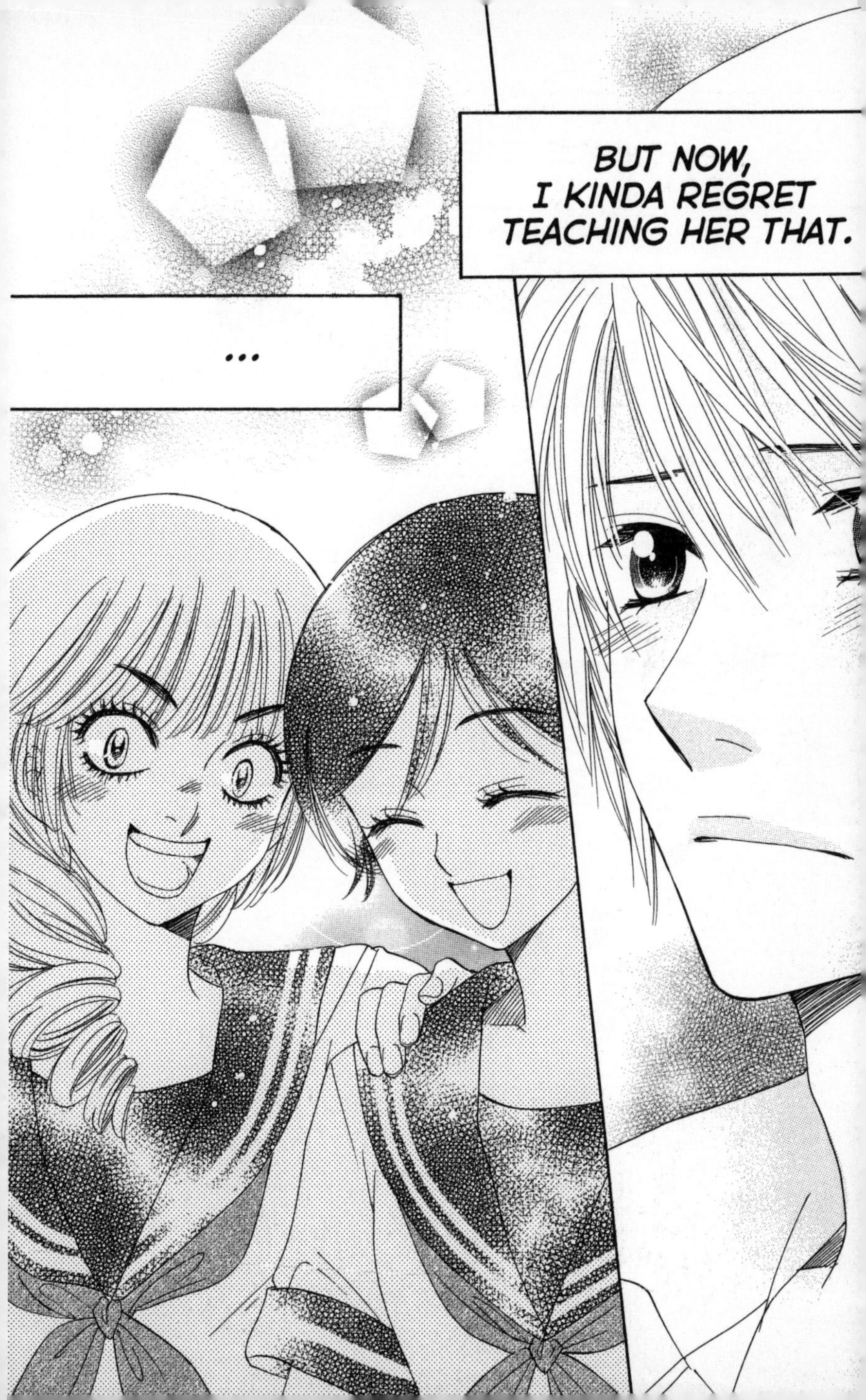
BUT NOW, I KINDA REGRET TEACHING HER THAT.
...

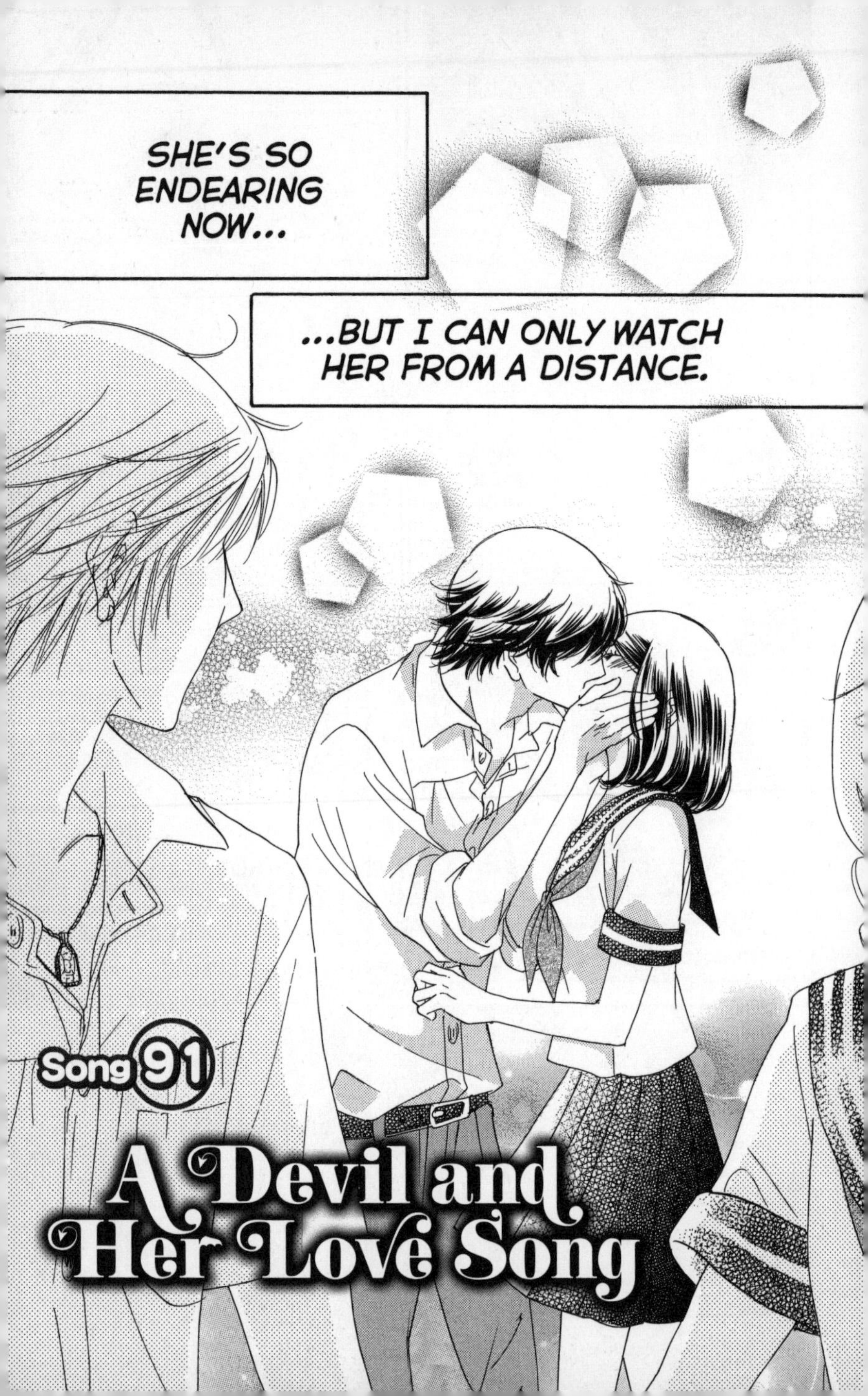
SHE'S SO ENDEARING NOW...
...BUT I CAN ONLY WATCH HER FROM A DISTANCE.
Song 91
A Devil and Her Love Song

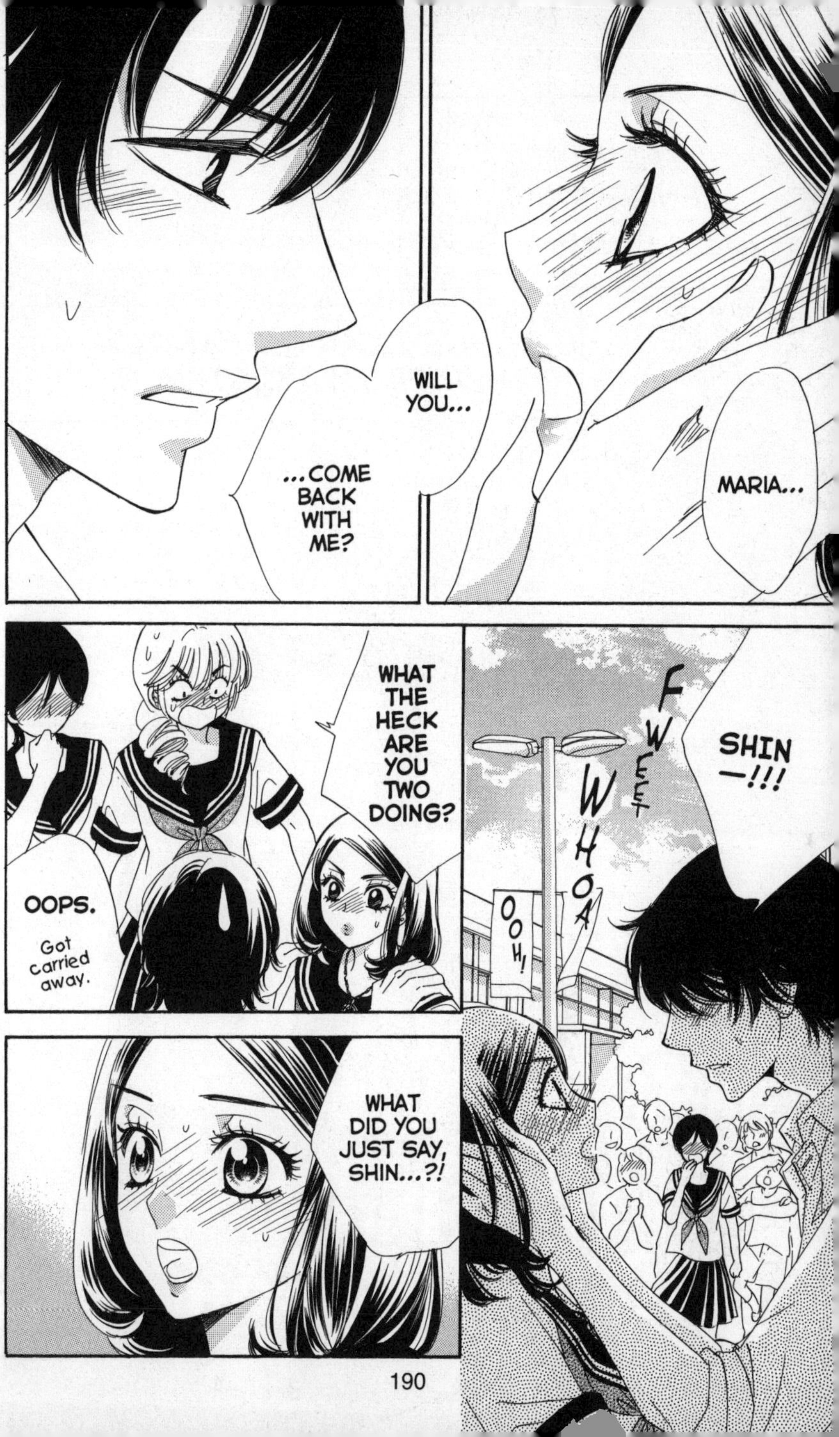
MARIA...
WILL YOU...
...COME BACK WITH ME?
SHIN—!!!
FWEET
WHOA
OOH!
WHAT THE HECK ARE YOU TWO DOING?
OOPS.
Got carried away.
WHAT DID YOU JUST SAY, SHIN...?!

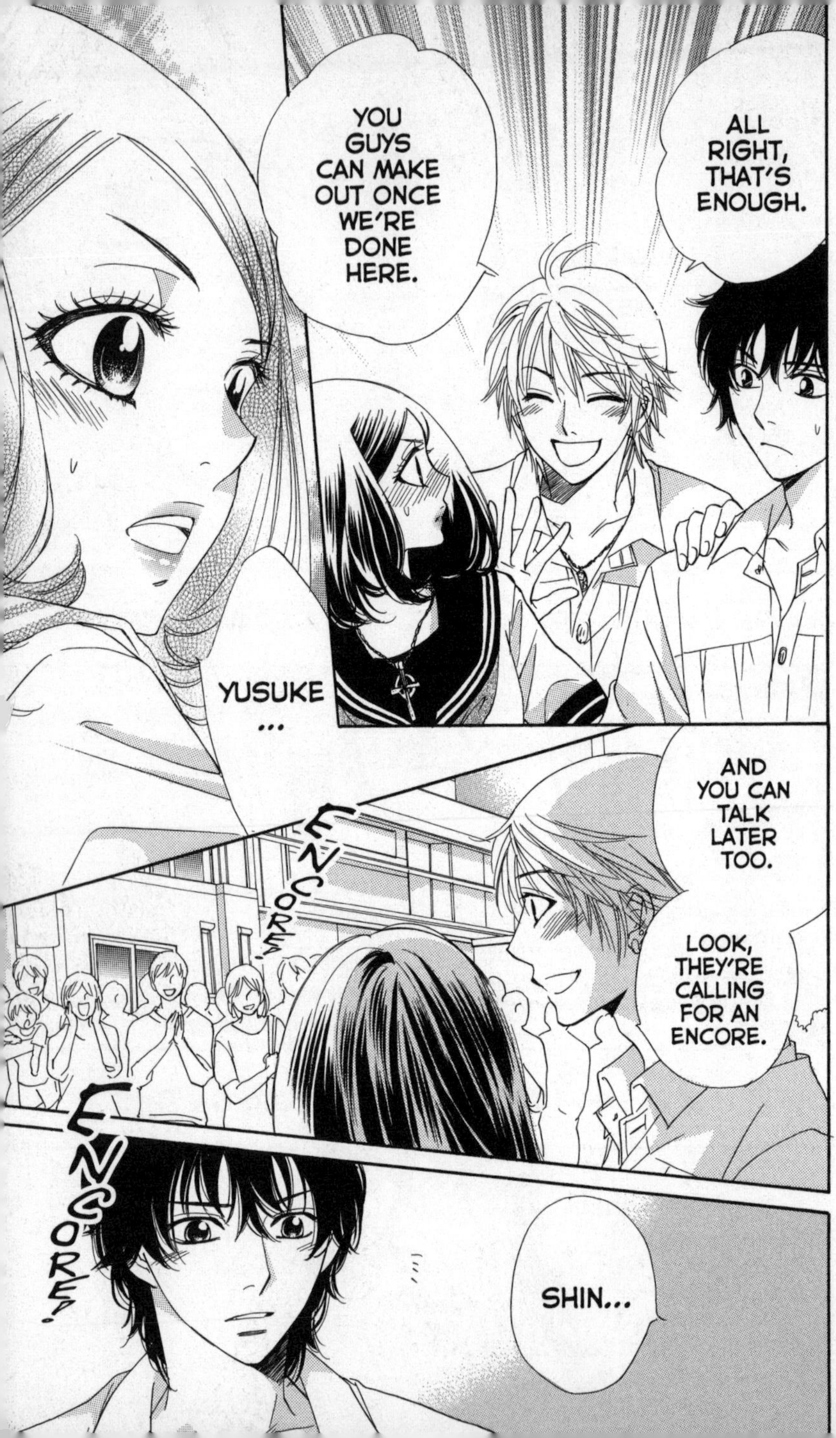
ALL RIGHT, THAT'S ENOUGH.
YOU GUYS CAN MAKE OUT ONCE WE'RE DONE HERE.
YUSUKE...
AND YOU CAN TALK LATER TOO.
LOOK, THEY'RE CALLING FOR AN ENCORE.
ENCORE!
ENCORE!
SHIN...

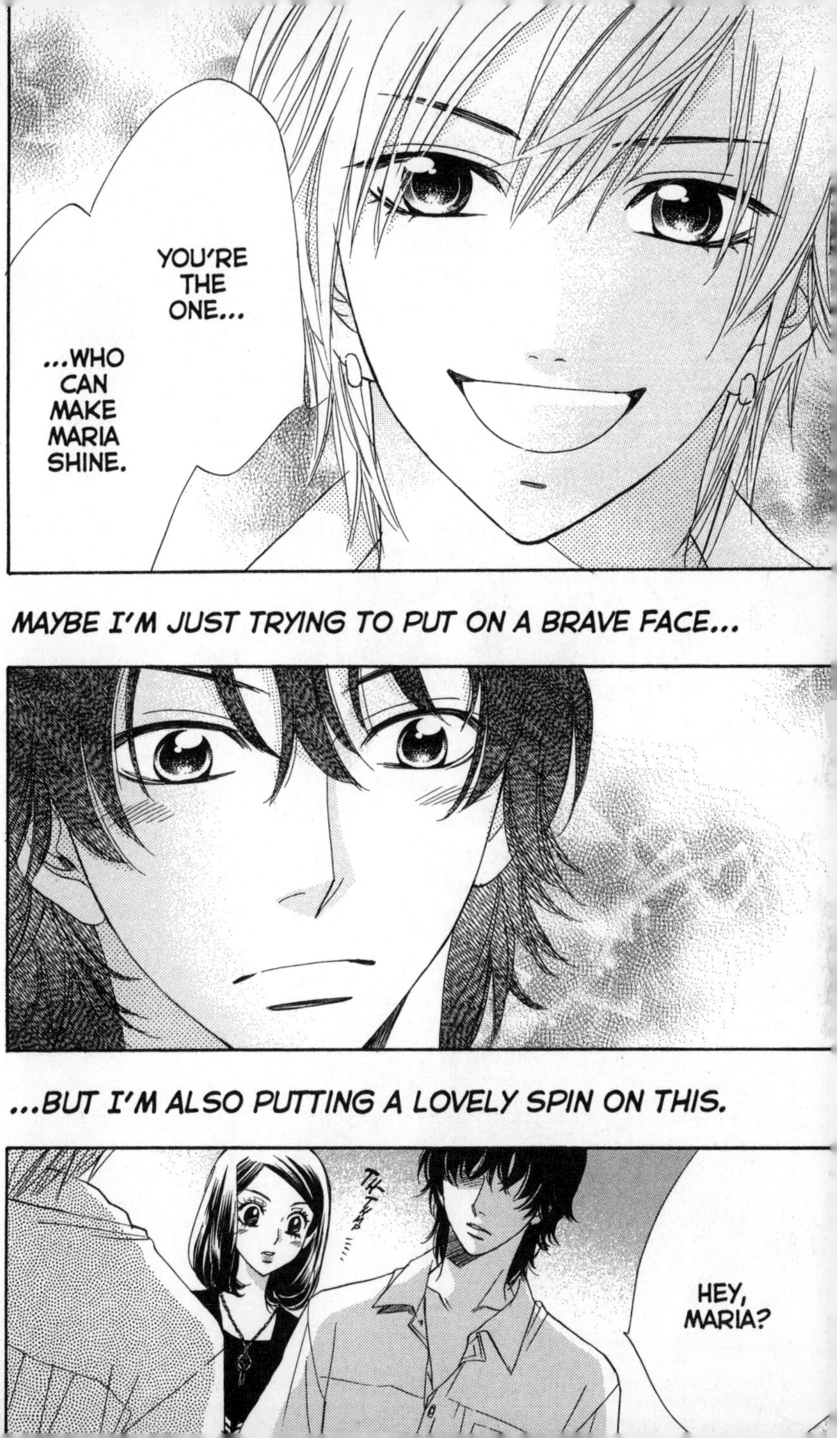
YOU'RE THE ONE...
...WHO CAN MAKE MARIA SHINE.
MAYBE I'M JUST TRYING TO PUT ON A BRAVE FACE...
...BUT I'M ALSO PUTTING A LOVELY SPIN ON THIS.
HEY, MARIA?

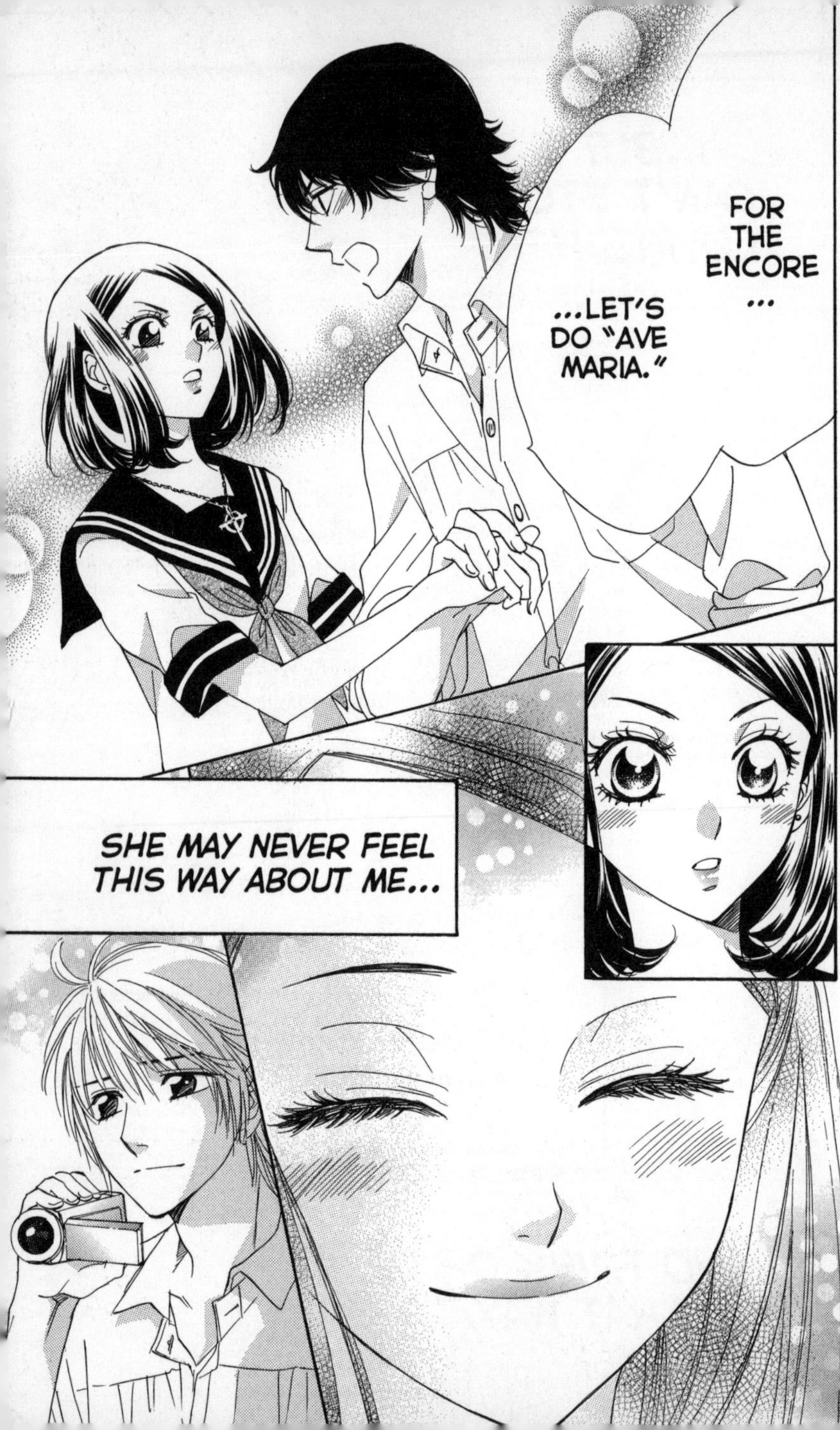
FOR THE ENCORE ...
...LET'S DO "AVE MARIA."
SHE MAY NEVER FEEL THIS WAY ABOUT ME...

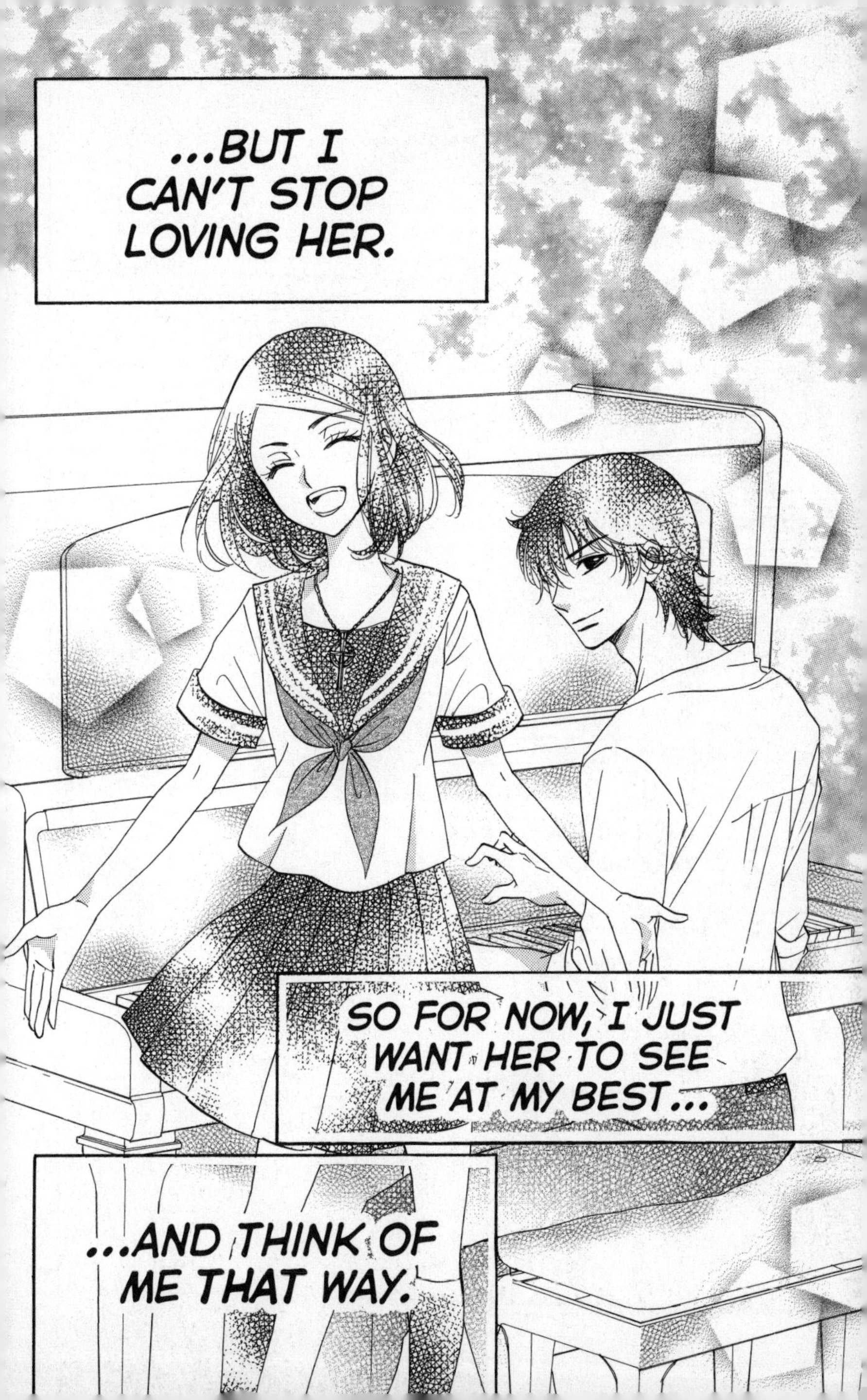
...BUT I CAN'T STOP LOVING HER.
SO FOR NOW, I JUST WANT HER TO SEE ME AT MY BEST...
...AND THINK OF ME THAT WAY.

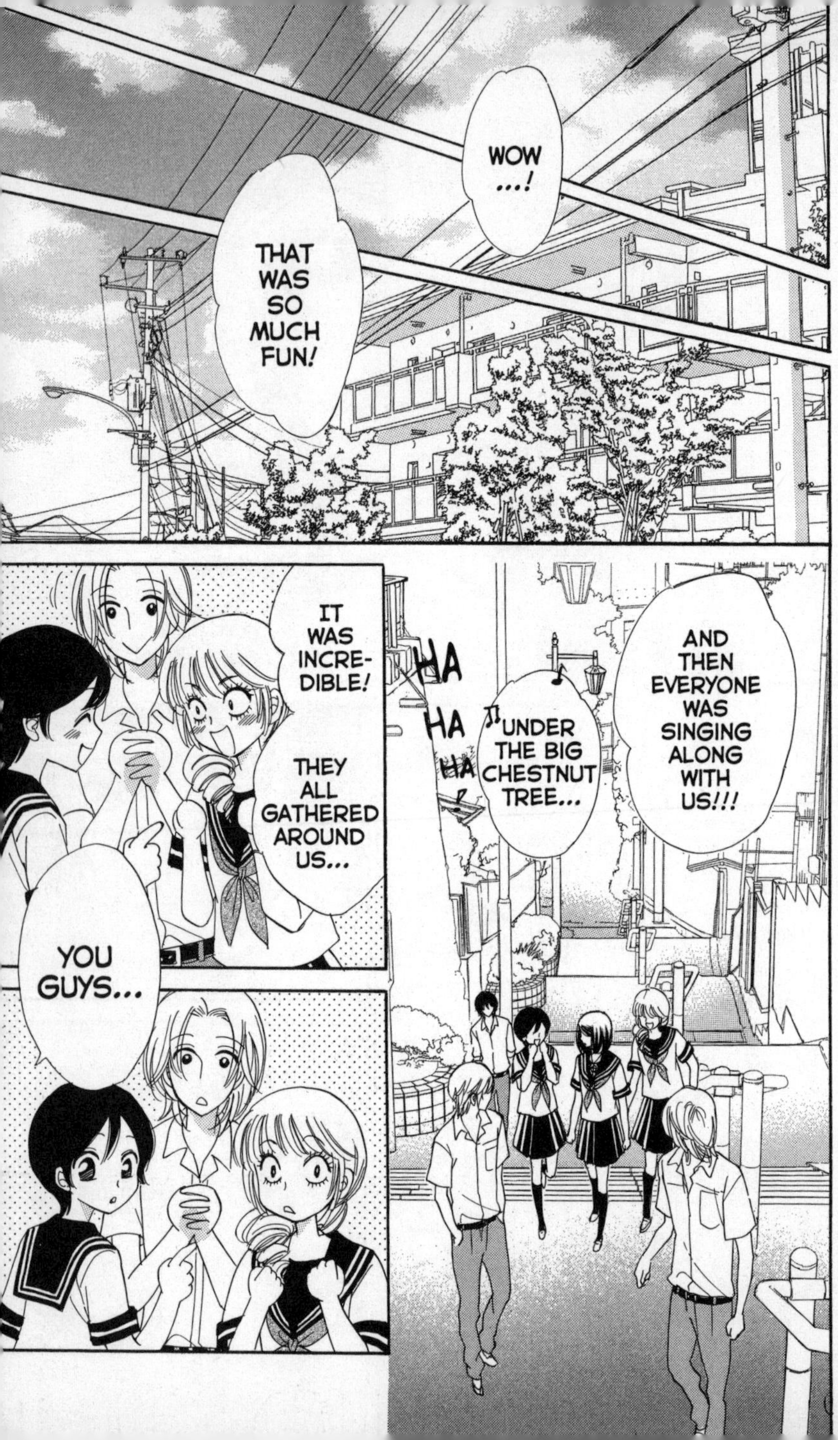
WOW...!
THAT WAS SO MUCH FUN!
AND THEN EVERYONE WAS SINGING ALONG WITH US!!!
UNDER THE BIG CHESTNUT TREE...
HA HA HA
IT WAS INCREDIBLE!
THEY ALL GATHERED AROUND US...
YOU GUYS...

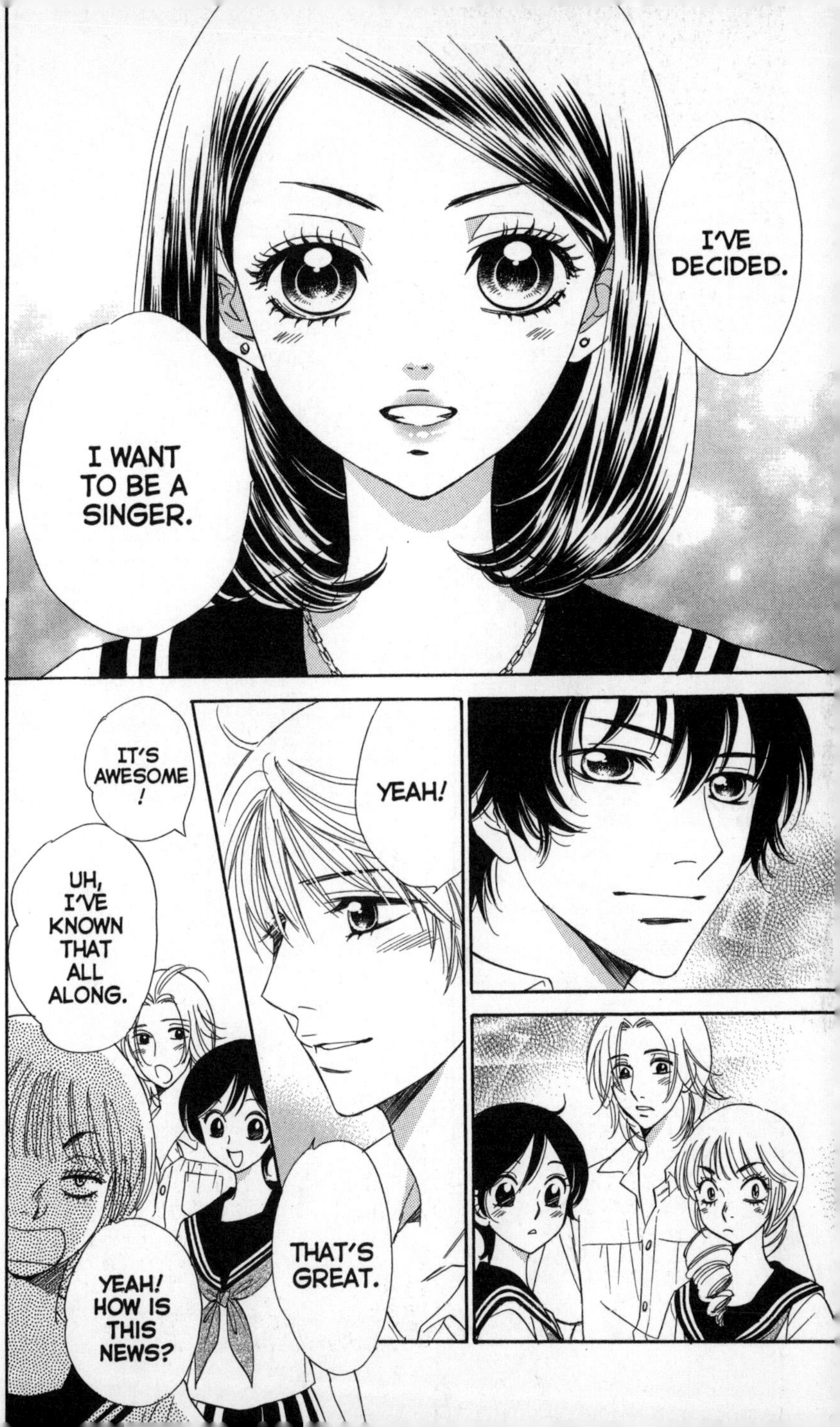
I'VE DECIDED.
I WANT TO BE A SINGER.
YEAH!
THAT'S GREAT.
IT'S AWESOME!
UH, I'VE KNOWN THAT ALL ALONG.
YEAH! HOW IS THIS NEWS?

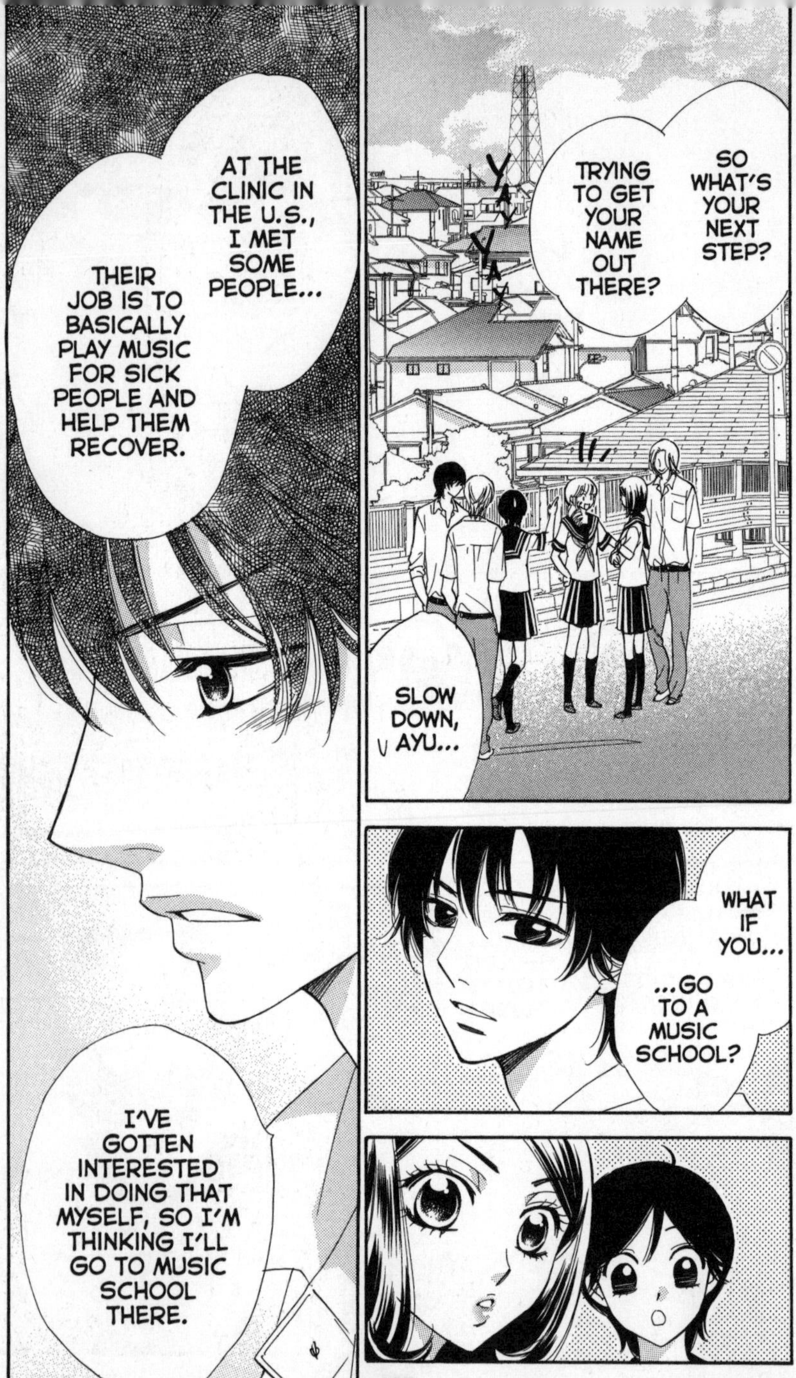
SO WHAT'S YOUR NEXT STEP?
TRYING TO GET YOUR NAME OUT THERE?
YAY YAY
SLOW DOWN, AYU...
WHAT IF YOU...
...GO TO A MUSIC SCHOOL?
AT THE CLINIC IN THE U.S., I MET SOME PEOPLE...
THEIR JOB IS TO BASICALLY PLAY MUSIC FOR SICK PEOPLE AND HELP THEM RECOVER.
I'VE GOTTEN INTERESTED IN DOING THAT MYSELF, SO I'M THINKING I'LL GO TO MUSIC SCHOOL THERE.

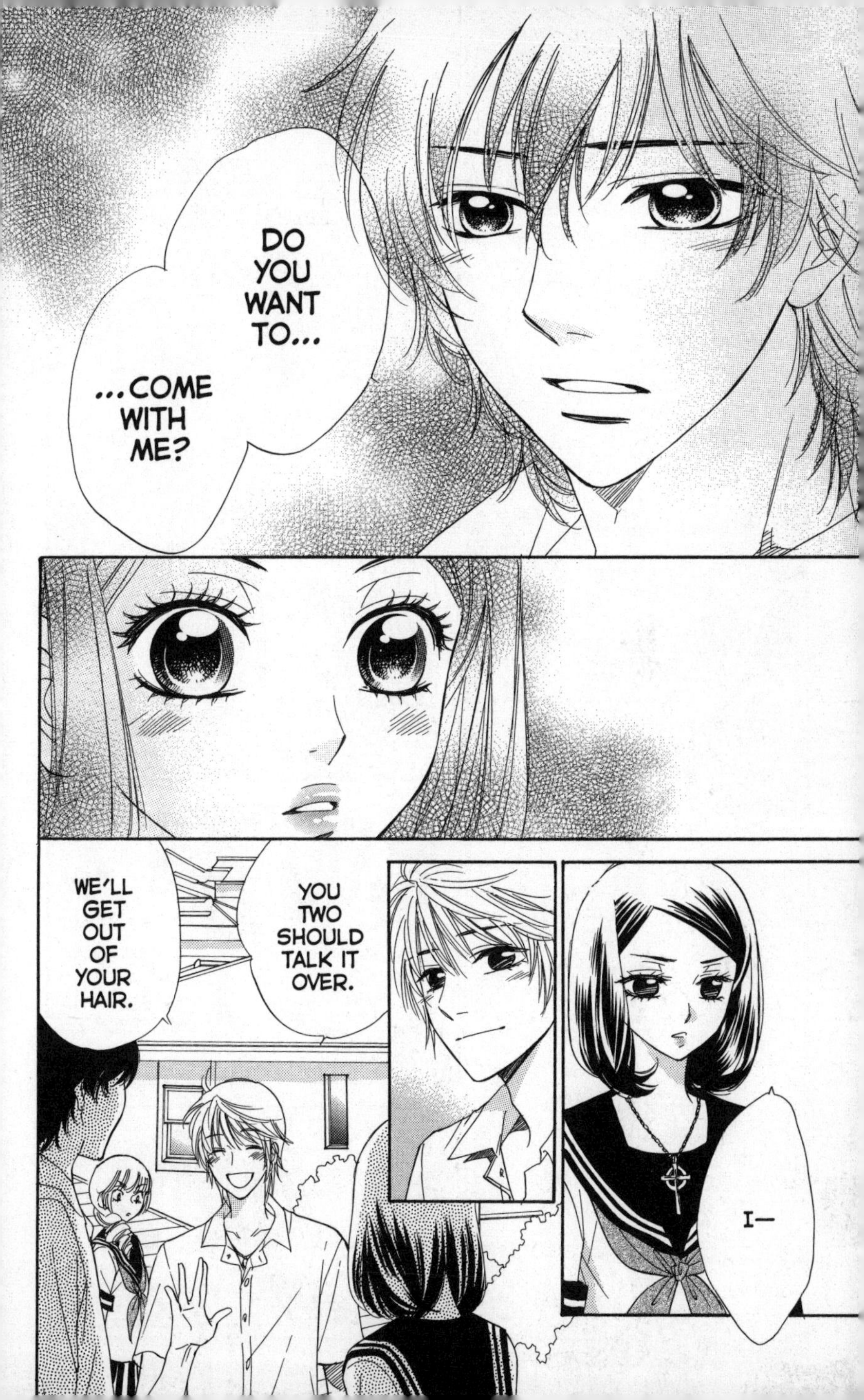
DO YOU WANT TO...
...COME WITH ME?
I—
YOU TWO SHOULD TALK IT OVER.
WE'LL GET OUT OF YOUR HAIR.

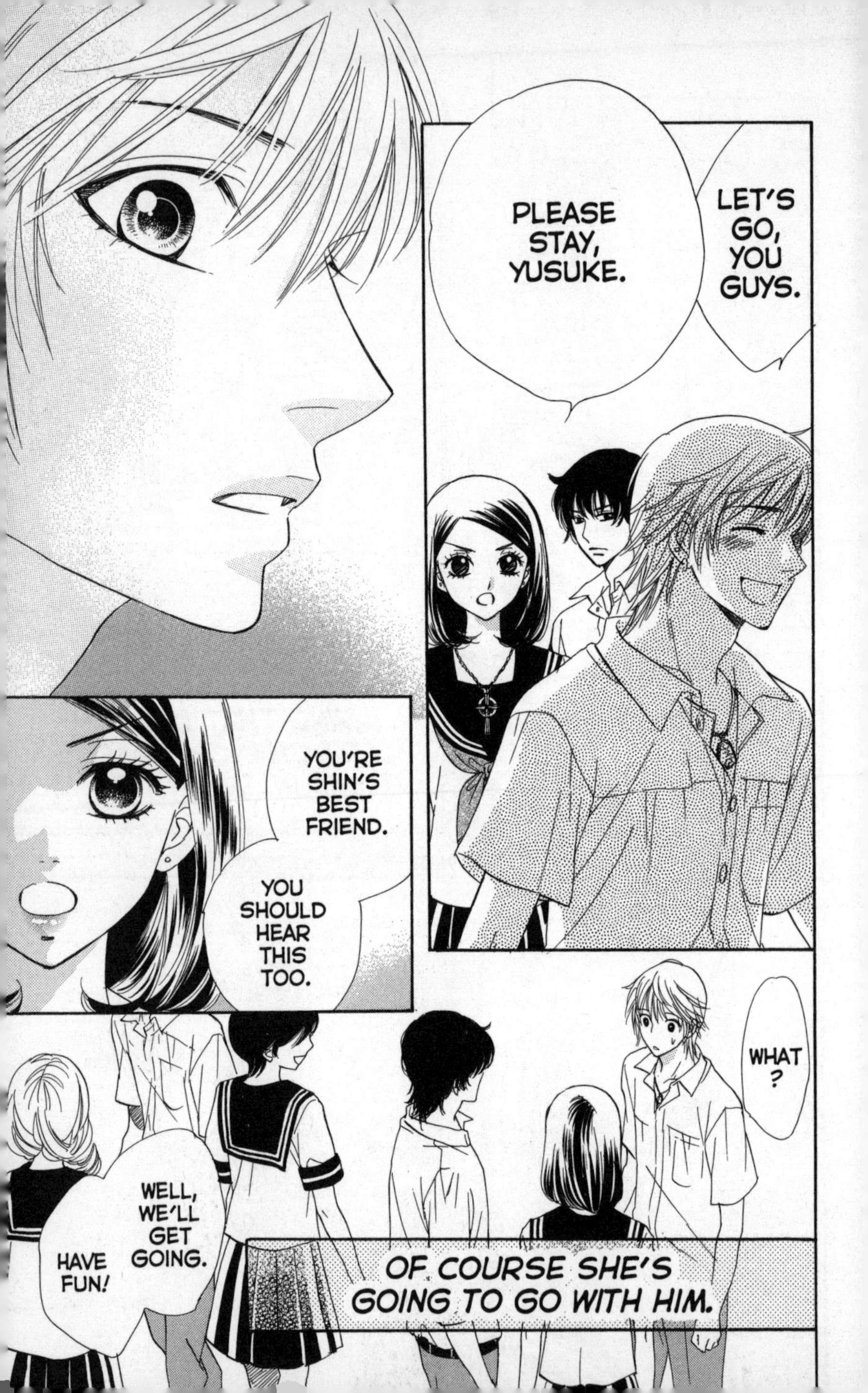
LET'S GO, YOU GUYS.
PLEASE STAY, YUSUKE.
YOU'RE SHIN'S BEST FRIEND.
YOU SHOULD HEAR THIS TOO.
WHAT?
OF COURSE SHE'S GOING TO GO WITH HIM.
WELL, WE'LL GET GOING.
HAVE FUN!

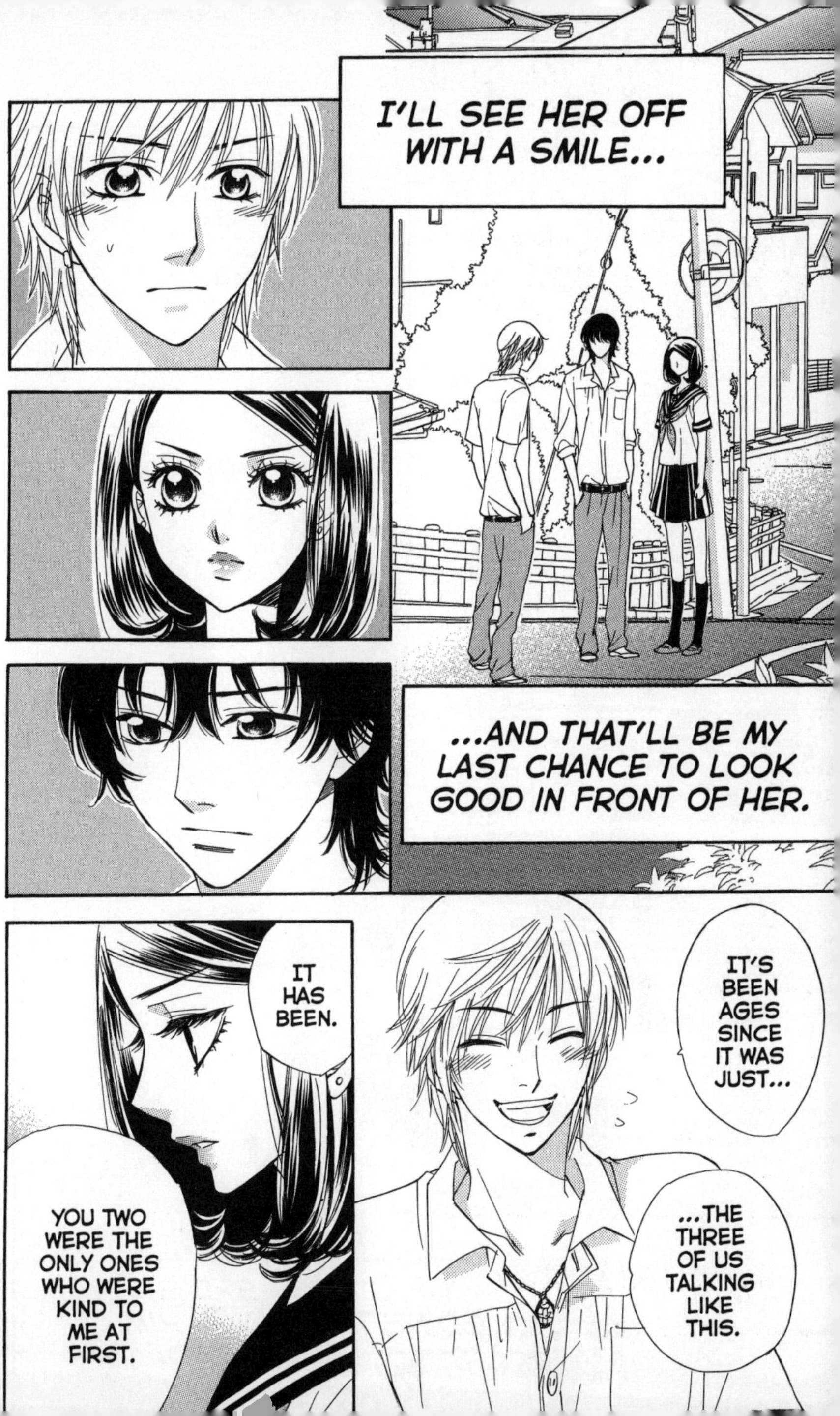
I'LL SEE HER OFF WITH A SMILE...
...AND THAT'LL BE MY LAST CHANCE TO LOOK GOOD IN FRONT OF HER.
IT'S BEEN AGES SINCE IT WAS JUST...
...THE THREE OF US TALKING LIKE THIS.
IT HAS BEEN.
YOU TWO WERE THE ONLY ONES WHO WERE KIND TO ME AT FIRST.

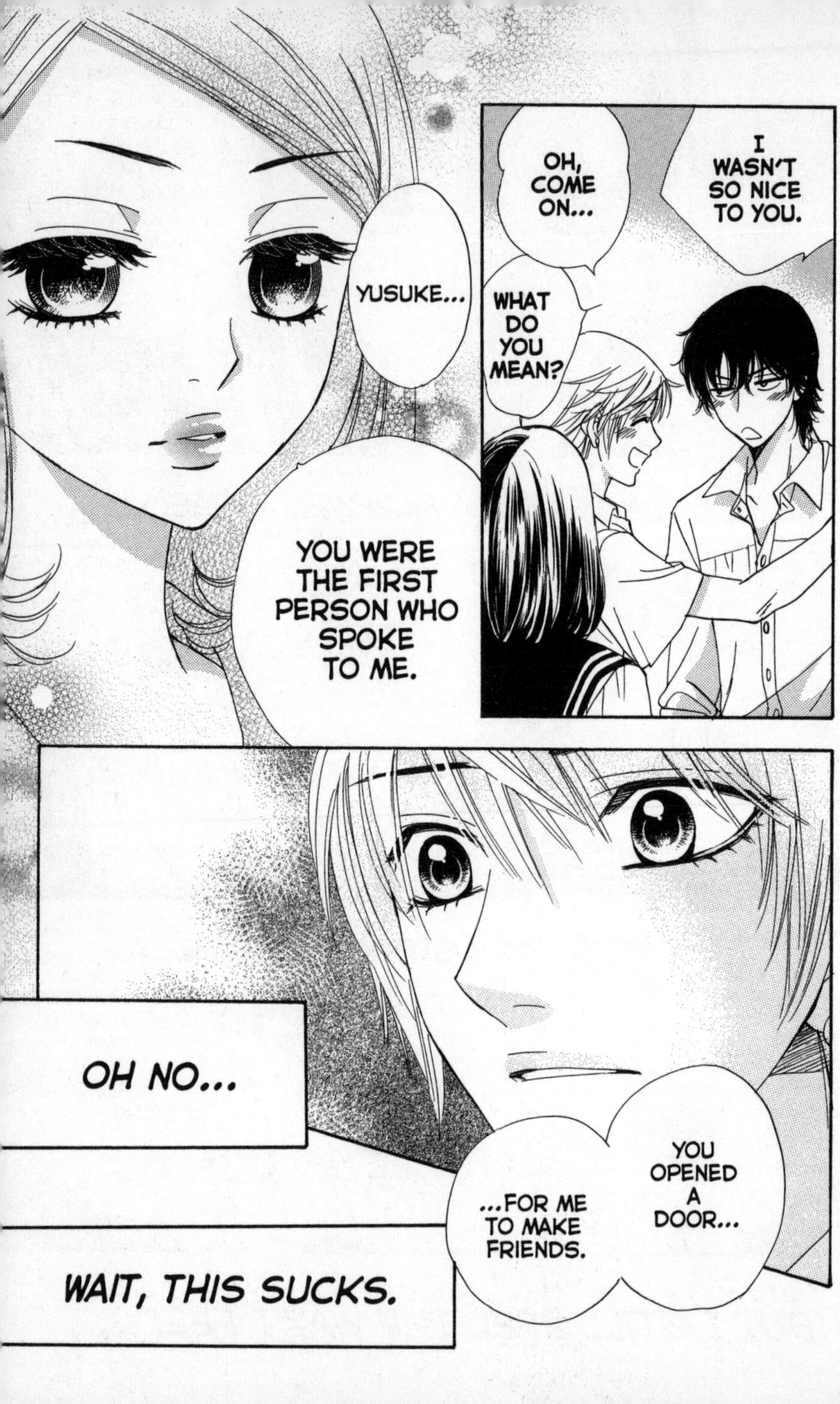
I WASN'T SO NICE TO YOU.
OH, COME ON...
WHAT DO YOU MEAN?
YUSUKE...
YOU WERE THE FIRST PERSON WHO SPOKE TO ME.
YOU OPENED A DOOR...
...FOR ME TO MAKE FRIENDS.
OH NO...
WAIT, THIS SUCKS.

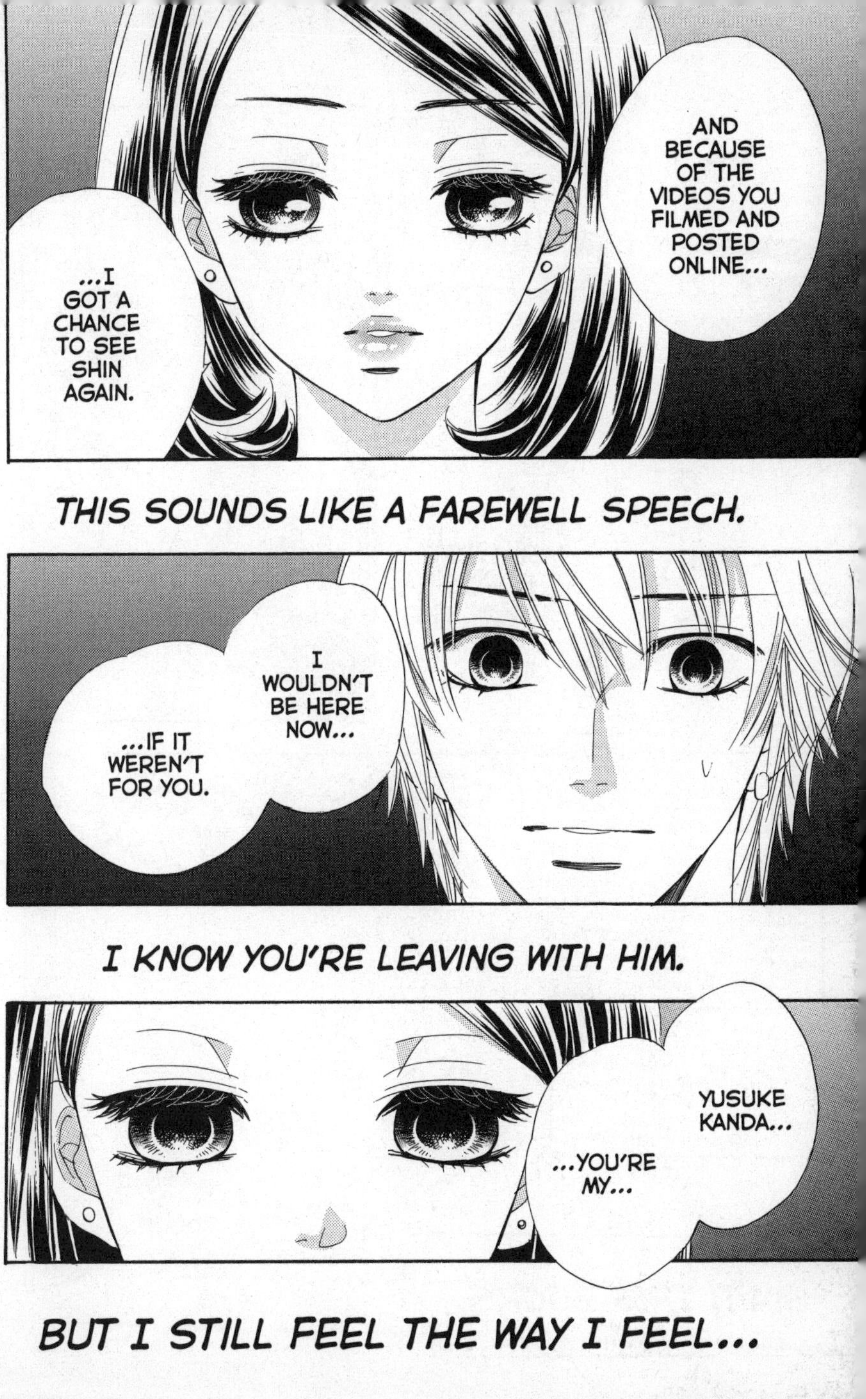
AND BECAUSE OF THE VIDEOS YOU FILMED AND POSTED ONLINE...
...I GOT A CHANCE TO SEE SHIN AGAIN.
THIS SOUNDS LIKE A FAREWELL SPEECH.
I WOULDN'T BE HERE NOW...
...IF IT WEREN'T FOR YOU.
I KNOW YOU'RE LEAVING WITH HIM.
YUSUKE KANDA...
...YOU'RE MY...
BUT I STILL FEEL THE WAY I FEEL...

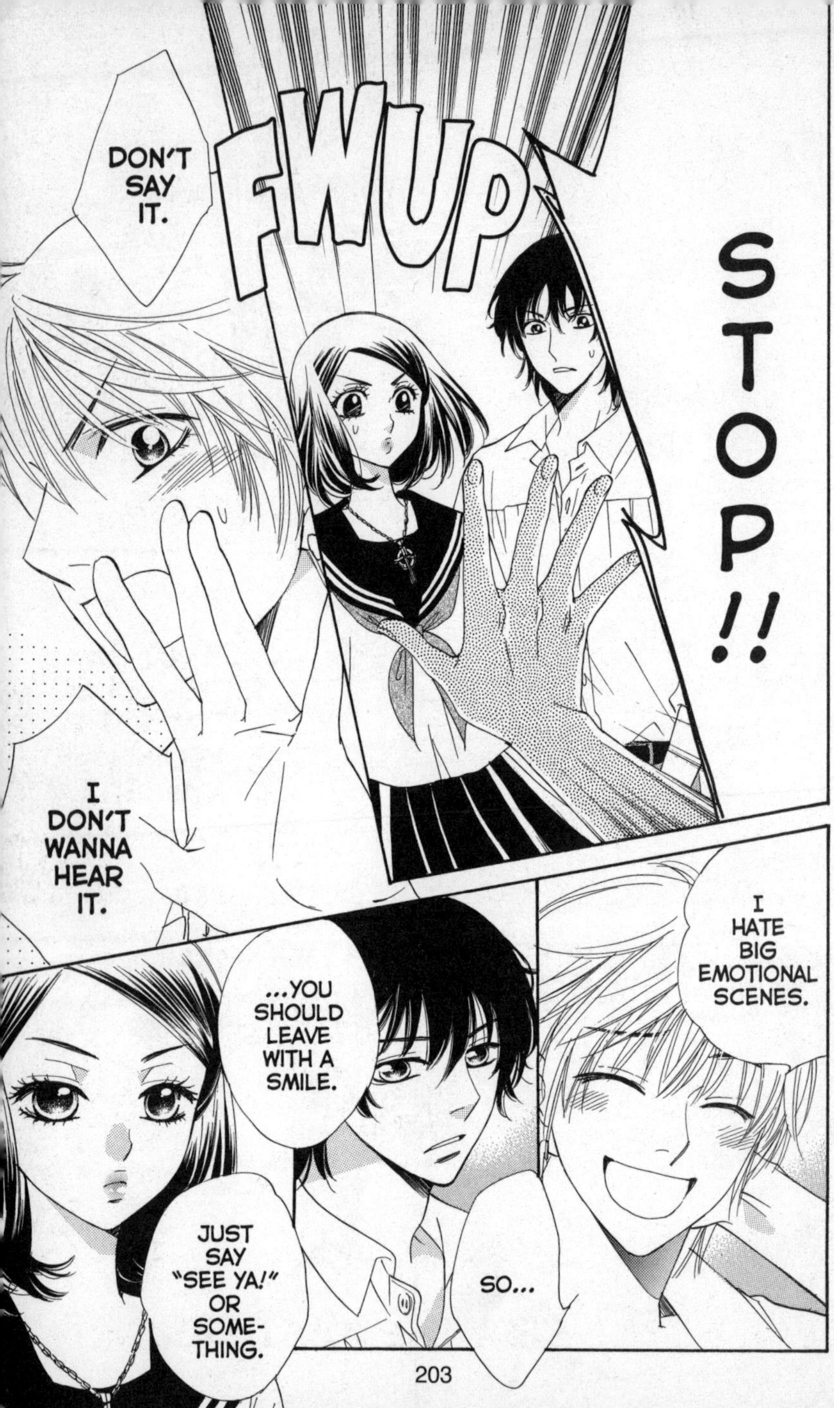
STOP!!
FWUP
DON'T SAY IT.
I DON'T WANNA HEAR IT.
I HATE BIG EMOTIONAL SCENES.
SO...
...YOU SHOULD LEAVE WITH A SMILE.
JUST SAY "SEE YA!" OR SOMETHING.

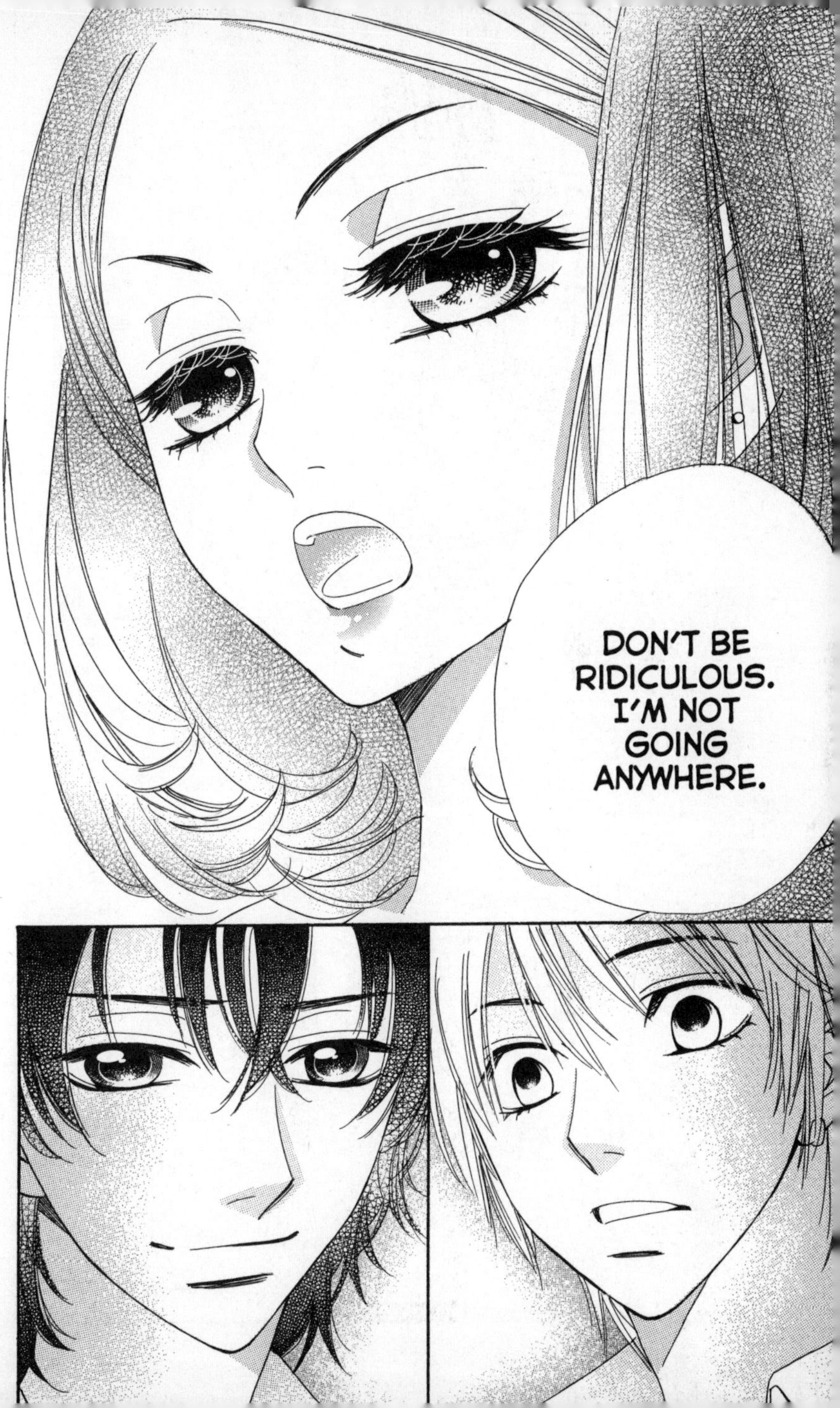
DON'T BE RIDICULOUS. I'M NOT GOING ANYWHERE.

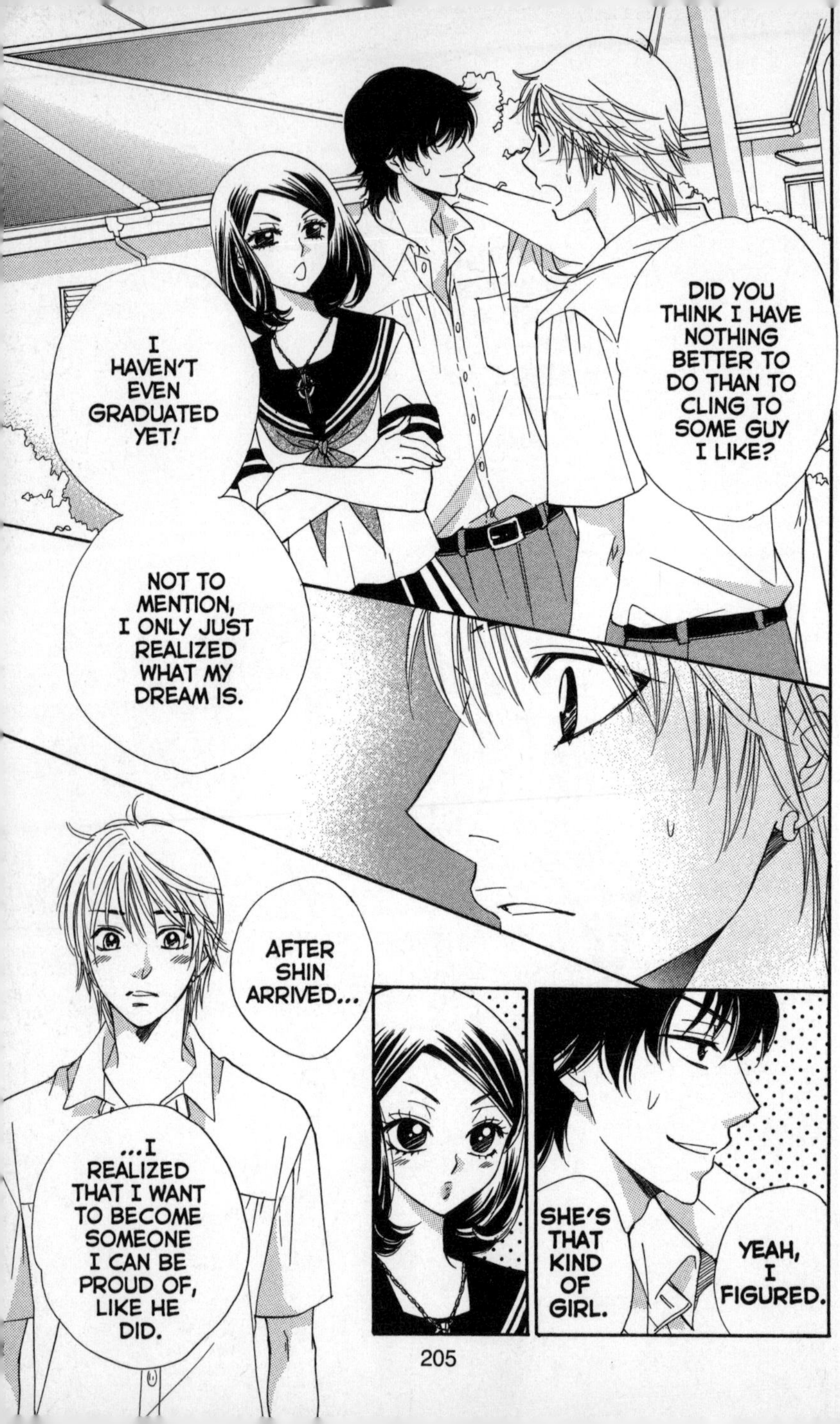
DID YOU THINK I HAVE NOTHING BETTER TO DO THAN TO CLING TO SOME GUY I LIKE?
I HAVEN'T EVEN GRADUATED YET!
NOT TO MENTION, I ONLY JUST REALIZED WHAT MY DREAM IS.
YEAH, I FIGURED.
SHE'S THAT KIND OF GIRL.
AFTER SHIN ARRIVED...
...I REALIZED THAT I WANT TO BECOME SOMEONE I CAN BE PROUD OF, LIKE HE DID.

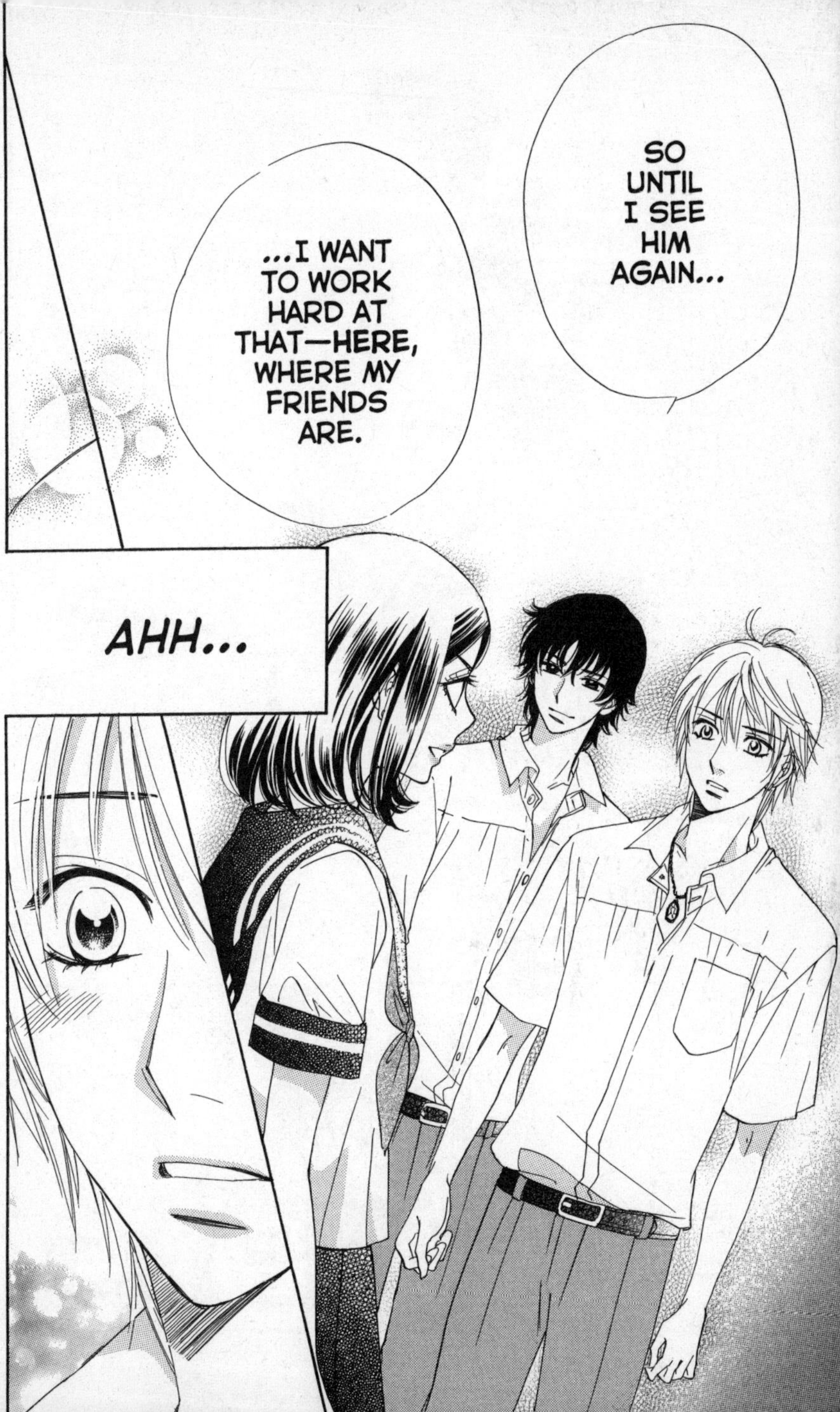
SO UNTIL I SEE HIM AGAIN...
...I WANT TO WORK HARD AT THAT—HERE, WHERE MY FRIENDS ARE.
AHH...

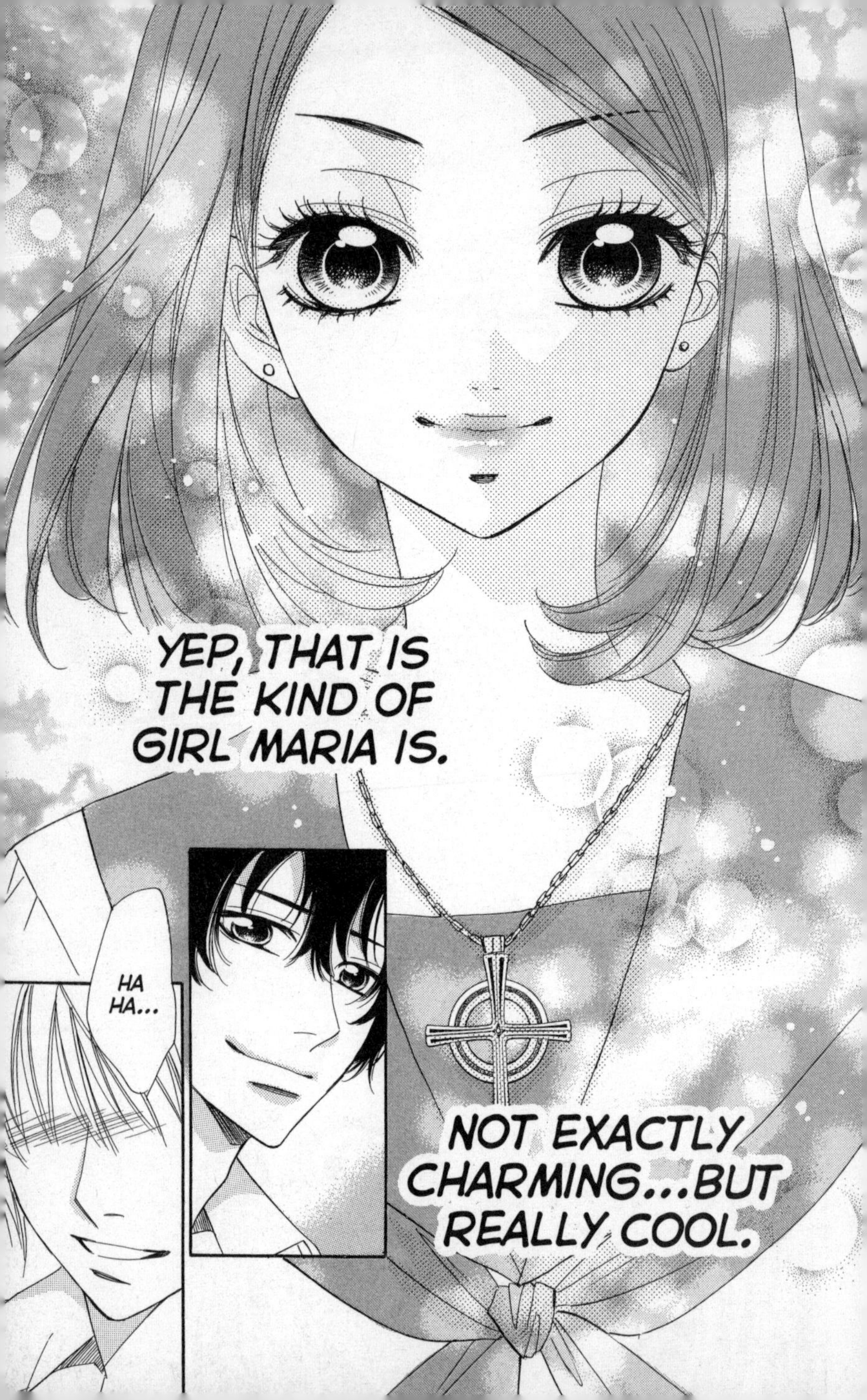
YEP, THAT IS THE KIND OF GIRL MARIA IS.
NOT EXACTLY CHARMING...BUT REALLY COOL.
HA HA...

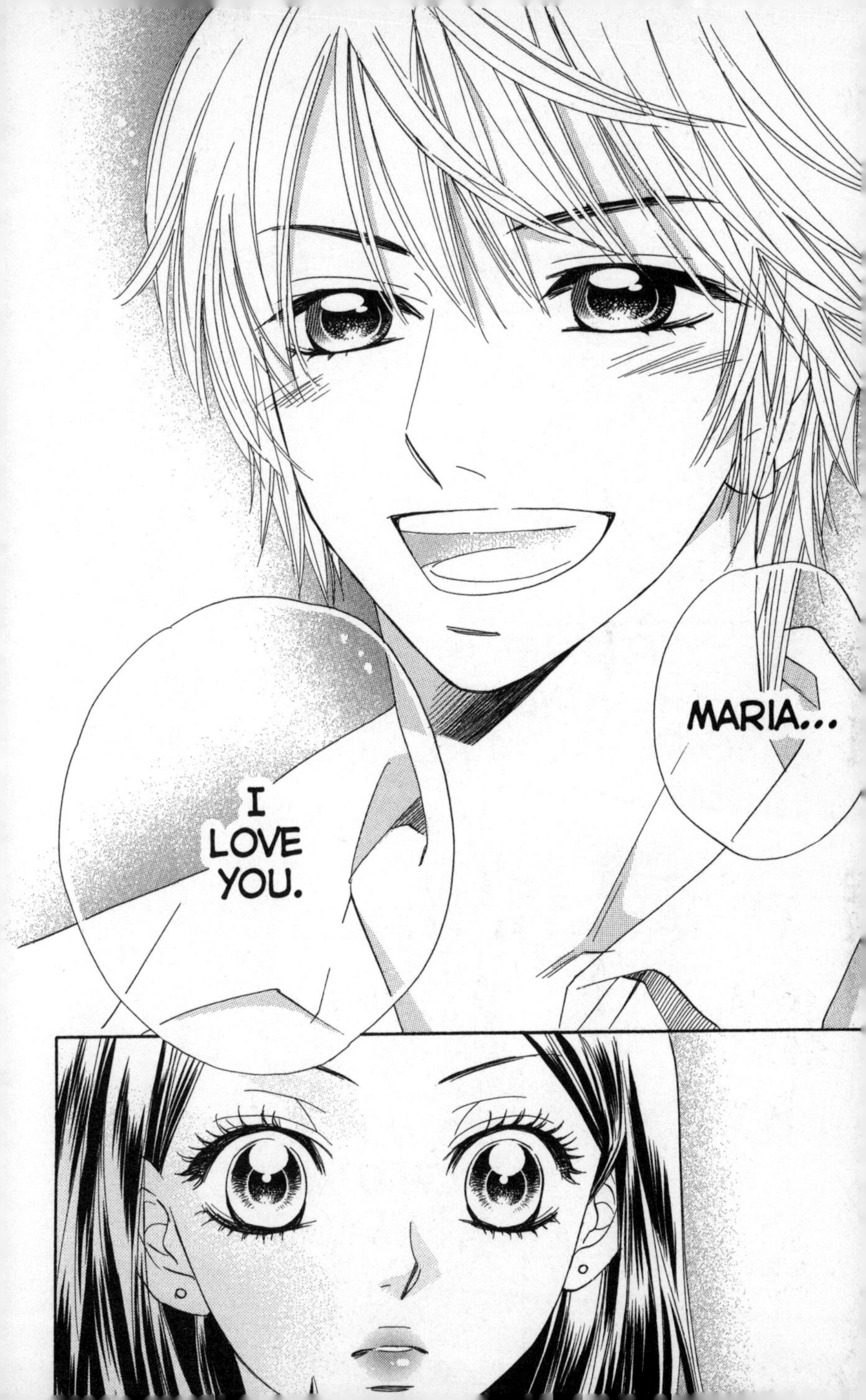
MARIA...
I LOVE YOU.

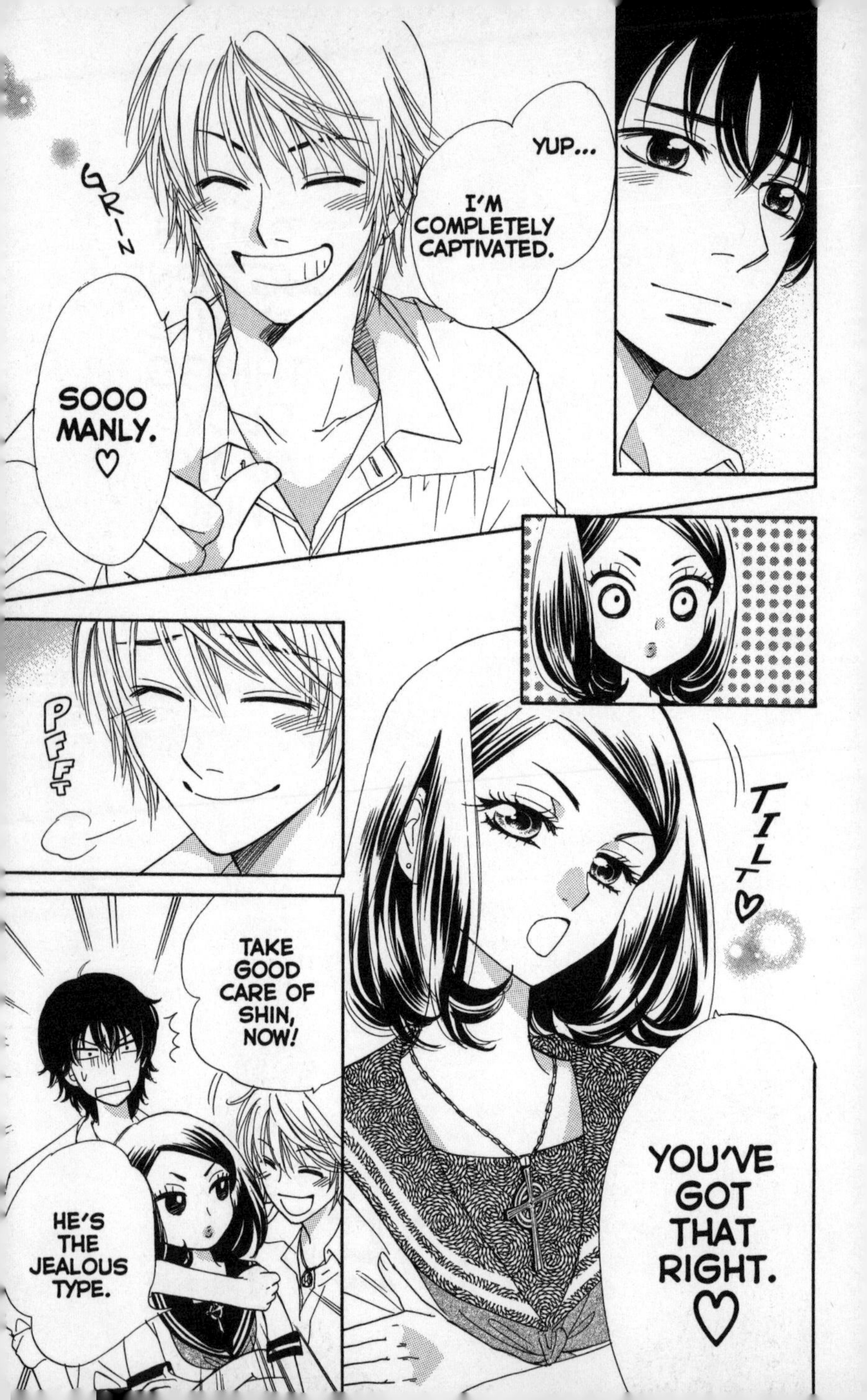
YUP... I'M COMPLETELY CAPTIVATED.
GRIN
SOOO MANLY. ♡
TILT ♡
YOU'VE GOT THAT RIGHT. ♡
PFFT
TAKE GOOD CARE OF SHIN, NOW!
HE'S THE JEALOUS TYPE.

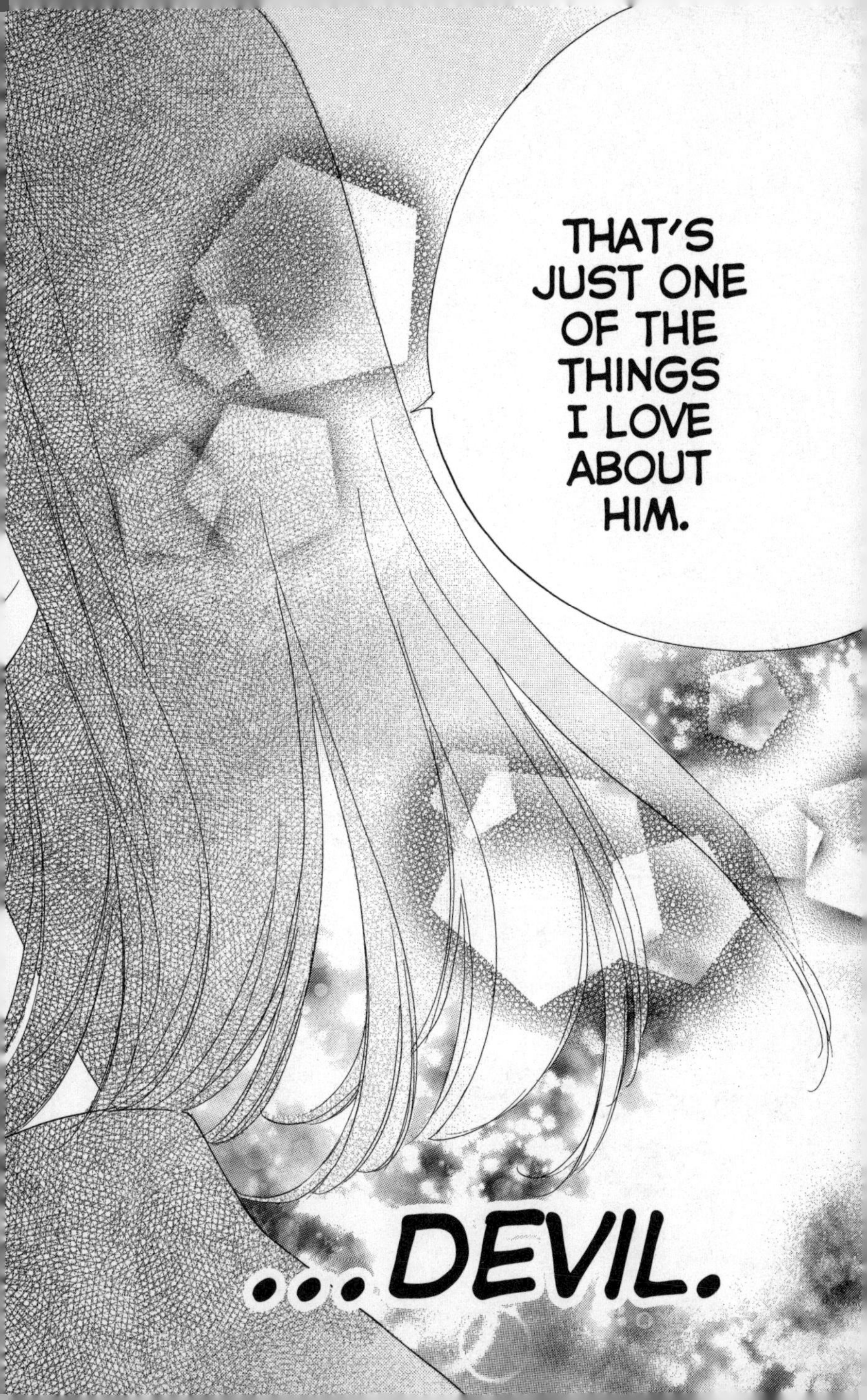
THAT'S JUST ONE OF THE THINGS I LOVE ABOUT HIM.
...DEVIL.

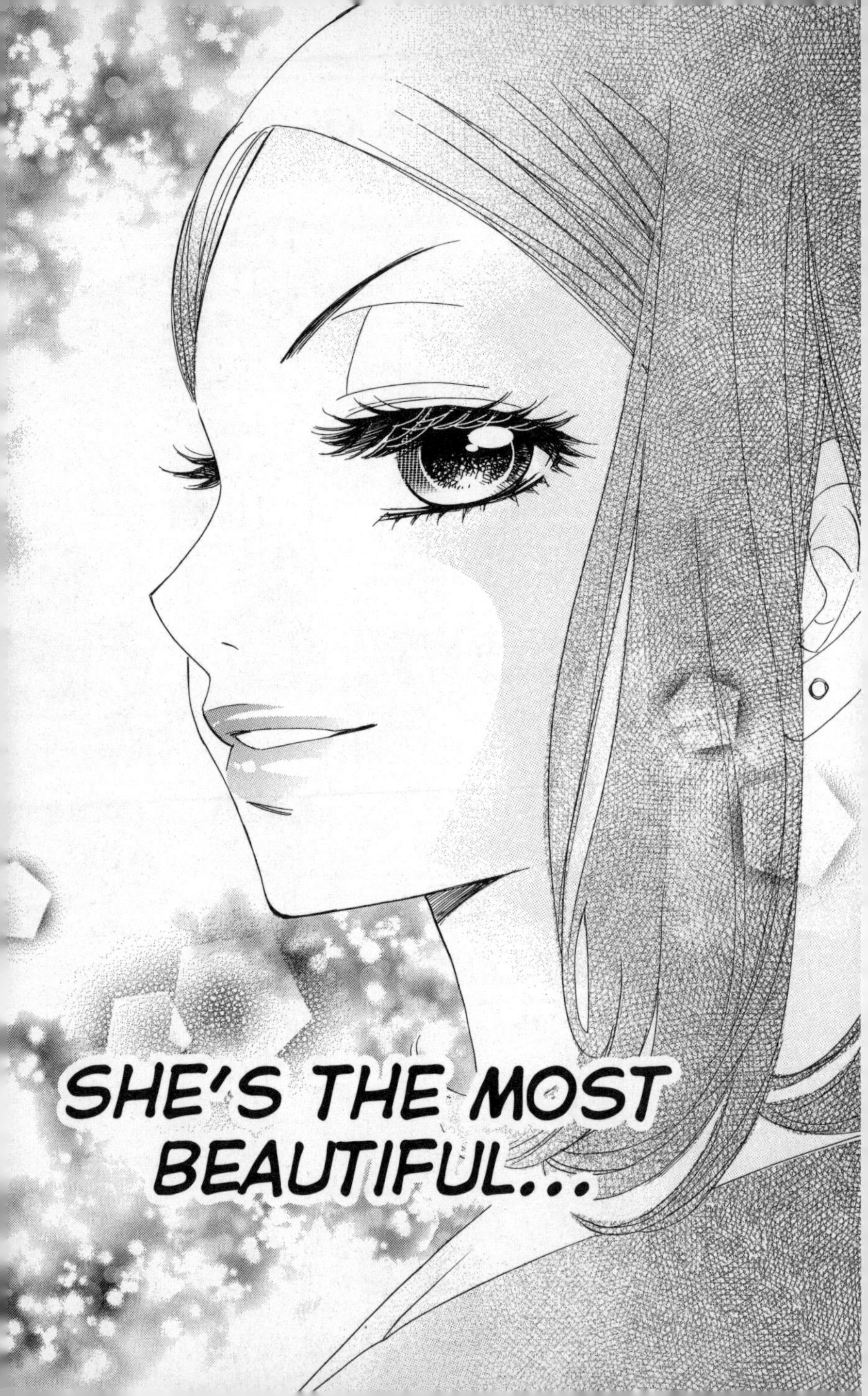
SHE'S THE MOST BEAUTIFUL...

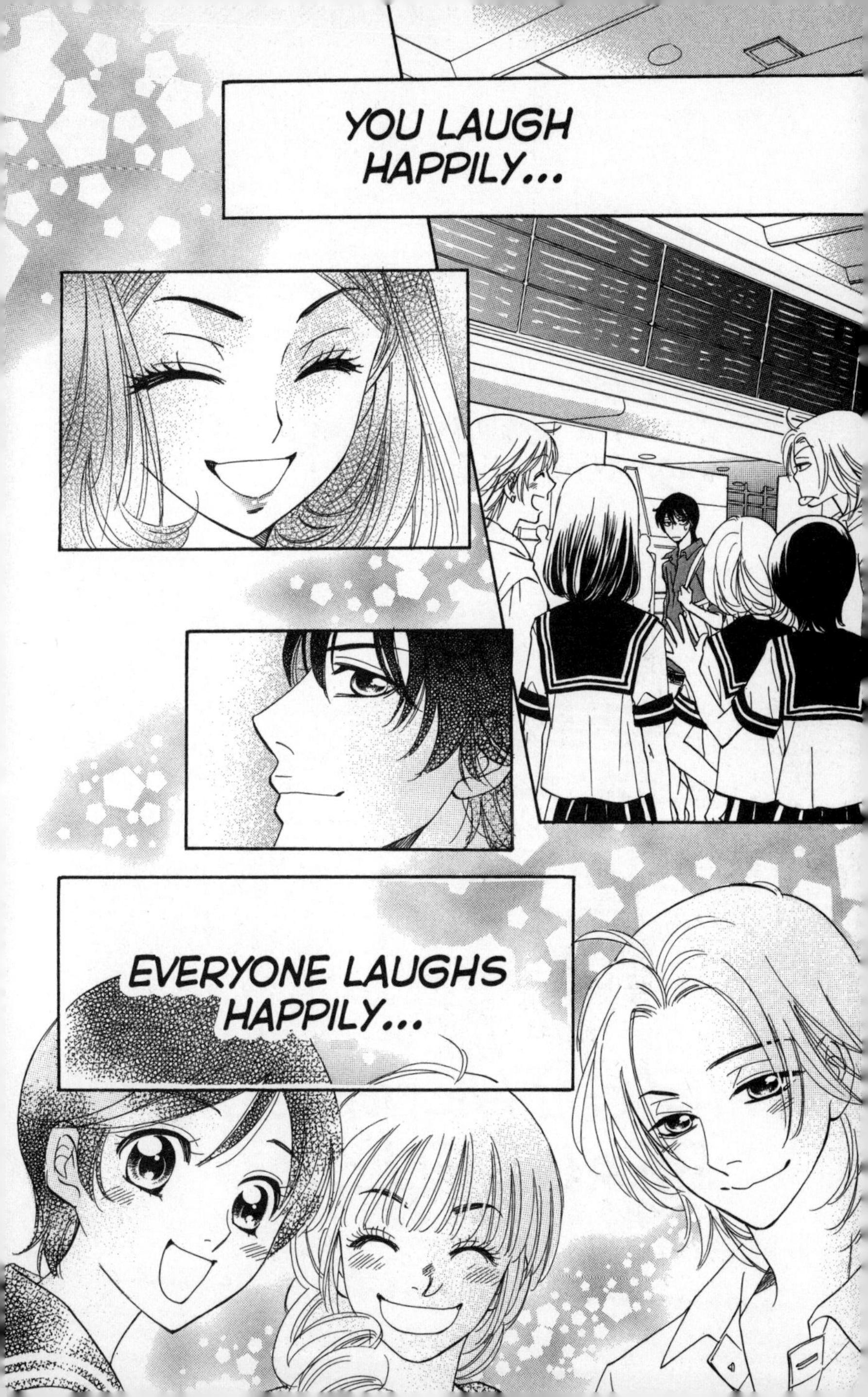
YOU LAUGH HAPPILY...
EVERYONE LAUGHS HAPPILY...

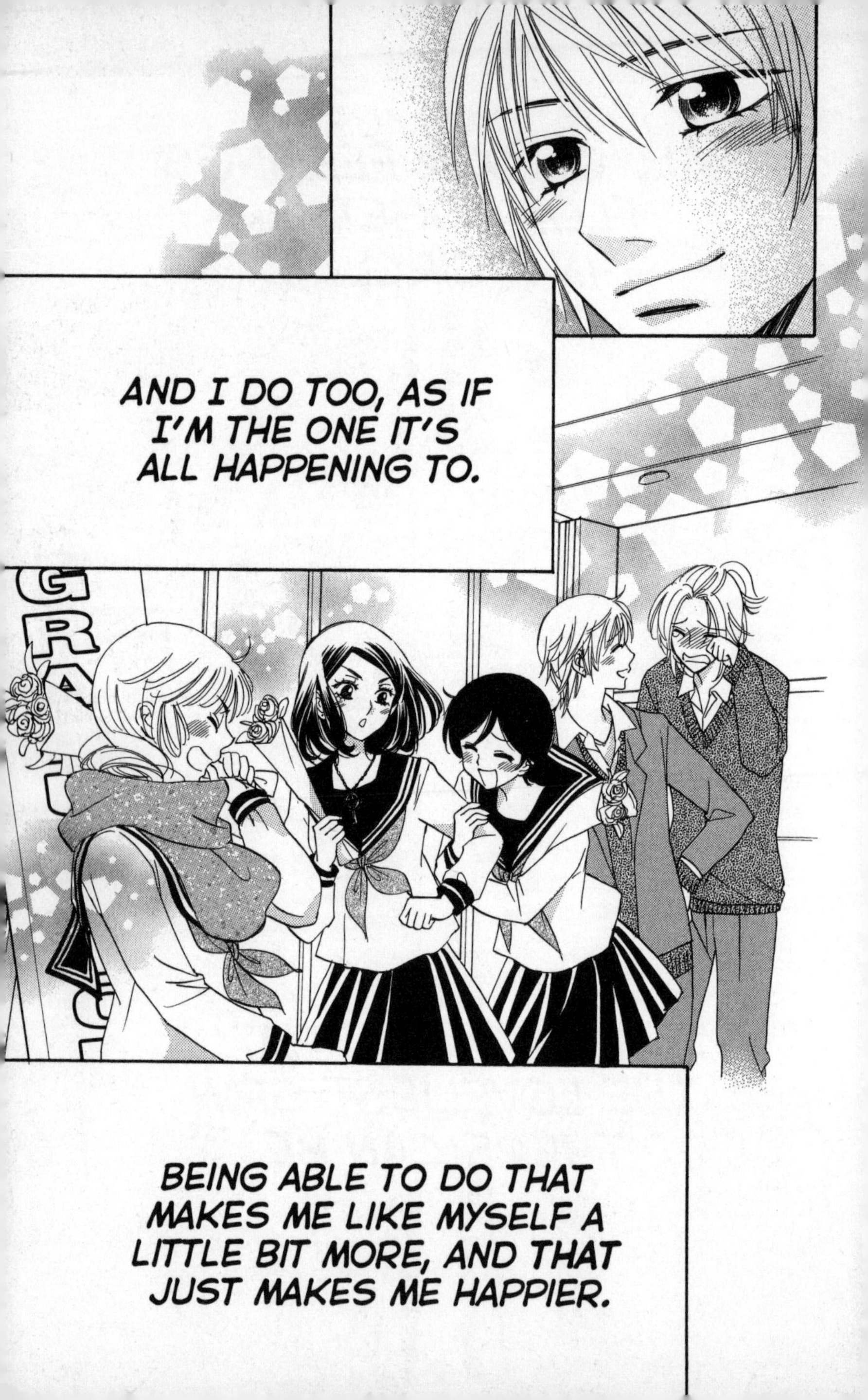
AND I DO TOO, AS IF I'M THE ONE IT'S ALL HAPPENING TO.
BEING ABLE TO DO THAT MAKES ME LIKE MYSELF A LITTLE BIT MORE, AND THAT JUST MAKES ME HAPPIER.

ALL OF OUR FEELINGS FLOW TOGETHER IN A CIRCLE...
...AND TO ME, THAT'S THE LOVELIEST SPIN THERE CAN BE.
THE END

Thank you so much for
reading to the very end!

Editor-in-chief from a while ago Suzuki-san
Last editor-in-chief Shimada-san
Editor-in-chief Sawano-san
Former editor Ono-san
Editor Matsui-san
Everyone in the editorial department
Everyone in the sales department
Everyone at the printing press
The designers who created
the logo and cover
Everyone who had a part in
A Devil and Her Love Song

S, my roommate, who helped
me with the manuscript

And to all the readers

Thank you so, so much!
I hope to see you again.

Miyoshi Tomori

A Devil and
Her Love Song

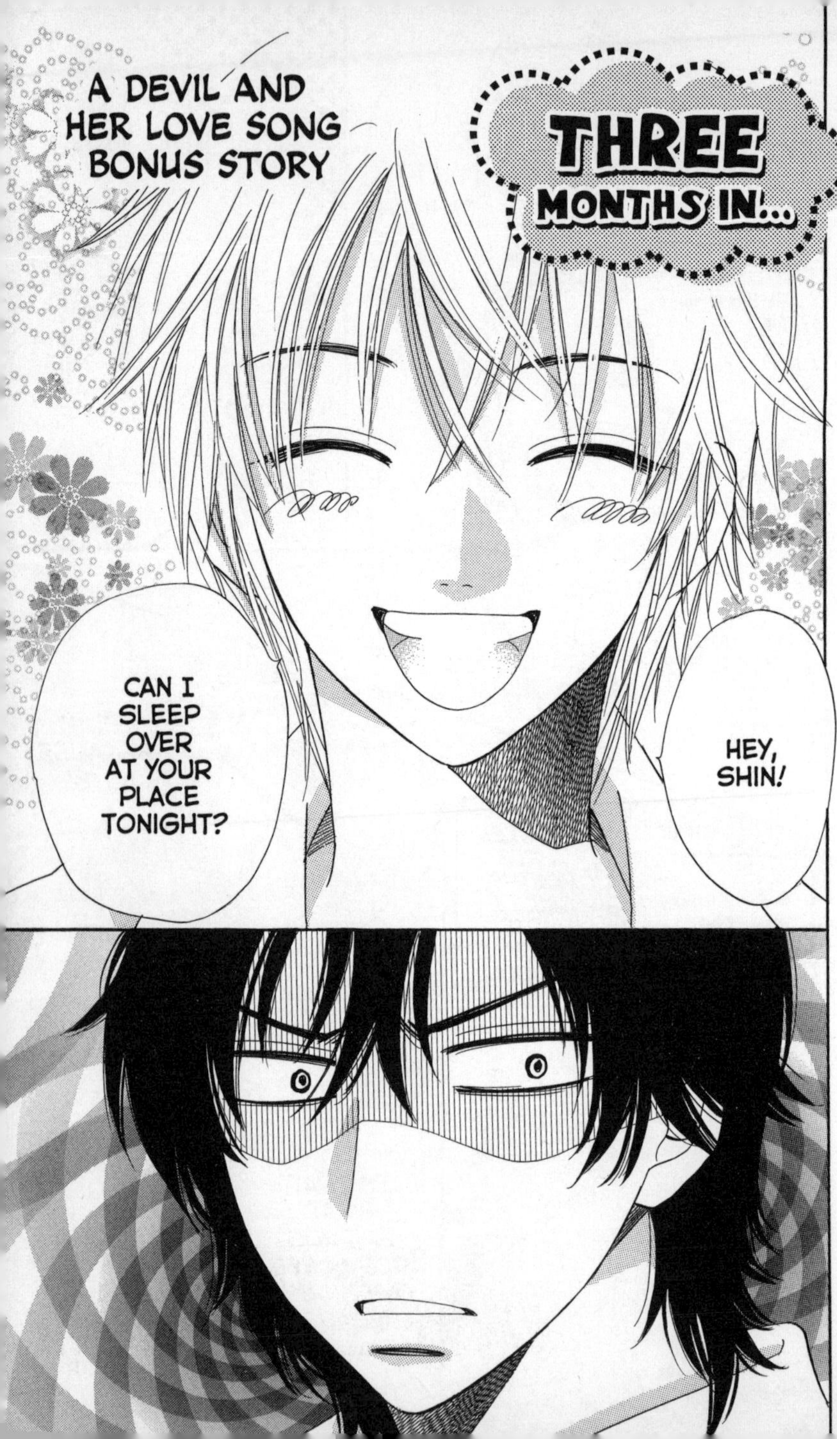
THREE MONTHS IN...
A DEVIL AND HER LOVE SONG BONUS STORY
HEY, SHIN!
CAN I SLEEP OVER AT YOUR PLACE TONIGHT?

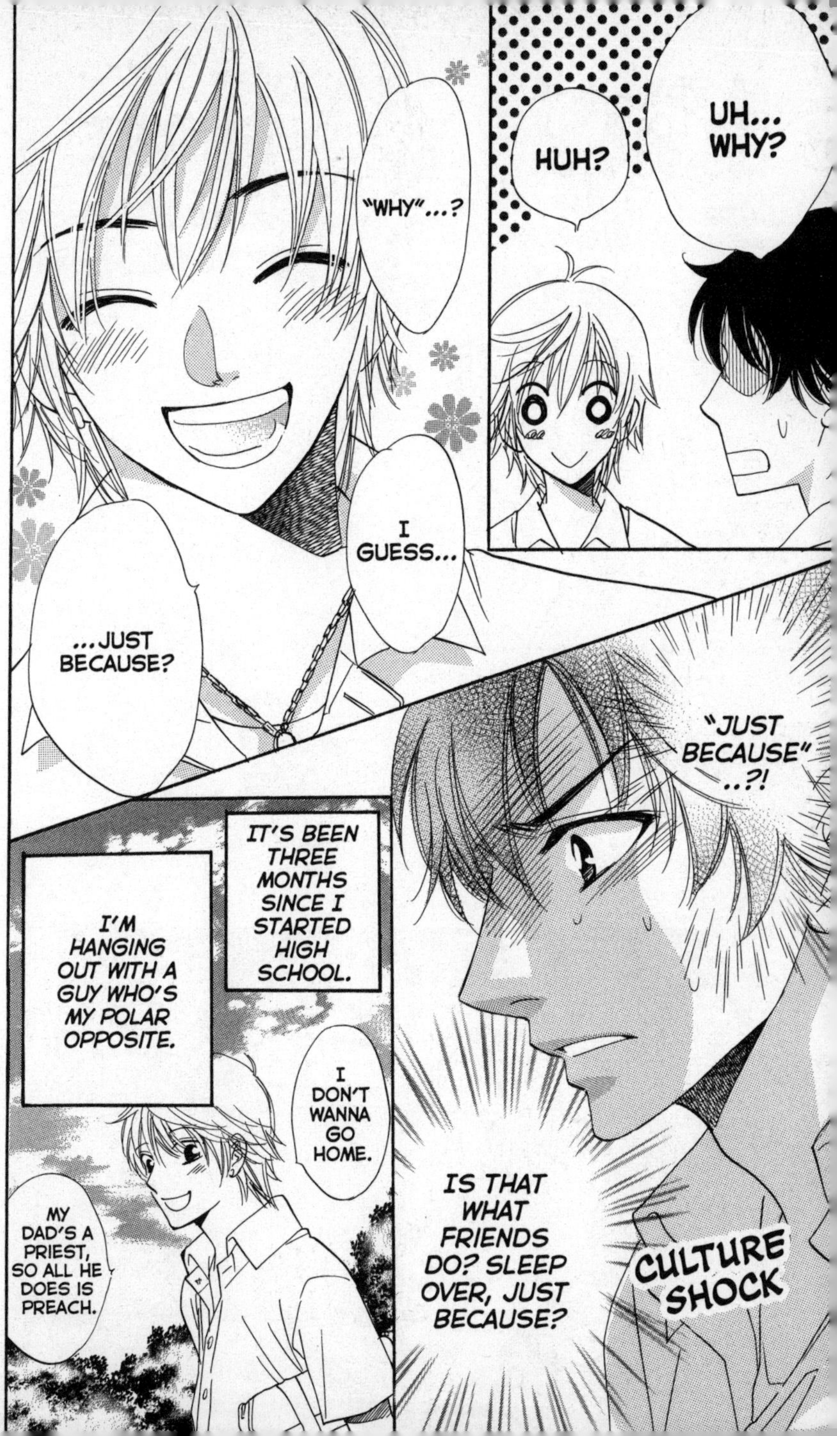
UH... WHY?
HUH?
"WHY"...?
I GUESS...
...JUST BECAUSE?
"JUST BECAUSE" ..?!
CULTURE SHOCK
IS THAT WHAT FRIENDS DO? SLEEP OVER, JUST BECAUSE?
IT'S BEEN THREE MONTHS SINCE I STARTED HIGH SCHOOL.
I'M HANGING OUT WITH A GUY WHO'S MY POLAR OPPOSITE.
I DON'T WANNA GO HOME.
MY DAD'S A PRIEST, SO ALL HE DOES IS PREACH.

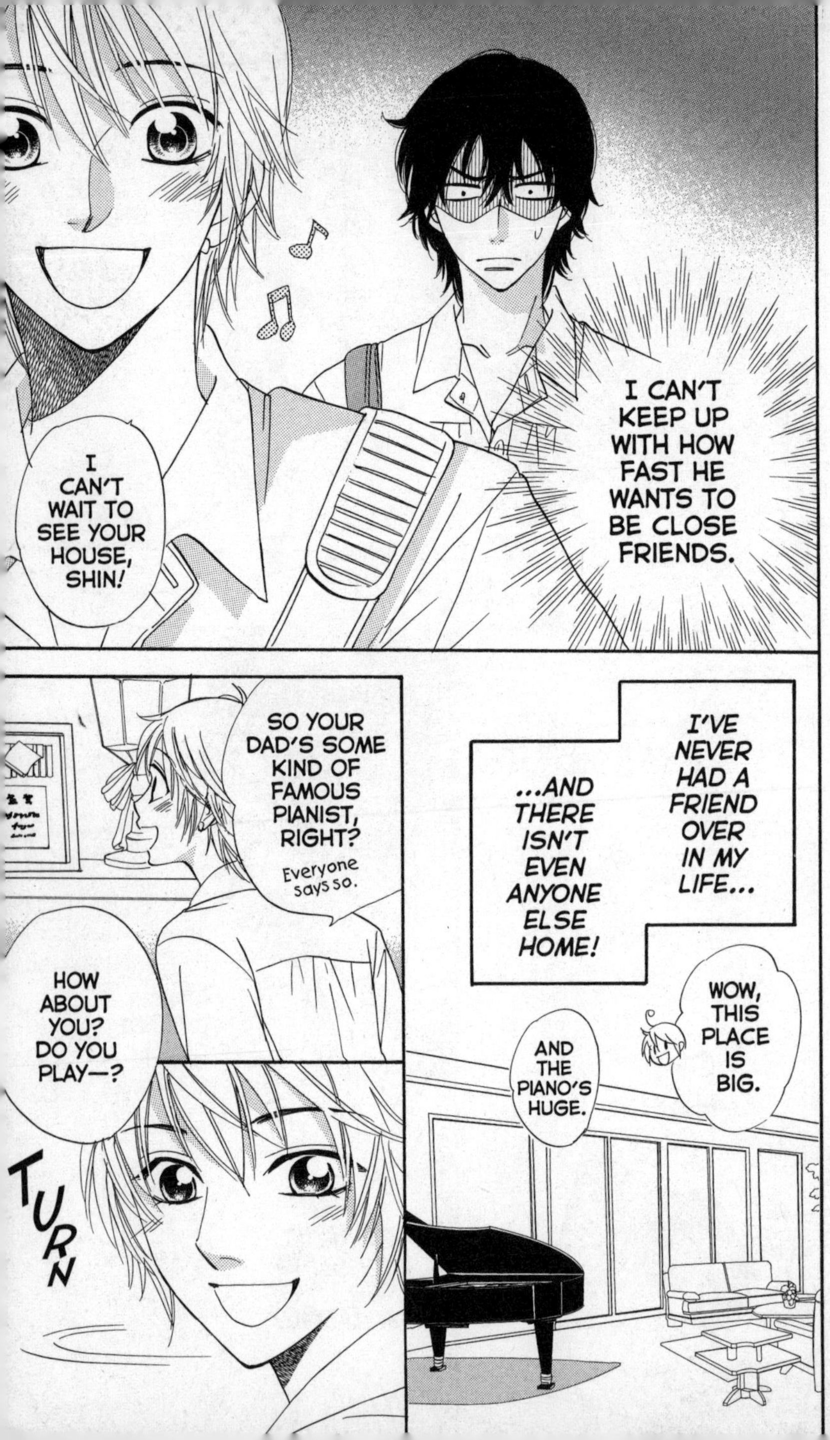
I CAN'T KEEP UP WITH HOW FAST HE WANTS TO BE CLOSE FRIENDS.
I CAN'T WAIT TO SEE YOUR HOUSE, SHIN!
I'VE NEVER HAD A FRIEND OVER IN MY LIFE...
...AND THERE ISN'T EVEN ANYONE ELSE HOME!
WOW, THIS PLACE IS BIG.
AND THE PIANO'S HUGE.
SO YOUR DAD'S SOME KIND OF FAMOUS PIANIST, RIGHT?
Everyone says so.
HOW ABOUT YOU? DO YOU PLAY—?
TURN

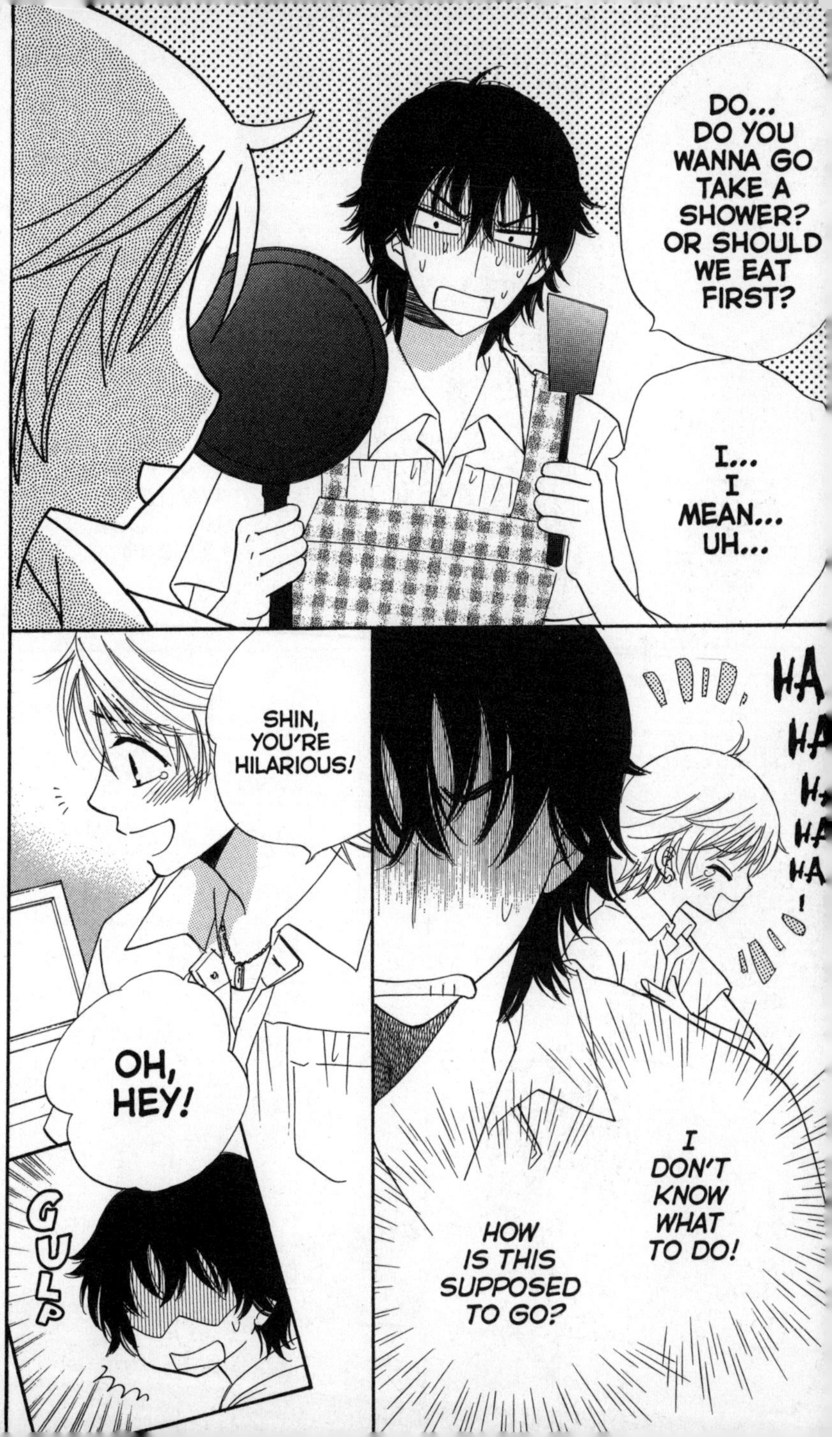
DO... DO YOU WANNA GO TAKE A SHOWER? OR SHOULD WE EAT FIRST?
I... I MEAN... UH...
HA HA HA HA HA!
I DON'T KNOW WHAT TO DO!
HOW IS THIS SUPPOSED TO GO?
SHIN, YOU'RE HILARIOUS!
OH, HEY!
GULP

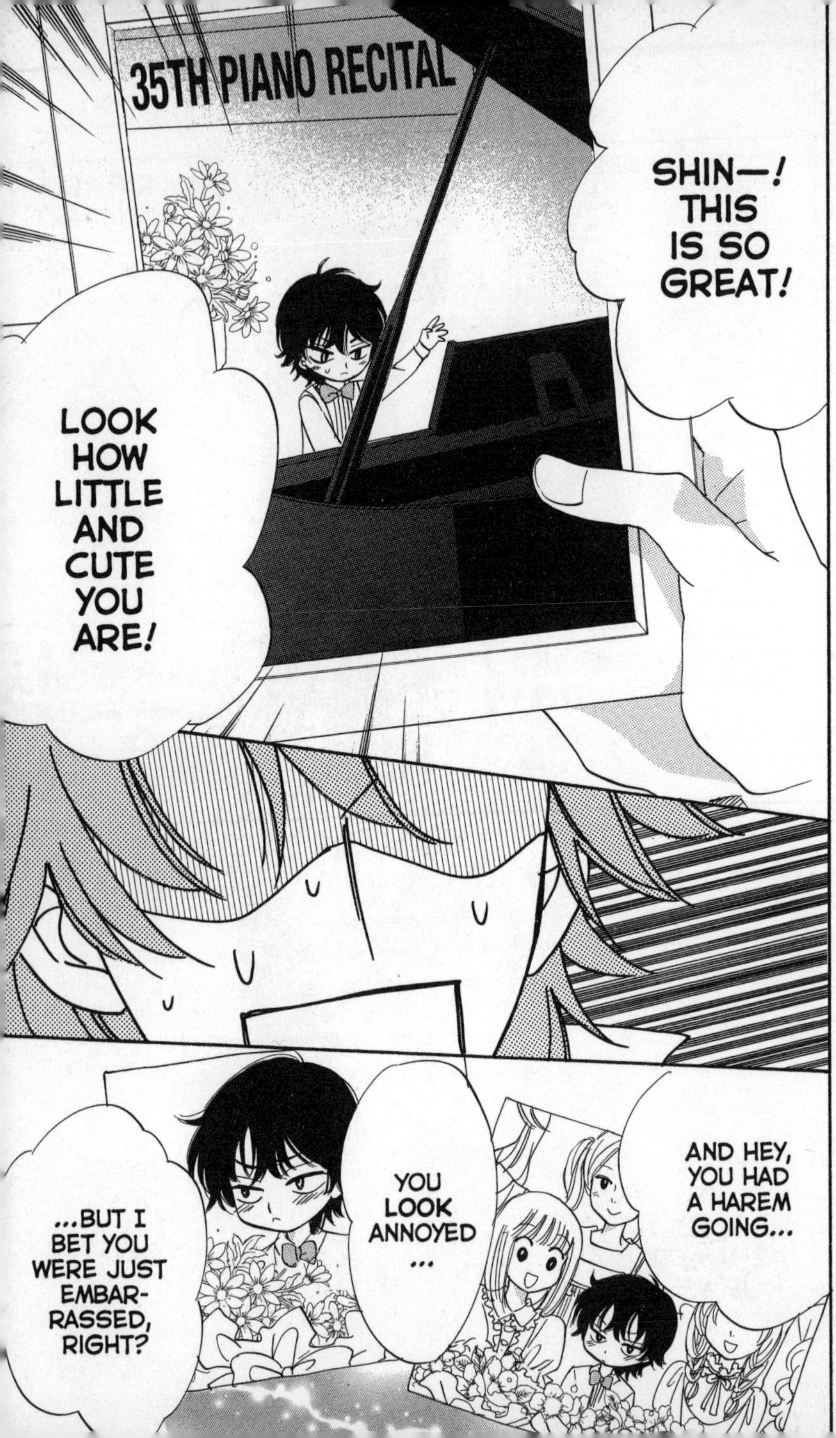
35TH PIANO RECITAL
SHIN—! THIS IS SO GREAT!
LOOK HOW LITTLE AND CUTE YOU ARE!
AND HEY, YOU HAD A HAREM GOING...
YOU LOOK ANNOYED ...
...BUT I BET YOU WERE JUST EMBARRASSED, RIGHT?

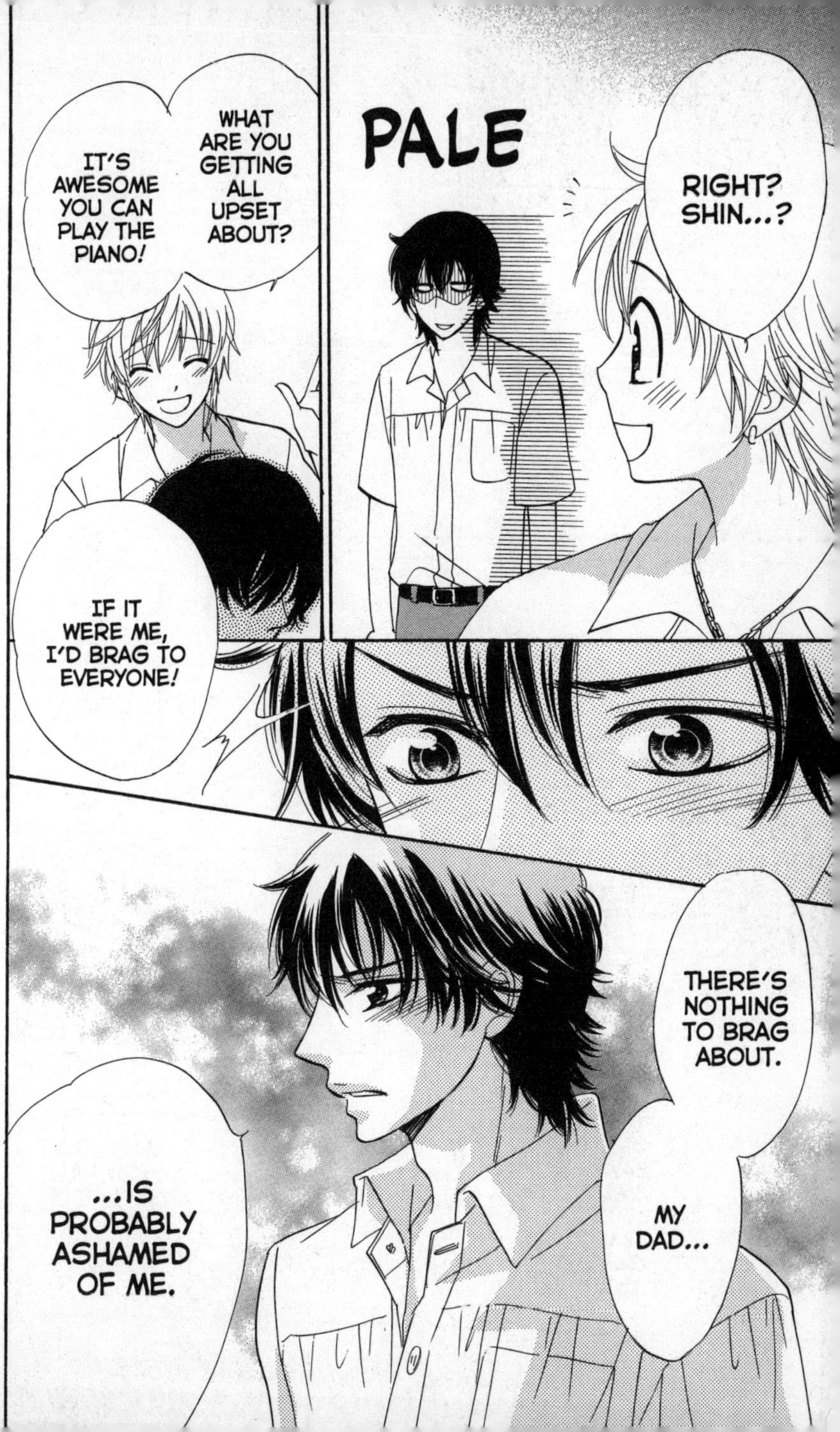
RIGHT? SHIN...?
PALE
WHAT ARE YOU GETTING ALL UPSET ABOUT?
IT'S AWESOME YOU CAN PLAY THE PIANO!
IF IT WERE ME, I'D BRAG TO EVERYONE!
THERE'S NOTHING TO BRAG ABOUT.
MY DAD...
...IS PROBABLY ASHAMED OF ME.

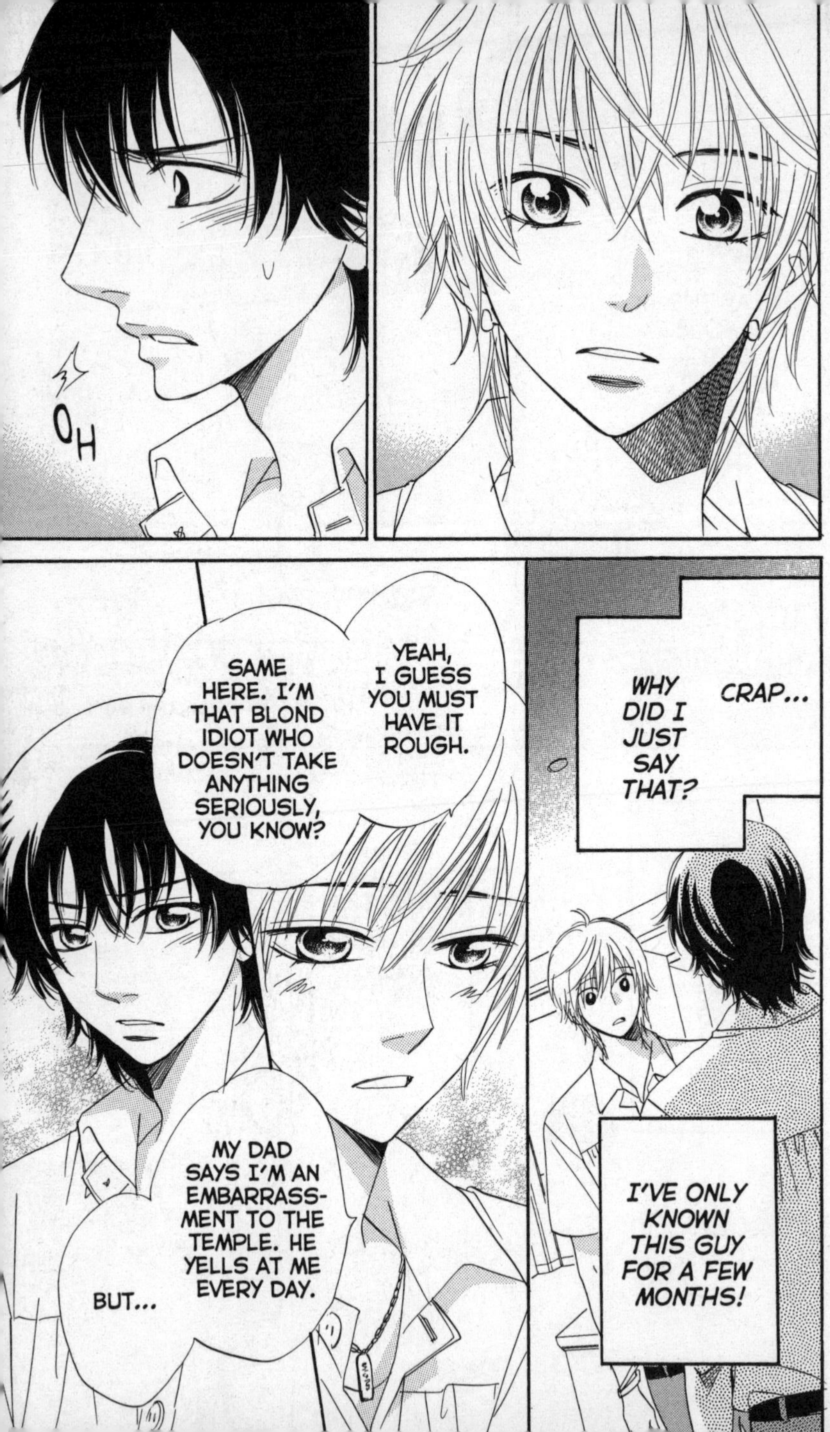
OH
CRAP...
WHY DID I JUST SAY THAT?
I'VE ONLY KNOWN THIS GUY FOR A FEW MONTHS!
YEAH, I GUESS YOU MUST HAVE IT ROUGH.
SAME HERE. I'M THAT BLOND IDIOT WHO DOESN'T TAKE ANYTHING SERIOUSLY, YOU KNOW?
MY DAD SAYS I'M AN EMBARRASS-MENT TO THE TEMPLE. HE YELLS AT ME EVERY DAY.
BUT...

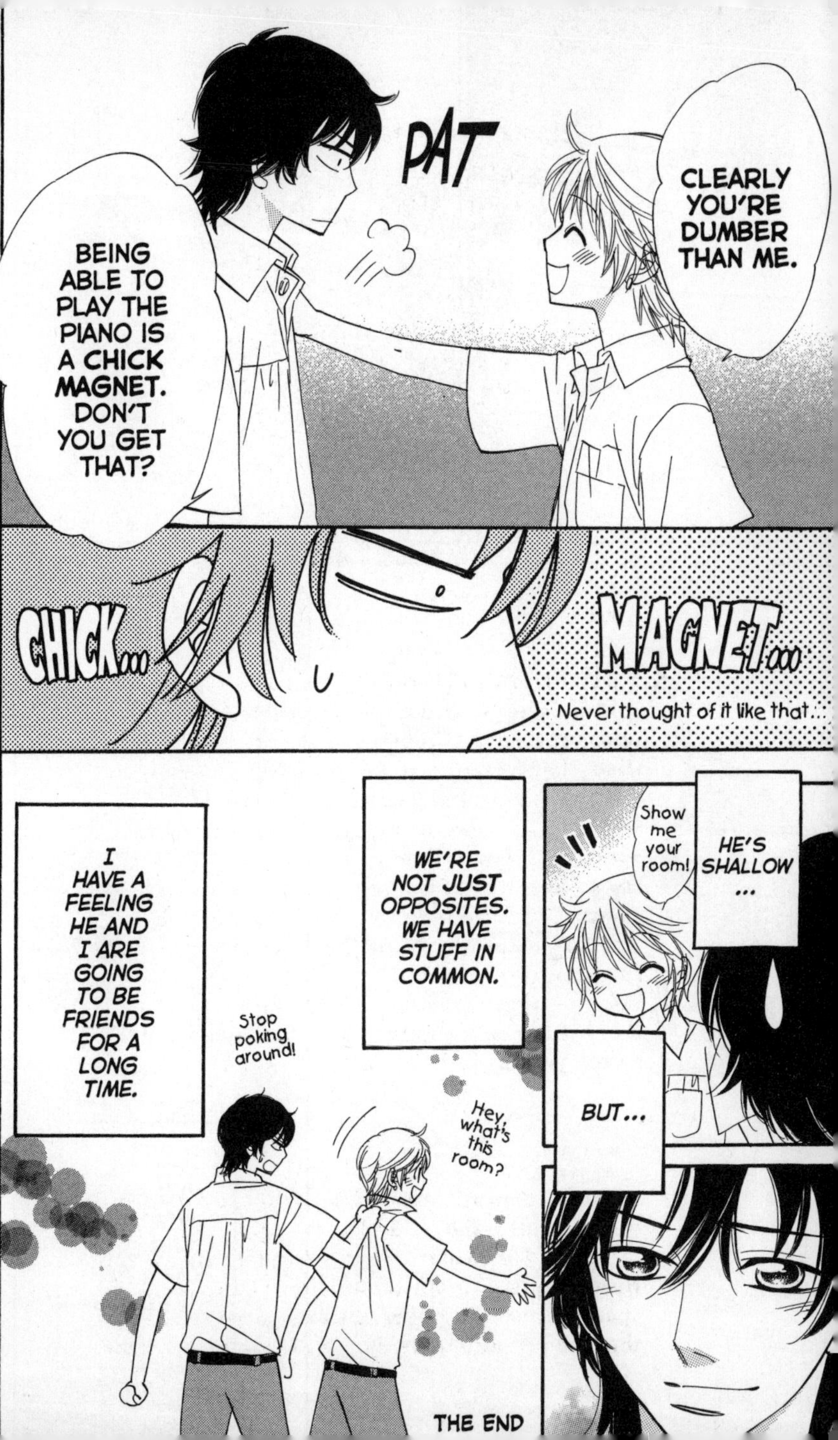
CLEARLY YOU'RE DUMBER THAN ME.
PAT
BEING ABLE TO PLAY THE PIANO IS A CHICK MAGNET. DON'T YOU GET THAT?
MAGNET...
CHICK...
Never thought of it like that...
HE'S SHALLOW ...
Show me your room!
BUT...
WE'RE NOT JUST OPPOSITES. WE HAVE STUFF IN COMMON.
I HAVE A FEELING HE AND I ARE GOING TO BE FRIENDS FOR A LONG TIME.
Hey, what's this room?
Stop poking around!
THE END

I asked them to increase the number of pages in this volume to the maximum pages possible without raising the price of the book. But even then, there were so many pages of the manga itself that I couldn't write an afterword. That's why I wasn't able to express my gratitude as much as I would have liked, but I just want to say to all my readers how much I appreciate them! Thank you very much! This has truly become a memorable series since many things happened to me personally while drawing it. I hope to work harder so that I can draw comics that will be enjoyed by everyone. I would love to see you again in another of my manga.

-Miyoshi Tomori

Miyoshi Tomori made her debut as a manga creator in 2001, and her previous titles include *Hatsukare* (First Boyfriend), *Tongari Root* (Square Root), and *Brass Love!!* In her spare time she likes listening to music in the bath and playing musical instruments.

A DEVIL AND HER LOVE SONG

Volume 13

Shojo Beat Edition

STORY AND ART BY
MIYOSHI TOMORI

English Adaptation/Ysabet MacFarlane
Translation/JN Productions
Touch-up Art & Lettering/Monalisa de Asis
Design/Courtney Utt
Editor/Amy Yu

Printed in the U.S.A.

Published by VIZ Media, LLC
P.O. Box 77010
San Francisco, CA 94107

10 9 8 7 6 5 4 3 2 1
First printing, February 2014

www.viz.com www.shojobeat.com

PARENTAL ADVISORY
A DEVIL AND HER LOVE SONG is rated T for Teen and is recommended for ages 13 and up. This volume contains suggestive themes.
RATED T FOR TEEN
ratings.viz.com